The Geography of Neandertals and Modern Humans in Europe and the Greater Mediterranean

Peabody Museum Bulletin 8

CONTRIBUTORS

Ofer Bar-Yosef
Amilcare Bietti
Eudald Carbonell
Jean-Jacques Hublin
Janusz K. Kozlowski
Steven L. Kuhn
Carolina Mallol
Julià Maroto
Paul Mellars
David Pilbeam
José M. Rando
Manuel Vaquero

The Geography of Neandertals and Modern Humans in Europe and the Greater Mediterranean

Ofer Bar-Yosef and David Pilbeam

Editors

Peabody Museum of Archaeology and Ethnology

Harvard University

Cambridge, Massachusetts, U.S.A.

2000

Cover illustration: Map of the Greater Mediterranean region with illustrations of typical Middle and Upper Paleolithic artifacts. Schematic drawings by Ofer Bar-Yosef. From left: Aterian point; Chatelperronian point; Aurignacian split-base point; Bohunician unifacial point, after J. Svoboda, "The Bohunician," in *Feuilles de Pierre: Les industries à pointes foliacées du Paléolithique supérieur européen*, ed. J. K. Kozlowski. Études et Recherches archéologiques de l'Université de Liège, no. 42 (1990), fig. 7; Sungirian point; Endscraper; Emireh point; Levallois point.
Adaptation of design and layout by Amy Hirschfeld and Josephine Dickinson.

First printing: 2000 (Henry N. Sawyer Co., Inc., Charlestown, Massachusetts)
Second printing: 2001 (Henry N. Sawyer Co., Inc. Charlestown, Massachusetts)
Third printing: 2012 (IBT/Hamilton, Troy, New York)

COPYRIGHT © 2000 BY THE PRESIDENT AND FELLOWS OF HARVARD COLLEGE
ISBN: 978-0-87365-958-1
LIBRARY OF CONGRESS CONTROL NUMBER 00-091057
MANUFACTURED IN THE UNITED STATES OF AMERICA

All rights reserved. This book, or any part thereof, may not be reproduced in any form or by any means, electronic or mechanical, including photocopying, recording, or any information storage or retrieval system now known or to be invented, without permission from the publisher.

Contents

CHAPTER 1. Introduction   1

Ofer Bar-Yosef and David Pilbeam

Acknowledgments   2
Bibliography   2

CHAPTER 2. A Geographic Perspective on the Middle to Upper Paleolithic Transition in the Iberian Peninsula   5

Eduald Carbonell, Manuel Vaquero, Julià Maroto, José M. Rando, and Carolina Mallol

INTRODUCTION   5
RELIEF OF IBERIAN PENINSULA   6
CLIMATE AND VEGETATION OF THE IBERIAN PENINSULA   8
    Present Climate and Vegetation   8
    Climatic Changes during OIS 5–3   9
REGIONAL DISTRIBUTION OF THE SITES   10
    Northern Zone   10
    Eastern Zone   18
    Southern Zone   23
    Western Zone   25
    Central Zone   25
CONCLUSIONS   28
    Historical Factors   28
    Geological and Geomorphological Factors   28

Acknowledgments   30
Bibliography   31

CHAPTER 3. The Archaeological Records of the Neandertal–Modern Human Transition in France   35

Paul Mellars

INTRODUCTION   35
ARCHAEOLOGICAL CONTEXT   36
CONCLUSIONS   44
Note   44
Bibliography   45

CHAPTER 4. The Late Middle and Early Upper Paleolithic in Italy   49

Steven L. Kuhn and Amilcare Bietti

INTRODUCTION   49
BACKGROUND   49
LATE MOUSTERIAN   50
ULUZZIAN   57
AURIGNACIAN   60
SYNTHESIS AND DISCUSSION   66
CONCLUSIONS   71
Notes   72
Bibliography   72

CHAPTER 5. The Problem of Cultural Continuity between the Middle and Upper Paleolithic in Central and Eastern Europe   77

Janusz K. Kozlowski

INTRODUCTION	77
EVOLUTIONARY TRENDS IN TECHNOLOGY BASED ON LEVALLOIS CORES	77
TECHNOLOGICAL EVOLUTION BASED ON BIFACIAL TOOL SHAPING	87
Szeletian	87
Bryndzenian	90
Streletskian	90
EVOLUTION BASED ON BLADES USED AS BLANKS FOR LEAF POINTS	92
EVOLUTIONARY TRENDS BASED ON BLADE TECHNOLOGY AND BACKED TOOLS	95
DISCUSSION	95
CONCLUSIONS	99
Bibliography	103

CHAPTER 6. The Middle and Early Upper Paleolithic in Southwest Asia and Neighboring Regions   107

Ofer Bar-Yosef

INTRODUCTION	107
THE PALEOCLIMATIC CONDITIONS	108
THE CHRONOLOGY OF THE LEVANTINE ENTITIES	111
THE HOMINIDS	111
THE STUDY OF LITHIC INDUSTRIES	113
THE LATE LEVANTINE MIDDLE PALEOLITHIC	116
The Definition of Lithic Industries	116
Mortuary Practices	119
Subsistence	119
Settlement Patterns	120
EARLY UPPER PALEOLITHIC ENTITIES IN THE LEVANT	123
The Dating of the Levantine Early Upper Paleolithic	128
The Ahmarian	130
Other Archaeological Aspects of the Levantine Early Upper Paleolithic	130
THE LEVANTINE AURIGNACIAN	132
THE MIDDLE AND UPPER PALEOLITHIC OF THE TAURUS-ZAGROS REGION	137
THE MIDDLE AND UPPER PALEOLITHIC IN NORTHEAST AFRICA	140
DISCUSSION	141
Note	143
Acknowledgments	143
Bibliography	143

CHAPTER 7. Modern–Nonmodern Hominid Interactions: A Mediterranean Perspective   157

Jean-Jacques Hublin

INTRODUCTION	157
GEOGRAPHICAL PRESENTATION	158
North Africa	159
Southwestern Asia	161
Europe	163
DISCUSSION AND CONCLUSIONS	169
Notes	172
Bibliography	172

CHAPTER 8. Afterword   183

David Pilbeam and Ofer Bar-Yosef

Bibliography	186

APPENDIX   189

Contents   vii

Figures

CHAPTER 2. A Geographic Perspective on the Middle to Upper Paleolithic Transition in the Iberian Peninsula

Figure 1. Location of the Iberian Peninsula in the European continent   6

Figure 2. Main geographical and geological units of the Iberian Peninsula   7

Figure 3. Bioclimatic zones of the Iberian Peninsula   8

Figure 4. Location of the site distribution zones   10

Figure 5. Distribution of Middle and Early Upper Paleolithic sites in the Northern Zone   16

Figure 6. Distribution of Neandertal and anatomically modern human remains in the Iberian Peninsula   18

Figure 7. Distribution of Middle Paleolithic and Early Upper Paleolithic sites in the Eastern Zone   19

Figure 8. Stratigraphic sequence of Abric Romaní   20

Figure 9. Retouched artifacts from level Jb of Abric Romaní   21

Figure 10. Retouched artifacts from level H of Arbreda Cave   22

Figure 11. Distribution of Middle Paleolithic and Early Upper Paleolithic sites in the Southern Zone   24

Figure 12. Distribution of Middle Paleolithic and Early Upper Paleolithic stes in the Western Zone   26

Figure 13. Distribution of Middle Paleolithic and Early Upper Paleolithic sites in the Central Zone   27

Figure 14. Distribution of Early Upper Paleolithic sites (Aurignacian and Chatelperronian) in the Iberian Peninsula   29

CHAPTER 3. The Archaeological Records of the Neandertal–Modern Human Transition in France

Figure 1. The distribution of Aurignacian sites in France   37

Figure 2. The distribution of Chatelperronian sites in France   38

Figure 3. Absolute age determinations for Chatelperronian sites in southwest France and northern Spain, and for early Aurignacian sites in northern Spain   39

Figure 4. Radiocarbon dates for early Aurignacian levels in southwest France and northern Spain   43

CHAPTER 4. The Late Middle and Early Upper Paleolithic in Italy

Figure 1. Dated and undated Mousterian sites in Italy discussed in the text   51

Figure 2. The S. Francesco "Denticulate Mousterian" assemblage   52

Figure 3. Stone tools from Buca della Iena and Grotta del Capriolo   53

Figure 4. Assemblage from most recent layers at Grotta Breuil, Monte Circeo   54

Figure 5. Assemblage from levels 9 and 10 at Riparo del Poggio, Campania   58

Figure 6. The early Uluzzian of Grotta del Cavallo   59

Figure 7. The Middle or "evolved" Uluzzian of Grotta del Cavallo   61

Figure 8. Uluzzian artifacts from Grotta la Fabbrica, Castelcivita   62

Figure 9. "Proto-Aurignacian" artifacts from Riparo Mochi, layer G   63

Figure 10. The earliest Aurignacian of more recent southern Italian sites   64

Figure 11. Artifacts from layer F of Riparo Mochi, Liguria   65

Figure 12. Relevant portions of key stratigraphic sequences, with absolute dates marked   67

Figure 13. Distribution of late Mousterian, Aurignacian, and Uluzzian sites from 40–35 ka B.P.   68

Figure 14. Distribution of late Mousterian, Aurignacian, and Uluzzian sites from 35–30 ka B.P.   68

CHAPTER 5. The Problem of Cultural Continuity Between the Middle and Upper Paleolithic in Central and Eastern Europe

Figure 1. General scheme of Early and Middle Upper Paleolithic units in Europe   78

Figure 2. Temnata Cave, Bulgaria, sector TD-II, layer VI. Levallois double platform blade cores   81

Figure 3. Temnata Cave, Bulgaria, sector TD-II, layer VI. Upper Paleolithic cores with narrow flaking face and lateral crests transformed into flat cores with broad flaking face   82

Figure 4. Temnata Cave, Bulgaria, sector TD-II, layer VI. Retouched tools: Mousterian points, side- and endscraper, endscrapers, burins   83

Figure 5. Korolevo II, complex II: Double platform blade core with central crest. Korolevo I, complex Ia: volumetric blade core with crest on the narrow side, volumetric residual blade core with sequence of detached tablets   85

Figure 6. Stranska Skala, Moravia. Bohunician reconstructed cores   86

Figure 7. Vedrovice V, Moravia. Discoidal core, single platform unprepared core, polyhedral-spherical flake cores, unprepared blade cores   88

Figure 8. Dzierzyslaw, Poland. Szeletian single and double platform unprepared blade-flake cores   89

Figure 9. Streletskian tools: Kostenki I, Russia, layer V; Kostenki 6 (Streletskaya). Endscrapers, triangular leaf points with concave base (Sungir points), sidescraper, blade with lateral retouch, unfinished foliates   91

Figure 10. Gorodtsovian tools: Kostenki 15, Russia. Sidescrapers, endscrapers   93

Figure 11. Jerzmanowician leaf points: Jerzmanowice, Nietoperzowa Cave, layer 6 and Wierzchowie, Poland, Mamutuwa Cave. Leaf points on blades (*pointes à face plane*), bifacially worked foliates   94

Figure 12. Arched backed blades from Kraków-Zwierzyniec I, Poland, layer 12–14, in sectors J3, 4a, and 4b   96

Figure 13. Arched backed blades and microlithic trucations from Klisoura Cave I, Greece, layer V   97

Figure 14. Chronological relationships between particular "transition units" and the Aurignacian in Central and Eastern Europe   98

Figure 15. Most important sites dated to the period 50–40 ka B.P.   100

Figure 16. Most important dated sites from the period 40–35 ka B.P.   101

Figure 17. Most important regions of settlement in the period 35–30 ka B.P   102

CHAPTER 6. The Middle and Early Upper Paleolithic in Southwest Asia and Neighboring Regions

Figure 1. Map of the regions discussed in the text   108

Figure 2. Generalized chronology of the Middle and Upper Paleolithic sites in the Levant   109

Figure 3. Map of Late Levantine Mousterian sites ("Tabun B-type")   112

Figure 4. Middle Paleolithic artifacts from Qafzeh Cave (a "Tabun C-type" industry)   117

Figure 5. Middle Paleolithic artifacts from Kebara Cave (a "Tabun B-type" industry)   118

Figure 6. Middle Paleolithic settlement patterns: Mt. Carmel/ Galilee; Southern Jordan   122

Figure 7. Map of the Levant with the earliest Upper Paleolithic sites   125

Figure 8. Early Upper Paleolithic artifacts from Ksar 'Akil and layers XXV–XXIV in Kebara: points, chamfered flakes and blades (*chanfreins*), endscrapers, cores   126

Figure 9. Early Upper Paleolithic tools from Boker
Tachtit, levels 1 and 2   127

Figure 10. Early Upper Paleolithic tools from Umm el
Tlel, layer IIIbase and III2a: Umm el Tlel points,
blade, cores   128

Figure 11. Dates of the Late Middle and Early Upper
Paleolithic in the Levant   129

Figure 12. Map of the Ahmarian sites in the Levant   131

Figure 13. Map of the Aurignacian sites in the
Eastern Mediterranean   133

Figure 14. Levantine Aurignacian stone artifacts from
Hayonim Cave: Dufour and retouched bladelets,
carinated and nosed scrapers, carinated burin, burin
on truncation, Aurignacian blades, endscrapers on
retouched blades   134

Figure 15. Levantine Aurignacian bone, tooth, and
antler artifacts from Hayonim Cave and Kebara Cave   135

Figure 16. Middle Paleolithic artifacts from
Karain Cave   138

Figure 17. Middle Paleolithic artifacts from Kunji
Cave in the Zagros   139

Figure 18. Hypothetical colonization routes in the
eastern Mediterranean   142

CHAPTER 8. Afterword

Figure 1. Map showing TL and ^{14}C dates for the Late
Mousterian in the Greater Mediterranean region   184

Figure 2. Map showing TL and ^{14}C dates for the
Early Upper Paleolithic in the Greater
Mediterranean region   185

Tables

CHAPTER 2. A Geographic Perspective on the Middle to Upper Paleolithic Transition in the Iberian Peninsula

Table 1. Absolute dates and dating methods for certain Middle and Early Upper Paleolithic sites in the Iberian Peninsula — 11–15

CHAPTER 3. The Archaeological Records of the Neandertal–Modern Human Transition in France

Table 1. Absolute age measurements for Châtelperronian and early Aurignacian levels in France and northern Spain — 41–42

CHAPTER 4. The Late Middle and Early Upper Paleolithic in Italy

Table 1. Dates for Middle and Upper Paleolithic sites in Italy — 56–57

CHAPTER 5. The Problem of Cultural Continuity Between the Middle and Upper Paleolithic in Central and Eastern Europe

Table 1. Most important sites dated to the period 50–40 ka B.P. — 79

Table 2. Most important sites dated to the period 40–35 ka B.P. — 80

CHAPTER 6. The Middle and Early Upper Paleolithic in Southwest Asia and Neighboring Regions

Table 1. Frequencies of large, medium, and small mammals from Mousterian and Upper Paleolithic sites in southwest Asia (excluding carnivores) — 120–121

Table 2. Percentages of tool types by level (XII–VI), from Ksar 'Akil 1937–1938 — 136

APPENDIX A.

Radiometric dates available at the time of publication — 189–197

CHAPTER 1 Introduction

Ofer Bar-Yosef and David Pilbeam
Peabody Museum, Harvard University

Long-term evolutionary processes and, in particular, the archaeological concept of cultural homeostasis—as frequently noted for the Lower and Middle Paleolithic—have important implications for paleo-anthropological interpretations. No less important is the geographical distribution of the set of archaeological entities that, according to the traditional terminology, are incorporated in the Middle Paleolithic. This period, once seen as relatively short, is now known to have lasted for a longer time. The dating accepted in the past, that this period began during the Last Interglacial and continued through the first part of the Last Glaciation, or from about 130 to 40 ka, has altered dramatically in the last two decades. The onset of the Middle Paleolithic is defined by the earliest manifestation of the Mousterian (in Africa known as the Middle Stone Age), and new dates move it back in time to around 250 to 270 ka. This shift is due to relatively new radiometric techniques such as TL and ESR, which, together with OSL and U/Th series dating, indicate that what had seemed to be a somewhat short "cultural stage" is in reality longer.

During the Middle Paleolithic, Africa was inhabited by various more or less "archaic" populations ancestral to modern *Homo sapiens*, while Europe was the homeland of the Neandertals. Archaeological projects since the early twentieth century have demonstrated that the transition from the Middle to the Upper Paleolithic was quite abrupt. The story is well known. Originally, the view was that Middle Paleolithic industries could be described as "flake-based," while the newer, "blade-based" industries that replaced them came to be more prevalent. The latter were seen as the products of modern *Homo sapiens* (or *Homo sapiens sapiens*). This misconception, sometimes still found in recent textbooks, led to the idea that supposed changes in basic knapping techniques reflect biological evolutionary phases. It was later discovered that the earliest European Upper Paleolithic blade industry, known as the Chatelperronian (or Castelperronian) was made by Neandertals. In addition, it was also subsequently shown that those blade industries or lithic methods that aimed to produce elongated blanks and points were of a much greater age (Bar-Yosef and Kuhn 1999, and references therein). The oversimplification "flake-based=Neandertal, blade-based=modern human" fell apart. The need to define entities or lithic traditions more clearly, both diachronically and geographically, became an urgent necessity.

During the last two decades, various types of genetic studies provided different and sometimes conflicting scenarios for the origins of modern humans, especially in terms of the estimated date (see, for example, Watson et al. 1997; Hawks et al., 2000; Jorde et al., 2000). In our view, the data support a recent rather than an ancient origin for modern humans; age estimates have ranged between 300,000 and 100,000 years, with the more recently published estimates clustering around 150,000 years ago (Watson et al. 1997; Tischkoff et al. 1996). If we consider the possibility that several groups of modern humans expanded throughout the Old World at different rates, several questions can be raised concerning their impact across Africa and Eurasia. Not the least of these is the relationship between the Neandertals, who had evolved in Europe since the Middle Pleistocene, and the incoming Cro-Magnons. Debates on the complex nature of interactions between these two populations continue to rage (e.g., Mellars et al. 1999, Zilhão and d'Errico 1999). Examples of potentially analogous relationships between populations of local and invading hunter-gatherers can be drawn from the prehistory of North America, as well as from the protagonists of the Neolithic Revolution. However, testing the complexity of these interactions requires archaeological sequences with better controlled chronology, not all of which, unfortunately, are in the circum-Mediterranean region.

That none of these topics is entirely new is exemplified by the publication of several conference proceedings and books that have focused on issues of the emergence of modern humans and the demise of the Neandertals (Akazawa et al. 1992, Gamble 1994, Mellars 1990, Mellars and Stringer 1989, Otte 1998, Stringer and Gamble 1993, Stringer and McKie 1996, Trinkaus 1989). Although several authors have attempted to examine general cultural or biological aspects from the perspective of a particular region, the notion of a geographic approach is not explicit. Often, the Eurocentric viewpoint dominates to the extent that the demise of the Neandertals is generally referred to as a western European problem. Paleo-biological events and cultural changes that took place in North Africa are rarely incorporated into the overall picture, and one notes a similar approach towards relevant data from areas such as Eastern Europe, the Caucasus, and beyond. Sporadically, particular papers (e.g., Foley and Lahr 1997) have made an effort to redirect attention to the issue as a broader subject, involving the examination of the archaeology of Africa and Eurasia.

We therefore felt that as we are interested in continuing to promote a holistic geographical view of the prehistoric change known as the Middle to Upper Paleolithic Transition, a hard look at the available evidence was called for, but starting on a quite local geographical-temporal scale. With a few colleagues (E. Carbonell, J.-J. Hublin, J. Kozlowski, P. Mellars, and S. Kuhn), we convened a two day seminar at the Peabody Museum on December 14–16, 1997. We later received the papers incorporated in this volume.

Acknowledgments

We would like to express our gratitude to the American School of Prehistoric Research for funding the project and its publication, and to the authors who participated in the vivid discussions and have demonstrated great patience in the time it took to complete this volume. We are very grateful to Josephine Dickinson, without whose meticulous editing and care this volume might not finally have been completed.

BIBLIOGRAPHY

Akazawa, T., K. Aoki, and T. Kimura (eds.)
1992 *The Evolution and Dispersal of Modern Humans in Asia.* Hokusen-Sha, Tokyo.

Bar-Yosef, O., and S. Kuhn
1999 "The Big Deal about Blades: Laminar Technologies and Human Evolution." *American Anthropology* 101(2):1–17.

Foley, R., and M. M. Lahr
1997 "Mode 3 Technologies and the Evolution of Modern Humans." *Cambridge Archaeological Journal* 7(1):3–36.

Gamble, C.
1994 *Timewalkers: The Prehistory of Global Colonization.* Harvard University Press, Cambridge.

Hawks, J., K. Hunley, S.-H. Lee, and M. Wolpoff
2000 "Population Bottlenecks and Pleistocene Human Evolution." *Molecular Biology and Evolution* 17: 2–22.

Hey, J.
1997 "Mitochondrial and Nuclear Genes Present Conflicting Portraits of Human Origins." *Molecular Biology and Evolution* 14:166–172.

Jorde, L., W. Watkins, M. Bamshad, M. Dixon, C. Ricker, M. Seielstad, and M. Batzer
2000 "The Distribution of Human Genetic Diversity: A Comparison of Mitochondrial, Autosomal, and Y-Chromosome Data." *American Journal of Human Genetics* 66:979–988.

Mellars, P. (ed.)
1990 *The Emergence of Modern Humans: An Archaeological Perspective.* Edinburgh University Press, Edinburgh.

Mellars, P., M. Otte, L. Straus, J. Zilhão, and F. d'Errico
1999 "The Neanderthal Problem Continued. CA Forum on Theory in Anthropology." *Current Anthropology* 40(3):341–364.

Mellars, P., and C. Stringer (eds.)
1989 *The Human Revolution: Behavioral and Biological Perspectives on the Origins of Modern Humans.* Edinburgh University Press, Edinburgh.

Otte, M. (ed.)
1998 *Préhistoire d'Anatolie: Genèse de deux mondes. Anatolian Prehistory: At The Crossroads of Two Worlds,* vol. 2. Etudes et Recherches

Archéologiques de l'Université de Liège 85. Service de Préhistoire, Liège.

Ruvolo, M.
1996 "A New Approach to Studying Modern Human Origins: Hypothesis Testing with Coalescence Time Distributions." *Molecular Phylogenetics and Evolution* 5(1):202–219.

Stringer, C., and C. Gamble
1993 *In Search of the Neanderthals*. Thames and Hudson, London.

Stringer, C. B., and R. McKie
1996 *African Exodus: The Origins of Modern Humanity*. Pimlico, London.

Tishkoff, S., E. Dietzsc, W. Speed, A. Pakstis, J. Kidd, K. Cheung, B. Bonne-Tamir, A. Santachiara-Benerecetti, P. Moral, M. Krings, S. Paabo, E. Watson, N. Risch, T. Jenkins, and K. Kidd
1996 "Global Patterns of Linkage Disequilibrium at the CD4 Locus in Modern Human Origins." *Science* 271:1380–1387.

Trinkaus, E. (ed.)
1989 *The Emergence of Modern Humans: Biocultural Adaptations in the Later Pleistocene*. Cambridge University Press, Cambridge.

Wise, C. A., M. Sraml, D. C. Rubinsztein, and S. Easteal
1997 "Comparative Nuclear and Mitochondrial Genome Diversity in Humans and Chimpanzees." *Molecular Biology and Evolution* 14:707–716.

Watson, E., P. Forster, M. Richards, and H.-J. Bandelt
1997 "Mitochondrial Footprints of Human Expansions in Africa." *American Journal of Human Genetics* 61:691–704.

Zilhão, J., and F. d'Errico
1999 "The Chronology and Taphonomy of the Earliest Aurignacian and Its Implications for the Understanding of Neanderthal Extinction." *Journal of World Prehistory* 13(1):1–68.

CHAPTER 2

A Geographic Perspective on the Middle to Upper Paleolithic Transition in the Iberian Peninsula

Eudald Carbonell, Manuel Vaquero, Julià Maroto,[1]
José M. Rando, and Carolina Mallol
Universitat Rovira i Virgili, Tarragona, Spain
[1]Universitat de Girona, Girona, Spain

INTRODUCTION

The goal of this paper is to present a geographic view of the Middle to Upper Paleolithic transition in the Iberian Peninsula, discussing the distribution of the major archaeological sites that have contributed information on this event. Chronologically, the sites included in this synthesis generally correspond to Oxygen Isotope Stage (OIS) 3, and more specifically, to the late Middle Paleolithic and Early Upper Paleolithic. The latter comprises assemblages attributed to the Chatelperronian and Aurignacian techno-complexes. Some of the stratigraphic sequences presented here also include occupations from OIS4 and 5. These isotopic stages will also be taken into consideration when describing the paleoclimatic reconstruction.

There are abundant sites within this period. However, few of these remain after disregarding surface findings, dubious stratigraphic contexts, and sites with problematic frameworks of interpretation due to poor excavation criteria. The criteria underlying the selection of sites that can provide information from the perspective of this paper are the following:
1. Long sequences in which both cultural periods are documented.
2. Excavations carried out with modern field methods and interdisciplinary teamwork that have yielded paleoenvironmental data aside from strictly cultural information.
3. Sites with radiometric dating, which enables accurate framing of them in the chronology considered.
4. Sites that are of particular significance for their place in the history of archaeological research or for the importance of the archaeological record documented.

The geographic perspective of the transition will be presented in distribution maps, from which the major issues can be approached by focusing on general site distribution as well as on the main cultural complexes involved in the transition. The uneven distribution of the sites and the radiometric dates recently obtained for the late Middle Paleolithic and Early Upper Paleolithic of the Iberian Peninsula have been employed to propose several scenarios concerning the biocultural change in Europe.

Two main conclusions can be drawn from the data currently available. First, one of the earliest appearances of the Upper Paleolithic, at similar dates to some east European sites, has been documented in the north of the peninsula, in the Cantabrian and Catalonian regions. Second, the latest persistence of Neandertals and Middle Paleolithic industries has been documented in the south and central regions (Andalucía, the Valencian Community, and central-western Portugal). The interpretation of this data suggests the existence of an overlap, lasting several millennia, between groups culturally ascribed to the Middle Paleolithic and other groups that had already adopted Upper Paleolithic features. In anthropological terms, this hypothesis implies a prolonged coexistence of Neandertals and anatomically modern humans (AMH), on a peninsular scale.

RELIEF OF THE IBERIAN PENINSULA

The Iberian Peninsula is located at the southwestern edge of the European subcontinent (fig. 1). The Pyrenean Ranges constitute a barrier separating the peninsula from the rest of the continent. The northernmost edge of Africa is located 14 km from the southernmost tip of the peninsula, separated by the Strait of Gibraltar. The superficial extension of the Iberian Peninsula is 581,422 km², featuring 3,144 km of coasts bathed by the Atlantic Ocean in the north and the west, and by the Mediterranean Sea in the rest of the peninsula. The mean altitude of its territory is 600 m (a.s.l.).

For its latitude and the diversity of its relief, the Iberian Peninsula constitutes the most singular Mediterranean structure. The internal relief of this territory is characterized by well-structured mountain ranges, massifs, and ridges, as well as by the plateau rising in the Central Peninsula (fig. 2). The most outstanding mountain systems are distributed throughout the peninsula: east-west to north are the Pyrenees, the Cantabrian Range, and the Galician Massif; north-south to east are the Betic Range and the Catalan Massif; north-south and east-west in the center are the Iberian Range, the Central Range, the Mounds of Toledo, and the Sierra Morena ridge.

Five large fluvial basins traverse the peninsular relief and constitute an asymmetrical water system. Only the Ebro River flows to the east, into the Mediterranean Sea. The other main watercourses, the Duero, Tajo, Guadiana, and Guadalquivir Rivers, run north-

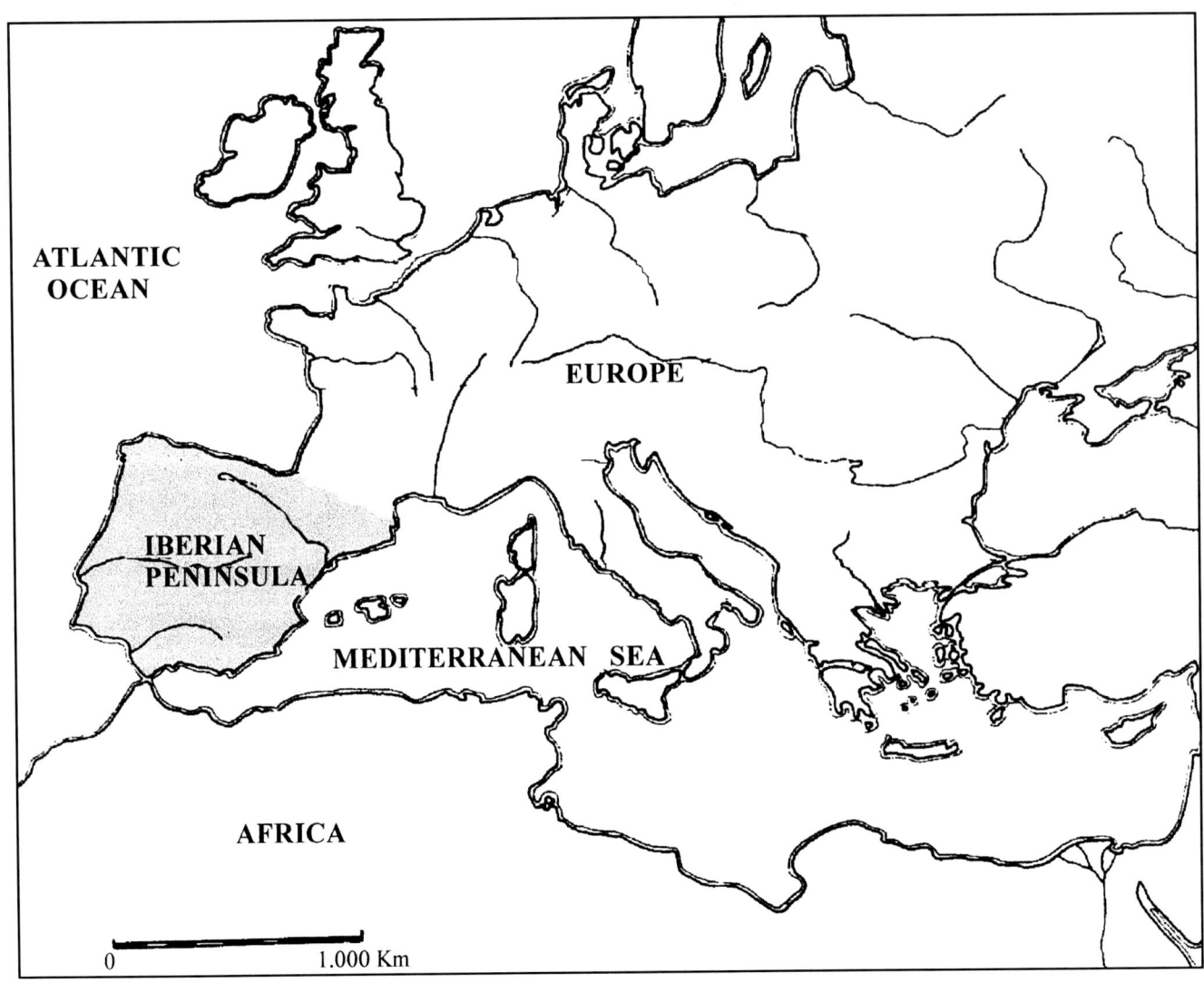

Figure 1. Location of the Iberian Peninsula in the European continent.

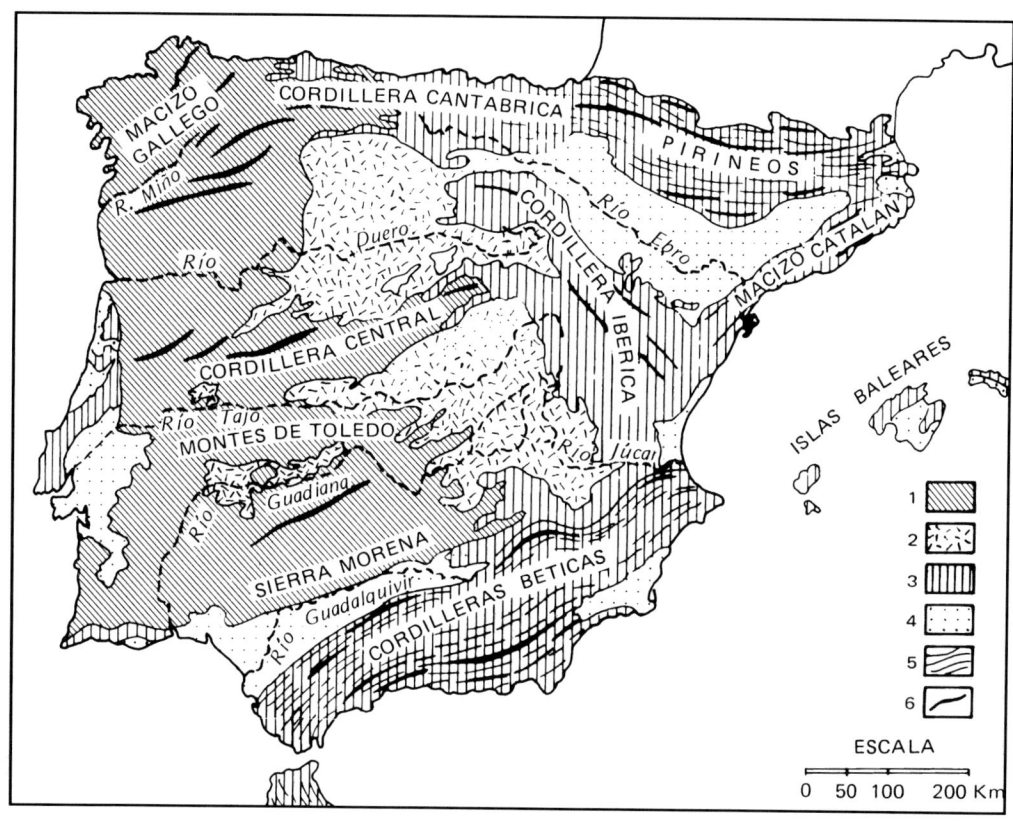

Figure 2. Main geographical and geological units of the Iberian Peninsula (from De Tèran et al. 1978): 1. Meseta's Hercinian massif, 2. Meseta's Tertiary depressions, 3. Meseta's Alpine ledges, 4. Peripheral depressions, 5. Alpine mountain range, 6. Main mountain alignments.

south and flow into the Atlantic Ocean. Undoubtedly, the valleys through which these rivers flow constitute the natural paths giving access to the different reliefs of the peninsula. They cross the littoral ranges reaching the interior of the peninsula and overcoming topographic accidents of all kinds. The main structural units are:

1. The Meseta. A quadrangular block rising in the center of the peninsula and forming an enormous, high plain. It is slightly tilted towards the Atlantic, with a 3 percent gradient.
2. The triangle formed by the Ebro Basin and the Pyrenees in the northeast.
3. The Betic Ranges and the Guadalquivir Basin in the south.
4. All coastal and littoral zones, reaching the Cantabrian range in the north and the littoral and pre-littoral chains in the east. They are natural corridors that communicate throughout the periphery and permit a peninsular circulation bypassing the center.

Undoubtedly, the relief has affected the mobility of hominids throughout the territory in an irreversible manner. In addition, the nature of the geologic composition has played an important role in the preservation of sites, its most significant substrata being the siliceous, calcareous, and clayey ones.

As regards the clay composition of Tertiary Age, the best-characterized formations are the high plains of the Meseta and the plains of the Ebro and Guadalquivir basins. The calcareous terrain generally belongs to the Secondary Age. It mostly comprises the eastern and southern half of the peninsula. The siliceous zone of Primary Age is concentrated in the western part. Although the human occupations of OIS 5 and 3 took place in the open air and in caves, there is more data available in the calcareous zones, which contain greatly developed karsts and usually reveal human occupations. These systems have preserved the archaeological record and therefore contain more information than the siliceous zones. Undoubtedly, the geologic substrata influence the distribution of the sites. The differential preservation produced among siliceous and calcareous terrain is basic to understanding this spatial issue.

CLIMATE AND VEGETATION OF THE IBERIAN PENINSULA

The climatic zone to which the Mediterranean region belongs is characterized by the interaction between the dry climates of the subtropical belt and the suboceanic climate of the temperate, forest zone, which is influenced by the storms associated with the polar fronts (fig. 3). According to Balairón (1997), the Mediterranean climate may vary according to four main parameters. The climate depends, first of all, on the interrelations existing between general and regional circulation; it receives the influx of the medium latitude general circulation patterns as well as the natural Saharan dynamics. Secondly, it depends on the singularity of the regional Mediterranean atmospheric circulation. Thirdly, it depends on a high local variability of precipitation in arid and semiarid Mediterranean areas; changes in frequency and intensity of droughts and rainfall, along with convective processes due to multiple causes. Finally, the climate depends on the potential influence of global climatic change, manifested through modifications of the polar and subtropical high circulation and of the vertical and horizontal temperature gradient, which affects the displacement of the convergent intertropical zone.

Present Climate and Vegetation

The present climate of the Iberian Peninsula, except the north and northwest, is Mediterranean. An Atlantic influence is noticeable in the northernmost part. The Iberian Range and Galician Massif act as buttresses and retain a strong Atlantic influence; this is reflected in the high rainfall regime and strong environmental humidity.

The Mediterranean climatic features originated in the end of the Pliocene, when the diverse zones belonging to this regime emerged. Despite the environmental changes produced in the course of the Pleistocene, the most representative arboreal and bushy taxa remain throughout the Iberian geography today.

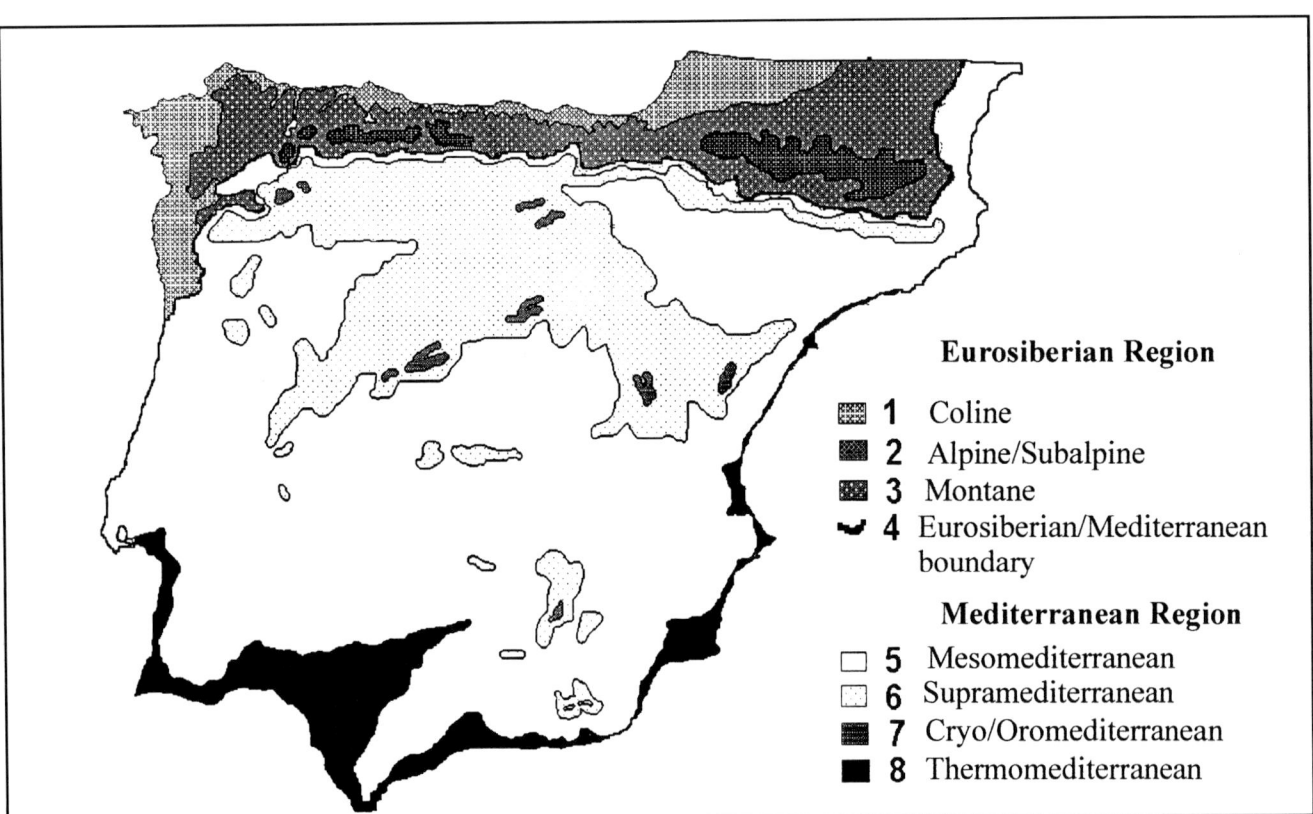

Figure 3. Bioclimatic zones of the Iberian Peninsula (after Rivas-Martinez 1987).

Spain can be divided into five bioclimatic clusters within the Mediterranean climate:

1. The Cryomediterranean zone is characterized by the presence of two species of fescue (*Festuca indigesta* and *Festuca clementei*).
2. The Oromediterranean zone is characterized by the presence of savin.
3. The Supramediterranean zone comprises beech, pyrenean oak, two species of holly (*ilex rotundifolia* and *ilex ilicifolia*), algerian oak, savin, incense juniper and spanish fir.
4. The Mesomediterranean zone comprises cork tree, holm oak, holly (*ilex ilicifolia*) and kermes oak, depending on the latitude and situation.
5. The Thermomediterranean zone includes algerian oak, holm oak, olive, lentisk, carob tree and common juniper.

Needless to say, the composition of the vegetation at this latitude depends on the altitude at which the sites are located, and the microclimates caused by certain kinds of relief must also be taken into account. For example, red pine (*Pinus sylvestris*) is abundant in elevated zones, and white pine (*Pinus halepensis*) in coastal zones. Many Mediterranean taxa are adapted to the cold. For instance, the holm oak (*Quercus ilex*) can resist temperatures of up to minus 20 degrees without suffering irreversible damage. The same is true for the olive tree (*Olea europea*), which is capable of resisting 5 degrees of frost in spring. The cork oaks and kermes oaks (*Quercus coccifera*) are less hardy (Di Castri and Mooney 1973).

The Atlantic climate is concentrated in the north, as has already been mentioned. It is characterized by the presence of beeches (*Fagus sylvatica*), chestnut trees (*Castanea*), birches (*Betula pendula* and *Betula alba*), and abundant undergrowth.

The river forests are characteristic of both climatic environments and are outstanding for the presence of black poplar (*Populus alba* and *Populus nigra*) and alder (*Alnus glutinosa*).

Climatic Changes during OIS 5–3

The analysis of cave stratigraphic sequences gives us an understanding of the arboreal and bushy evolution of the Iberian Peninsula in the past. Our main interest is climatic knowledge of OIS 5, 4, and 3. A diachronic climatic reconstruction is based on archaeological complexes with important stratigraphic sequences, as well as on other sites with systematic dates that can explain any isotopic stage in a coherent manner. Among these sites are the following: El Castillo and Lezetxiki (northern zone); Can Garriga, Arbreda, Abric Romaní and Cova Beneito (eastern zone); and Carihuela (southern zone).

OIS 5 (130 to 70 ka) is characterized by the Eemian interglacial in its initial phase (substage 5e). The climate of the Iberian Peninsula was Mediterranean (warm). Stage 5 is reflected in Can Garriga, with dates oscillating between 129 and 87 ka B.P. (Giralt et al. 1995). In the northern zone, the analyses carried out in Lezetxiki indicate the presence of *Pinus*, *Quercus*, *Castanea*, and *Juglans* in levels VI, Va, IVa and IVb. This arboreal formation indicates a temperate, humid climate (Sánchez Goñi 1993). Also, in Carihuela, the basal sequences (units XI and XII) indicate a Mediterranean humid climate that can be attributed to OIS 5 (Vega and Carrión 1993).

In Abric Romaní, OIS 4 was preceded by thermofilous vegetation interrupted by grasses and an expansion of the steppe. In the same shelter, a high proportion of arboreal pollen reaches 72 percent of total. This situation indicates a cold, humid climate (Burjachs and Julià 1994). In Carihuela, the disappearance of mesothermofilous taxa documents this stage, with a cold but still Mediterranean climate (Vega and Carrión 1993).

Oxygen Isotope Stage 3 is very well documented in the pollen sequence of Abric Romaní. From 57 to 50 ka B.P. it is characterized by strong climatic oscillations. Mesofilous taxa only develop in short warm phases with increasing humidity. In general, the climate is relatively cold. Subsequently, the emergence and increase of *Olea* and *Quercus* indicate a warm, humid climate. Towards 49 ka B.P. the steppe extends, and there is abundant *Artemisia*, indicating an arid climatic situation. An improvement is documented from 46 to 40 ka B.P., characterized by the presence of *Juniperus*, *Quercus*, *Pinus*, and *Olea*. Finally, between 40 and 37 ka B.P., *Olea* and *Phillyrea* have been documented at the site of Arbreda (lower assemblage A). There is a decrease in grasses, and conifers prevail (Burjachs and Renault-Miskovsky 1992). Everything seems to indicate the existence of a warming phase that has been associated with the Hengelo interstadial. Both in Arbreda and in Cova Beneito, an important climatic deterioration has been corroborated from 35 ka B.P., accompanied by an extension of the steppe (Carrión et al. 1993).

Around 40 ka B.P. a replacement of human populations is observed in the Iberian Peninsula. It would have been during the Hengelo interstadial that the progression of anatomically modern humans occurred in the northern part of the peninsula. However, it is very difficult to establish a direct relationship between climatic change and occupation of territory in Iberia.

REGIONAL DISTRIBUTION OF THE SITES

In the following sections, we will show the main characteristics of the Middle to Upper Paleolithic transition according to five geographical zones (fig. 4). The archaeological and paleoenvironmental sequences of the most important sites will be briefly presented, and the anthropological remains documented in each zone. Dates are shown in table 1.

Northern Zone

As a consequence of the important research tradition introduced in the Cantabrian cornice from the end of the past century, this zone of the peninsula comprises one of the major site concentrations in Europe (fig. 5). However, the number of sites varies considerably for each of the periods into which the Paleolithic is divided. From this viewpoint, the advanced Upper Paleolithic stages contain a bulk of information that diminishes as we go back in time. For the Early Upper Paleolithic and Middle Paleolithic, the number of locations is considerably reduced. Accordingly, the uneven character of the distribution can also be observed spatially. Most of the sites are located in the eastern part of the area corresponding to the Basque Country and Cantabrian Communities. On the contrary, the western part (Asturias and Galicia) only contains three relevant sites from the perspective of this paper. In addition, a good deal of the available data corresponds to excavations carried out at the beginning of this century, and their results are often not comparable to those obtained nowadays. Many sites have serious problems of stratigraphic interpretation and even disregard the location of some of the materials. On the other hand, some of the levels attributed to the Early Upper Paleolithic in the literature correspond to assemblages with few diagnostic elements, whose identification is based on their location and comparison of Upper Paleolithic sequences with Solutrean and Gravettian occupations.

From a geographic point of view, the region appears as a narrow corridor with an east-west orientation between the Cantabrian range, which separates it from the south, and the Cantabrian Sea to the north. The zone is crossed by numerous rivers flowing transversely to the range. During the Middle Paleolithic and Early Upper Paleolithic, the majority of sites were located in valleys close to the coast. Most of the sites documenting Middle Paleolithic occupations also comprise levels corresponding to the Early Upper Paleolithic, which indicates a continuous use of caves and shelters. Among the locations attributed to the Middle Paleolithic we must mention the sequences of El Pendo Cave, El Castillo, and Cueva Morín, for they have contributed the greatest amount of data, especially the latter two. However, we must also note other sites such as Cueva del Conde, La Flecha, Cueva del Otero, Axlor, Lezetxiki, and Amalda. The last three are located in the Basque Country. To these locations we must add recently excavated sites, especially the La Viña rockshelter, in which late Middle Paleolithic and Early Upper Paleolithic occupations have been documented.

Of all these sequences, especially noteworthy is that of El Castillo, which contains an estimated 18–20 meters of sediment and has been divided into 26 layers. In this sequence, a complete series of levels corresponding to the Middle Paleolithic and Early Upper Paleolithic has been documented. The top of the Middle Paleolithic (level 20) presents sedimentary characteristics corresponding to harsh climatic conditions (Cabrera et al. 1993; Cabrera and Bernaldo de Quirós 1996) attributed to a cold phase from Würm II immediately prior to the Hengelo interstadial. It is separated from the first Upper Paleolithic level by an archaeologically sterile layer (level 19) that reflects conditions of strong humidity identified with the Hengelo interstadial. The base of the Upper Paleolithic (level 18) has provided a broad series of dates that tends to locate the beginning of the Cantabrian Aurignacian around 40 ka B.P. This level would correspond to a slightly

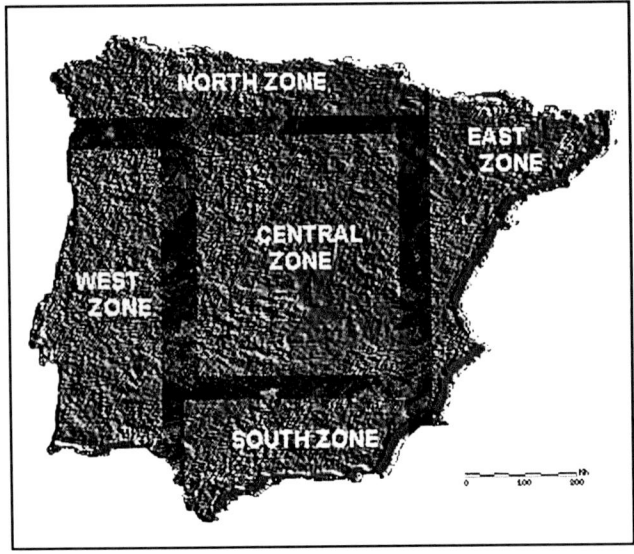

Figure 4. Location of the site distribution zones.

TABLE 1
Absolute dates and dating methods for certain Middle and Early Upper Paleolithic sites in the Iberian Peninsula

Site	Level	Date (kyr B.P.)	Method	Lab No.	Source
NORTHERN ZONE					
Middle Paleolithic					
Lezetxiki	V	57.0±2.0	U-Series		1
	V	70.0±9.0	U-Series		1
	V	140.0±17.0	ESR		1
Kurtzia		41.4±2.5	Conv ^{14}C	UGRA-293	2
La Flecha	Flowstone	31.6±0.0	Conv ^{14}C	SI-4460	3
Early Upper Paleolithic					
A Valiña	I	34.8+1.9/-1.5	Conv ^{14}C	GrN-17729	4
Cueva Morín	10	36.96±6.5	Conv. ^{14}C		5
	8A	28.43±0.5	Conv. ^{14}C	SI-952	5
	8A	28.15±0.7	Conv. ^{14}C	SI-952A	5
	8A	28.6±1.2	Conv. ^{14}C	SI-956	5
	7	29.51±0.8	Conv. ^{14}C	SI-955	5
	7	28.05±1.4	Conv. ^{14}C	SI-955A	5
	7/6	32.41±0.8	Conv. ^{14}C	SI-954	5
El Castillo	18b1	38.5±1.8	^{14}C AMS	AA-2406	6
	18b2	37.1±2.2	^{14}C AMS	OxA-2473	7
	18b2	37.7±1.8	^{14}C AMS	AA-2407	6
	18b2	38.5±1.3	^{14}C AMS	OxA-2474	7
	18b2	40.7±1.6	^{14}C AMS	OxA-2475	7
	18c	39.8±1.4	^{14}C AMS	OxA-2478	7
	18c	40.0±2.1	^{14}C AMS	AA-2405	6
	18c	40.7±1.5	^{14}C AMS	OxA-2476	7
	18c	41.1±1.7	^{14}C AMS	OxA-2477	7
	18c	42.2±2.1	^{14}C AMS	GifA-89147	7
Ekain	IXb	>30.6	Conv. ^{14}C	I-11056	8
La Viña	XIII Inf.	36.5±0.7	Conv. ^{14}C	Ly-6390	9
Labeko	IX bottom	34.21±1.2	Conv. ^{14}C	Ua-3324	10
	IX bottom	26.57±0.5	Conv. ^{14}C	Ua-3034	10
	IX	29.75±0.7	Conv. ^{14}C	Ua-3325	10
	VII bottom	26.91±0.5	Conv. ^{14}C	Ua-3320	10
	VII top	31.45±0.9	Conv. ^{14}C	Ua-3321	10
	V	30.61±0.8	Conv. ^{14}C	Ua-3322	10
	V	23.36±0.3	Conv. ^{14}C	Ua-3035	10
	IV	21.66±0.3	Conv. ^{14}C	Ua-3323	10
EASTERN ZONE					
Middle Paleolithic					
Roca dels Bous	R3	38.8±1.2	^{14}C AMS	AA-6481	11
	S1	>46.9	^{14}C AMS	AA-6480	11

TABLE 1 CONTINUED
Absolute dates and dating methods for certain Middle and Early Upper Paleolithic sites in the Iberian Peninsula

Site	Level	Date (kyr B.P.)	Method	Lab No.	Source
Ermitons	IV	36.43±1.8	Conv. ^{14}C	CSIC-197	12
	IV	33.19±0.6	^{14}C AMS	OxA-3725	12
Arbreda	I	39.4±1.4	^{14}C AMS	AA-3776	13
	I	34.1±0.7	^{14}C AMS	AA-3777	13
	I	41.4±1.6	^{14}C AMS	AA-3778	13
	I	44.56±2.4	^{14}C AMS	OxA-3731	12
	Basal MP	83.0+10.7/-8.7	Pa/U		14
	Basal MP	85.1+38.2/-26.7	Th/U		14
	Basal MP	89.1+36.8/-24.3	Ra/U		14
Banyoles		45.0±4.0	U-Series		15
Abric Romaní	Travert.	43.8±1.5	U-Series		16
	Travert.	46.3±1.5*	U-Series		17
	Travert.	42.7±1.3*	U-Series		17
	B	43.5±1.2	^{14}C AMS	NZA-2312	17
	Travert.	43.4±1.5	U-Series		16
	Travert.	45.6±3.5*	U-Series		16
	Travert.	43.2±1.1*	U-Series		16
	Travert.	44.4±0.2*	U-Series		16
	D	40.6±0.9	^{14}C AMS	NZA-2313	18
	E	43.2±1.1	^{14}C AMS	NZA-2314	18
	H	44.5±1.2	^{14}C AMS	NZA-2315	18
	Travert.	46.5±1.7*	U-Series		16
	Travert.	48.0±1.6	U-Series		16
	Travert.	49.3±1.6	U-Series		16
	Travert.	50.4±0.5*	U-Series		16
	Travert.	52.3±0.6*	U-Series		16
	Travert.	52.2±1.6	U-Series		16
	Travert.	54.5±0.5*	U-Series		16
	Travert.	54.2±1.1*	U-Series		16
	Travert.	56.8±3.2*	U-Series		16
	Travert.	58.6±1.2*	U-Series		16
	Travert.	60.0±1.4*	U-Series		16
	Travert.	59.2±1.1*	U-Series		16
	Travert.	70.2±2.6	U-Series		19
Cova 120		57.9+6.8/-6.5	U-Series		20
Gabasa	e	46.5+4.4/-2.8	Conv. ^{14}C	GrN-12809	21
Cova Beneito	D1	38.8±1.9	^{14}C AMS	AA-1387	22
	D1	30.16±0.6	Conv. ^{14}C	Gif	22
Cova Negra	V	28.9±5.6	Conv. ^{14}C	C-847	23
	V	>28.7	Conv. ^{14}C	C-848	23
	V	>28.7	Conv. ^{14}C	C-849	23
Early Upper Paleolithic					
Arbreda	H	37.7±1.0	^{14}C AMS	AA-3779	13
	H	37.7±1.0	^{14}C AMS	AA-3780	13

TABLE 1 CONTINUED
Absolute dates and dating methods for certain Middle and Early Upper Paleolithic sites in the Iberian Peninsula

Site	Level	Date (kyr B.P.)	Method	Lab No.	Source
	H	39.9±1.3	^{14}C AMS	AA-3781	13
	H	38.7±1.2	^{14}C AMS	AA-3782	13
	H	37.34±1.0	^{14}C AMS	OxA-3729	12
	H	35.48±0.8	^{14}C AMS	OxA-3730	12
	H	>33.5	Conv. ^{14}C	Beta-46690	24
Reclau Viver	B	30.19±0.5	^{14}C AMS	OxA-3726	12
	A	40.0±1.4	^{14}C AMS	OxA-3727	12
Mollet		33.78±0.7	^{14}C AMS	OxA-3728	12
Abric Romaní	Travert.	40.8±1.5*	U-Series		16
	Travert.	39.4±1.5	U-Series		16
	Travert.	42.9±1.6	U-Series		16
	Travert.	39.1±1.5	U-Series		16
	Travert.	44.4±1.6*	U-Series		17
	Travert.	41.8±0.8*	U-Series		17
	Travert.	36.3±1.3	Conv. ^{14}C		17
	A	37.29±0.9	^{14}C AMS	AA-7395	17
	A	35.4±0.8	^{14}C AMS	AA-8037A	17
	A	37.9±1.0	^{14}C AMS	AA-8037B	17
	A	36.59±0.6	^{14}C AMS	NZA-2311	17
Cova Beneito	C4	26.04±0.8	Conv. ^{14}C	Gif-7650	22
	C4	33.9±1.1	^{14}C AMS	AA-1388	22
Mallaetes	XII	29.69±0.5	Conv. ^{14}C	KN-1/926	25

SOUTHERN ZONE

Middle Paleolithic

Site	Level	Date (kyr B.P.)	Method	Lab No.	Source
Gorham's Cave	G	47.7±1.5	Conv. ^{14}C		26
	G	49.2±3.2	Conv. ^{14}C		26
	Context 24	32.28±0.42	^{14}C AMS	OxA-7857	35
	Context 18	42.20±1.10	^{14}C AMS	OxA-7791	35
	Context 22	45.30±1.7	^{14}C AMS	OxA-6075	35
	Context 22D	51.70±3.3	^{14}C AMS	OxA-7790	35
Vanguard Cave	Top section	45.20±2.4	^{14}C AMS	OxA-7389	35
	Unit 53	54.00±3.3	^{14}C AMS	OxA-6891	35
	Unit 53	46.90±1.5	^{14}C AMS	OxA-6892	35
	Unit 54	>49.4	^{14}C AMS	OxA-7127	35
	Unit 55	41.80±1.4	^{14}C AMS	OxA-6998	35
	SideChamber	>44.1	^{14}C AMS	OxA-70778	35
Devil's Tower	3	>30.0	Conv. ^{14}C		26
	4	c.29.0	Conv. ^{14}C		26
Bajondillo		27.3±1.7	U-Series		31
	bottom	25.3-26.5±10/15%	ESR		31
Zafarraya	I-3/7	25.1±1.3	U-Series		27
	I-3/7	26.9±2.7	U-Series		27
	I-3/7	28.9±4.2	U-Series		27

TABLE 1 CONTINUED
Absolute dates and dating methods for certain Middle and Early Upper Paleolithic sites in the Iberian Peninsula

Site	Level	Date (kyr B.P.)	Method	Lab No.	Source
	I-3/7	29.8±0.6	Conv. ^{14}C	Gif-9140-II	27
	I-8	31.7±3.6	U-Series		27
	I-8	31.8±0.5	Conv. ^{14}C	Gif/LSM-9140-I	27
	D	33.4±0.2	U-Series		27
Carihuela	VI.9	45.2±1.2	^{14}C AMS	Beta-74381	32
Early Upper Paleolithic					
Gorham's Cave	D	27.86±0.3	Conv. ^{14}C	GrN-1363	26
	D	28.70±0.2	Conv. ^{14}C	GrN-1455	26
	Context 7	25.68±0.28	^{14}C AMS	OxA-6997	35
	Context 9	30.20±0.7	^{14}C AMS	OxA-7074	35
	Context 9	29.80±0.7	^{14}C AMS	OxA-7075	35
	Context 9	30.25±0.7	^{14}C AMS	OxA-7076	35
	Context 9	29.25±0.65	^{14}C AMS	OxA-7077	35
	Context 13a	29.25±0.75	^{14}C AMS	OxA-7110	35
	Context 15	28.68±0.24	^{14}C AMS	OxA-7792	35
WESTERN ZONE					
Middle Paleolithic					
Columbeira	20	28.9±0.9	Conv. ^{14}C	Gif-2704	28
	16	26.4±0.7	Conv. ^{14}C	Gif-2703	28
Figueira Brava	inf.	30.05±0.5	Conv. ^{14}C	ICEN-386	28
	ind.	30.93±0.7	Conv. ^{14}C	ICEN-387	28
	2	30.56+11.7/-10.7	U-Series	SMU-232	29
	2	44.80+15.8/-13.9	U-Series	SMU-233	29
Caldeirao	K	27.6±0.6	Conv. ^{14}C	OxA-1941	28
Foz do Enxarrique	C	32.93±1.0	U-Series	SMU-255	29
	C	34.08±0.8	U-Series	SMU-226	29
	C	34.09±0.9	U-Series	SMU-224	29
Salemas (quarry)	inf.	27.17+1.0/-0.9	Conv. ^{14}C	ICEN-361	29
	inf.	>29.2	Conv. ^{14}C	ICEN-371	29
	inf.	29.89+1.1/-0.9	Conv. ^{14}C	ICEN-366	29
Salemas (cave)	tvb	20.74±0.47	Conv. ^{14}C	ICEN-384	29
	tvb	23.83±0.58	Conv. ^{14}C	ICEN-383	29
	tvb	24.82±0.55	Conv. ^{14}C	ICEN-379	29
Escoural	3a	48.9+5.8/-5.5	U-Series	SMU-250	29
Vilas Ruivas	B	51.0+13.0/-12.0	TL	BM-VRU1	29
	B	68.0+35.0/-26.0	TL	BM-VRU2	29
Early Upper Paleolithic					
Gato Preto		38.1±3.9*	TL		28
Pego do Diabo	2	28.12+0.8/-0.7	Conv. ^{14}C	ICEN-732	28
	2	23.08±0.4	Conv. ^{14}C	ICEN-490	28

Table 1 continued
Absolute dates and dating methods for certain Middle and Early Upper Paleolithic sites in the Iberian Peninsula

Site	Level	Date (kyr B.P.)	Method	Lab No.	Source
CENTRAL ZONE					
Middle Paleolithic					
Cueva Millán	1a	37.6±0.7	Conv. ^{14}C	GrN-11021	30
	1b	37.45±0.6	Conv. ^{14}C	GrN-1161	30
Peña Miel	e	45.0+1.4/-1.2	Conv. ^{14}C	GRN-12123	21
	e	39.9±10.5	Conv. ^{14}C	UGRA-128	21
	g	>40.0	Conv. ^{14}C	CSIC-546	21
La Ermita	5a-b	31.1±0.5	^{14}C AMS	OxA-4603	33
Jarama VI	2	29.5±2.7	^{14}C AMS	Beta-56638	34
	2	32.6±1.8	^{14}C AMS	Beta-56639	34
	2	23.3±0.5	^{14}C AMS	Beta-56639	34

Chatelperronian levels are underlined

* Average

Sources: 1. Baldeon 1993, 2. Muñoz et al. 1990, 3. Butzer 1981, 4. Fernández Rodríguez et al. 1993, 5. Bernaldo de Quirós 1982, 6. Cabrera & Bischoff 1989, 7. Cabrera & Bernaldo de Quirós 1996, 8. Marieskurrena 1990, 9. Fortea 1996, 10. Barandiarán 1996, 11. Terradas et al. 1993, 12. Maroto et al. 1996, 13. Bischoff et al. 1989, 14. Yokoyama et al. 1987, 15. Julià & Bischoff 1991, 16. Bischoff et al. 1988, 17. Bischoff et al. 1994, 18. Vaquero 1997, 19. Burjachs & Julià 1994, 20. Agustí et al. 1991, 21. Utrilla & Montes 1993, 22. Iturbe et al. 1993, 23. Villaverde & Fumanal 1990, 24. Soler & Maroto 1993, 25. Fortea & Jordá 1976, 26. Barton 1988, 27. Hublin et al. 1995, 28. Zilhão 1993, 29. Raposo 1995, 30. Moure & García-Soto 1983, 31. Cortés & Simón 1997, 32. Vega et al. 1997, 33. Moure et al. 1997, 34. Garcia Valero 1997, 35. Barton et al. 1999.

cold and humid period in which the rigorous conditions tend to be accentuated from bottom to top, which would be comparable to one of the first of the cold pulsations of Würm III. The temperate character of the environmental conditions during the Middle to Upper Paleolithic transition has also been manifested in Cueva Morín, where pollen analyses indicate that the end of the Middle Paleolithic, the Chatelperronian, and the archaic Aurignacian are situated in a phase of climatic amelioration correlated with the Hengelo interstadial (González Echegaray et al. 1971). The Middle Paleolithic of Kurtzia would also correspond to an interstadial period dated around 41 ka B.P. (Muñoz et al. 1990).

The Middle to Upper Paleolithic transition has also been documented in La Viña rockshelter, which has been excavated during the last few years (Fortea 1996). The lower levels of this site correspond to the Middle Paleolithic, dated to more than 47 ka B.P. in level XIV and to 42 ka B.P. in the boundary between levels XIV and XIII. Lower level XIII, attributed to the Aurignacian and yielding numerous carinated tools and Dufour bladelets, has provided a date of around 36 ka B.P. The sedimentary features of the deposit indicate that both the Middle and Early Upper Paleolithic are located in an interstadial-type climate. This is consistent with the results obtained for El Castillo and Cueva Morín.

As we have previously indicated, most of these sites also contain Early Upper Paleolithic levels, generally attributed to the Aurignacian, although some Chatelperronian levels are also documented. Several succeeding stadia have been distinguished within the Aurignacian sequence (archaic, typical, and evolved Aurignacian), whose chronological validity must be evaluated in light of currently available radiometric dates. The initial Aurignacian would be represented in Cueva Morín (levels 9, 8, and 8b), Cueva del Pendo

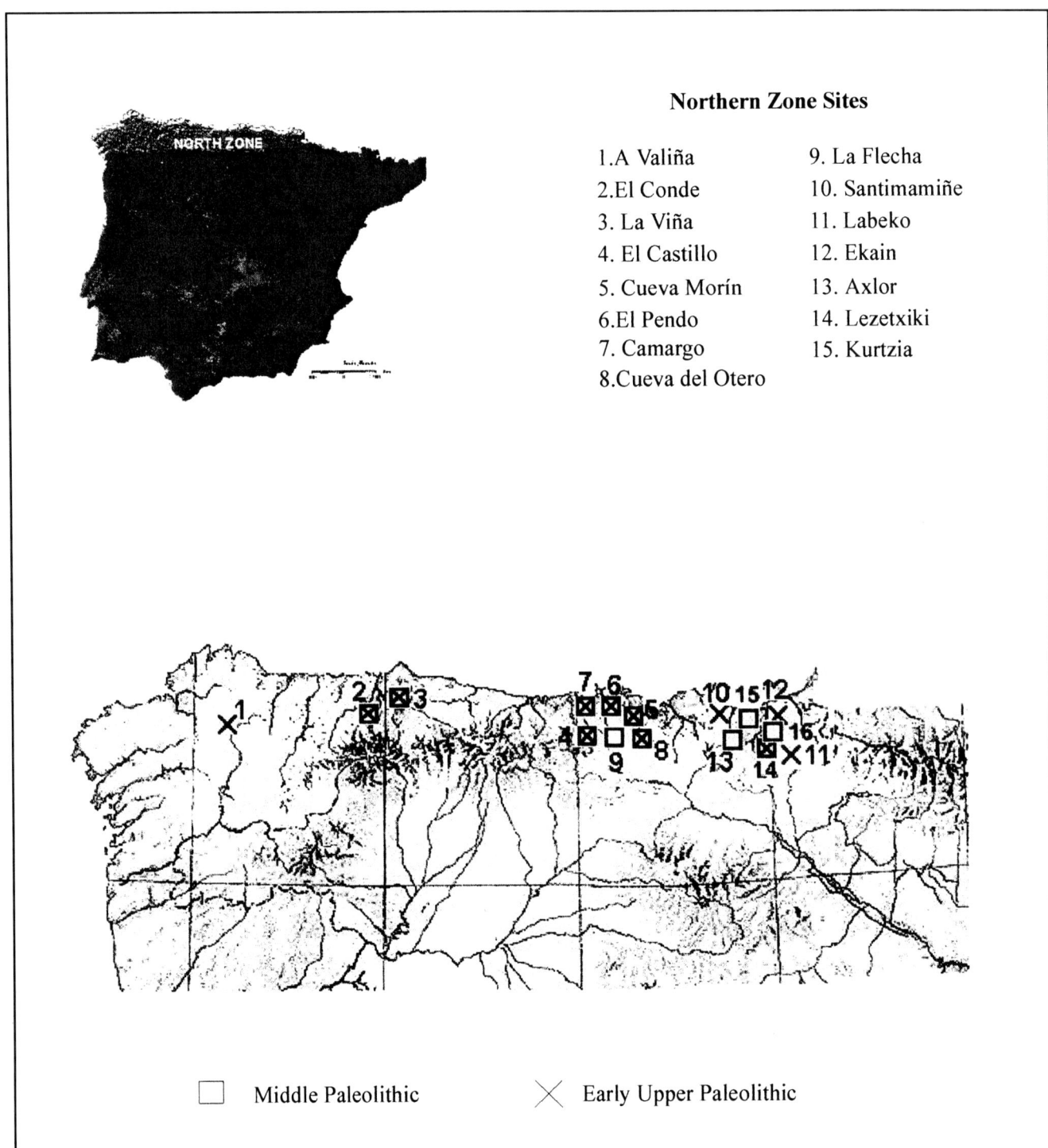

Figure 5. Distribution of Middle and Early Upper Paleolithic sites in the Northern Zone.

(levels 8a and 8b) and Cueva del Castillo (level 18). The levels corresponding to the typical Aurignacian are levels 6 and 7 of Cueva Morín and level 7 of El Pendo. Finally, level 5I of Cueva Morín, levels 6 and 5b of El Pendo, and levels 6, 4, and 5 of Cueva del Otero have been ascribed to an evolved Aurignacian (Bernaldo de Quirós 1982).

In the Basque Country, the most relevant sequence is that of Lezetxiki cave, where according to some interpretations, the Middle to Upper Paleolithic transition has been documented. One of the most relevant aspects of this transition is the identification of an assemblage of Neandertal dental remains in level III, which has been ascribed to the Aurignacian by some authors (Esparza 1993). However, the latest revisions of these materials tend to qualify considerably the importance of this site from the point of view of the Middle to Upper Paleolithic transition. The radiometric dates are not conclusive, although they tend to make the base of the deposit older, according to the interpretation supported by Baldeón (1993) and Sánchez Goñi (1993), who locate levels VIII and VII in the antepenultimate glaciation, while level VI would correspond to OIS 5. In the context of the Middle to Upper Paleolithic transition, the main problems are found in the attribution of levels IV and III. To Baldeón, the industry from level IV is fully framed in the Middle Paleolithic, while level III, which contains diagnostic Upper Paleolithic elements in a Mousterian matrix, would have resulted from a mix of industries coming from different cultural periods. In any case, the contextual problems of these levels weaken their utility in the framework of the issue analyzed here.

The Chatelperronian is represented in level 10 of Cueva Morín, which has provided a radiocarbon date of around 37 ka B.P., and in level 8 of El Pendo, which documents a situation similar to some French sites such as Roc-de-Combe and Le Piage, intercalated in the Aurignacian sequence between the archaic Aurignacian and the typical Aurignacian. This situation has been used as an argument in favor of the contemporaneous nature of both techno-complexes. Nevertheless, this interstratification could be the result of stratigraphic mistakes (Zilhão and d'Errico 1999) produced by processes of redeposition and admixture. Among the most significant results of research carried out in recent years, we must point out the identification of Chatelperronian assemblages at both boundaries of the studied zone: the Basque Country and Galicia.

In the site of Labeko Koba (Arrasate-Mondragón, Guipuzcoa), an Early Upper Paleolithic sequence with a Chatelperronian basal level has been identified, although this identification was based on a very limited number of remains (Arrizabalaga 1993). This site has yielded several dates between 26 and 34 ka B.P. On top, there is a series of Aurignacian levels, and the lowest of these contains a high percentage of bladelets with Dufour-type semi-abrupt retouch, ascribed to the Proto-Aurignacian. In the Aurignacian sequence of Labeko, a series of dates has been obtained of between 31 and 21 ka B.P. (Barandiarán 1996). The existence of Chatelperronian levels has been claimed in other sites in the Basque Country (Esparza 1993), although they are problematic attributions, either because of the reduced number of diagnostic elements (Ekain, Deba, Guipuzcoa) or because these are old references with no corroboration from the revision of the materials (Santimamiñe, Cortezubi, Vizcaya). At the other boundary of the northern zone, the excavations carried out in A Valiña cave (Castroverde, Lugo) have revealed the existence of an Early Upper Paleolithic level (presumably Chatelperronian) dated around 34 ka B.P. and set in a temperate, humid climatic context (Fernández Rodríguez et al. 1993).

Human remains attributed to the Middle and Early Upper Paleolithic are scarce (fig. 6), and many of them were recovered during excavations at the beginning of the century at currently unknown locations (Garralda 1993). We must point out, however, that most of the human remains associated with peninsular Upper Paleolithic assemblages are located in this zone. Until now, Neandertal remains have only been found in the Basque Country, in the sites of Axlor and Lezetxiki. However, both of these cases involve dental remains, and, in the case of Lezetxiki, their stratigraphic position presents the aforementioned problems. For the Early Upper Paleolithic, the main data comes from the Castillo and Camargo caves, although in both cases the remains come from non-revised, old excavations and were lost after the initial studies. In El Castillo, the remains were found at the base of the Aurignacian (level 18) and consisted of several skull fragments, dental pieces, and a mandibular fragment from two or three individuals, one of them juvenile. The description of these remains evidenced a considerable robusticity, as well as archaic characteristics, about which doubts were voiced regarding their taxonomic association. In Camargo, a cranial fragment attributed to *Homo sapiens sapiens* was found, also in an Aurignacian level. Finally, we must cite the evidence from Cueva Morín; although there are no bone remains in this case, the cast of the body of a tall individual was found in an archaic Aurignacian burial. The scarcity of remains, together with contextual problems impedes the reliable establishment of the morphology of the populations related to the Middle to Upper Paleolithic transition.

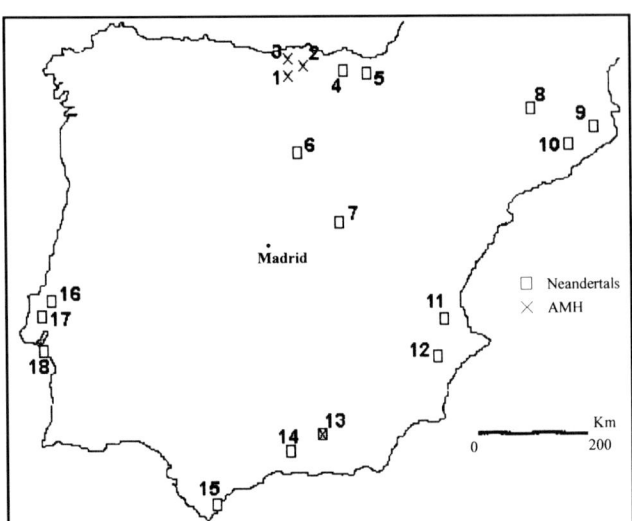

Figure 6. Distribution of Neandertal and anatomically modern human remains in the Iberian Peninsula. 1. El Castillo, 2. Cueva Morín, 3. Camargo, 4. Azlor, 5. Lezetxiki, 6. Valdegoba, 7. Los Casares, 8. Gabasa, 9. Banyoles, 10. Abric Agut, 11. Cova Negra, 12. El Salt, 13. Zafarraya, 14. Carihuela, 15. Devil's Tower, 16. Columbeira, 17. Salemas, 18. Figueira Brava.

Eastern Zone

In the eastern part of the peninsula, the distribution of sites shows the same uneven pattern observed in the northern zone (fig. 7). While they are relatively abundant in some of the areas for which there is available data (e.g., Northern Catalonia, Central Valencia), the information in other areas is very fragmentary (e.g., Southern Catalonia, Northern Valencia). In this zone, we must point out the role played by a series of long sequences that have served to structure the cultural dynamics at a regional level, including those from Abric Romaní (Capellades, Barcelona) and Cova Negra (Xàtiva, Valencia) for the Middle Paleolithic and the Cueva de l'Arbreda (Serinyà, Girona) for the Upper Paleolithic.

In Catalonia, the sites are found in two main geographic areas. The first area consists of the Pre-Pyrenaic ranges, where several Middle Paleolithic occupations have been documented in recent years (e.g., Gabasa, Roca dels Bous, and Cova 120), and can be added to those previously known (Ermitons). However, no occupation that could reliably be attributed to the Early Upper Paleolithic has been documented in this zone. On the other hand, in the Catalanides area, which comprise the littoral and pre-littoral Catalan mountain ranges, we can recognize two principal nuclei: (a) the north-east nucleus, around the lake of Banyoles, where the sites of Arbreda, Reclau Viver, and Mollet I are located and where the Banyoles mandible was found; and (b) the central part of the Catalanides, around the locality of Capellades, where the sites of Abric Romaní and Abric Agut are found. Here, Middle and Early Upper Paleolithic levels have been identified. In the Valencian Community, the main sites have been documented in the eastern foothills of the Betic Ranges: Cova Negra, Mallaetes, Cova Beneito (Muro, Alicante), and El Salt (Alcoi, Alicante).

Both Abric Romaní and Arbreda document the Middle to Upper Paleolithic transition around 40 ka B.P., which has been corroborated by dates provided by the Early Upper Paleolithic of Reclau Viver (Maroto et al. 1996). Abric Romaní contains a sequence of almost 20 meters, dated between 70 and 40 ka B.P. (fig. 8); most of the 27 archaeological levels documented correspond to the Middle Paleolithic (fig. 9) with the exception of the most recent level (level A), attributed to the archaic Aurignacian. The uppermost part of the sequence, which documents the cultural change, is dated by both uranium/thorium series and ^{14}C AMS (Bischoff et al. 1988, 1994). The ^{14}C AMS dates are situated in the Early Upper Paleolithic around 37 ka B.P., while the U/Th dates indicate a date of around 42 ka B.P. These data suggest an age difference between the radiocarbon date and the U/Th date that may be greater than 5 ka at around 40 ka B.P. The Aurignacian lithic industry from Abric Romaní shows similarities to the industry from Arbreda, especially in the abundant presence of bladelets with Dufour-type abrupt retouch (Carbonell et al. 1996), which seem to characterize the first phases of the Aurignacian in Catalonia. As mentioned above, the pollen analysis has identified five climatic phases in the Abric Romaní sequence (Burjachs and Julià 1994), from OIS 5 to a period of climatic tempering corresponding to the Hengelo interstadial. The Middle to Upper Paleolithic transition would have occurred during the final part of the interstadial, when the climatic conditions started to degenerate (Burjachs and Julià 1996).

In Arbreda, the Middle Paleolithic sequence has been dated between 83 ka and about 40 ka B.P. The first Upper Paleolithic level (level H) appears immediately above, with no significant sedimentary ruptures. It has yielded a series of ^{14}C AMS dates of 38.3±0.5 ka B.P. on average. The pollen analysis indicates a prevalence of relatively temperate conditions during the final Middle Paleolithic, with equivalencies in the Moershoofd-Hengelo interstadials. In contrast, the Early Upper Paleolithic was located during a cold phase immediately following the Hengelo interstadial (Burjachs and Renault-Miskovsky 1992). From a typological point of view, in Arbreda, as in Abric Romaní, the Early Upper Paleolithic is characterized by a significant presence of Dufour-type bladelets with semi-abrupt retouch (Maroto et al. 1996) (fig. 10).

In the context of the pre-Pyrenees foothills, several Middle Paleolithic occupations have been documented. These contrast with the practical absence of reliable references for the Early Upper Paleolithic (Terradas et al. 1993; Utrilla and Montes 1993). With the exception of Cova 120 (Agustí et al. 1991), which comprises dates prior to 60 ka B.P., the remaining sites (Ermitons, Roca dels Bous, and Gabasa) have provided dates from the end of the Middle Paleolithic. For some of these sites, the persistence of the Middle Paleolithic during periods following the Würm interstadial has been proposed. The most solid evidence in favor of this relatively late persistence of the Middle to Upper Paleolithic transition in the interior of Catalonia is currently provided by the Ermitons cave (Sales de Llierca, Girona), where ^{14}C AMS dates of 33.19±0.66 ka B.P. have been obtained (stratum IV). This is a particularly recent date, especially when compared with that from the Middle to Upper Paleolithic transition in Arbreda, located only 20 km east.

The sedimentary study of the Gabasa cave, however, would indicate, according to Hoyos et al. (1992), that most of the Middle Paleolithic occupations correspond to the Würm interstadial, while the last level (level A) was integrated in Würm III. Nevertheless, as Blasco et al. (1996) admit, the dates from level C, which indicates a date more recent than 46.9 ka B.P., seems to contradict this interpretation of the sedimentary data. Furthermore, the argument used to give context to the lithic industry of levels A and C in an

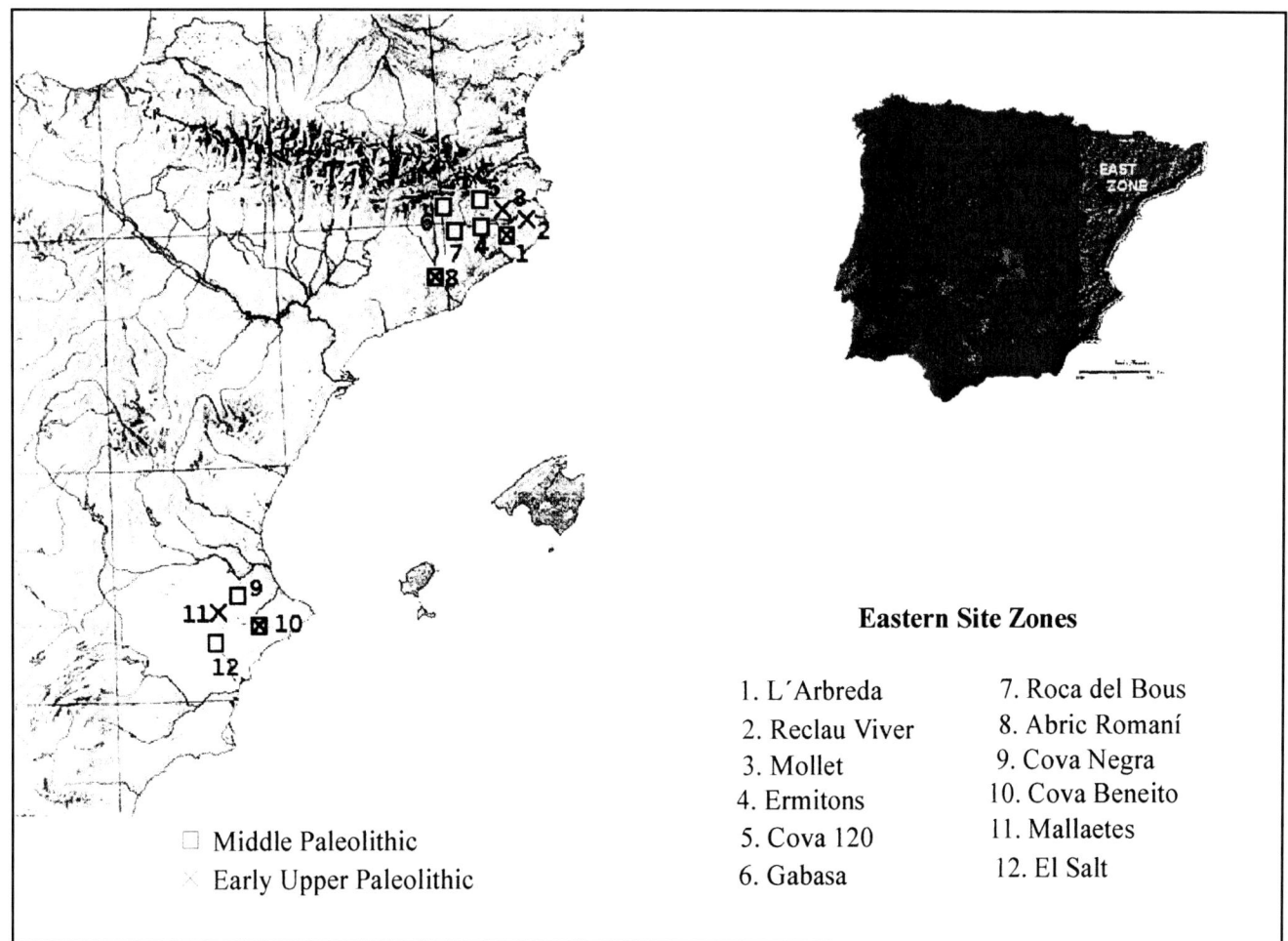

Figure 7. Distribution of Middle Paleolithic and Early Upper Paleolithic sites in the Eastern Zone.

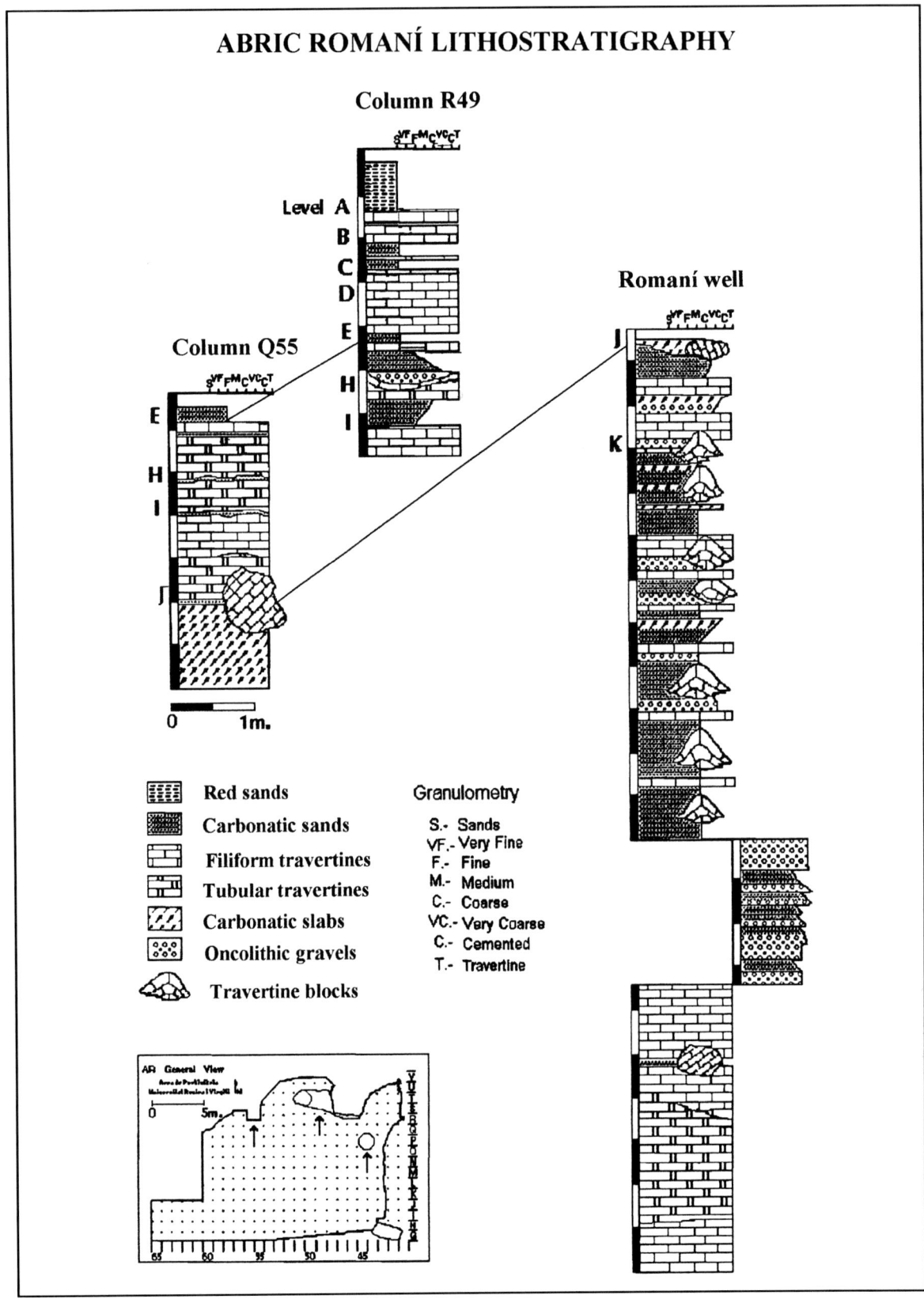

Figure 8. Stratigraphic sequence of Abric Romaní.

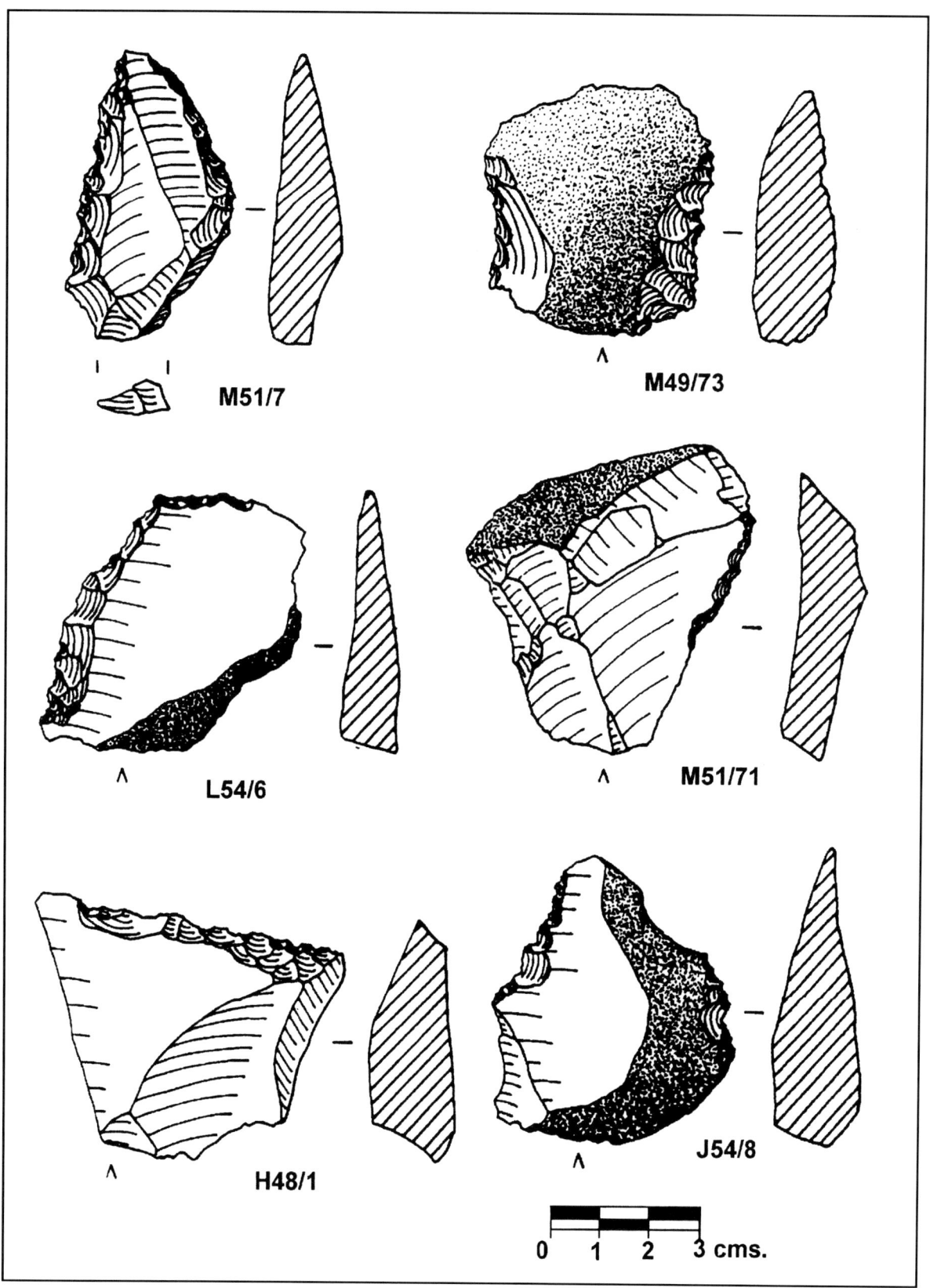

Figure 9. Retouched artifacts from level Jb of Abric Romaní.

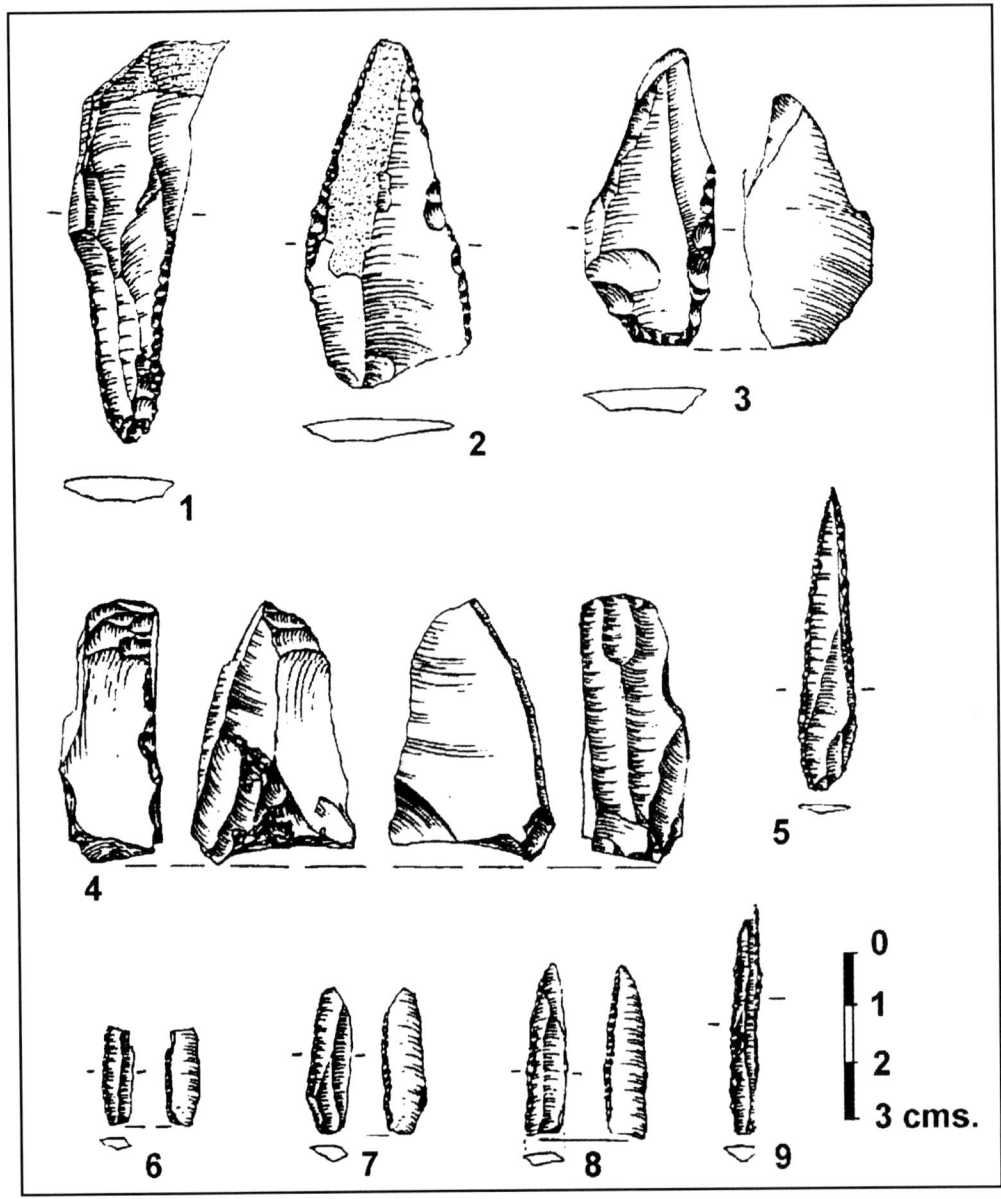

Figure 10. Retouched artifacts from level H of Arbreda Cave (from Maroto et al. 1996); Aurignacian blade (1), Retouched blade (2), Burin (3), Core (4), Font Yves Point (*perçoir*) (5), Dufour bladelets (6–9).

evolved stage of the Middle Paleolithic (the existence of a high proportion of *débordant* flakes) also fails to convince. Finally, the Middle Paleolithic of Roca dels Bous has provided a date of around 38 ka B.P., which, although it would render the site contemporaneous with the early Aurignacian of Arbreda and Abric Romaní, is not as recent as the date documented at Ermitons (Terradas et al. 1993).

In the Valencia region, the site of Cova Negra contains one of the most important Middle Pale-olithic sequences. Six sedimentary phases have been differentiated (Cova Negra A–F), and the paleoclimatic interpretation places the base of the stratigraphy (CN–A) in OIS 5a (Villaverde and Fumanal 1990). The CN–E phase has been correlated with the Würm interstadial, for which the top of the sequence (CN–F) would fully correspond to the recent Würm. All the Cova Negra levels can be attributed to the Middle Paleolithic, despite the finding of some characteristic Upper Paleolithic artifacts in archaeological level 1. This level was found partially disturbed and in any case, such pieces cannot be related to the Early Upper Paleolithic. Hence, this interpretation suggests that the Middle Paleolithic followed the Würm II–III interstadial here, while some sites from the northern peninsula (e.g., El Castillo, Arbreda, and Abric Romaní) already contained Upper Paleolithic industries. Among the remaining sequences of the Levantine regions attributed to the Middle Paleolithic, we must point out the site of El Salt, the base of which has been dated to around 80 ka B.P. (Galván 1992).

The only site of this Levantine area in which the Middle to Upper Paleolithic transition has been documented is Cova Beneito. Its stratigraphic sequence has been structured in 12 levels (Fumanal and Carrión 1992); the two lower levels (XII–XI) show mild and humid climatic conditions that would correspond to the Würm II–III interstadial. The identification of Middle Paleolithic occupations during the subsequent environmental degradation (level X) stresses the prevalence of this industry at relatively late dates (Carrión et al. 1993), as was the case for Cova Negra. Finally, the Aurignacian has been documented in level XII from Mallaetes, with a date of 29.6 ± 0.5 ka B.P., providing a characteristic bone industry that suggests it belongs to a relatively advanced stage of this techno-complex.

In this zone, the number of human remains is also limited, and all belong to cultural contexts attributed to the Middle Paleolithic. We must first cite the finding of the Banyoles mandible, although the taxonomic attribution of this, as well as its chronological position, have been the subject of debate. While most evaluations attribute this specimen to the Pre-Neandertal group, placing it earlier than the Upper Pleistocene, the recently obtained date (Julià and Bischoff 1991) on travertine adhering to the mandible is 44 ka B.P., which puts it within the final Middle Paleolithic. In this context, the evolved characteristics this mandible exhibits acquire new significance. An assemblage of human remains was also found in Cova Negra (a parietal, a juvenile mandibular fragment, and several tooth remains) located in the Middle Paleolithic sequence and attributed to *Homo sapiens neanderthalensis.* Aside from Banyoles and Cova Negra, other sites with Neandertal remains (Abric Agut, Gabasa, and El Salt) have only provided some isolated remains. However, we should mention the possible existence of a cranial fragment among the materials from Abric Agut. This specimen is currently under study, and judging from its archaeological context, it may belong to a Neandertal (Campillo, pers. comm.).

Southern Zone

From a geomorphological point of view, three major units can be recognized in the southern zone: Sierra Morena, the Guadalquivir Basin, and the Betic Range. The main sites are found within the Betic Range, where lithologic features favor the existence of caves and shelters. In Sierra Morena and the Guadalquivir River valley, the main references correspond to open-air sites, which often lack a clear stratigraphic context. Numerous sites excavated during the first third of this century exhibit serious problems regarding the stratigraphic provenience and cultural ascription of their materials. This is the case of the sites excavated by Louis Siret in the southeast quadrant (Vermeja, Palomarico, Perneras, and Zájara I), and the contribution of this area to the issue of the Middle to Upper Paleolithic transition has been questioned (Vega 1993). In this context, the number of sites retained in this synthesis is quite limited (fig. 11). Other sites present great potential, although data available from chronostratigraphic and cultural sequences are very scarce. This is especially so in the case of Cueva Horá (Darro, Granada), which contains one of the most important stratigraphic sequences of the peninsula, covering from the end of the Middle Pleistocene to the Holocene. Unfortunately, the data available for the work carried out at this site are scarce and fragmentary.

Of special relevance regarding the sites in the southern Peninsula in the frame of the Middle to Upper Paleolithic transition is the persistence of the Middle Paleolithic after the Würm Interstadial. This has already been suggested from the paleoenvironmental interpretation of certain stratigraphic sequences, especially that of Carihuela cave. As we have mentioned previously, some of the central sites of the eastern zone point in this direction, and the dates recently obtained in Boquete de Zafarraya tend to corroborate this interpretation.

Fifty stratigraphic levels have been identified in Carihuela (Píñar, Granada). These are structured in 12 units that cover from OIS 5 to the Holocene in a practically continuous sequence, with no significant sedimentary ruptures. Most of the levels (units XII–IVb) correspond to the Middle Paleolithic and have yielded some human remains attributed to archaic *Homo sapiens.* The Upper Paleolithic levels, located in the most poorly documented segment of the sequence, lack a precise cultural ascription, and whether they belong to the Early Upper Paleolithic can not be corroborated. In these levels, some remains of anatomically modern humans were recovered, although the determination of their stratigraphic position is subject to some problems

(Vega 1988). The paleoclimatic interpretation of the variations in the sedimentary deposit indicates the prevalence of the Middle Paleolithic after the Würm interstadial, as do the pollen analyses, which locate the top of the Middle Paleolithic (Unit V) at the beginning of OIS 2 (Vega and Carrión 1993). Although a series of TL dates are available, the results must be considered with caution, as they were carried out when this method was still in an experimental phase. Moreover, some of the dated samples display stratigraphic problems. However, the new AMS and U/Th dates currently being obtained are consistent with the stratigraphic interpretation proposed (Vega et al. 1997).

The most consistent evidence of the late prevalence of the Middle Paleolithic in the south of the peninsula has been provided by the excavations in Boquete de Zafarraya (Málaga). An assemblage of Neandertal remains associated with a characteristic Middle Paleolithic industry has been documented at this site, dates between 33 and 25 ka B.P. (Hublin et al. 1995). These dates corroborate the previous evaluations made from micromammal studies, which indicated cold conditions. This is consistent with a period following the Würm II–III Interstadial.

Gibraltar comprises one of the major concentrations of sites in the Iberian Peninsula. Disregarding those excavated during the last century, for which there are only inaccurate data, the most relevant sites from the point of view of the issue analyzed here are Devil's Tower and Gorham's Cave. Devil's Tower has a stratigraphic sequence structured in three major units. The paleontological data suggest the important contribution of carnivores in the formation of the archaeological site, at which a Neandertal human skull was found. The excavations of Gorham's Cave by Waechter revealed a sequence of almost 8 meters, subdivided into 26 levels, most of which correspond to the Middle Paleolithic. The base of the sequence has been correlated with OIS 5e, while the top of the Middle Paleolithic (level G) has been dated at around 47–49 ka

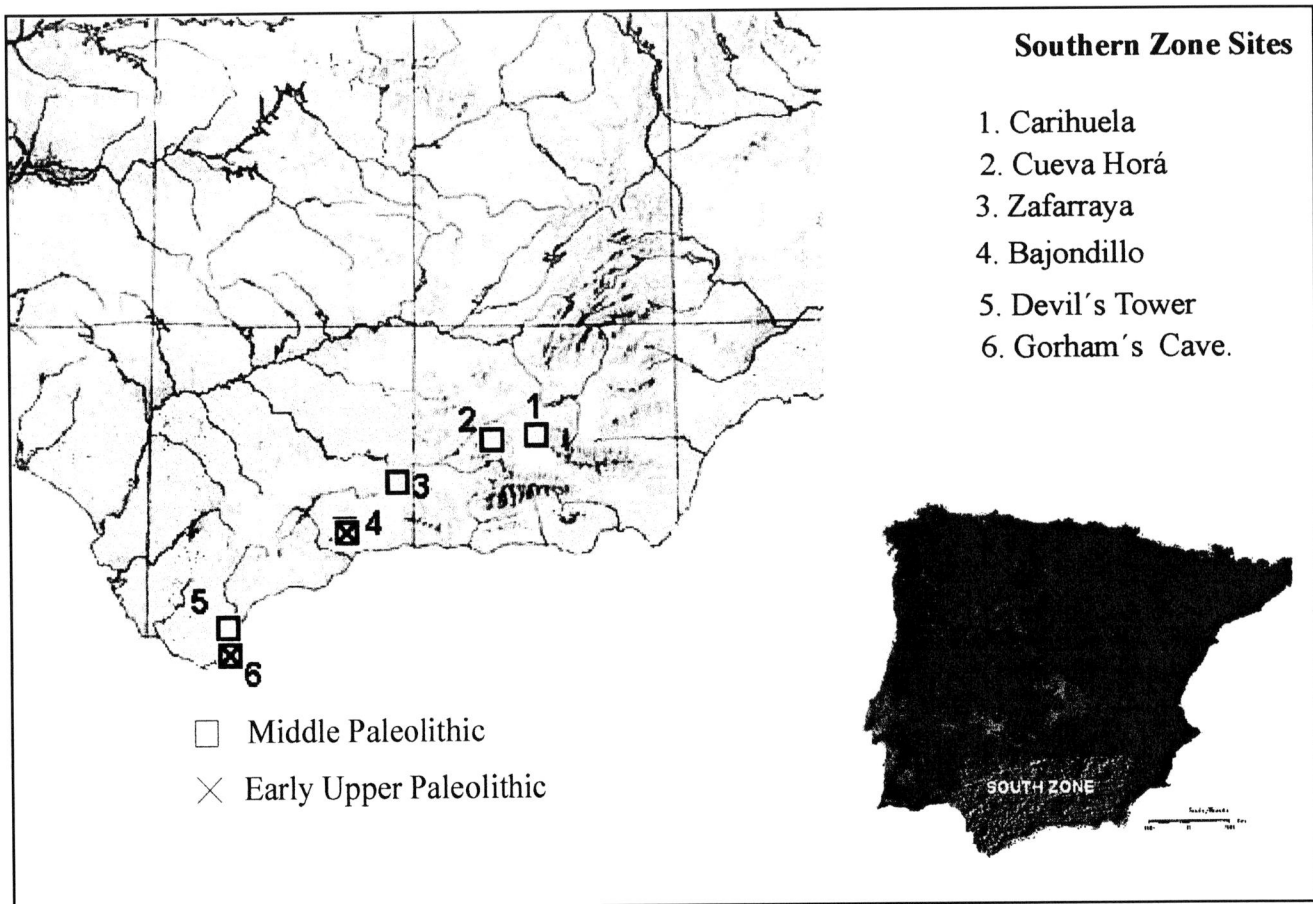

Figure 11. Distribution of Middle Paleolithic and Early Upper Paleolithic sites in the Southern Zone.

B.P. Recent excavations in Gorham's and Vanguard Caves have provided new information on Middle and early Upper Paleolithic occupations (Barton et al. 1999). New dates from Gorham's Cave tend to support a late chronology for the Middle/Upper Paleolithic boundary in southern Iberia.

The occupations attributed to the Early Upper Paleolithic are very scarce and often involve problems of identification, since they are from old excavations. Although these interpretations have been made from very small collections, some levels, such as stratum D of Gorham's Cave, have traditionally been assigned to the Aurignacian. From these data, it has been established that despite the possibility of earlier series of occupations, it was only during the Solutrean that the Upper Paleolithic technical systems became generalized in this zone. We must also take into account some sites excavated in the past few years that may indicate the presence of Aurignacian sites. These include the basal level of Cueva de Nerja and especially the site of Bajondillo (Torremolinos, Málaga), where the existence of Aurignacian materials, including carinated scrapers and Dufour bladelets has been suggested (Cortés and Simón 1997).

Some of the most significant human remains from the point of view of the Middle to Upper Paleolithic transition have been found in this zone. More importantly, they are associated with an accurate stratigraphic context. These are the Neandertal remains found in Boquete de Zafarraya, where a mandible and a femoral fragment were recovered. Although they are quantitatively significant, the remains found in Carihuela display serious stratigraphic problems of contextualization. As Gerardo Vega (1993) has pointed out, among this material there is an assemblage of Neandertal remains, as well as a series of anatomically modern human specimens from Units III and IVa. However, the unknown character of the lithic industry from these units hampers the cultural ascription of these remains to the Early Upper Paleolithic. Finally, the Neandertal remains recovered from the Gibraltar sites also exhibit problems of contextualization, especially those from Forbes Quarry and Genista, which prevents the establishment of an even approximate chronology. The stratigraphic provenience of the materials found in Devil's Tower is also unclear. These correspond to a juvenile individual and might belong to level A2 or A3.

Western Zone

In the west of the peninsula, most of the sites selected are located in the Portuguese littoral central zone, around the Tajo River mouth. In this zone we must mention the sites of Foz do Enxarrique, also found in the Tajo River valley, although close to the Spanish border, and Escoural, in Alentejo (fig. 12). In general, the Middle Paleolithic sites tend to be located along principal or secondary river valleys, while those of the Upper Paleolithic are rarely related to principal watercourses (Raposo 1995).

Among the Middle Paleolithic sites with documented occupations, a good number have provided considerably late dates, even later than 30 ka B.P. These are similar to those documented in the southern zone of the peninsula. Among such sites we must mention Columbeira, Salemas, Figueira Brava, Caldeirao, and Foz do Enxarrique. While sites documenting Middle and Upper Paleolithic assemblages in a single sequence are relatively numerous, their cultural ascription is generally inaccurate and can only be correlated with some of the characteristic Early Upper Paleolithic technocomplexes in a few cases (Zilhão 1993). A poor archaeological assemblage has been documented in level 2 of Pego do Diabo. Zilhão (1993) has assigned this assemblage to the Aurignacian on the basis of the presence of bladelets with semi-abrupt retouch. Especially significant is the open-air site of Gato Preto, where a lithic industry with abundant Aurignacian scrapers has provided a slightly older date than the rest of the Portuguese Early Upper Paleolithic assemblages.

Much of the scarce anthropological evidence documented in this zone is comprised of Neandertal specimens: a fragment of decidual tooth found in Salemas, a molar germ in Columbeira, and a second molar, a metacarpal, and a phalange in Figueira Brava (Raposo 1995). The recent discovery of an early Upper Paleolithic human burial at the Abrigo do Lagar Velho, dated to around 24.5 ka B.P. is, however, of note. These remains show a mosaic of early modern human and Neandertal features, and have been interpreted as the result of Neandertal/early modern human interbreeding (Duarte et al. 1999).

Central Zone

From a geomorphologic point of view, the central zone basically consists of the Meseta (Central Plain), although we have also included the western sector of the Ebro valley. The Meseta can be divided into two subunits, north and south, which are separated by the Central System. Of all of the zones analyzed here, this yields the smallest bulk of information, especially as regards the Early Upper Paleolithic (fig. 13). Middle Paleolithic sites with the criteria established at the beginning of this article are scarce. While there are numerous open-air sites that have provided materials initially ascribed to this period, their chronological and cultural attribution remains problematic, making them unreliable from the point of view of the issue we are analyzing.

Among the sites that correspond to the Middle Paleolithic, we note Cueva Millán (Hortigüela, Burgos), which has provided one of the few radiometric dates for this region. Located in the northern Submeseta, in the middle of the Arlanza River valley, this site consists of a sequence of three Middle Paleolithic levels, two of which have been dated around 37 ka B.P. (Moure and García-Soto 1983). The faunal assemblages and the pollen analyses suggest a prevalence of temperate conditions that have been correlated with the Würm II–III interstadial. Another Middle Paleolithic site, Cueva de la Ermita (Hortigüela, Burgos) is located near Cueva Millán. Its archaeological record is very similar to that documented for the last mentioned site and the dates so far obtained suggest very recent dates, around 31 ka B.P., although this is considered problematic due to the low protein content of the bone samples dated (Moure et al. 1997). Also in the province of Burgos is Cueva de Valdegoba, which has a few archaeological levels with characteristic Middle

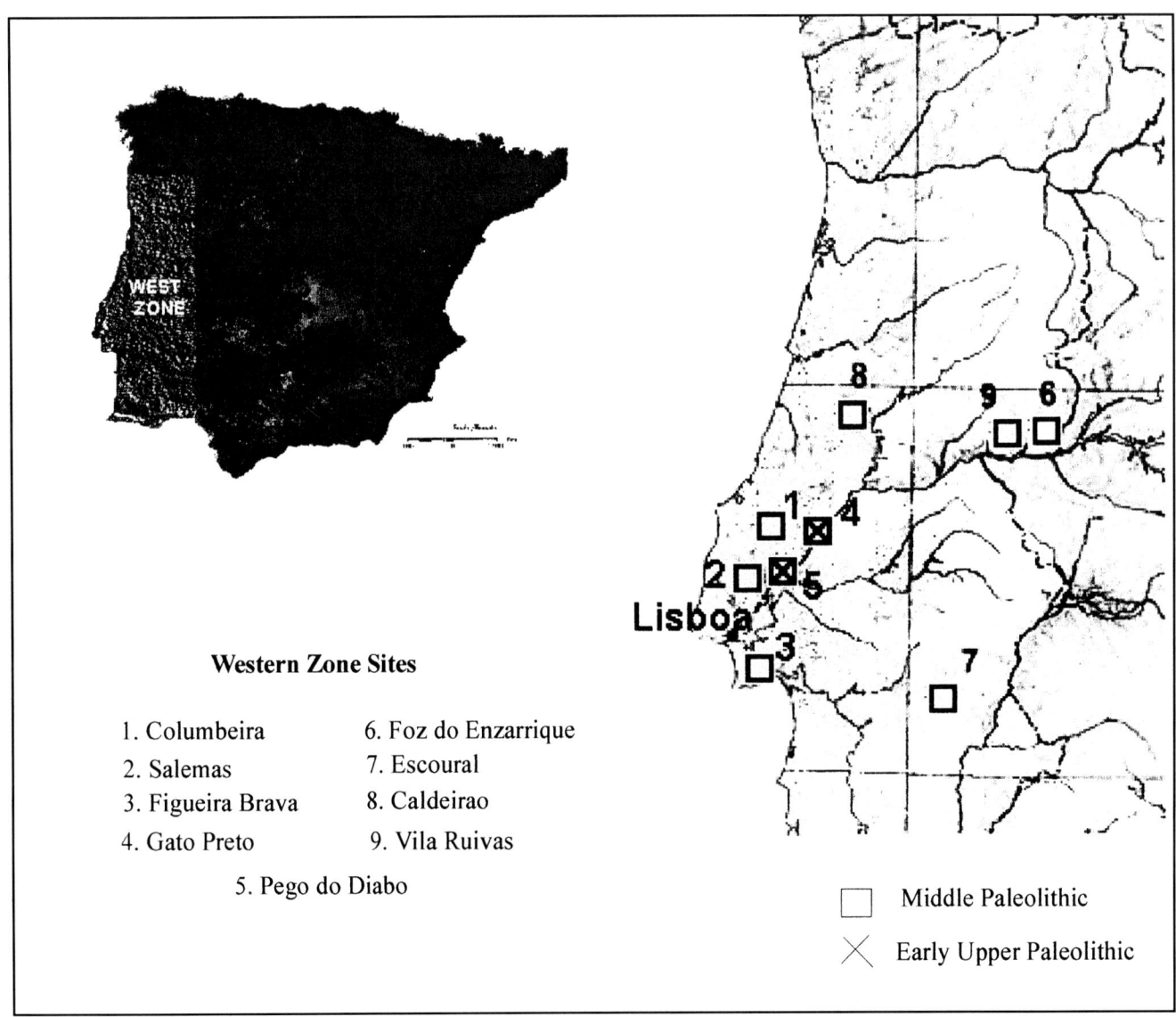

Figure 12. Distribution of Middle Paleolithic and Early Upper Paleolithic sites in the Western Zone.

Paleolithic industries documented, although an accurate chronological ascription is not available at present (Diez et al. 1988–1989).

The number of sites in the southern Submeseta is even smaller. Cueva de los Casares (Guadalajara) contains various Middle Paleolithic levels, whose climatic context is characterized by quite warmer and more humid conditions, which have been correlated with a Lower Würm interstadial. Recently excavated Cueva de Jarama VI (Valdesotos, Guadalajara) has shown a stratigraphic sequence with several occupation levels attributed to the Middle Paleolithic; the radiocarbon dates obtained indicate, as for La Ermita, a very recent chronology between 23 and 32 ka B.P. (Garcia Valero 1997).

The only site of the zone that registers Middle Paleolithic and Early Upper Paleolithic levels in a single sequence is Cueva de Peña Miel (Nieva de Cameros, La Rioja), located in the Ebro River valley. The stratigraphic sequence includes three Middle Paleolithic levels and one level that has been described as possibly Aurignacian (Utrilla and Montes 1993). The top of the Middle Paleolithic (level e) has yielded several dates placing these levels around 40–45 ka B.P. The sedimentary study indicates cool and humid conditions for the Middle Paleolithic, while the Early Upper Paleolithic is correlated with a cold and dry context attributed to the beginnings of Würm III.

In consonance with the rest of the data collected from this zone, we can only mention some outstanding anthropological evidence. The human mandible found in Cueva de Valdegoba, although attributed to *Homo sapiens neanderthalensis*, was found out of stratigraphic context. We note the absence of an accurate chronology for this site. A metacarpal found in Cueva de los Casares has also been identified as Neandertal.

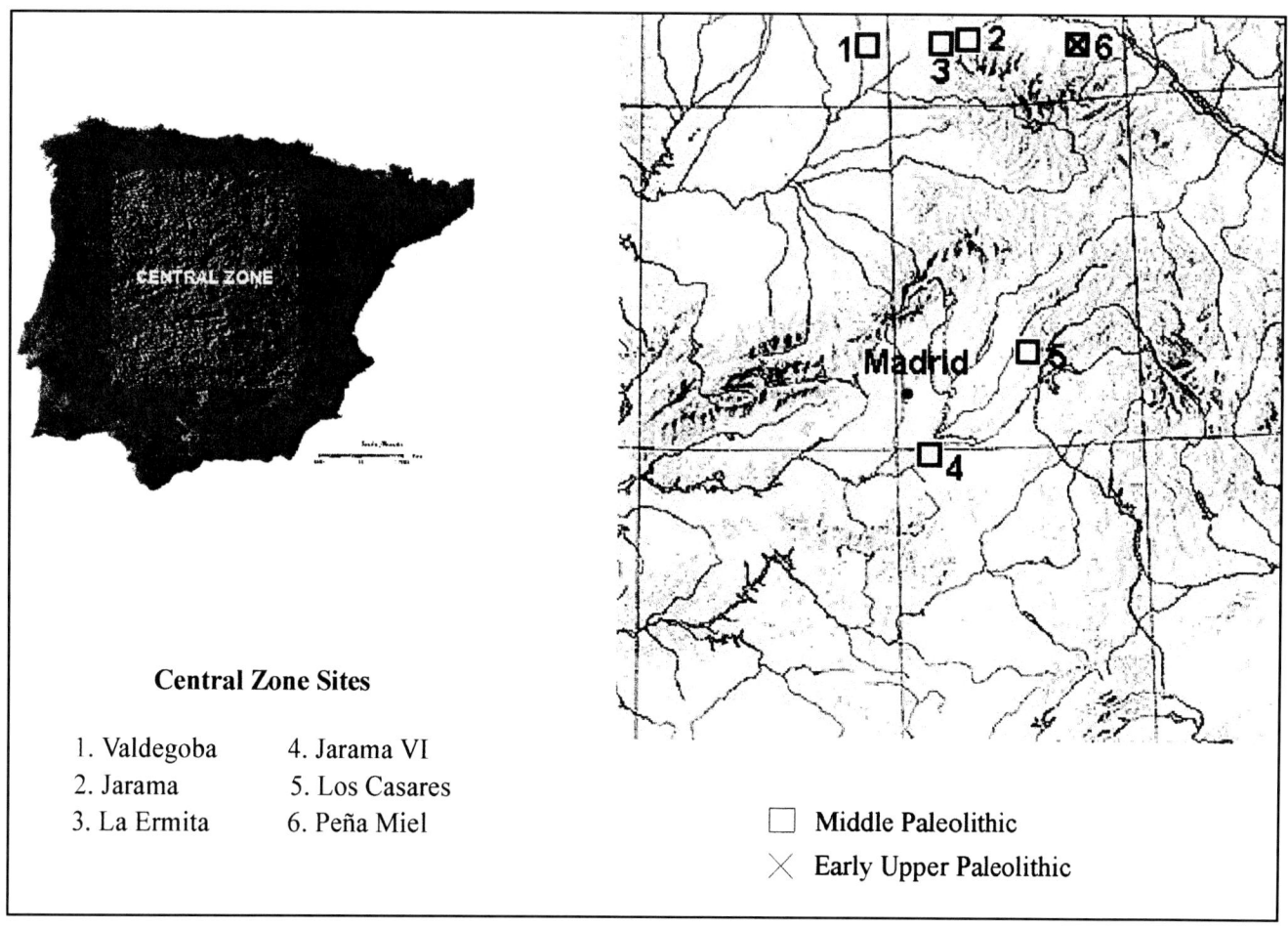

Figure 13. Distribution of Middle Paleolithic and Early Upper Paleolithic sites in the Central Zone.

Conclusions

The irregular distribution of the Middle and Early Upper Paleolithic sites in the Iberian Peninsula can be clearly observed in the maps presented here. There are zones with a relatively significant concentration of sites and others for which the available information is very scarce or nonexistent. The causes of this distribution can be summarized by considering two kinds of factors: those of a historical character, affecting the general development of prehistoric research, and others of a geological character, related to the lithological variability of the Iberian Peninsula.

Historical Factors

While prehistoric research in the Iberian Peninsula began in the nineteenth century, it was during the first decades of the twentieth that many of the sites presented here were discovered, especially some of the most important sequences (e.g., Cova Negra, El Castillo, or Abric Romaní). These works were framed in an incipient research tradition concentrated in Paleolithic studies, closely related to the tradition that was also evolving in the rest of Europe. This process was suddenly interrupted by the Spanish Civil War and the subsequent political situation. During the 1950s and 60s, the excavations carried out are fragmentary, as is the case with Carihuela, Cueva Morín, or Lezetxiki. These sites often depended on the participation of foreign researchers in the midst of underdeveloped educational and research institutions. Beginning in the 60s and through the 80s and coinciding with the political changes taking place in Spain and Portugal, Paleolithic research acquired a new impulse triggered by both the discovery of new sites (e.g., Arbreda, Zafarraya, and Beneito) and modern excavations of previously known sites (e.g., Abric Romaní, Cova Negra, Castillo, and Carihuela).

The existence of dictatorial regimes in the peninsular states during a good part of this century led directly to the absence of a political framework adequate to administer the research, and influenced the distribution of the sites excavated. On the one hand, the absence of effective administrative control favored the work of amateur archaeologists, resorting to inadequate field interventions. To this we must add the accentuated regionalization of the research as well as a lack of archaeological interest in the big public works that were carried out during this period. This situation, clearly visible from the distribution maps, was a consequence of the impact of specific research centers that performed investigations in some zones, while other zones were not explored at all (e.g., the centers of Valencia, Girona, or Santander).

In this context, we must include the scarcity of research efforts directed towards the construction of geological and paleoenvironmental frameworks at a regional level to integrate the findings that were being produced. For this reason many of the sites, particularly open-air sites, remained out of context. On the other hand, the research tradition basically centered on cave and shelter sites, while open-air sites were neglected. This especially affected some regions in which karstic structures were rare.

Geological and Geomorphological Factors

The orography of the Iberian Peninsula may have influenced the site distribution. The difference between the conditions of the Meseta and of the peninsular periphery, as well as that between the altitude of the center and of the periphery, produced strong climatic gradients between both areas. To this we must add the localized character of the pathways and a trend towards regionalization derived from a mountainous relief. On the other hand, at a lithological level, we must point out the location of most of the sites in a predominantly calcareous area, while the scarcity of caves and shelters, together with the differential preservation of the record, has reduced the number of sites in siliceous areas. This is especially the case of the central and western regions of the peninsula such as the Meseta, Galicia, and Portugal. This factor is particularly significant, as research has been preferentially oriented towards cave occupations.

Regarding the spatial distribution of Middle and Early Upper Paleolithic sites, as well as their distribution in time, additional issues could be set forward from the point of view of the Middle to Upper Paleolithic transition:

1. The emergence of the Upper Paleolithic in the north of the peninsula has provided some of the oldest dates in Europe (Arbreda, Castillo, and Abric Romaní), around 40 ka B.P. These dates appear in the northern zone and in the north of the eastern zone and resemble those documented in other European sites, calling into question the hypothesis of an east-west Aurignacian diffusion. It should be mentioned, however, that Zilhão and d'Errico (1999) have questioned the Aurignacian ^{14}C dates older than 36.5 ka B.P., particularly those from El Castillo and L'Arbreda. According to these researchers, the dates reported from these sites

are not secure, due to taphonomic and stratigraphic problems. The character of the transition regarding the underlying Middle Paleolithic varies according to different regions. In the northern zone, a Middle to Upper Paleolithic continuity has been proposed based on data from El Castillo. This continuity would be manifested on technological as well as on typological grounds (Cabrera and Bernaldo de Quirós 1996), although there is some disagreement among the researchers who have worked in this geographic zone (Freeman 1993). The same criteria indicate a sudden substitution entailing a clear discontinuity between the late Middle Paleolithic and the first Aurignacian assemblages in the northeast of the peninsula (Maroto et al. 1996; Carbonell et al. 1996). In both zones, the Middle to Upper Paleolithic transition occurs in a climatic context of interstadial character.

2. In conjunction with this, the latest persistence of Middle Paleolithic assemblages has been documented in the south, center, and west of the peninsula, which have provided dates later than 30 ka B.P. (Zafarraya, Jarama VI, Columbeira, and Salemas). The site of Zafarraya indicates that this persistence is also associated with the presence of Neandertals. From a climatic point of view, such persistence would be reflected in the generalization of Middle Paleolithic occupations from the first cold phases following the Würm Interstadial.

3. The so-called transitional industries are very scarce in the Iberian Peninsula (fig. 14). The Chatelperronian has been documented only in the north of the peninsula, in Morín, Pendo, A Valiña, Ekain, and Labeko. However, there are no sequences similar to those documented in other parts of Europe. To this must be added the occurrence of isolated elements in sites such as Arbreda that raise problems of cultural ascription, although they would not imply the existence of Chatelperronian levels. In any case, we must appreciate the influence of the differences in the criteria used for the classification of the lithic industry. If, in some cases, the presence of a Chatelperronian point is enough to define an occupational level as Chatelperronian, in others, additional criteria are required to define it as such.

4. The rest of the Early Upper Paleolithic lithic assemblages tend to be concentrated in the north of the peninsula. In the south, and coinciding with the persistence of the Middle Paleolithic, the full emergence of the Upper Paleolithic is much more recent, with generalized existence only coming as late as the Solutrean (Vega 1993).

5. Within the general framework described in the previous paragraphs, we must note some contradic-

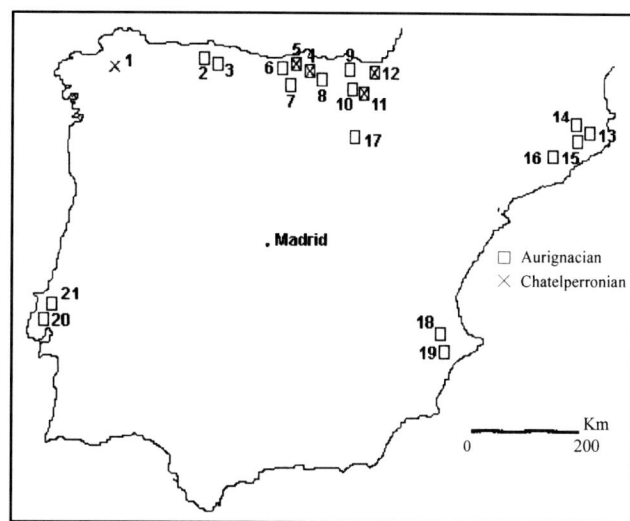

Figure 14. Distribution of Early Upper Paleolithic sites (Aurignacian and Chatelperronian) in the Iberian Peninsula. 1. A Valiña, 2. El Conde, 3. La Viña, 4. Cueva Morín, 5. El Pendo, 6. Camargo, 7. El Castillo, 8. Cueva del Otero, 9. Santimamiñe, 10. Lezetxiki, 11. Labeko, 12. Ekain, 13. Reclau Viver, 14. Mollet, 15. Arbreda, 16. Abric Romaní, 17. Peña Miel, 18. Mallaetes, 19. Cova Beneito, 20. Pego do Diabo, 21. Gato Preto.

tions of regional character. For example, in Catalonia, along with the presence of an Early Upper Paleolithic dated to around 40 ka B.P. in several sites (Arbreda, Abric Romaní, and Reclau Viver), the existence of a late Middle Paleolithic in the interior regions has been documented (Ermitons and Roca dels Bous). This implies that the coexistence between Middle and Upper Paleolithic occurred not only on a peninsular scale, but also in the interior of some zones. We could propose an early apparition of the Aurignacian in littoral areas, while the Middle Paleolithic remained limited to the interior, more marginal regions. This coexistence within a single geographic zone (the northeast of the peninsula) has been repeatedly proposed during the last few years (Maroto et al. 1996; Terradas et al. 1993; Utrilla and Montes 1993).

The interpretation of these data must be framed within the problem of the cultural transition in the whole of the European continent and of its association with the biological change that entailed the replacement of the Neandertals by anatomically modern humans. In this sense, the "Out of Africa" hypothesis, proposing an African origin for the AMH, implies the migration of these human groups towards Eurasia, appearing in Europe around 40 ka B.P. and replacing

Neandertal populations without any genetic interchange. This diffusionist hypothesis has been associated with the abrupt emergence of Upper Paleolithic techno-complexes in a good part of Europe, which would imply a cognitive change corresponding to a biological transformation. Independent of the evaluation that the diffusionist hypothesis deserves, we don't believe that the time and space distribution of the Early Upper Paleolithic in the Iberian Peninsula can be used as an argument against it.

These data do not suggest a sudden transition, but a long period of coexistence of at least 10 ka. However, coexistence does not necessarily imply occupation of the same areas. The spatial segregation of both technological systems has been observed. The emergence of the Upper Paleolithic in a certain geographic area does not imply the definite disappearance of the Middle Paleolithic, as its presence remains in more or less proximal, although marginal, areas. This situation is well adjusted to the model of the transition in mosaic proposed by Straus (1996), which contemplates a diversity of regional situations.

The geographic distribution of the Early Upper Paleolithic also suggests that the first emergence of this techno-complex is related, in one way or another, to the phenomenon of mobility between the peninsula and the rest of Europe. The sites in which the earliest Aurignacian occupations have been documented (Castillo, Arbreda, Abric Romaní, and Reclau Viver) are located in zones of easiest access from the continent: the Cantabrian cornice and the Catalan pre-littoral formations. These areas constitute corridors directly linking the natural passageways between the Iberian Peninsula and Europe; for this reason, they would represent the zones occupied the earliest, given the case of a migration of human groups along such routes.

In the zones documenting Early Upper Paleolithic occupations, the "corridors" appear in valleys that are relatively close to the coast, at a low altitude. On the other hand, the influence of geographic barriers must be contemplated in the distribution of these techno-complexes. The clearest case is that of the Cantabrian Range, which separates the narrow coastal strip in which we find sites such as El Castillo, Cueva Morín, El Pendo, etc., from the Northern Meseta. No evidence has been documented in this last zone that may reliably be attributed to the Early Upper Paleolithic. A similar situation occurs in the north of the eastern zone, particularly in the foothills of the pre-Pyrenees, where Middle Paleolithic occupations are well documented, although clear evidence of the Early Upper Paleolithic has not been documented to the present. In general, a prolonged persistence of the Middle Paleolithic in the mountainous regions and in areas with high altitude has been observed.

The irregular character of the distribution of the sites allows us to propose a series of issues for future research:

1. It is necessary to articulate the research politically, emphasizing salvage excavations, big engineering enterprises, and the administrative integration of different research teams. Special attention must be paid to the major issues surrounding the discussion of the Middle to Upper Paleolithic transition, with the goal of reaching a greater interchange and collaboration among the teams.
2. Quaternary geological studies have been notably developed in recent years, but it is necessary to extend work to the entire peninsula and to foment greater interdisciplinary collaboration among archaeologists, geologists, and botanists.
3. We must emphasize the further research of those sequences that can serve as referential frames at a regional level, in addition to integrating the context of the transition at a European level.
4. It is necessary to set forward a research protocol for open-air sites that responds to the deficit currently occurring in this aspect of Paleolithic archaeology. Important diachronic open-air sequences similar to those documented in caves and shelters would be of great value.
5. These lines of future research must be framed within a critical perspective regarding the interpretation and evaluation of the archaeological record, establishing a breakthrough from the mechanical, fragmentary traditions that have characterized the research in the past. Technical and methodological progress, such as interdisciplinary collaboration, can not be completely developed without reconsideration of the important theoretical questions.

Acknowledgments

We would like to thank Ofer Bar-Yosef and David Pilbeam for inviting us to participate in this book and Dr. Luis Raposo for his very helpful comments. We would also thank Rolf Quam for his collaboration in the translation of this text.

BIBLIOGRAPHY

Agustí, B., G. Alcalde, A. Güell, N. Juan-Muns, J. M. Rueda, and X. Terradas
  1991 "La Cova 120, parada de caçadors-recollectors del paleolític mitjà." *Cypsela* IX:7–20.

Arrizabalaga, A.
  1993 "El yacimiento arqueológico de Labeko Koba (Arrasate-Mondragón-Guipúzcoa). Aportación al Paleolítico Superior inicial vasco," in *El origen del hombre moderno en el suroeste de Europa*, V. Cabrera, ed., pp. 195–208. UNED, Madrid.

Balairón, L.
  1997 "El clima mediterráneo y sus caraterísticas en el contexto de la Circulación Atmosférica Global," in *El paisaje Mediterráneo a través del espacio y el tiempo. Implicaciones en la desertificación*, J. J. Ibáñez, B. L. Valero, and C. Machado, eds., pp. 27–31. Geoforma, Logroño.

Baldeón, A.
  1993 "El yacimiento de Lezetxiki (Gipuzkoa, País Vasco). Los niveles musterienses." *Munibe* 45:3–97.

Barandiarán, I.
  1996 "Le Paléolithique supérieur au Pays Basque et dans le Bassin de l'Ebre (1990–1995)," in *Le Paléolithique supérieur européen. Bilan quinquennal 1991–1996*, M. Otte, ed., pp. 319–322. Etudes et Recherches Archeologiques de l'Université de Liège 76. Université de Liège, Liège.

Barton, C. M.
  1988 *Lithic Variability and Middle Paleolithic Behavior. New Evidence from the Iberian Peninsula.* British Archaeological Reports International Series, 408. Oxford.

Barton, R. N. E., A. P. Currant, Y. Fernandez-Jalvo, J. C. Finlayson, P. Goldberg, R. Macphail, P. B. Pettitt, and C. B. Stringer
  1999 "Gibraltar Neanderthals and Results of Recent Excavations in Gorham's, Vanguard and Ibex Caves." *Antiquity* 73:13–23.

Bernaldo de Quirós, F.
  1982 *Los inicios del Paleolítico Superior Cantábrico.* Memorias del Centro de Investigaciones y Museo de Altamira, 8. Ministerio de Cultura, Madrid.

Bischoff, J. L., R. Julià, and R. Mora
  1988 "Uranium-Series Dating of the Mousterian Occupation at Abric Romaní, Spain." *Nature* 332:68–70.

Bischoff, J. L., K. Ludwig, J. F. García, E. Carbonell, M. Vaquero, T. W. Stafford, and A. J. T. Jull
  1994 "Dating of the Basal Aurignacian Sandwich at Abric Romaní (Catalunya, Spain) by Radiocarbon and Uranium-Series." *Journal of Archaeological Science* 21:541–551.

Bischoff, J. L., N. Soler, J. Maroto, and R. Julià
  1989 "Abrupt Mousterian/Aurignacian Boundary at c. 40 ka B.P.: Accelerator ^{14}C Dates from L'Arbreda Cave (Catalunya, Spain)." *Journal of Archaeological Science* 16:563–576.

Blasco, F., L. Montes, and P. Utrilla
  1996 "Deux modeles de strategie occupationelle dans le Moustérien tardif de la vallée de l'Ebre: les grottes de Peña Miel et Gabasa," in *The Last Neandertals, the First Anatomically Modern Humans: A Tale about the Human Diversity: Cultural Change and Human Evolution: The Crisis at 40 ka B.P.*, E. Carbonell and M. Vaquero, eds., pp. 289–313. Universitat Rovira i Virgili, Tarragona.

Burjachs, F., and R. Julià
  1994 "Abrupt Climatic Changes during the Last Glaciation Based on Pollen Analysis of the Abric Romani, Catalonia, Spain." *Quaternary Research* 42:308–315.
  1996 "Paleoenvironmental Evolution during the Middle-Upper Paleolithic Transition in the NE of the Iberian Peninsula," in *The Last Neandertals, the First Anatomically Modern Humans: A Tale about the Human Diversity: Cultural Change and Human Evolution: The Crisis at 40 ka B.P.*, E. Carbonell and M. Vaquero, eds., pp. 377–383. Universitat Rovira i Virgili, Tarragona.

Burjachs, F., and J. Renault-Miskovsky
  1992 "Paléoenvironnement et paléoclimatologie de la Catalogne durant près de 30000 ans (du Würmien ancien au début de l'Holocène) d'apres la palynologie du site de l'Arbreda (Gérone, Catalogne)." *Quaternaire* 3(2):75–85.

Butzer, K.
  1981 "Cave Sediments, Upper Pleistocene Stratigraphy and Mousterian Facies in Cantabrian Spain." *Journal of Archaeological Science* 8:133–183.

Cabrera, V., and F. Bernaldo de Quirós
  1996 "The Origins of the Upper Palaeolithic: A Cantabrian Perspective," in *The Last Neandertals, the First Anatomically Modern Humans: A Tale about the Human Diversity: Cultural Change and Human Evolution: The Crisis at 40 ka B.P.*, E. Carbonell and M. Vaquero, eds., pp. 251–265. Universitat Rovira i Virgili, Tarragona.

Cabrera, V., and J. L. Bischoff
1989 "Accelerator ^{14}C Dates for Early Upper Paleolithic (Basal Aurignacian) at El Castillo Cave (Spain)." *Journal of Archaeological Science* 16:577–584.

Cabrera, V., M. Hoyos, and F. Bernaldo de Quirós
1993 "La transición del Paleolítico Medio al Superior en la cueva de El Castillo: características paleoclimáticas y situación cronológica," in *El origen del hombre moderno en el suroeste de Europa*, V. Cabrera, ed., pp. 81–101. UNED, Madrid.

Carbonell, E., A. Cebrià, E. Allué, I. Cáceres, Z. Castro, R. Díaz, M. Esteban, A. Ollé, I. Pastó, X. P. Rodríguez, J. Rosell, R. Sala, J. Vallverdú, M. Vaquero, and J. M. Vergés
1996 "Behavioural and Organizational Complexity in the Middle Palaeolithic from the Abric Romaní," in *The Last Neandertals, the First Anatomically Modern Humans: A Tale about the Human Diversity: Cultural Change and Human Evolution: The Crisis at 40 ka B.P.*, E. Carbonell and M. Vaquero, eds., pp. 385–434. Universitat Rovira i Virgili, Tarragona.

Carrión, J., M. P. Fumanal, and G. Iturbe
1993 "La secuencia polínica de Cova Beneito en su marco litoestratigráfico, arqueológico y geocronológico," in *Estudios sobre Cuaternario. Medios sedimentarios, cambios ambientales, hábitat humano*, M. P. Fumanal and J. Bernabeu eds., pp. 139–148. AEQUA, Valencia.

Cortés, M., and M. D. Simón
1997 "Cueva Bajondillo (Torremolinos, Málaga). Aportaciones al Paleolítico en Andalucía," in *El mon mediterrani després del Pleniglacial (18–12.000 B.P.)*, J. M. Fullola and N. Soler, eds., pp. 275–287. Museu d'Arqueologia de Catalunya, Girona.

De Terán, M., and L. Solé Sabarís
1978 *Geografía General de España*. Ariel. Barcelona.

Di Castri, F., and H. A. Mooney (eds.)
1973 *Mediterranean Type Ecosystems. Origin and Structure*. Chapman and Hall Limited/Springer Verlag, London.

Díez, C., M. A. García, E. Gil, J. F. Jordá, A. I. Ortega, A. Sánchez, and B. Sánchez
1988–1989 "La cueva de Valdegoba (Burgos). Primera campaña de excavaciones." *Zephyrus* 41–42:55–74.

Duarte, C., J. Maurício, P. B. Pettitt, P. Souto, E. Trinkaus, H. van der Plicht, and J. Zilhão
1999 "The Early Upper Paleolithic Human Skeleton from the Abrigo do Lagar Velho (Portugal) and Modern Human Emergence in Iberia." *Proceedings of the National Academy of Sciences, USA* 96:7604–7609.

Esparza, X.
1993 "Los complejos Preauriñacienses: El Castelperroniense y el Protoauriñaciense en el Pirineo occidental," in *El origen del hombre moderno en el suroeste de Europa*, V. Cabrera, ed., pp. 209–218. UNED, Madrid.

Fernández Rodríguez, C., P. Ramil, A. Martínez Cortizas, J. M. Rey, and P. Peña
1993 "La cueva de A Valiña (Castroverde, Lugo): Aproximación estratigráfica, paleobotánica y paleontológica al Paleolítico superior inicial de Galicia," in *Estudios sobre Cuaternario. Medios sedimentarios, cambios ambientales, hábitat humano*, M. P. Fumanal and J. Bernabeu, eds., pp. 159–165. AEQUA, Valencia.

Fortea, J.
1996 "Le Paléolithique supérieur en Espagne: Galice et Asturies (1991–1995)," in *Le Paléolithique supérieur europeen. Bilan quinquennal 1991–1996*, M. Otte, ed., pp. 329–344. Etudes et Recherches Archeologiques de l'Université de Liège 76. Université de Liège, Liège.

Fortea, J., and F. Jordá
1976 "La Cueva de Les Mallaetes y los problemas del Paleolítico Superior del Mediterráneo Español." *Zephyrus* 26–27:129–166.

Freeman, L. G.
1993 "La "transición" en Cantabria. La importancia de Cueva Morín y sus vecinos en el debate actual," in *El origen del hombre moderno en el suroeste de Europa*, V. Cabrera, ed., pp. 171–193. UNED, Madrid.

Fumanal, M. P., and J. S. Carrión
1992 "El tránsito del Paleolítico Medio-Superior en la Cueva de Beneito (Muro, Alicante). Avance del estudio estratigráfico y sedimentopolínico," in *Aragón/litoral mediterráneo: intercambios culturales durante la prehistoria*, P. Utrilla, ed., pp. 107–116. Institución Fernando el Catolico, Zaragoza.

Galván, B.
1992 "El Salt (Alcoi, Alicante): estado actual de las investigaciones." *Recerques del Museu d'Alcoi* 1:73–80.

Garcia Valero, M. A.
1997 "Aproximación al Paleolitico Medio en la vertiente sur del Sistema Central: Guadalajara," in *Il Congreso de Arqueología Peninsular. Tomo I. Paleolítico y Epipaleolítico*, R. de Balbin and P. Bueno, eds., pp. 85–103. Fundacion Rei Afonso Henriques, Zamora.

Garralda, M. D.
1993 "La transición del Paleolítico Medio al Superior en la Península Ibérica. Perspectivas antropológicas," in *El origen del hombre moderno en el suroeste de Europa*, V. Cabrera, ed., pp. 373–389. UNED, Madrid.

Giralt, S., J. Vallverdú, R. Sala, and X. P. Rodríguez
1995 "Cronoestratigrafia i paleoclimatologia de l'ocupació humana a la vall mitjana del Ter al pleistocè mitjà i superior inicial," in *Excavacions d'urgència a sant Julià de Ramis, anys 1991–1993*, B. Agustí, J. Burch, and J. Merino, eds., pp. 23–6. Centre d'Investigacions Arqueològiques de Girona, Girona.

González Echegaray, J., L. G. Freeman, K. W. Butzer, Arl. Leroi-Gourhan, J. Altuna, B. Madariaga, and J. M. Apellániz
1971 *Cueva Morín. Excavaciones 1966–1968*. Publicaciones del Patronato de las Cuevas, Santander.

Hoyos, M., P. Utrilla, L. Montes, and J. A. Cuchi
1992 "Estratigrafía, sedimentología y paleoclimatología de los depósitos musterienses de la cueva de los Moros de Gabasa." *Geomorfología y Cuaternario* 4:143–145.

Hublin, J.-J., C. Barroso, P. Medina, M. Fontugne, and J. L. Reyss
1995 "The Mousterian Site of Zafarraya (Andalucia, Spain): Dating and Implications on the Paleolithic Peopling Processes of Western Europe." *Comptes Rendus de l'Academie des Sciences de Paris* 321:931–937.

Iturbe, I., M. P. Fumanal, J. S. Carrión, E. Cortell, R. Martínez, P. M. Guillem, M. D. Garralda, and B. Vandermeersch
1993 "Cova Beneito (Muro, Alicante): una perspectiva interdisciplinar." *Recerques del Museu d'Alcoi* 2:23–88.

Julià, R., and J. L. Bischoff
1991 "Radiometric Dating of Quaternary Deposits and the Hominid Mandible of Lake Banyolas, Spain." *Journal of Archaeological Science* 18:707–722.

Mariezkurrena, C.
1990 "Dataciones Absolutas para la Arqueología Vasca." *Munibe* 42:287–304.

Maroto, J., N. Soler, and J. M. Fullola
1996 "Cultural Change between Middle and Upper Paleolithic in Catalonia," in *The Last Neandertals, the First Anatomically Modern Humans: A Tale about the Human Diversity: Cultural Change and Human Evolution: The Crisis at 40 ka B.P.*, E. Carbonell and M. Vaquero, eds., pp. 219–250. Universitat Rovira i Virgili, Tarragona.

Moure, J. A., and E. García-Soto
1983 "Cueva Millán y la Ermita. Dos yacimientos musterienses en el valle medio del Arlanza." *Boletín del Seminario de Arte y Arqueología* 42:5–30.

Moure, A., G. Delibes, I. Castanedo, M. Hoyos, J. C. Canaveras, R. A. Housley, and M. J. Iriate
1997 "Revision y nuevos datos sobre el Musteriense de la cueva de La Ermita (Hortigüela, Burgos)," in *Il Congreso de Arqueologia Peninsular. Tomo I. Paleolitico y Epipaleolitico*, R. de Balbin and P. Bueno, eds., pp. 67–83. Fundacion Rei Afonso Henriques, Zamora.

Muñoz, M., M. F. Sánchez, and F. Ugarte
1990 "El entorno geoambiental del yacimiento arqueológico de Kurtzia." *Munibe* 41:107–115.

Raposo, L.
1995 "Ambientes, territorios y subsistencia en el Paleolítico Medio de Portugal." *Complutum* 6:57–77.

Rivas-Martínez, S.
1987 *Memoria del mapa de las series de vegetación de España (1:400.000)*. Public, ICONA, Madrid.

Sánchez Goñi, M. F.
1993 "Criterios de base tafonómica para la interpretación de análisis palinológicos en cueva: el ejemplo de la región cantábrica," in *Estudios sobre Cuaternario. Medios sedimentarios, cambios ambientales, hábitat humano*, M. P. Fumanal and J. Bernabeu, eds., pp. 117–130. AEQUA, Valencia.

Soler, N., and J. Maroto
1993 "Les nouvelles datations de l'Aurignacien dans la Peninsule Iberique," in *Actes du XIIe Congrès International des Sciences Préhistoriques et Protohistoriques*, pp. 162–173. Institut archéologique de l'Académie Slovaque des Sciences, Bratislava.

Straus, L. G.
1996 "Continuity or Rupture; Convergence or Invasion; Adaptation or Catastrophe; Mosaic or Monolith: Views on the Middle to Upper Paleolithic Transition in Iberia," in *The Last Neandertals, the First Anatomically Modern Humans: A Tale about the Human Diversity: Cultural Change and Human Evolution: The Crisis at 40 ka B.P.*, E. Carbonell and

M. Vaquero, eds., pp. 203–218. Universitat Rovira i Virgili, Tarragona.

Terradas, X., R. Mora, J. Martínez, and S. Casellas
1993 "La Roca dels Bous en el contexto de la transición Medio-Superior en el NE de la Península Ibérica," in *El origen del hombre moderno en el suroeste de Europa*, V. Cabrera, ed., pp. 247–257. UNED, Madrid.

Utrilla, P., and L. Montes
1993 "El final del Musteriense en el Valle del Ebro. Datos y reflexiones," in *El origen del hombre moderno en el suroeste de Europa*, V. Cabrera, ed., pp. 219–246. UNED, Madrid.

Vaquero, M.
1997 "Tecnología lítica y comportamiento humano: organización de las actividades y cambio diacrónico en el Paleolítico Medio del Abric Romaní." Tesis doctoral inédita. Universitat Rovira i Virgili, Tarragona.

Vega, L. G.
1988 *El Paleolítico Medio del sureste peninsular y Andalucía Oriental*. Universidad Complutense, Madrid.
1993 "El tránsito del Paleolítico Medio al Paleolítico Superior en el sur de la Península Ibérica," in *El origen del hombre moderno en el suroeste de Europa*, V. Cabrera, ed., pp. 147–170. UNED, Madrid.

Vega, L. G., and J. S. Carrión
1993 "Secuencia paleoclimática y respuesta vegetal durante el Pleistoceno superior de la cueva de la Carihuela (Píñar, Granada, SE de España," in *Estudios sobre Cuaternario. Medios sedimentarios, cambios ambientales, hábitat humano*, M. P. Fumanal and J. Bernabeu, eds., pp. 131–138. AEQUA, Valencia.

Vega, L. G., P. Cosano, A. Villar, O. Escarpa, and T. Rojas
1997 "Las industrias de la interfase Pleistoceno Medio-Superior en la cueva de la Carihuela (Píñar, Granada)," in *II Congreso de Arqueologia Peninsular. Tomo I. Paleolitico y Epipaleolitico*, R. de Balbin and P. Bueno, eds., pp. 105–131. Fundacion Rei Afonso Henriques, Zamora.

Villaverde, V., and M. P. Fumanal
1990 "Relations entre le Paléolithique moyen et le Paléolithique supérieur dans le versant méditerranéen espagnol," in *Paléolithique moyen recent et Paléolithique supérieur ancien en Europe. Ruptures et transitions: examen critique des documents archéologiques*, C. Farizy, ed., pp. 177–183. Mémoires du Musée de Préhistoire d'Ile de France 3, Nemours.

Yokoyama, Y., H. Nguyen, J. P. Quaegebeur, G. Le Hasif, and O. Romain
1987 "Datation par l'spectrométrie gamma non destructive et la résonance de spin électronique (ESR) du remplissage de la grotte de l'Arbreda." *Cypsela* 6:137–143.

Zilhão, J.
1993 "Le passage du Paléolithique moyen au Paléolithique supérieur dans le Portugal," in *El origen del hombre moderno en el suroeste de Europa*, V. Cabrera, ed., pp. 127–145. UNED, Madrid.

Zilhão, J., and F. d'Errico
1999 "The Chronology and Taphonomy of the Earliest Aurignacian and its Implications for the Understanding of Neandertal Extinction." *Journal of World Prehistory* 13(1):1–68.

CHAPTER 3

The Archaeological Records of the Neandertal–Modern Human Transition in France

Paul Mellars
Department of Archaeology, Cambridge University

INTRODUCTION

France has always been seen as the classic region for Upper Palaeolithic studies, both historically and in terms of the sheer wealth of the archaeological evidence from this area and the intensity of research on this material over the past century. The probable reasons for the exceptional density of occupation in this region—and especially in the classic Perigord area—have been discussed elsewhere (Mellars 1985). They are likely to have involved at least three or four factors: the high productivity of these rich, southern tundra and steppe environments—the most southerly areas of such vegetation in last-glacial Europe; the relative mildness of the oceanic winters and the correspondingly increased length of the growing season; and (above all) the density and diversity of the different animal communities that thrived in these habitats, clearly reflected in the rich and varied faunal assemblages recovered from archaeological sites. The exceptional concentration of sites in one or two river valleys (especially those of the Dordogne and the Vézère) seems to reflect at least in part the role of these valleys as major migration routes for reindeer herds and perhaps other species, such as bison and horse. It should be added that this wealth and concentration of Upper Palaeolithic occupation in western France seems to be reflected equally in the archaeological records of the preceding Middle Palaeolithic populations, especially perhaps in those of the later phases of the Middle Palaeolithic represented by the so-called Mousterian of Acheulian tradition industries (Mellars 1996). All of the documented human skeletal records of the Mousterian in this region (as at La Ferrassie, La Chapelle-aux-Saints, La Quina, Le Moustier, etc.) are, of course, associated with essentially "classic" Neandertal remains (Stringer and Gamble 1993).

The recent publication of surprisingly well preserved mitochondrial DNA from the original Neandertal type-specimen from Neandertal itself (Krings et al. 1997) leaves little doubt that in at least most areas of Europe, the Neandertals became extinct without, apparently, leaving any genetically detectable descendants in later populations. Most of the recent debate has now shifted to the precise mechanisms by which the replacement of the Neandertal by anatomically modern humans took place and, in particular, the extent of any contact or interaction between the two populations. Most recent opinion has favored the view that in many parts of Europe there was a prolonged period of about 5,000 years of coexistence of the two populations (probably within separate but adjacent territories) and that this is reflected in a substantial degree of "acculturation" in the archaeological records of the final Neandertal populations—as reflected, for example, by the presence of bone and ivory tools, personal ornaments, and extensive use of red ochre in the "Chatelperronian" levels at Arcy-sur-Cure in Central France (e.g., Harrold 1989; Demars 1990; Graves 1991; Stringer and Gamble 1993; Djindjian 1993; Kozlowski 1993; Hublin et al. 1996; Mellars 1989, 1998, 1999). Recently, this view has been challenged by d'Errico et al. (1998), who argue instead for an extremely rapid replacement of Neandertal by anatomically modern populations in most areas of Europe, with apparently no discernible evidence for contact, behavioral interaction, or "acculturation" between the two groups. This view, in turn, has radical implications for the nature of the social and cognitive contrasts between the two populations and for the demographic or other mechanisms by which the Neandertals became extinct (Zubrow 1989, Mellars 1998). The aim of the present paper is to review the available data on the chronology of the final Neandertal populations in western France and the immediately adjacent areas of northern Spain, and to reassess the available evidence for the extent of the chronological overlap between the late Neandertal and early anatomically modern populations (see also Mellars 1999).

Archaeological Context

There is now fairly general agreement on the basic patterns of the archaeological and associated human skeletal records associated with the transition from Neandertal to anatomically modern populations in these regions. In both France and northern Spain, it is generally accepted that the earliest archaeological traces of anatomically modern populations are represented by the so-called Aurignacian industries (fig. 1)—industries that are clearly intrusive in western Europe and show evidence for a whole range of behavioral innovations that are not found in the preceding Mousterian industries, including the extensive use of bone, antler and ivory implements, perforated animal teeth and other forms of personal ornamentation, long-distance trading of decorative sea shells, and the earliest evidence of several forms of both representational and abstract art and musical instruments (Djindjian 1993; Kozlowski 1993; Mellars 1992; Gambier 1993; White 1993). These industries have recently been dated at a number of sites in both northeastern and northwestern Spain (L'Arbreda, Abric Romaní, Reclau Viver, and El Castillo) by both radiocarbon-accelerator and uranium-series dating to around 38–40,000 B.P. in radiocarbon terms (Bischoff et al. 1989, 1994; Hedges et al. 1994; Cabrera-Valdés et al. 1996).

Recent debate has focused mainly on the significance and chronology of the so-called Chatelperronian industries (see fig. 2). These industries occur over broadly the same geographical range as the Aurignacian industries (principally in central and western France, with rare outliers in northern Spain) but reveal a technology that contrasts sharply with that of the Aurignacian and is clearly rooted in the immediately preceding late Neandertal Mousterian technologies of the same region—specifically those of the "Mousterian of Acheulian tradition" group (Harrold 1989; Mellars 1989, 1996, 1998; Pelegrin 1995; d'Errico et al. 1998). Skeletal discoveries at both Saint-Césaire in western France and Arcy-sur-Cure in central France reveal beyond doubt that the Chatelperronian was manufactured by typically Neandertal hominids (Lévêque and Vandermeersch 1980; Hublin et al. 1996). Significantly, however, many of the Chatelperronian industries show a number of typically Upper Palaeolithic features, analogous to those of the Aurignacian, including increased use of blade technology, some typically Upper Palaeolithic stone tool forms (notably end scrapers and burins), and in at least one well-documented site (the Grotte du Renne at Arcy-sur-Cure), carefully shaped bone and ivory tools and a range of animal tooth pendants (Leroi-Gourhan and Leroi-Gourhan 1965; Baffier and Julien 1990; Pelegrin 1995; d'Errico et al. 1998). The central issue is whether these characteristically Upper Palaeolithic features in the late Neandertal Chatelperronian industries were simply "copied" or "borrowed" from contemporaneous and adjacent Aurignacian populations, or whether they reflect a totally independent, autonomous invention of Upper Palaeolithic technology and related "symbolic" expression among the final Neandertal populations of western Europe. Clearly, the chronological relationship of the Chatelperronian to the Aurignacian is fundamental and pivotal to this debate.

In view of the apparently clear and undisputed evidence that typically Aurignacian industries were being produced in northern Spain by about 40,000 (radiocarbon) years ago, the whole of the present issue hinges on whether the Chatelperronian industries are essentially contemporaneous with the early Aurignacian industries—as most recent workers have assumed—or whether they are entirely earlier than the Aurignacian, as recently argued by d'Errico et al. The purpose of what follows is to show that the totality of the current chronological evidence strongly favors the former view and conflicts with the hypothesis of a clear chronological separation between the two technologies.

1. From the pattern of radiocarbon dates dates displayed in figure 3, it is immediately clear that the available dates for Chatelperronian levels in France and northern Spain are almost entirely younger than 40,000 B.P. and are concentrated mainly between 38,000 and 33,000 B.P., with dates within this range now available for 16 separate samples from seven different sites. A number of new AMS radiocarbon dates recently secured by the Oxford radiocarbon laboratory for the Chatelperronian levels at the rock-shelter site of Combe-Saunière in the Isle valley (Dordogne) of southwest France confirm this pattern (Mellars et al., n.d.),

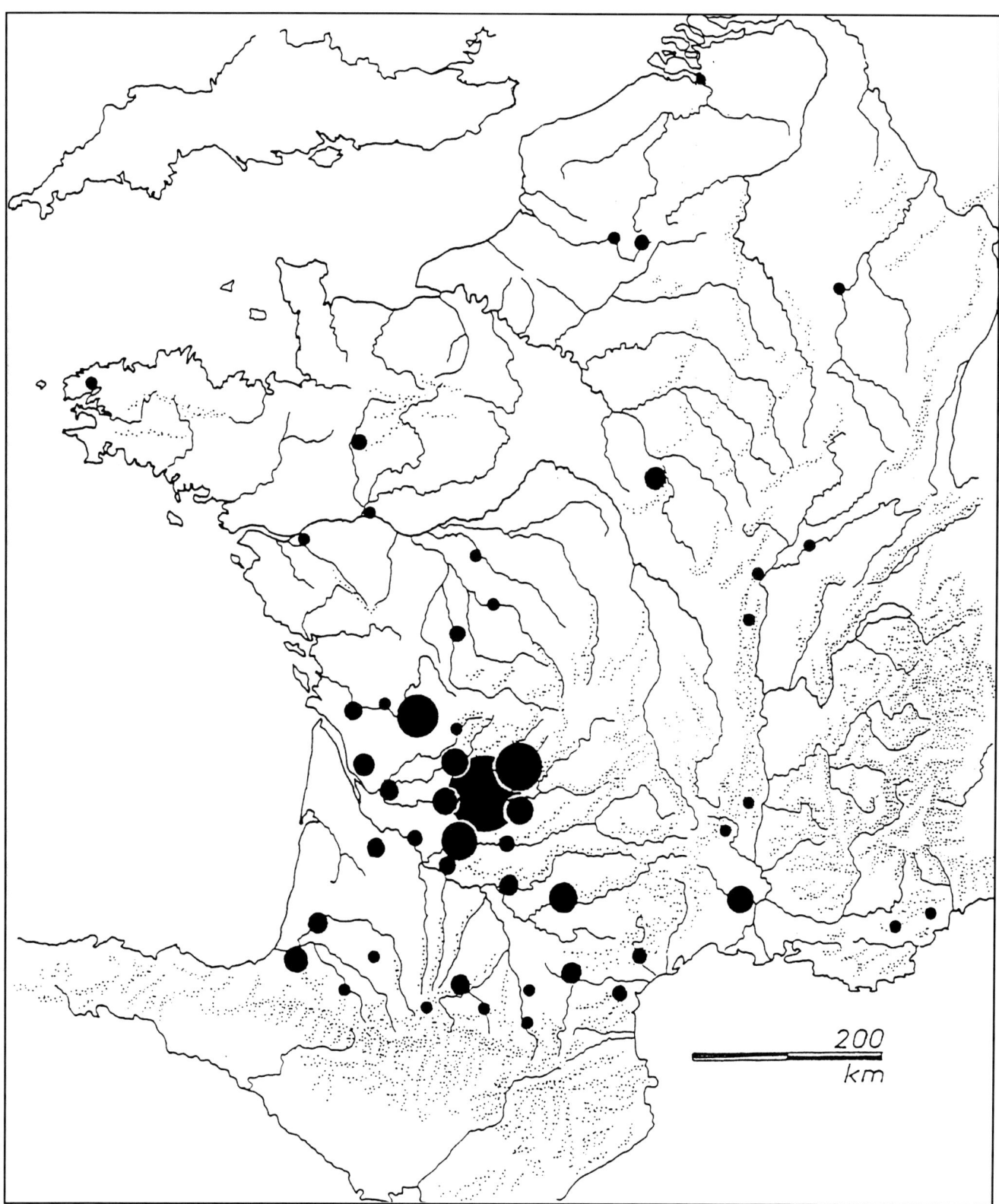

Figure 1. The distribution of Aurignacian sites in France, according to Demars (1996). The sizes of the symbols are proportional to the numbers of sites in each location. The total numbers of recorded sites is 211, of which 48 are open-air sites.

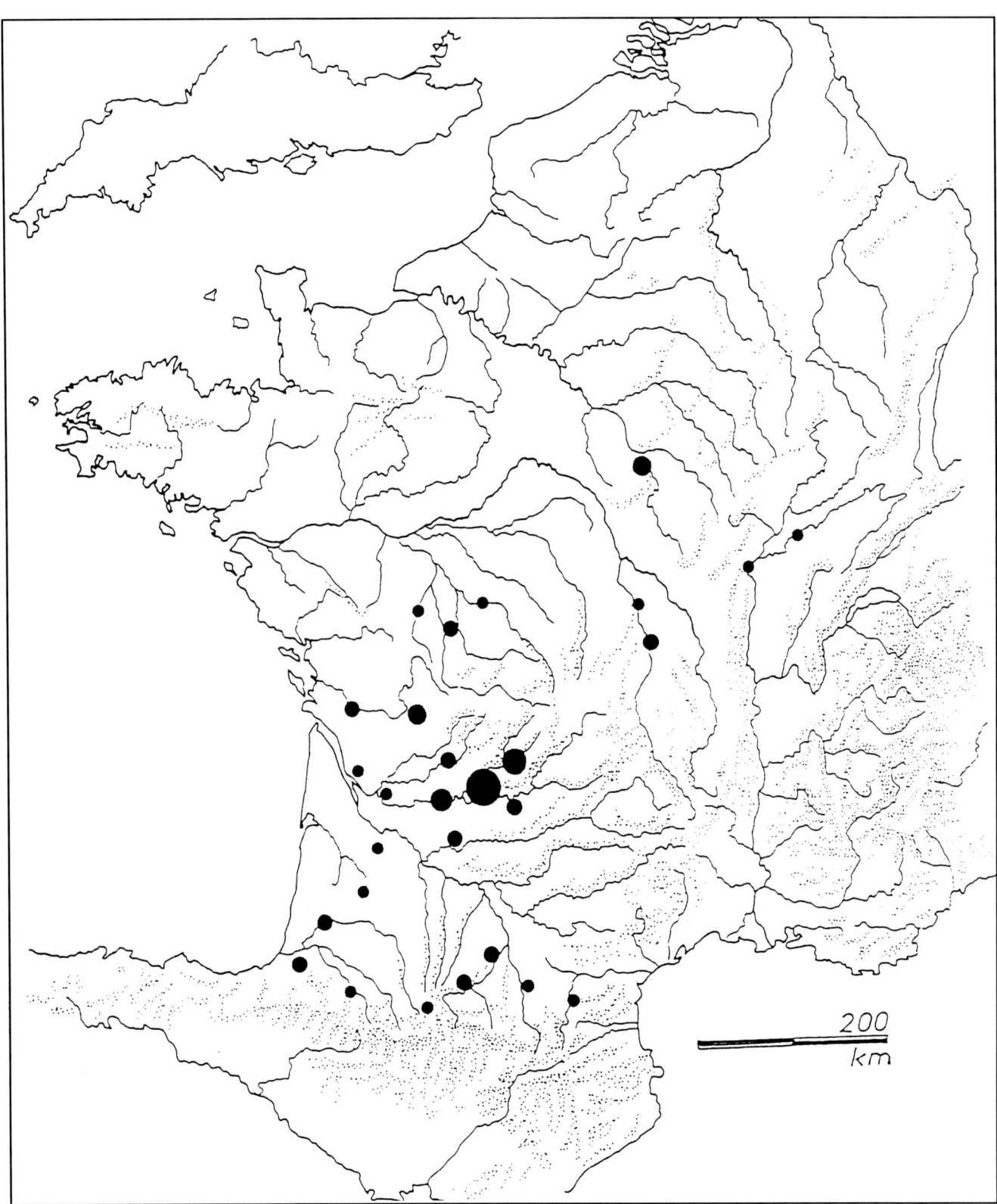

Figure 2. The distribution of Chatelperronian sites in France, according to Demars (1996). The sizes of the symbols are proportional to the numbers of sites in each location. The total number of recorded sites is 61, of which 10 are open-air sites.

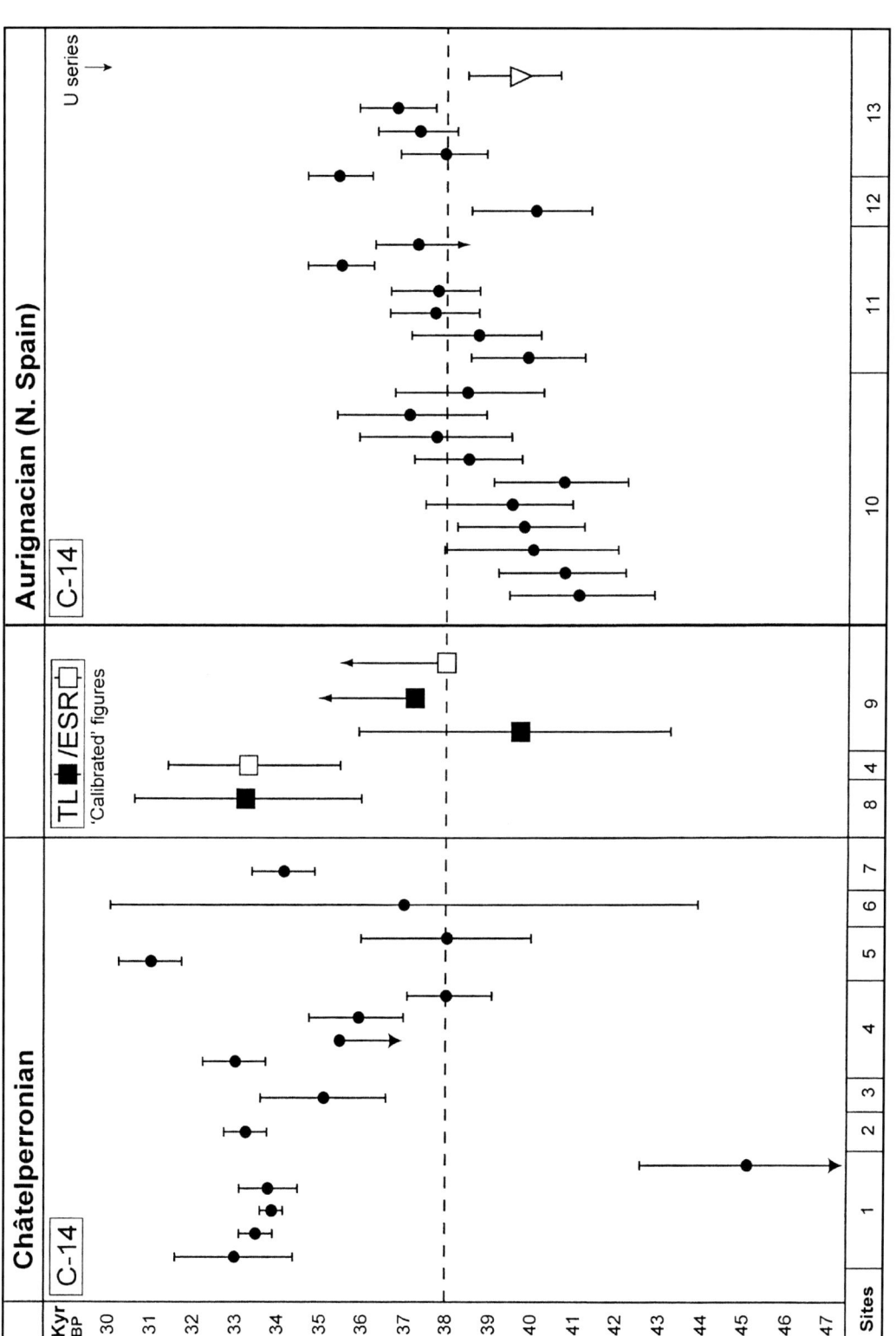

Figure 3. Absolute age determinations for Chatelperronian sites in southwest France and northern Spain, and for early Aurignacian sites in northern Spain. Note that the thermoluminescence (TL), electron spin resonance (ESR), and uranium series dates have been "calibrated" to radiocarbon terms by the subtraction of 3,000 years — as implied by the calibration studies of Bard et al. (1990, 1993) and Laj et al. (1996). The "younger than" dates for the Chatelperronian levels at Le Moustier are based on the TL and ESR ages for the underlying Mousterian levels at the site. It will be seen that while virtually all the dates for the Chatelperronian levels are younger than 38,000 B.P., most of the dates for Spanish early Aurignacian levels lie between 38,000 and 40,000 B.P. Note that if the discrepancy between radiocarbon and "absolute" dates were greater than 3,000 years, this would make the TL and ESR dates for the Chatelperronian levels even younger than those shown here. The sites are as follows: 1. Arcy-sur-Cure, 2. Les Cottés, 3. Camiac, 4. Combe-Saunière, 5. Roc-de-Combe, 6. Cueva Morín, 7. Labeko Kova, 8. Saint-Césaire, 9. Le Moustier, 10. El Castillo, 11. L'Arbreda, 12. Reclau Viver, 13. Abric Romaní. For further details of samples and dates, see table 1.

including one measurement produced by the "tripeptide" extraction technique, which has been developed specifically to eliminate contamination effects by recent, intrusive carbon (Van Klinken et al. 1994). The only measurement that departs strikingly from this pattern is the single date of 45,100±2800 B.P. based on a single bone fragment from the middle Chatelperronian level (level IX) at Arcy-sur-Cure. This measurement is more than 10,000 years older than six other radiocarbon measurements (by both conventional and AMS dating) for the Chatelperronian levels on the site and, as the radiocarbon laboratory has already suggested (Hedges et al. 1994), almost certainly represents a stratigraphically misplaced sample derived from the underlying Mousterian levels on the site.

The contrast between these dates for the Chatelperronian and the available dates for early Aurignacian levels in northern Spain is clearly apparent in figure 3. While all except one of the 16 dates for Chatelperronian levels are younger than 38,500 B.P., 11 of the 21 dates for the Spanish early Aurignacian levels lie between 38,500 and 41,000 B.P.—a pattern that clearly supports the view that the appearance of the Aurignacian technology in western Europe, and the seemingly associated appearance of anatomically modern populations, precedes most, if not all, of the known occurrences of Chatelperronian industries in this region.

2. Absolute age measurements by other dating methods fully support this conclusion (see table 1, fig. 3). Here it must be recalled that there is now clear evidence that radiocarbon dates in the 30–40,000 year age span substantially underestimate the true (calendrical) ages of samples in comparison with those of other chronometric methods, as a result of the enrichment of the ^{14}C component of the atmosphere over this period—probably by a factor of about 3,000–4,000 years (Bard et al. 1990, 1993; Laj et al. 1996). When this displacement is taken into account, all of the available dates for Chatelperronian levels by these other (non-radiocarbon) dating methods point to the same chronological pattern as that of the radiocarbon dates (see table 1). A series of six thermoluminescence dates on burnt flint samples from the upper Chatelperronian layer (associated with the partial Neandertal skeleton) at Saint-Césaire ranged between 33,700±5400 and 38,200±5300 in "uncalibrated" terms and converge on a central figure of around 36,300±2700 years (Mercier et al. 1991). Translated into radiocarbon terms, this is equivalent to a ^{14}C age of around 33,300±3000 B.P. Similarly, a series of six ESR measurements on animal teeth recently obtained for the Chatelperronian levels at Combe-Saunière centres once again on about 36,400±2500 B.P.—again equivalent to around 33,400±3000 B.P. in radiocarbon terms (Mellars et al. n.d.). Equally, if not more, significant is the TL dating of the Mousterian levels, which clearly underlie the Chatelperronian levels at Saint-Césaire, to about 40,000 B.P. (approximately 37,000 radiocarbon B.P.) and the dating of similar late Mousterian levels at Le Moustier (by both TL and ESR techniques) to about 40–41,000 B.P. (approximately 37–38,000 radiocarbon B.P.) (Mercier et al. 1991; Valladas et al. 1986; Mellars and Grün 1991). Unless all of these mutually consistent age determinations, by two different dating methods, are grossly underestimating the true ages of the associated archaeological levels, they confirm that the whole of the time span of the Chatelperronian industries, at least in the "classic" region of southwestern France must be younger than about 38–40,000 B.P. in radiocarbon terms. Certainly, this dating leaves little scope for pushing the whole of the Chatelperronian—including the long stratified sequences at Quinçay, Arcy-sur-Cure, and elsewhere—to before 40,000 B.P. in radiocarbon terms, as the dating proposed recently by d'Errico et al. would imply.

3. As a further, direct confirmation of the same pattern, it should be recalled that three and possibly four separate sites in France and northern Spain have been reported to show a direct interstratification of Chatelperronian and early Aurignacian occupations in the same stratigraphic succession—at Le Piage and the Roc-de-Combe in the Lot region of southwestern France, El Pendo in Cantabria, and probably at Châtelperron itself in northern Burgundy (Demars 1990; White 1998). Unless all of these sequences have been subjected to some strange geological disruptions, they provide further unmistakable evidence of a significant chronological overlap between the time ranges of the Chatelperronian and Aurignacian industries in these regions. It should be recalled that exactly the same conclusion was drawn over 15 years ago by Leroyer and Leroi-Gourhan (1983) on the basis of the climatic and palaeobotanical associations of the two groups of industries (see also Leroyer 1988).

4. Finally, it is interesting to compare the available radiocarbon and other age measurements for the earliest Aurignacian levels in northern Spain with those from the adjacent areas of southwestern France. As shown in figure 4, this points clearly to a rather later appearance of Aurignacian technologies—and presumably the associated anatomically modern populations—in southwestern France than in northern Spain, with dates for the earliest Aurignacian in the

TABLE 1
Absolute age measurements for Chatelperronian and early Aurignacian levels in France and northern Spain

Layer	Lab. Number/Method	Date (B.P.)	Source
CHATELPERRONIAN: 14C Dates			
Arcy-sur-Cure (Grotte du Renne)			
Layer VIII	GrN-1736	33,500±400	Vogel & Waterbolk 1963
	GrN-1742	33,860±250	"
	Ly-2163	33,000±1,400	Delibrias & Fontugne 1990
Layer IX	OxA-3465	45,100±2,800	Hedges et al. 1994
Layer X	OxA-3464	33,820±720	"
	GrN-4251	25,500±380	Vogel & Waterbolk 1967
	GrN-4216	24,500±360	"
Les Cottés			
Layer G	GrN-4333	33,300±500	Vogel & Waterbolk 1967
Camiac			
Layer D	Ly-1104	35,100±1,500	Delibrias & Fontugne 1990; Guadelli & Laville 1990
Combe Saunière			
Layer X	OxA-6503	35,900±1,100	Mellars et al. n.d.
	(tripeptide)	38,100±1,000	"
	OxA-6504	33,000±900	"
Roc-de-Combe			
Layer X	OxA-1264	31,000±750	Hedges et al. 1990
	OxA-1443	38,000±2,000	"
Brassempouy			
Layer 2g	Gif-8172	31,690±810	Bon et al. 1998
Cueva Morín			
Layer 10	SI-951	36,950±6,777	Harrold 1989
Labeko Kova			
Chatelperronian	Ua-3324	34,215±1,265	Barandiarán Maetzu 1996
CHATELPERRONIAN: TL/ESR Dates			
Saint-Césaire	TL		
Layer EJOP sup.		33,700±5,400	Mercier et al. 1991, 1993
		35,600±4,600	"
		36,600±5,000	"
		36,600±4,900	"
		37,400±5,200	"
		38,200±5,300	"
	Average:	36,300±2,700	"
Combe-Saunière	ESR		
Layer X (Châtelperronian)		36,400±2,500 (average)	Mellars et al. n.d.
Le Moustier	TL/ESR		
Layer K (Châtelperronian)	TL	42,600±3,700 (average)	Valladas et al. 1986
Layer J (Mousterian)	TL	40,300±2,600	"
Layer I (Mousterian)	TL	40,900±5,000	"
Layer H (MTA Type B)	TL	42,500±2,000	"
Layer H "	ESR	41,000±2,600	Mellars & Grün 1991

Table 1 continued
Absolute age measurements for Chatelperronian and early Aurignacian levels in France and northern Spain

Layer	Lab. Number/Method	Date (B.P.)	Source
AURIGNACIAN, NORTHERN SPAIN			
El Castillo			
Layer 18b1	AA-2406	38,500±1,800	Cabrera-Valdés & Bischoff 1989
Layer 18b2	AA-2407	37,700±1,800	"
	OxA-2473	37,100±2,200	Hedges et al. 1994
	OxA-2474	38,500±1,300	"
	OxA-2475	40,700±1,600	"
Layer 18c	OxA-2476	40,700±1,500	"
	OxA-2477	41,100±1,700	"
	AA-2405	40,000±2,100	"
	OxA-2478	39,800±1,400	"
	GifA-89147	39,500±2,000	Cabrera-Valdés et al. 1996
L'Arbreda			
Layer H	AA-3779	37,700±1,000	Bischoff et al. 1989
	AA-3780	37,700±1,000	"
	AA-3781	39,900±1,300	"
	AA-3782	38,700±1,200	"
	OxA-3729	37,340±820	Hedges et al. 1994
	OxA-3730	35,480±820	"
Reclau Viver			
Layer III	OxA-3727	40,000±1,400	Hedges et al. 1994
Abric Romaní			
Layer A	AA-8037A	35,400±810	Bischoff et al. 1994
	AA-8037B	37,900±1,000	"
	AA-7395	37,290±990	"
	AA-6608	36,740±920	"
	U-series	42,600±1,100	"
AURIGNACIAN, SOUTHWEST FRANCE			
La Rochette			
Layer 7	GrN-4362	36,000±450	Vogel & Waterbolk 1967
La Ferrassie			
Layer K6	Gif-4279	35,000	Delibrias & Fontugne 1990
	GrN-5751	33,220±570	"
Combe-Saunière			
Layer VIII	OxA-6507	34,000±850	Mellars et al. n.d.
Roc-de-Combe			
Layer 7b	OxA-1262	33,400±1,100	Hedges et al. 1990
Layer 7c	OxA-1263	34,800±1200	"
Abri Pataud			
Layer 12	GrN-4327	33,000±500	Vogel & Waterbolk 1967
Layer 14	GrN-4507	34,250±675	"
	GrN-4720	33,330±410	"
	GrN-4610	33,300±760	"
Le Flagéolet			
Layer XI	OxA-598	33,800±1,800	Mellars et al. 1987

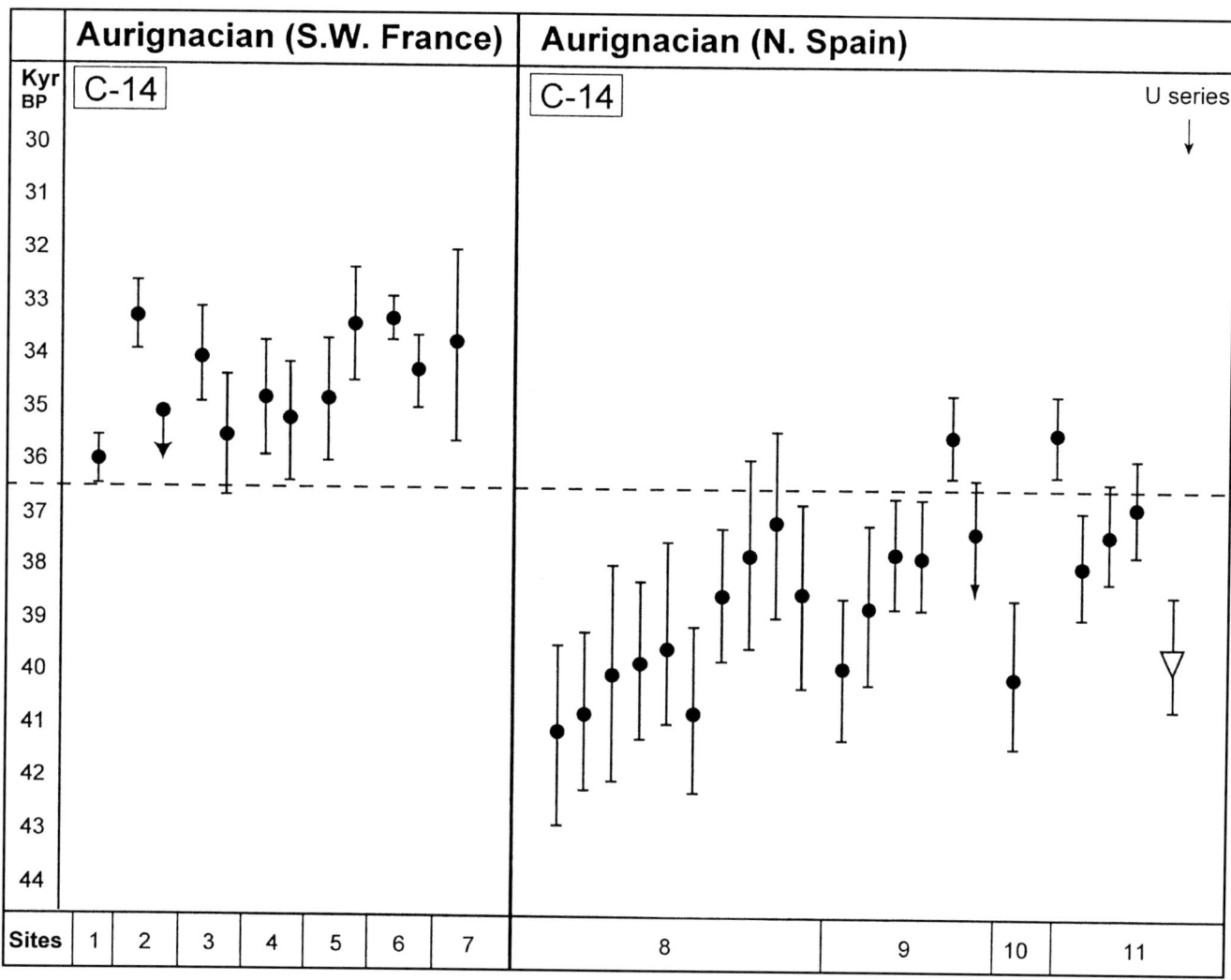

Figure 4. Radiocarbon dates for early Aurignacian levels in southwest France (left) and northern Spain (right). The sites are as follows: 1. La Rochette, 2. La Ferrassie, 3. Combe-Saunière, 4. Abri Castanet, 5. Roc-de-Combe, 6. Abri Pataud, 7. Le Flageolet, 8. El Castillo, 9. L'Arbreda, 10. Reclau Viver, 11. Abric Romaní. For further details of samples and dates, see table 1. Provisional unpublished dates for the Abri Castanet were kindly provided by J. Pelegrin, R. White, H. Valladas, and N. Mercier.

former area centering on around 34–36,000 B.P., while those in the latter area center on 38–40,000 B.P. The possible reasons for the delayed penetration of anatomically modern populations into the southwest region of France have been discussed elsewhere and were probably related partly to different climatic and ecological conditions in the two areas and (above all) to the exceptionally high population densities of the later Neandertal populations in the southwest French region, clearly implied by the exceptionally high concentration of late Mousterian sites in this region (Mellars 1996, 1998). It is precisely in this region that we also find the densest concentration of Chatelperronian sites—approximately 90 percent of the known Chatelperronian occurrences (see fig. 2; d'Errico et al. 1998; Pelegrin 1995). This confirms that this was indeed one of the latest regions of survival of the final Neandertal populations in Europe and suggests that the ability of the two populations to coexist over a period of apparently several thousand years was largely due to the occupation of ecologically discrete territories—though probably with occasional episodes of interpenetration of the two territories in response to short-term ecological or demographic fluctuations, as the occasional cases of interstratification of Chatelperronian and Aurignacian levels at the three sites referred to above would imply.

CONCLUSIONS

From the totality of the dating evidence discussed above—including the results of the new radiocarbon and ESR dating at Combe-Saunière and other sites—there can be no serious doubt that the time ranges of the Chatelperronian and early Aurignacian industries in France and northern Spain overlapped by a period of several thousand years, implying a similar overlap between the final Neandertal and earliest, intrusive anatomically modern populations in these areas. The most important implication of this dating is that it leaves entirely open the possibility that the appearance of a range of distinctively "modern" behavioral features among the late Neandertal populations of western Europe—including the presence of simple bone and ivory tools and perforated pendants at Arcy-sur-Cure—was the product of some form of contact and interaction between the two populations, regardless of whether we refer to this as "acculturation," or by some other term. The alternative is that after a period of around 200,000 years of typically Middle Palaeolithic technology and behaviour, the local Neandertal populations in western Europe independently, coincidentally, and almost miraculously "invented" these distinctive features of Upper Palaeolithic technology at almost exactly the same time as anatomically and behaviorally modern populations are known to have been expanding across Europe (Kozlowski 1993; Mellars 1992; Gambier 1993; d'Errico et al. 1998). It should be recalled here that we are speaking of not just one or two Upper Palaeolithic features, but a range of around ten or a dozen behavioural innovations, including increased blade technology, abundant and typical forms of end scrapers and burins, several forms of bone or ivory points, regularly notched bones, several forms of perforated or grooved pendants (including a preferential use of fox canine teeth for pendants), bone tubes, ivory rings, and liberal use of powdered red ochre scattered across living areas (d'Errico et al. 1998). In purely statistical terms, the entirely independent evolution of all these features would seem to demand an extraordinary degree of convergent and coincidental cultural development—in scientific terms, perhaps not the most economical hypothesis. Certainly, if the independent-development hypothesis were substantiated, this would have profound implications for our understanding of both the social and cognitive dimensions of Neandertal populations and the entire processes by which typically "modern" behavioral patterns emerged (cf. Bar-Yosef 1998).

There are, of course, several different ways in which various forms of contact and interaction between the intrusive anatomically modern and resident Neandertal populations could be visualized (Graves 1991; d'Errico et al. 1998; Mellars 1998), and these allow for a range of different perspectives on the relative cognitive and intellectual capacities of the two populations. If we allow for the prolonged period of genetic separation of the Neandertal and modern lineages implied by the recent DNA evidence (Krings et al. 1997), the possibility of some significant divergences in neurological structures between the two populations can hardly be ruled out. One could also argue that the survival of the Aurignacian and Chatelperronian industries as clearly identifiable and sharply separated technological traditions over a period of several thousand years must imply some fundamental barrier to communication and interbreeding between the two groups, which prevented their total assimilation and integration over this span of time. This would be fully consistent with recent suggestions that the Neandertal and anatomically modern humans were biologically separate species (Stringer and Mackie 1996), and also with the mitochondrial DNA evidence for the clear genetic differences between the two groups (Krings et al. 1997). At the same time, it implies a very high degree of adaptation of the Neandertal groups to the specific environments of western Europe, which is hardly surprising in view of the 200,000 years or so of essentially continuous Neandertal occupation in the area under a range of fluctuating environmental conditions (Stringer and Gamble 1993, Mellars 1996). Clearly, the issues of chronology discussed above are central to all of the current debates over the character of the final Neandertal populations in Europe, their relationships to the incoming anatomically modern populations, and their eventual demise.

Note

This is an expanded and amended version of a paper given at the conference on "The First Europeans" in Gibraltar in August 1998.

BIBLIOGRAPHY

Baffier, D., and M. Julien
1990 "L'outillage en os des niveaux châtelperroniens d'Arcy-sur-Cure," in *Paléolithique moyen récent et Paléolithique supérieur ancien en Europe*, C. Farizy, ed., pp. 329–334. A.P.R.A.I.F. Mémoires du Musée de Préhistoire d'Ile de France no. 3, Nemours.

Bar-Yosef, O.
1998 "On the Nature of Transitions: The Middle to Upper Palaeolithic and the Neolithic Revolution." *Cambridge Archaeological Journal* 8:141–163.

Barandiarán Maetzu, I.
1996 "Le Paléolithique supérieur au Pays Basque et dans le bassin de l'Ebre (1990–1995)," in *Le Paléolithique Supérieur Européen: Bilan Quinquennal 1991–1996*, M. Otte, ed., pp. 319–322. Etudes et Recherches Archeologiques de l'Université de Liège, Liège.

Bard, E., M. Arnold, R. G. Fairbanks, and B. Hamelin
1993 "^{230}Th–^{234}U and ^{14}C Ages Obtained by Mass Spectrometry on Corals." *Radiocarbon* 35:191–199.

Bard, E., B. Hamelin, R. G. Fairbanks, and A. Zindler
1990 "Calibration of the ^{14}C Timescale Over the Past 30,000 Years using Mass Spectrometric U-Th Ages from Barbados Corals." *Nature* 354:405–410.

Bischoff, J. L., K. Ludwig, J. F. Garcia, E. Carbonell, M. Vaquero, T. Stafford, and A. Jull
1994 "Dating of the Basal Aurignacian Sandwich at Abric Romaní (Catalunya, Spain) by Radiocarbon and Uranium-Series." *Journal of Archaeological Science* 21:541–551.

Bischoff, J. L., N. Soler, J. Maroto, and R. Julia
1989 "Abrupt Mousterian/Aurignacian Boundary at ca. 40 ka B.P.: Accelerator ^{14}C Dates from L'Arbreda Cave (Catalunya, Spain)." *Journal of Archaeological Science* 16:563–576.

Bon, F., C. Ferrier, D. Gambier, and P. Gardère
1998 "Gisement de Brassempouy (Landes): les recherches de 1995 à 1997, bilan et perspectives." *Bulletin de la Société Borda*, pp. 203–222.

Cabrera-Valdés, V., and J. L. Bischoff
1989 "Accelerator ^{14}C Dates for Early Upper Palaeolithic (Basal Aurignacian) at El Castillo Cave (Spain)." *Journal of Archaeological Science* 16:577–584.

Cabrera-Valdés, V., H. Valladas, F. Bernaldo de Quiros, and M. H. Gomez
1996 "La transition Paléolithique moyen—Paléolithique supérieur a El Castillo (Cantabrie): nouvelles datations par le carbone-14." *Comptes Rendus de l'Académie des Sciences de Paris* 322 (Ser. IIa) 1093-1098.

Delibrias, G., and M. Fontugne
1990 "Datations des gisements de l'Aurignacien et du Moustérien en France," in *Paléolithique moyen récent et Paléolithique supérieur ancien en Europe*, C. Farizy, ed., pp. 39–42. A.P.R.A.I.F. Mémoires du Musée de Préhistoire d'Ile de France no. 3, Nemours.

Demars, P. Y.
1990 "Les interstratifications entre Aurignacien et Châtelperronien à Roc-de-Combe et au Piage (Lot): approvisionnement en matières premières et position chronologique," in *Paléolithique Moyen Récent et Paléolithique Supérieur Ancien en Europe*, C. Farizy, ed. pp. 235–240. A.P.R.A.I.F. Mémoires du Musée de Préhistoire d'Ile de France no. 3, Nemours.
1996 "Demographie et occupation de l'espace au Paléolithique supérieur et au Mésolithique en France." *Préhistoire Européenne* 8:3–26.

d'Errico, F., J. Zilhao, M. Julien, D. Baffier, and J. Pelegrin
1998 "Neanderthal Acculturation in Western Europe? A Critical Review of the Evidence and Its Interpretation." *Current Anthropology* 39:S1–S44.

Djindjian, F.
1993 "Les origines du peuplement Aurignacien en Europe," in *Aurignacien en Europe et au Proche Orient*, L. Banesz and J. K. Kozlowski, eds., pp. 136–154. Acts of 12th International Congress of Prehistoric and Protohistoric Sciences, Bratislava.

Gambier, D.
1993 "Les hommes modernes du debut du Paléolithique supérieur en France: bilan des données anthropologiques et perspectives," in *El Origen del Hombre Moderno en el Suroeste de Europa*, V. Cabrera-Valdés, ed., pp. 409–430. Universidad Nacional de Educacion a Distancia, Madrid.

Graves, P.
1991 "New Models and Metaphors for the Neanderthal Debate." *Current Anthropology* 32:513–541.

Guadelli, J.-L., and H. Laville
1990 "L'environnement climatique de la fin du Moustérien à Combe-Grenal et à Camiac. Confrontation des données naturalistes et implications,"

in *Paléolithique moyen récent et Paléolithique supérieur ancien en Europe*, C. Farizy, ed., pp. 43–48. A.P.R.A.I.F. Mémoires du Musée de Préhistoire d'Ile de France no. 3, Nemours.

Harrold, F. B.
1989 "Mousterian, Châtelperronian, and Early Aurignacian in Western Europe: Continuity or Discontinuity?" in *The Human Revolution: Behavioural and Biological Perspectives on the Origins of Modern Humans*, P. Mellars and C. Stringer, eds., pp. 677–713. Princeton University Press, Princeton.

Hedges, R. E. M., R. A. Housley, C. Bronk Ramsey, and G. J. Van Klinken
1994 "Radiocarbon Dates from the Oxford AMS System: Archaeometry Datelist 18." *Archaeometry* 36:337–374.

Hedges, R. E. M., R. A. Housley, I. A. Law, and C. R. Bronk
1990 "Radiocarbon Dates from the Oxford AMS System: Archaeometry Datelist 10." *Archaeometry* 32:101–108.

Hublin, J.-J., F. Spoor, M. Braun, F. Zonneveld, and S. Condemi
1996 "A Late Neanderthal Associated with Upper Palaeolithic Artefacts." *Nature* 381:224–226.

Kozlowski, J. K.
1993 "L'Aurignacien en Europe et au Proche Orient," in *Aurignacien en Europe et au Proche Orient*, L. Banesz and J. K. Kozlowski, eds., pp. 283–291. Acts of 12th International Congress of Prehistoric and Protohistoric Sciences, Bratislava.

Krings, M., A. Stone, R. W. Schmitz, H. Krainitzki, M. Stoneking, and S. Pääbo
1997 "Neandertal DNA Sequences and the Origin of Modern Humans." *Cell* 90:19–30.

Laj, C., A. Mazaud, and J.-C. Duplessy
1996 "Geomagnetic Intensity and ^{14}C Abundance in the Atmosphere and Ocean During the Past 50 kyr." *Geophysical Research Letters* 23:2045–2048.

Leroi-Gourhan, Arl., and A. Leroi-Gourhan
1965 "Chronologie des grottes d'Arcy-sur-Cure." *Gallia-Préhistoire* 7:1–64.

Leroyer, C.
1988 "Des occupations castelperroniennes et aurignaciennes dans leur cadre chrono-climatique," in *L'Homme de Néandertal*, vol. 8, M. Otte, ed., pp. 103–108. Etudes et Recherches Archéologiques de l'Université de Liège 35, Liège

Leroyer, C., and A. Leroi-Gourhan
1983 "Problèmes de chronologie: le castelperronien et l'aurignacien." *Bulletin de la Société Préhistorique Française* 80:41–44.

Lévêque, F., and B. Vandermeersch
1980 "Découverte de restes humains dans un niveau castelperronien à Saint-Césaire (Charente-Maritime)." *Comptes Rendus de l'Académie des Sciences de Paris*, series 2, 291:187–189.

Mellars, P. A.
1985 "The Ecological Basis of Social Complexity in the Upper Paleolithic of Southwestern France," in *Prehistoric Hunter-Gatherers: The Emergence of Cultural Complexity*, T. D. Price and J. A. Brown, eds., pp. 271–297. Academic Press, Orlando.
1989 "Major Issues in the Emergence of Modern Humans." *Current Anthropology* 30:349–385.
1992 "Archaeology and the Population–Dispersal Hypothesis of Modern Human Origins in Europe," in *The Origin of Modern Humans and the Impact of Chronometric Dating*, M. J. Aitken, C. B. Stringer, and P. A. Mellars, eds., pp. 225–234. Philosophical Transactions of the Royal Society Series B 337 no. 1280, London.
1996 *The Neanderthal Legacy: An Archaeological Perspective from Western Europe*. Princeton University Press, Princeton.
1998 "The Impact of Climatic Changes on the Demography of Late Neanderthal and Early Anatomically Modern Populations in Europe," in *Neandertals and Modern Humans in Western Asia*, T. Akazawa, K. Aoki, and O. Bar-Yosef, eds., pp. 493–507. Plenum Press, New York.
1999 "The Neanderthal Problem: Replies to d'Errico and Colleagues." *Current Anthropology* 40(3):341–364.

Mellars, P. A., H. M. Bricker, J. A. J. Gowlett, and R. E. M. Hedges
1987 "Radiocarbon Accelerator Dating of French Upper Palaeolithic Sites." *Current Anthropology* 28:128–133.

Mellars, P., and R. Grün
1991 "A Comparison of the Electron Spin Resonance and Thermoluminescence Dating Methods: The Results of ESR Dating at Le Moustier (France)." *Cambridge Archaeological Journal* 1:269–276.

Mellars, P. A., L. P. Zhou, P. Pettitt, R. E. M. Hedges, and J.-M. Geneste
n.d. "Electron Spin Resonance and Radiocarbon-Accelerator Dating of Combe-Saunière, Dordogne." In Preparation.

Mercier, N., H. Valladas, J.-L. Joron, and J.-L. Reyss
    1993 "Thermoluminescence Dating of the Prehistoric Site of La Roche à Pierrot, Saint-Césaire," in *Context of a Late Neandertal*, F. Lévêque, M. A. Backer, and M. Gilbaud, eds., pp. 15–22. Prehistory Press, Madison.

Mercier, N., H. Valladas, J.-L. Joron, J.-L. Reyss, F. Lévêque, and B. Vandermeersch
    1991 "Thermoluminescence Dating of the Late Neanderthal Remains from Saint-Césaire." *Nature* 351:737–739.

Pelegrin, J.
    1995 *Technologie lithique: Le Châtelperronien de Roc-de-Combe (Lot) et de la Côte (Dordogne)*. CNRS, Paris.

Stringer, C., and C. Gamble
    1993 *In Search of the Neanderthals: Solving the Puzzle of Human Origins*. Thames and Hudson, London.

Stringer, C. B., and R. Mackie
    1996 *African Exodus: The Origins of Modern Humanity*. Jonathan Cape, London.

Valladas, H., J.-M. Geneste, J.-L. Joron, and J.-P. Chadelle
    1986 "Thermoluminescence Dating of Le Moustier (Dordogne, France)." *Nature* 322:452–454.

Van Klinken, G. J., A. D. Bowles, and R. E. M. Hedges
    1994 "Radiocarbon Dating of Peptides Isolated from Contaminated Fossil Bone Collagen by Collagenase Digestion and Reversed-Phase Chromatography." *Geochimica et Cosmochimica Acta* 58(11): 2543–2551.

Vogel, J. C., and H. T. Waterbolk
    1963 "Groningen Radiocarbon Dates IV." *Radiocarbon* 5:163–202.
    1967 "Groningen Radiocarbon Dates VII." *Radiocarbon* 9:107–155.

White, R.
    1993 "Technological and Social Dimensions of 'Aurignacian Age' Body Ornaments across Europe," in *Before Lascaux: The Complex Record of the Early Upper Paleolithic*, H. Knecht, A. Pike-Tay, and R. White, eds., pp. 277–300. CRC Press, Boca Raton
    1998 "Comment on F. d'Errico et al., 'Neanderthal Acculturation in western Europe? A Critical Review of the Evidence and its Interpretation.'" *Current Anthropology* 39:S30–S32.

Zubrow, E.
    1989 "The Demographic Modeling of Neanderthal Extinction," in *The Human Revolution: Behavioural and Biological Perspectives on the Origins of Modern Humans*, P. Mellars and C. Stringer, eds., pp. 212–231. Princeton University Press, Princeton.

CHAPTER 4

The Late Middle and Early Upper Paleolithic in Italy

Steven L. Kuhn
Department of Anthropology, University of Arizona

Amilcare Bietti
Dipartimento di Biologia Animale e dell'Uomo,
Università di Roma, "La Sapienza"

INTRODUCTION

Recent fossil discoveries and advances in chronometric techniques have forced Paleolithic prehistorians to reevaluate comfortable, unilinear models of cultural and biological succession in Europe and western Asia. It is now evident that Neandertals and anatomically modern humans could have coexisted for significant spans of the late Pleistocene in both Europe and the Levant. Although modern humans and Upper Paleolithic technologies eventually won through, we must take seriously the possibility that these populations lived in close proximity and even interacted for many generations before the Neandertals were displaced or genetically and culturally swamped. The types of interaction most commonly discussed are overt conflict and the borrowing of Upper Paleolithic technological innovations by the (presumably backward) Mousterian hominids. However, processes like conflict or acculturation, which characterize relations between recent human populations or cultures, provide inappropriate analogical models for the Pleistocene. We should not focus exclusively on direct, face-to-face relations. For example, indirect competition between two populations or two species may have important consequences for the evolution of both, without involving a great deal of actual confrontation between individuals. The hypothetical interactions between populations of the genus *Homo* during the late Pleistocene can only be studied at evolutionary time scales and with evolutionary understanding.

In order to begin approaching the question of interactions between different human (sub)species during the Pleistocene, it is first necessary to establish the chronologic and geographic limits of their possible coexistence. The late Pleistocene archaeological record of Italy provides a provocative, if somewhat incomplete, range of evidence. As in other parts of Europe, several distinct varieties of lithic assemblages were manufactured in different parts of the Italian peninsula during the later Pleistocene. The changing distributions of these assemblage types over time are consistent with the gradual, discontinuous spread of an intrusive population of modern humans bearing a distinctive techno-complex ("proto-Aurignacian"), with a corresponding persistence of indigenous groups producing different kinds of Middle and Upper Paleolithic artifact assemblages. Although there is little evidence for the adoption of specific Upper Paleolithic traits by preexisting Middle Paleolithic groups, demographic factors may have had significant consequences for human behavior and human adaptations in the region.

BACKGROUND

Italy is extremely rich in karstic terrain, with many deeply stratified caves containing Middle and/or Upper Paleolithic deposits. The country also has a long and active history of research on paleoanthropology and Paleolithic archaeology extending back well into the previous century. At least ten sites excavated in the recent era[1] contain both Middle Paleolithic and Early Upper Paleolithic deposits in stratified context. Even though there are many sites, human remains are surprisingly scarce. As a consequence, this discussion concentrates mainly on the archaeological evidence.

In addressing the Middle and especially the Upper Paleolithic record of Italy, it is important to recognize that the majority of research has been conducted using approaches quite different from those normally employed in other parts of Europe, and particularly in France. With a few notable exceptions, Italian Upper Paleolithic researchers employ the typological system of G. Laplace (1961, 1966). The descriptive conventions, typological units, and comparative statistics developed by Laplace differ markedly from the more widely employed Upper Paleolithic typological system of Sonneville-Bordes and others (Sonneville-Bordes and Perrot 1954–1956; Bietti 1976–1977). Until very recently, Paleolithic researchers in Italy have focused almost exclusively on typological issues. Consequently, information on lithic technology is scattered, incomplete, and largely anecdotal. Taphonomic and zooarchaeological studies are even less common, and for most sites, little more than a list of species present is available regarding the faunal assemblage.

The geography of Italy, with well-defined routes of movement and communication and a more-or-less isolated southern extreme, makes the peninsula (potentially) an ideal place for examining hypothetical migrations, invasions, refugia, and other forms of population interaction during the Pleistocene. The Italian peninsula is commonly divided into three major provinces. Of course, many smaller environmental, topographic, and geological subdivisions may be recognized, but these three broad geographic zones appear to have had some significance throughout prehistory, and indeed they continue to play a role in modern political discourse. The northern part of the country, including the provinces of Liguria, Piemonte, Lombardia, Trentino/Alto Adige, Veneto, Emilia-Romagna, and Trieste, is more or less contiguous with the rest of south-central Europe, although the Alps do present a formidable barrier. The most southerly provinces, including Apulia, Calabria, Campania, Molise, and Basilicata, represent a true geographic "cul de sac," spatially isolated from the rest of the continent. The provinces of central Italy, including Latium, Umbria, Abruzzo, and Tuscany, are intermediate in space, but historically they have retained their own identities. There is also a significant division between the western (Tyrrhenian) and eastern (Adriatic) coasts. Today, and undoubtedly in the past as well, the Apennines present a major barrier to movement and communication across the central part of the peninsula.

During historic times, Italy maintained its closest political and cultural links with western Europe. This was not necessarily the case during the late Pleistocene. During glacial periods, the most open routes of communication and human movement would have been to the *east*, across the open plains exposed at the north end of the Adriatic by lowered sea levels. Movement to the west through the narrow gap between mountains and sea in Liguria would have been possible, but the Alps represented a substantial impediment, if not an essentially impenetrable barrier, to communication with areas directly to the north during much of the later Pleistocene.

Three main cultural/stratigraphic/typological units—late Mousterian, Uluzzian, and Aurignacian—are particularly relevant to the discussion at hand. It would be impractical to provide complete, assemblage-by-assemblage descriptions for all late Middle and early Upper Paleolithic sites or layers in Italy. In the next three sections, we instead summarize both the general characteristics of and patterns of variation within each of these broadly defined entities.

LATE MOUSTERIAN

The Mousterian is widespread throughout the Italian peninsula. Middle Paleolithic cave and open-air sites are found from the coasts up to elevations in excess of 2000 meters (e.g., Bietti and Mancini 1990, Taraborrelli 1969). The density of sites is highest along the Tyrrhenian coast, but this probably reflects the longer history of exploration as well as a greater concentration of easily identified caves in the area. Mousterian assemblages from several sites from throughout the peninsula have been attributed to the later part of "Würm II" or the "Würm II–III," or Hengelo, interstadial. Rather than discussing all supposedly late Mousterian assemblages, we focus on a few of the best documented cases, as well as on general trends in the later Middle Paleolithic. The locations of sites discussed below are shown in figure 1.

In the northern province of Veneto, the upper Mousterian levels (33–31) in the long sequence at Riparo Tagliente directly underlie early Aurignacian layers. Though not directly dated, this late Mousterian has been attributed to the "Hengelo" interstadial (Palma di Cesnola 1986:148). According to Peretto (1992), there is a regular decline in the frequency of Levallois and an increase in numbers of denticulates through the deep stratigraphic sequence at Tagliente. Among the tools, the percentage of unretouched Levallois pieces drops from a high of 46.4% to a low of

2.5% from the bottom of the sequence (horizon 1) to the top (horizon 9), while the percentage of denticulates rises from 12.7% to more than 27%. At the nearby site of Grotta di Fumane, Mousterian deposits are separated from very early Aurignacian strata by a very thin sedimentary layer. At Fumane there are hints of a trend within the Mousterian similar to that observed at Riparo Tagliente, but the decline in Levallois and increase in denticulates over time are less clear and regular (Bartolomei et al. 1992; Palma di Cesnola 1996:153). Although the Mousterian at this site is not dated, a very good set of dates is available for the Aurignacian (see below). Still in Veneto, Grotta del Broion, excavated in the 1950s (Leonardi 1964), yielded finite radiocarbon dates from the upper layers of a very long sequence of 46,400±1,500 and 40,000±1270 B.P. In the sequence at Grotta del Broion, there is no evidence for the decline in Levallois noted at Tagliente; in fact, the Levallois indices increase slightly over time (Broglio 1964).

There are no dated terminal Middle Paleolithic assemblages in Liguria, but the open-air site of S. Francesco is commonly attributed to the "Würm II–III," and the assemblage is often cited as an example of the terminal Mousterian (de Lumley and Isetti 1965, Tavoso 1988). Even though it is classified as "Denticulate Mousterian," the S. Francesco assemblage contains many Upper Paleolithic tool forms including truncated and retouched blades. Overall it is highly laminar, and large blades seem to have been especially favored as tool blanks (fig. 2). Unfortunately, the industry from S. Francesco has no close parallels elsewhere in Italy. At Riparo Mochi, just east of the French-Italian border, a deep series of Mousterian layers (stratum I) is separated from a dated early Aurignacian stratum by a nearly sterile layer (H) less than 1/2 meter thick. Again without dates, the most recent Mousterian deposits have been attributed to the latter part of the "Würm II," whereas layer H is correlated with the "Würm II–III" (de Lumley 1969). As at Tagliente, the frequency of denticulates increases over time within Mousterian stratum I at Riparo Mochi. Interestingly, the degree of laminarity and relative proportion of blades actually declines in the more recent deposits (Kuhn and Stiner 1992).

A stalagmite (stratum C) underlying the Mousterian layers at Buca della Iena (Hole of the Hyena) in Tuscany has been dated by the U/Th method to about 41,000 B.P. (Pitti and Tozzi 1971). The small assemblage from the site is dominated by denticulates and artifacts with irregular marginal "retouch" (fig. 3, 1–10) and exhibits comparatively low Levallois indices. The nature of the assemblage may well reflect

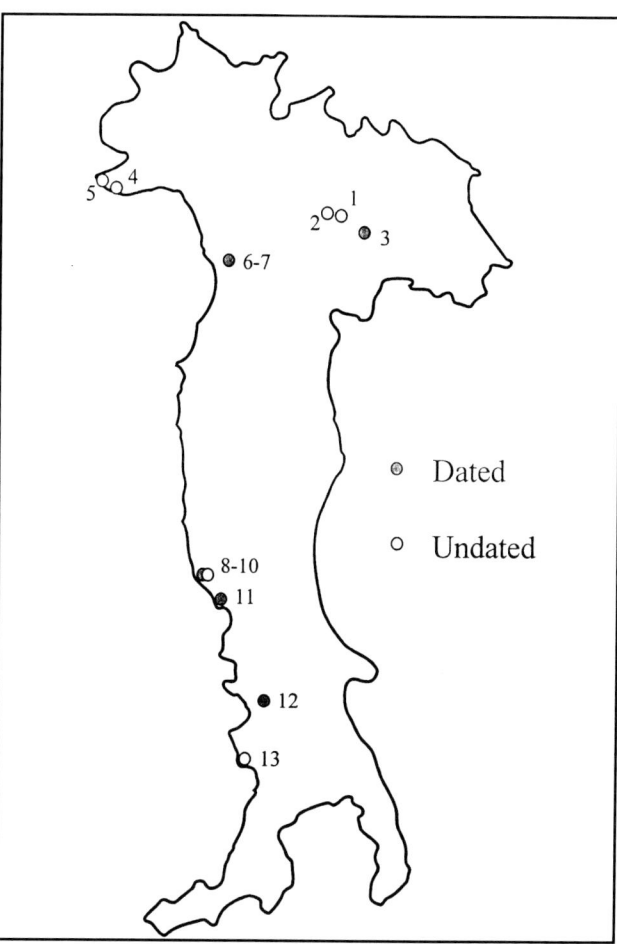

Figure 1. Dated and undated Mousterian sites in Italy discussed in the text: 1. Riparo Tagliente, 2. Grotta di Fumane, 3. Grotta di Broion, 4. S. Francesco, 5. Riparo Mochi, 6. Buca dell'Iena, 7. Grotta all'Onda, 8. Grotta Breuil, 9. Grotta del Fossellone, 10. Grotta Barbara, 11. Grotta di Sant'Agostino, 12. Grotta di Castelcivita, 13. Riparo del Poggio.

the unusual circumstances of the occupation. As the name implies, taphonomic evidence indicates that this site was used as a den by hyenas (Stiner 1994), and the human presence was probably quite ephemeral. At Grotta all'Onda, the Mousterian layers are also stratified above a stalagmite layer, this one dated to 39,300±3200 B.P. The Middle Paleolithic collections from Grotta all'Onda are from old excavations (the most recent in 1931) and are probably selected. Denticulates predominate among the retouched tools, and a number of Levallois pieces are present (Peretto 1992:181). Mousterian layers at the nearby site of Grotta del Capriolo are thought to be just slightly older than the stalagmites at Buca della Iena and Grotta

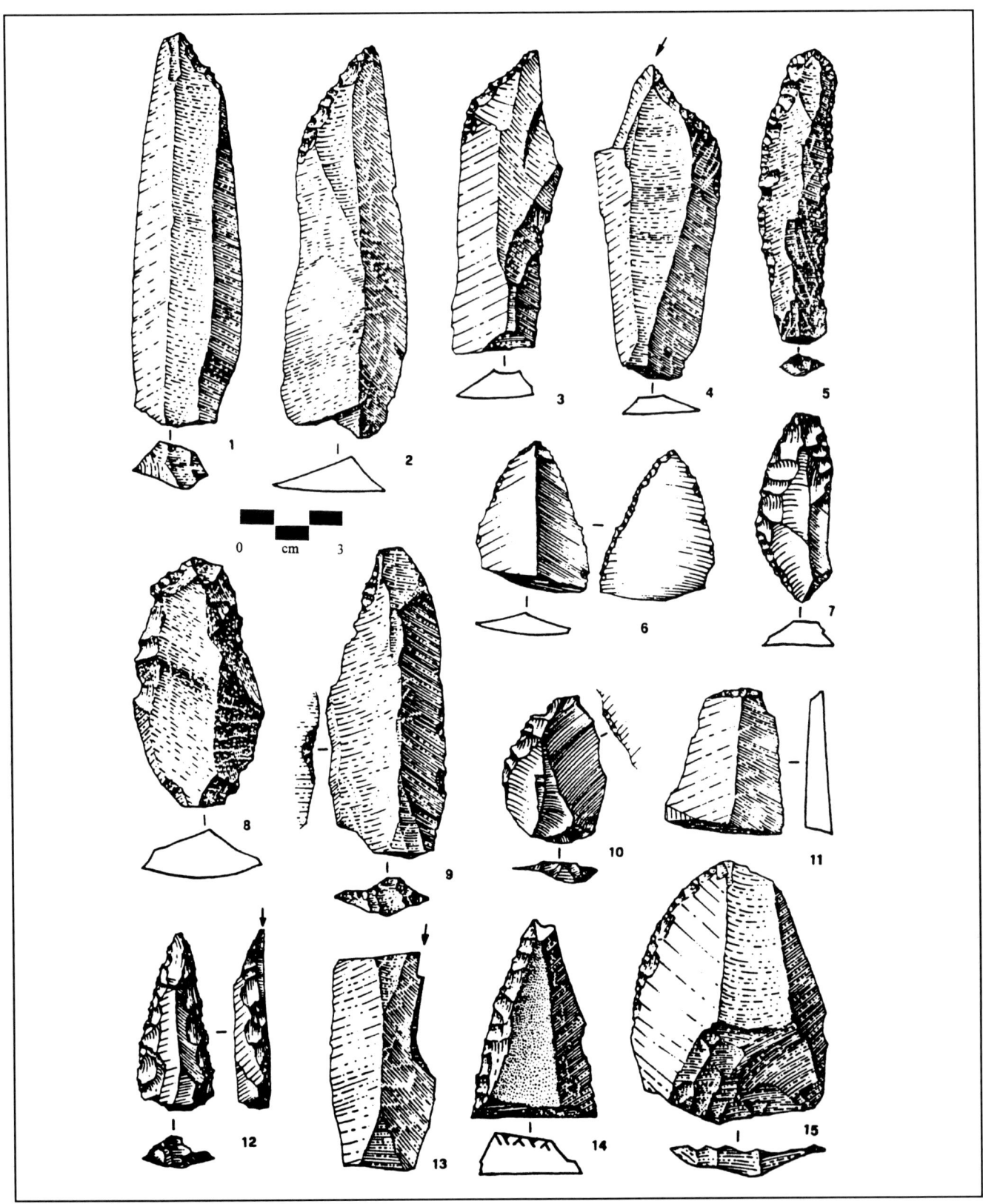

Figure 2. The S. Francesco "Denticulate Mousterian" assemblage. Adapted from de Lumley 1969, figs. 32, 35, 36, and 37.

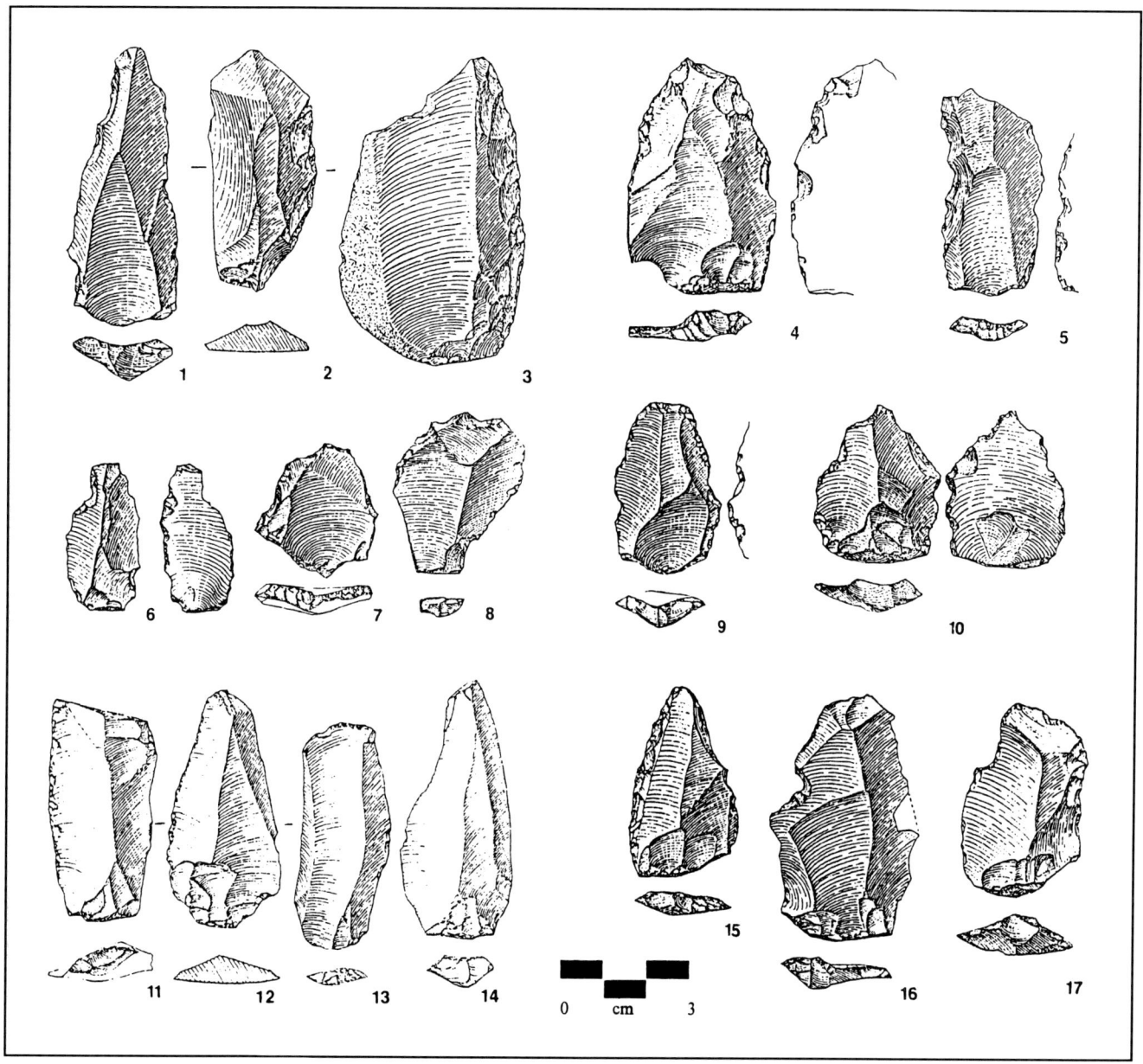

Figure 3. Stone tools from Buca della Iena (1–10) and Grotta del Capriolo (11–17) (Tuscany). Adapted from Pitti and Tozzi 1971, figs. 9, 10, 11, and 13.

all'Onda. The lithic assemblages at Grotta del Capriolo are notably rich in blades (fig. 3, nos. 11–17). Denticulates and notches slightly outnumber points and scrapers, but the majority of tools are simple retouched flakes (Pitti and Tozzi 1971).

The site of Grotta Breuil on Monte Circeo in the province of Latium has been under investigation since 1986 (Bietti et al. 1990–1991). The long Middle Paleolithic sequence at Grotta Breuil appears to span the latter part of Oxygen Isotope Stage (OIS) 4 and the first part of OIS 3 (Bietti et al. 1990–1991). The upper layers (3–6) yield a series of "terminal" Mousterian assemblages dated by the ESR technique to as late as 33,000 B.P. (Bietti 1997; Schwarcz et al. 1990–1991). The assemblage from the most recent layers (fig. 4), while sharing with other local Mousterian assemblages a series of characteristics conferred by the use of very small flint pebbles, has several distinctive features. The method of debitage is highly laminar, and the majority of tool blanks were detached from cores with one or

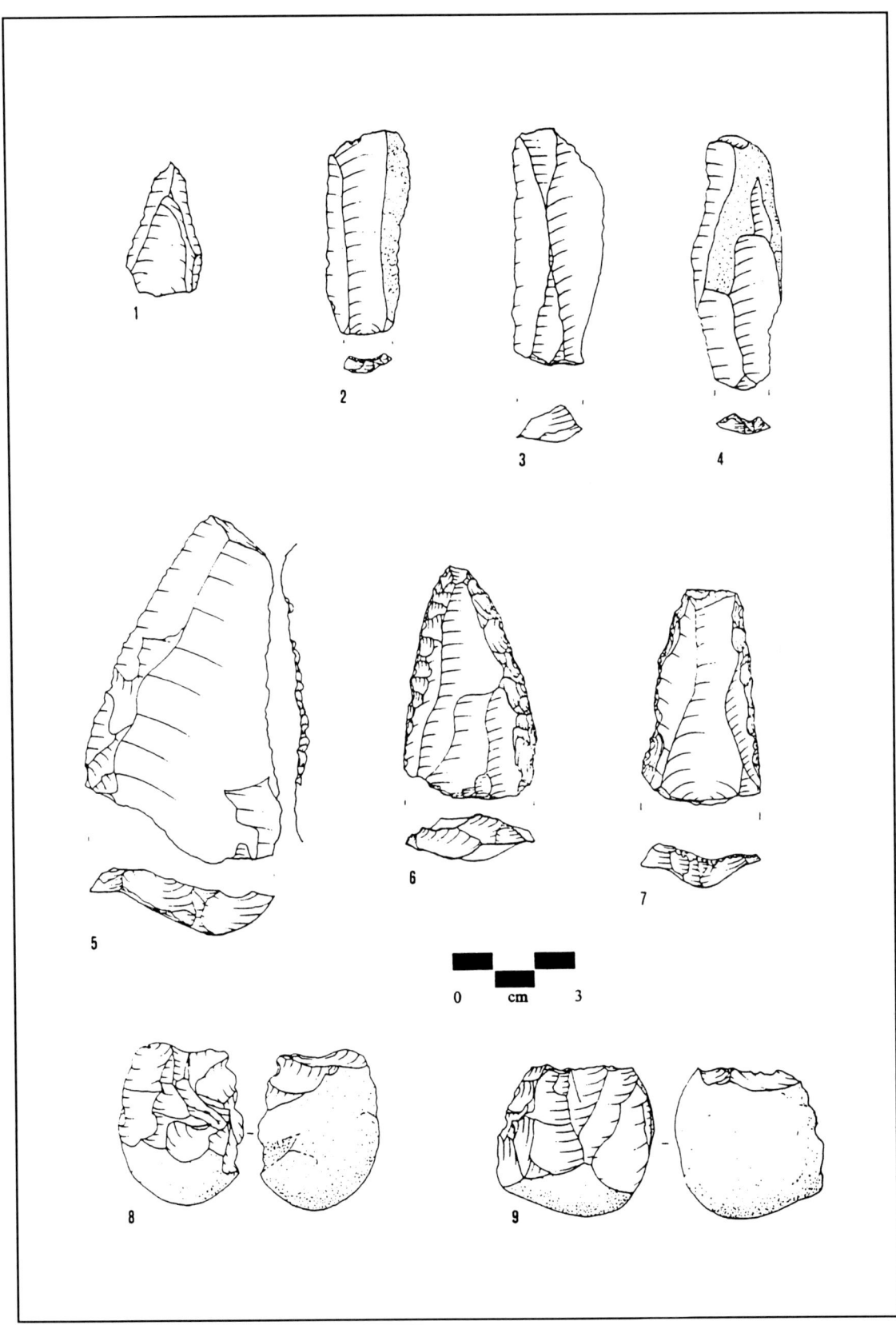

Figure 4. Assemblage from most recent layers at Grotta Breuil, Monte Circeo.

two opposed striking platforms. Like "bladey" Mousterian assemblages from other parts of the world (e.g., Baumler 1988), but unlike earlier Mousterian assemblages from coastal Latium (Kuhn 1995:99–106), centripetal cores form the most recent layers at Grotta Breuil seem to represent only the final stages of core reduction (Bietti and Grimaldi 1995; Rosetti and Zanzi 1990–1991). Although the methods of blank production are somewhat reminiscent of Upper Paleolithic techniques, almost all retouched tools are Middle Paleolithic forms. As in most of the other Mousterian sites of coastal west-central Italy, denticulates are rare and sidescrapers predominate.

The faunal assemblages from the upper levels at Grotta Breuil have been the subject of intensive zooarchaeological study (Stiner 1990–1991, 1994). In many respects, the most recent faunas from Grotta Breuil represent the culmination of long-term trends observed in the Mousterian of Latium (Stiner 1994, Stiner and Kuhn 1992). Anatomical representation is relatively complete among medium to large game species (mainly *Cervus elaphus*, *Capra ibex*, *Bos taurus*, and *Capreolus capreolus*, in order of abundance), indicating early and unhindered access to carcasses. More important, the assemblages are dominated by prime-aged adult individuals. Prime-dominated faunas seem to be a particular indicator of human ambush hunting. This pattern first appears in the Mousterian (Stiner 1990, Speth and Tchernov 1998) and continues through the Upper Paleolithic and on into the Holocene (Stiner 1990, 1993). The focus on the largest, fattest, but most difficult-to-obtain individuals in a prey population implies a high degree of control over potential prey, facilitated perhaps by humans' unique cooperative abilities.

Grotta Barbara (Mussi and Zampetti 1990–1991) is situated on Monte Circeo, just a few kilometers from Grotta Breuil. This very small cave contains both late Mousterian and Aurignacian components, but these have yet to be fully described. According to the excavators, however, the Mousterian industry, claimed to date to OIS 3, is especially rich in naturally backed knives (Mussi and Zampetti 1990–1991). Also on Monte Circeo, Grotta del Fossellone (Blanc and Segre 1953) contains a long Mousterian sequence capped with Aurignacian and later Upper Paleolithic layers. Although it has not been dated, the so-called "Denticulate Micro-Mousterian" from layers 26 and 27 near the top of the Middle Paleolithic sequence is often assumed to be late (Palma di Cesnola 1986; Vitagliano and Piperno 1990–1991). Due to the presence of *Dicerorhinus mercki* and *Paleoloxodon antiquus*, however, it can be argued that this stratum should actually be assigned to OIS 4 (Bietti 1997:135).

South of Monte Circeo, a short distance north of the town of Gaeta, is Grotta di Sant'Agostino (Tozzi 1970). The four arbitrary levels at Sant'Agostino have yielded ESR dates ranging from 43,000 to 54,000 years B.P. The lithic industry and fauna from the most recent level (level 1) exhibit characteristics intermediate between the very late Mousterian at Grotta Breuil and more ancient Mousterian from sites such as Grotta Guattari and Grotta dei Moscerini (Kuhn 1995). For example, a bias towards uni- or bidirectional (as opposed to centripetal) reduction is evident in the assemblages from Sant'Agostino, though it is not as strong as in the upper layers at Grotta Breuil. The Sant'Agostino fauna shows some tendency towards a prime-dominated mortality profile, but again, this pattern is less strongly expressed than at Breuil (Stiner 1994).

Moving still farther south, radiocarbon dates (table 1) suggest that the upper Mousterian (layer cgr) at the key site of Grotta di Castelcivita in Campania may be less than 40,000 years old. The assemblage from the highest levels is relatively small, and in a recent monograph, all Mousterian layers are lumped together (Gambassini 1997). Typologically, the assemblage has a strong Levallois component. Although little technological information is provided, illustrations suggest that elongated points, flakes, and blades produced from uni- or bidirectional cores are quite abundant (Bietti 1997; Gambassini 1997). Another comparatively late Mousterian assemblage from Campania, unfortunately without absolute dates, comes from levels 9 and 10 of Riparo del Poggio (fig. 5). Unlike the material from Castelcivita, the Levallois indices are quite low. Denticulates are the largest class of retouched tool, but Upper Paleolithic tool forms (endscrapers, burins) are common. Many of the tools are manufactured on blades or elongated flakes (Bartolomei et al. 1975; Palma di Cesnola 1996:172–173), and technologically the assemblage is quite reminiscent of the upper Layers of Grotta Breuil, albeit manufactured using larger raw materials.

A number of authors have argued for the existence of long-term trends within the Italian Mousterian. Most notably, Palma di Cesnola and others (Palma di Cesnola 1986, 1996; Mussi 1990:257) perceive a general increase in the frequencies of denticulates and a decline in Levallois flakes and points over time. Although this pattern may be clearly indicated in some sites, it is far from universal. Even Palma di Cesnola recognizes a number of important exceptions, including Grotta di Castelcivita (e.g., 1996:158, 181). In Latium, where assemblages from several sites can be ordered using radiometric dates, no such trend is

TABLE 1
Dates for Middle and Upper Paleolithic sites in Italy

Site	Layer(s)	Technique	Date(s)	Source
MOUSTERIAN				
Grotta Breuil	3/4	ESR (LU)	36,600±2700	1
	6	ESR (LU)	33,000±5000	2
Grotta Broion	1	^{14}C	46,400±1500	3
	1	^{14}C	40,600±1200	
Grotta di Castelcivita	cgr, cuts 27/28	^{14}C	33,800±1300	4
	cgr, cuts 29/30	^{14}C	39,100±1300	
		^{14}C	42,700±900	
Buca dell'Iena	stalagmite underlying MP	U/Th	41,000	5
Grotta all'Onda	stalagmite underlying MP	U/Th	39,300±3200	5
Grotta di Sant'Agostino	1	ESR (LU)	43,000±9000	1
ULUZZIAN				
Grotta del Cavallo	Ei-Eii	^{14}C	>31,000	6
Grotta di Castelcivita	rsa, lower 4	^{14}C	32,470±650	4
	rpi	^{14}C	33,300±430	
	pie	^{14}C	33,200±780	
PROTO-AURIGNACIAN (WITH RETOUCHED BLADELETS)				
Grotta della Cala	R (upper)	^{14}C	29,850(870	7
Grotta di Castelcivita	rsa, upper	^{14}C	31,950±650	4
		^{14}C	32,930±720	
Grotta di Fumane	D3b	^{14}C	31,700+1200/-1100	8
		^{14}C	32,300±400	
	D6	^{14}C	32,300±500	
	A1 (exterior)	^{14}C	31,900±500	
	A2 (exterior)	^{14}C	32,800±400	
		^{14}C	32,100±500	
		^{14}C	40,000+900/-1100	
	A2 (interior)	^{14}C	34,200+900/-1100	
		^{14}C	35,400+1100/-1300	
		^{14}C	36,500±600	
		^{14}C	36,800+1200/-1400	
Riparo Mochi	G, cut 51	^{14}C	33,400±750	9
	G, cut 56/57	^{14}C	34,680±760	
	G, cut 59	^{14}C	35,700±850	
	G, cut 60	^{14}C	34,870±800	
	G, base	^{14}C	37,400	
Grotta Paglicci	24Ai	^{14}C	29,300±600	10
	24Bi	^{14}C	34,000+900/-800	
Grotta di Paina	9	^{14}C	37,900±800	11
		^{14}C	38,600+1400/-1800	
Serino	12	^{14}C	31,200±650	12

TABLE 1 CONTINUED
Dates for Middle and Upper Paleolithic sites in Italy

Site	Layer(s)	Technique	Date(s)	Source
AURIGNACIAN (WITH MICROPOINTS)				
Grotta di Castelcivita	gic-ars	^{14}C	32,930±490	4
AURIGNACIAN ("CLASSIC")				
Riparo Mochi	top of G or base of (cut 50)	^{14}C	32,280±580	9

Sources for dates in table 1. 1. Schwarcz et al. 1990–1991, 2. H. Schwarcz and J. Rink, personal communication, 1997, 3. Vogel and Waterbolk 1967, 4. Gambassini 1997, 5. Pitti and Tozzi 1971, 6. Alessio et al. 1970, 7. Azzi et al. 1977, 8. Bartolomei et al. 1992, 9. Hedges et al. 1994, 10. Gambassini et al. 1995:25, 11. Broglio 1994, 12. Azzi and Gulisano 1979.

apparent. On the other hand, the most recent Mousterian assemblages in Latium do contain more blades and more laminar methods of blank production than do earlier assemblages. The intensity of artifact reduction also declines over time in this region (Kuhn 1995). The late Mousterian assemblages of S. Francesco, Grotta del Broion, and Riparo del Poggio are also rich in blades, but in other areas and at other sites, there is actually a decline in laminarity over time (Kuhn and Stiner 1992, Palma di Cesnola 1986). In the final analysis, most or all of these trends within the Mousterian are probably highly localized, representing behavioral adaptations to local conditions rather than general evolutionary developments on a peninsula-wide scale.

Virtually all Middle Paleolithic hominid fossils from Italy are highly fragmentary. A recent publication (Mallegni 1996) shows that Italy boasts thirteen sites that have yielded Neandertal remains, second only to France (31 sites). While some extremely important fossils, including the Circeo 1 Neandertal cranium from Grotta Guattari, have been found in Italy, none of the Italian Neandertal specimens represents a complete or even near-complete skeleton. The recently discovered specimen from Altamura/Lamalunga (Pesce-Delfino and Vacca 1994) is an exception, but it apparently represents an individual trapped in a highly unusual depositional context. Whether the highly fragmentary nature of human remains is due to a peculiar taphonomic situation or some feature of the behavior of Italian Neandertals remains uncertain. As far as the recent Mousterian is concerned, several fragmentary hominid fossils have been collected from Grotta Breuil. Most important for the current discussion is a molar (Breuil 3) from layer 6 that has been attributed to a Neandertal (Manzi and Passarello 1990–1991, 1995). This layer also yielded the ungulate tooth that provided an ESR date of 33,000±5,000 B.P. (table 1). Although the standard deviation is large, this date still indicates a very recent Neandertal and Mousterian presence at the site. A mandibular corpus (Fossellone 3/Circeo IV) from an immature individual, probably a Neandertal (Mallegni 1992), was found in the upper Mousterian levels at Grotta del Fossellone; as mentioned above, the age of these layers remains open to question.

ULUZZIAN

The term "Uluzzian" refers to a complex of Early Upper Paleolithic assemblages unique to Italy. Conventionally, the Uluzzian is thought to be the earliest form of Upper Paleolithic in the peninsula, but radiometric dates demonstrate otherwise. The name derives from the Bay of Uluzzo, on the Ionian coast of Apulia, where the industry was first identified. Sites yielding Uluzzian industries fall into two rather tight geographic clusters (Guerreschi 1992:199; Palma di Cesnola 1993). The southern cluster consists of a series of caves and open-air localities in Apulia, Calabria, and Campania. The northern cluster of Uluzzian sites is confined to Tuscany. With the exception of Grotta la Fabbrica (Pitti et al. 1976), all of the Tuscan assemblages are from undated, unstratified, open-air sites. Uluzzian assemblages are unknown in well-explored regions between

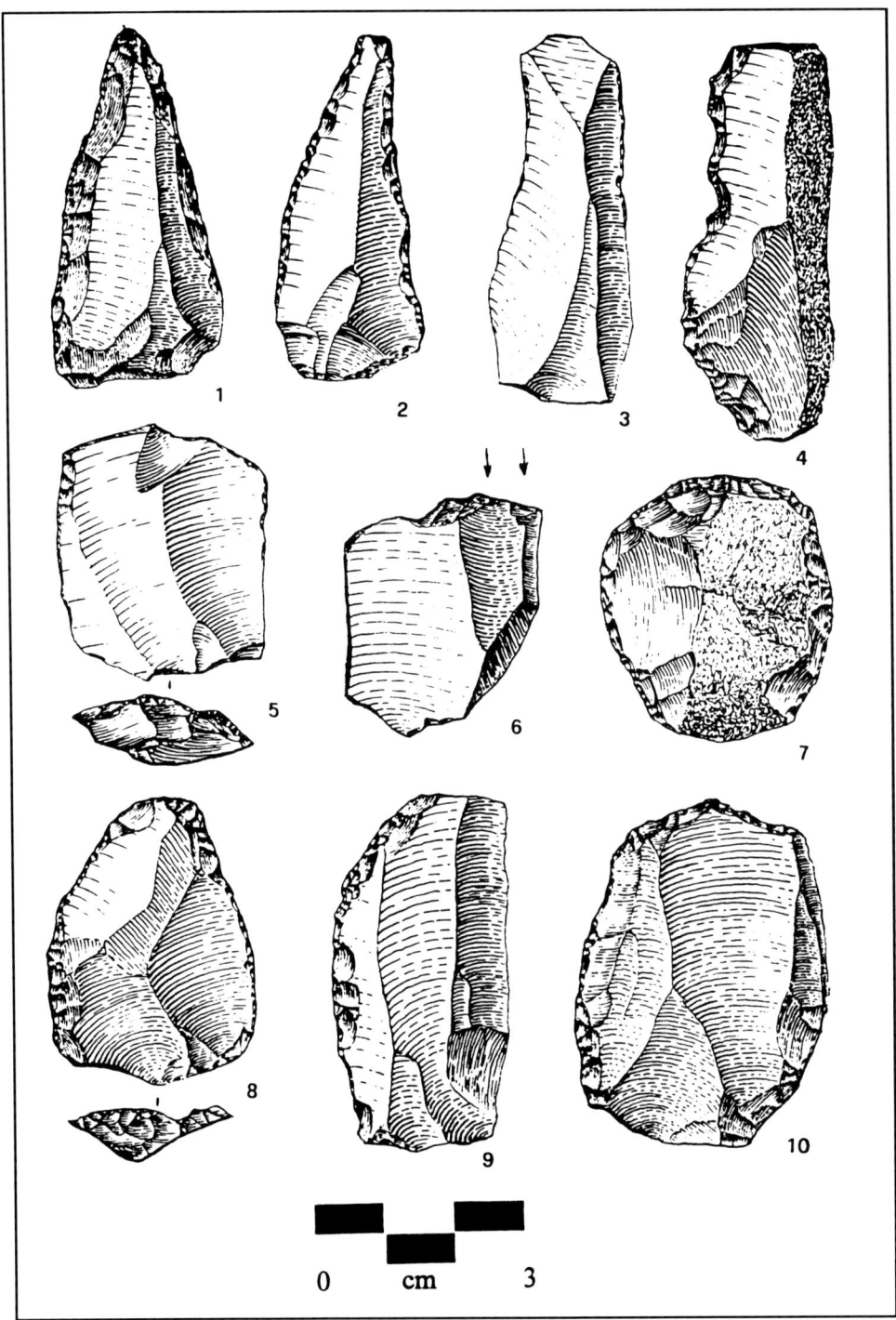

Figure 5. Assemblage from levels 9 and 10 at Riparo del Poggio, Campania. Adapted from Bartolomei et al. 1976, figure 5.

these two areas (i.e., Latium), as well as in the northern part of the country (Liguria, Veneto).[2]

Retouched tool forms in Uluzzian assemblages include a variety of endscrapers, along with sidescrapers and denticulates; burins are generally quite scarce (Gioia 1988, 1990; Palma di Cesnola 1993). Many assemblages appear to be dominated by generic Middle Paleolithic rather than Upper Paleolithic tool types.

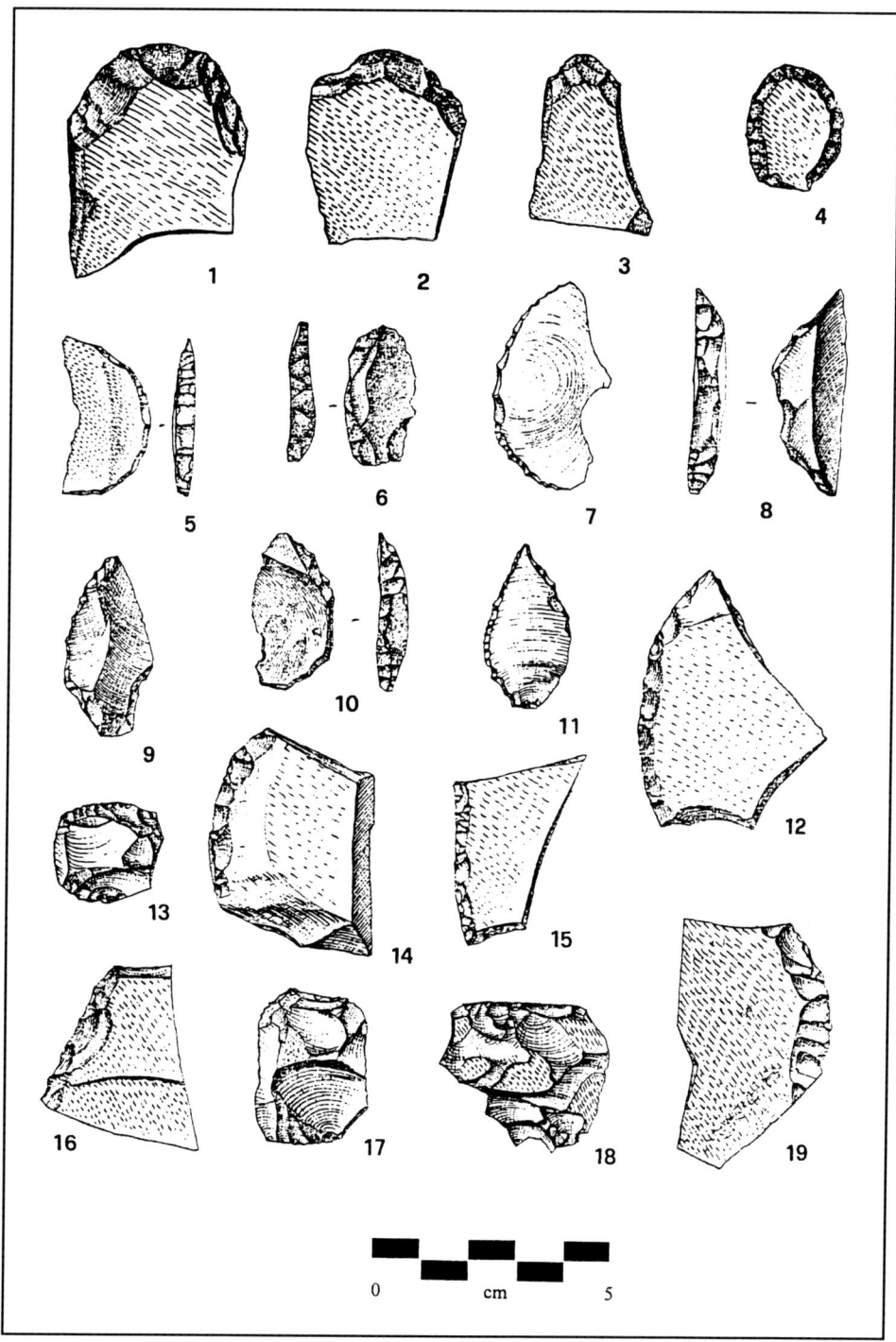

Figure 6. The early Uluzzian of Grotta del Cavallo. Adapted from Palma di Cesnola 1993, fig. 3.

The "type fossils" of the Uluzzian are implements with curved or arched backs resembling crescents or lunates. Except in so-called "middle" or "evolved" Uluzzian layers, however, these backed pieces are not especially abundant. The most common class of modified artifact in a great many Uluzzian assemblages is splintered pieces (*pièces esquilées*) (Palma di Cesnola 1993; Gioia 1990), which may be either wedges or bipolar cores, or perhaps both. It is worth noting that the tools in many assemblages, especially the putatively early ones, are made of thin, flat slabs of chert, flint, or jasper (Palma di Cesnola 1993:93), and it is possible that the high frequency of splintered pieces is somehow linked with the use of this kind of raw material. Very little information is available about technology in the Uluzzian. Quite clearly, however, it is not a blade industry: blades are few, and many of those that exist have faceted butts. Other than this, there are few concrete data on the technology of blank production. Uni- and bidirectional cores are reported (Palma di Cesnola 1993:82), but disc cores are illustrated as well (e.g., Pitti et al. 1976:fig. 3). Bone tools, mainly awls and points, are known from two sites, Grotta del Cavallo and Grotta la Fabbrica. Several perforated marine shells are also reported from the Uluzzian layers at Grotta del Cavallo (Guerreschi 1992:200).

Palma di Cesnola (1993:93–99) has proposed a chronological sequence for Uluzzian industries based mainly on the stratigraphic sequence of Grotta del Cavallo (see also Bietti 1997). The early Uluzzian (fig. 6) is dominated by denticulates and sidescrapers, with smaller numbers of endscrapers and backed pieces. Many artifacts are manufactured from the aforementioned thin slabs of stone. The middle or "evolved" Uluzzian sees more use of flint-pebble raw materials. Small, backed pieces, some approaching microlithic dimensions, are the predominant retouched tool forms (fig. 7). In the upper Uluzzian, backed pieces are extremely scarce, while denticulates as well as "Aurignacian-like" tool forms become more common once again.

Although it is possible to produce a generalized description of the Uluzzian, many assemblages, including some from key stratified sites (e.g., Grotta la Fabbrica [fig. 8], Castelcivita) simply do not fit well with the type sequence from Grotta del Cavallo. There appears to be a great deal more variability within the Uluzzian than is commonly recognized (Bietti 1997; Mussi 1998). The category of "Uluzzian" may well turn out to be a generic one, encompassing a whole range of assemblages that postdate the Mousterian but are not Aurignacian, and that represent localized adaptations to a particular set of environmental and demographic conditions (Bietti 1997:140–141). The ambiguity of what exactly constitutes the Uluzzian is exacerbated by the fact that so many collections are from unstratified and possibly mixed surface sites (Gioia 1988, 1990).

For the most part, Uluzzian assemblages have been assigned a chronological position based on either paleoclimatic indicators or typological resemblance to the different phases described at Grotta del Cavallo. Absolute dates are available for only two sites. Layers Ei–ii at Grotta del Cavallo (middle Uluzzian) yielded a single radiocarbon determination of >31,000 B.P. (table 1). The key site of Castelcivita has provided a series of dates placing the Uluzzian between 32,500 and 33,500 B.P. (Gambassini 1997).

The only human fossils associated with the Uluzzian are two deciduous molars from the lower levels at Grotta del Cavallo. The two teeth came from different geological levels but differed in absolute depths by only 15–20 cm. In keeping with the ambiguous nature of the industry, these remains provide no clear answer about its makers. The stratigraphically older specimen (from layer Eiii) is more modern in appearance, whereas the tooth from the higher level (EII) appears more "Neandertaloid" (Palma di Cesnola and Messeri 1967).

AURIGNACIAN

Aurignacian deposits are more common in Italy than are the Uluzzian. Palma di Cesnola (1996) lists 25 sites yielding Aurignacian industries, but other authors put the number as high as 45 (Chilardi et al. 1996). The Aurignacian is also more evenly distributed geographically. Aurignacian deposits are found from the extreme southern end of the peninsula, and even on Sicily (Chilardi et al. 1996), to the foothills of the Alps (Bartolomei et al. 1992; Lanzinger 1984). Most researchers divide the Italian Aurignacian into at least two groups, which show both chronological and geographic separation.

The first group consists of assemblages sometimes called "proto-Aurignacian," which are characterized by large numbers of marginally retouched or backed bladelets. These bladelets, which make up as much as 85% of retouched pieces in some layers, are generally straight or ventrally convex (e.g., Bartolomei et al. 1992, Kuhn and Stiner 1998). They are clearly the products of a fully developed system of blade manufacture employing the crested blade technique and single-platform cores, and were not produced from carinated core/scrapers such as the smaller, twisted *lamelles Dufours* (e.g., Lucas 1997). Some assemblages classified as proto-Aurignacian (e.g., Riparo Mochi layer G [fig. 9]) actually contain very few classic Aurignacian "type fossils," such as carinated and nosed endscrapers or blades with heavy scalar retouch, so that it is not obvious why they should be linked to the Aurignacian at all. Other contemporaneous assemblages (e.g.,

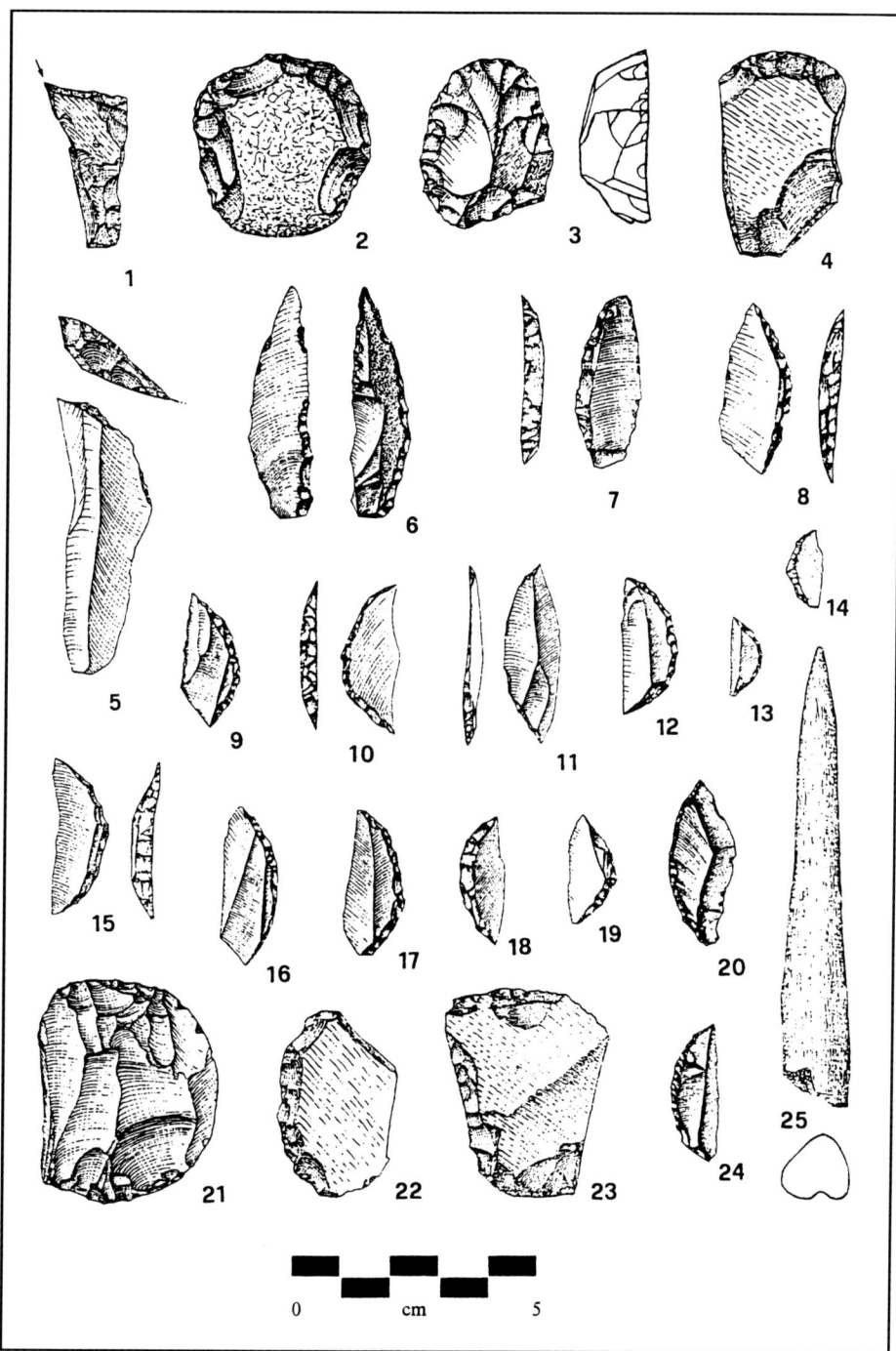

Figure 7. The Middle or "evolved" Uluzzian of Grotta del Cavallo. Adapted from Palma di Cesnola 1993, fig. 4.

Grotta di Fumane, Riparo Tagliente) contain large numbers of the more typical Aurignacian artifact types along with the retouched bladelets, however. Functional or situational factors may explain variation in the frequencies of heavy-duty Aurignacian tool forms at these sites.

The earliest Aurignacian assemblages from some southern Italian sites (e.g., Grotta di Castelcivita [layer gic], Grotta della Cala) are characterized by very small, triangular "marginally backed points" in addition to retouched bladelets and typical Aurignacian tool types (fig. 10). These southern assemblages are also consider-

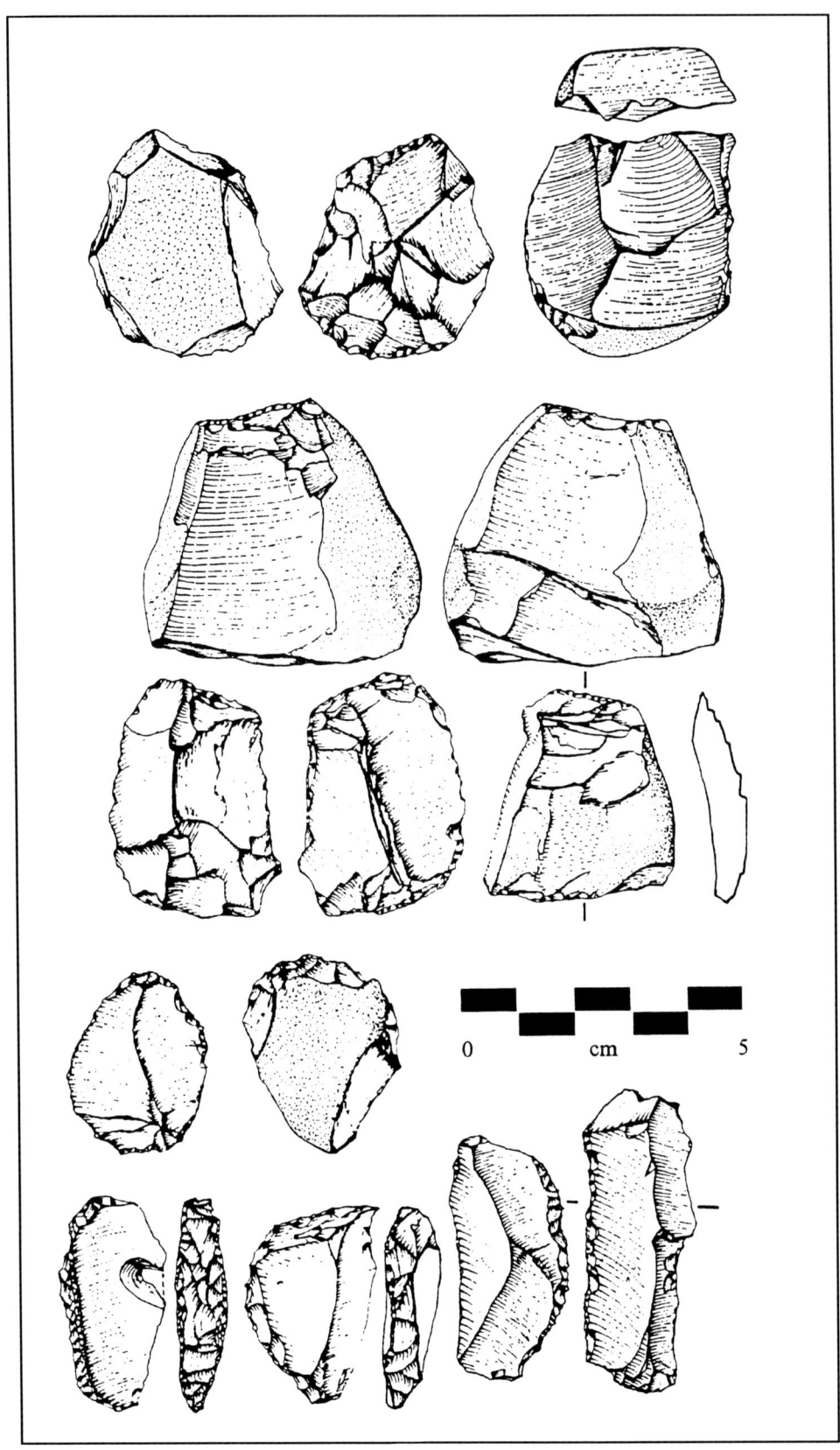

Figure 8. Uluzzian artifacts from Grotta la Fabbrica, Castelcivita. Adapted from Pitti et al. 1977, figs. 3, 4, and 5.

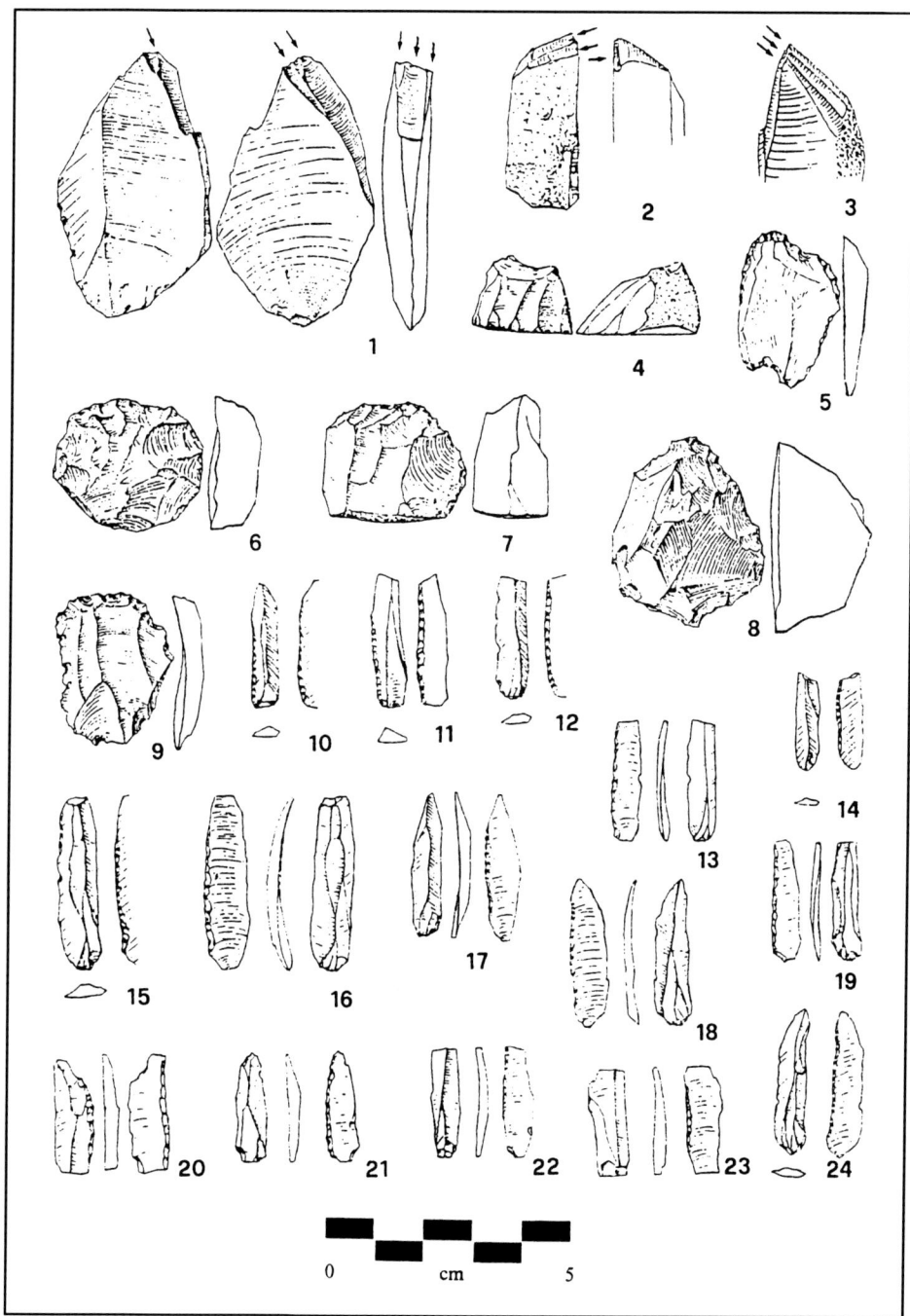

Figure 9. "Proto-Aurignacian" artifacts from Riparo Mochi, layer G.

ably more recent than the northern Italian ones. The early Aurignacian assemblage from Layer 24 at Grotta Paglicci, on the Adriatic coast of northern Apulia, appears to resemble the southern Italian variant, although it has its own unique characteristics (Palma di Cesnola 1991).

In the north of the country at least, even the earliest of the proto-Aurignacian assemblages contains substantial quantities of bone and antler artifacts, as well as large numbers of beads made of marine shells and other materials (Bartolomei et al. 1992; Kuhn and Stiner 1998).

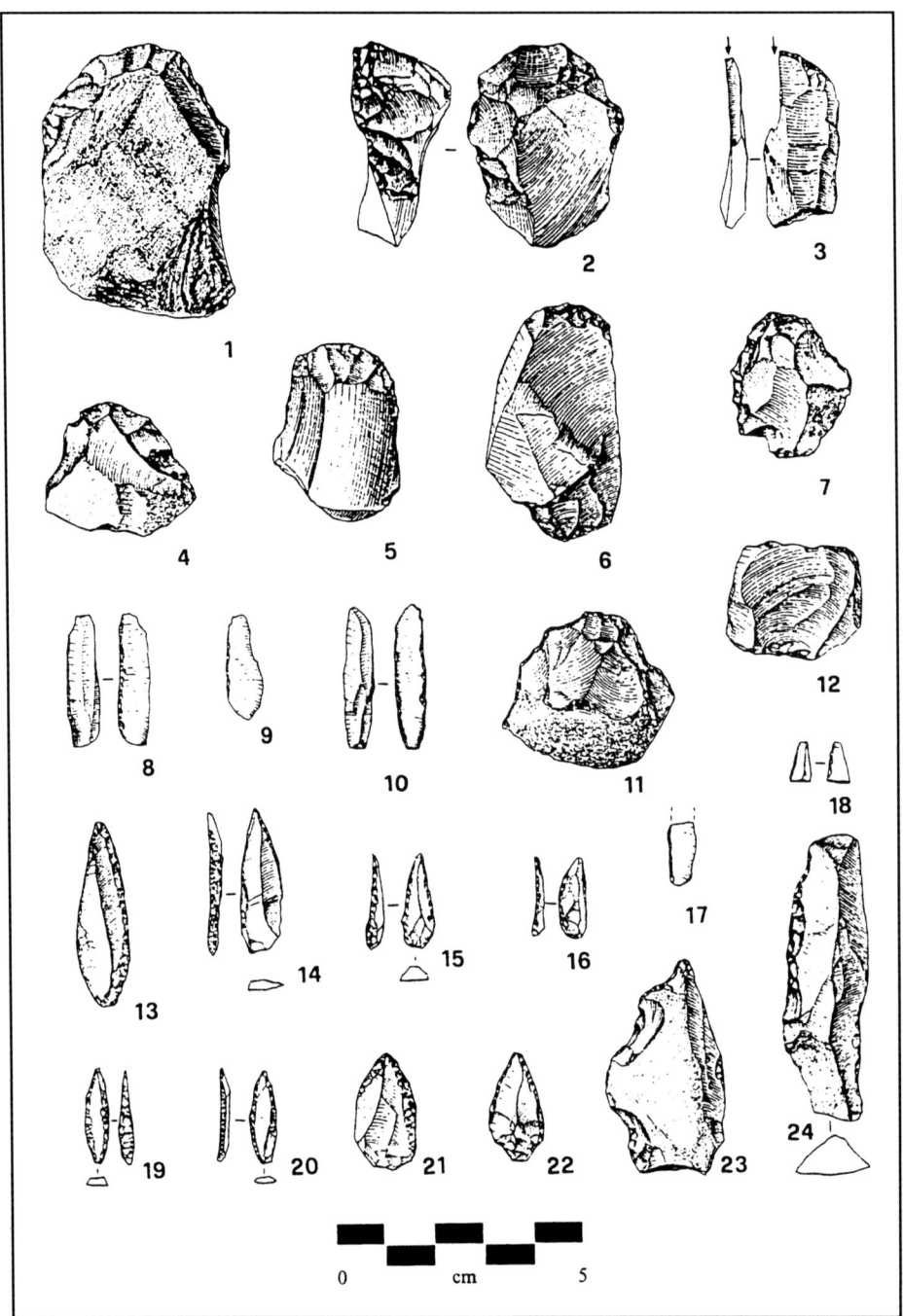

Figure 10. The earliest Aurignacian of more recent southern Italian sites. Adapted from Palma di Cesnola 1993, fig. 17.

A second, less numerous group of assemblages can best be characterized as "classic" Aurignacian by virtue of the presence of numerous carinated and nosed scrapers, retouched and "strangulated" Aurignacian blades, as well as bone points with split and conical bases. This kind of assemblage occurs in only a few stratified contexts, including Riparo Mochi in Liguria (layer F [fig. 11]), perhaps Grotta la Fabbrica in Tuscany (Bietti 1997:144; cf. Palma di Cesnola 1993:131), layer 21 at Grotta del Fossellone, and at Grotta Barbara on Monte Circeo. The material from Fossellone, which exhibits unique properties resulting from the use

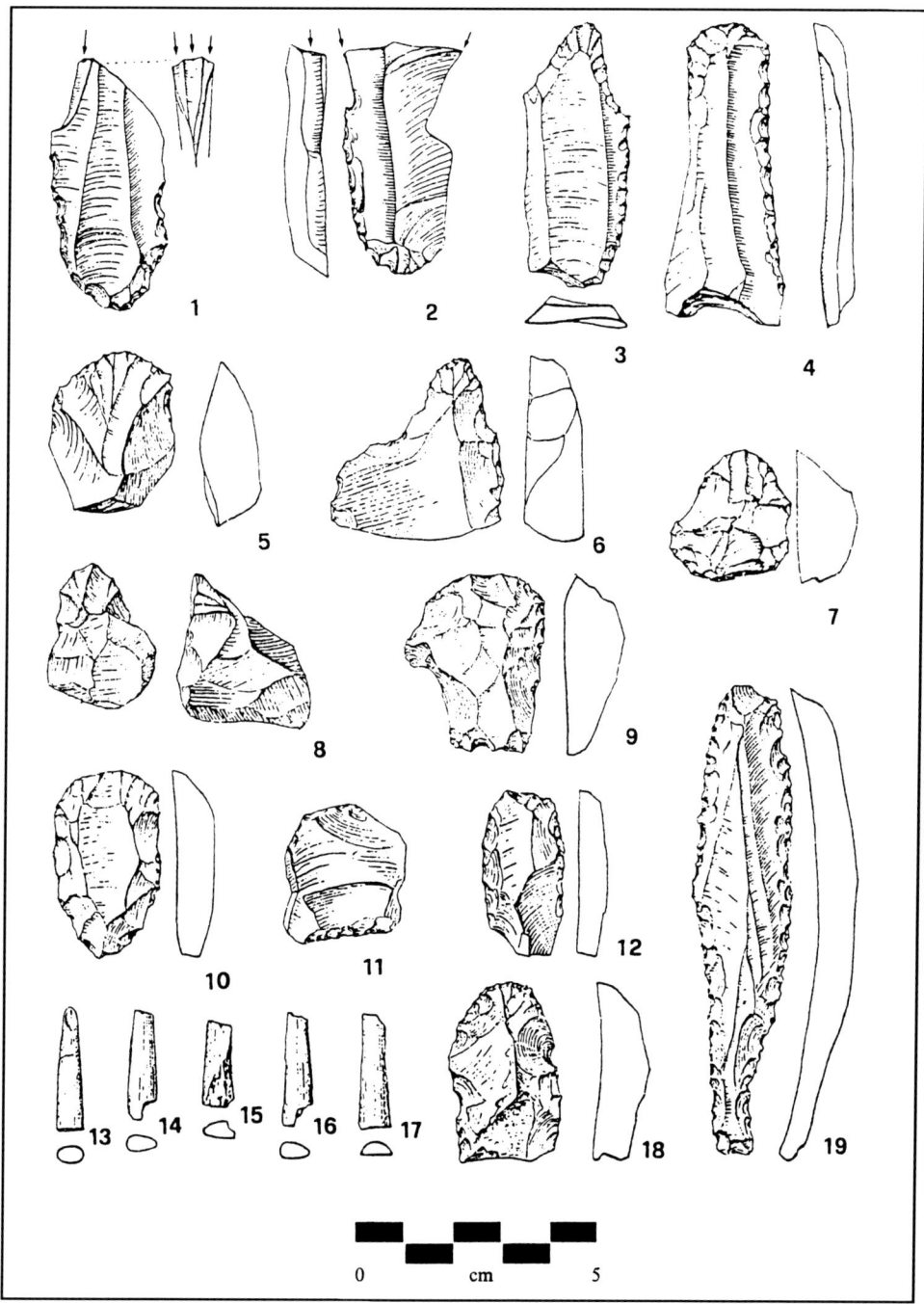

Figure 11. Artifacts from layer F of Riparo Mochi, Liguria. Adapted from Blanc 1953.

of small-pebble raw materials, is sometimes referred to as the "Circean" Aurignacian. Fontana Nuova di Ragusa, a small rockshelter in southern Sicily (Chilardi et al. 1996), apparently documents an unsuccessful colonization of Sicily by Aurignacian groups. The undated assemblage has been described as "Aurignacian I"

(Chilardi et al. 1996; Gioia 1988). Palma di Cesnola (1993:146) includes the industry from layers D1 through D6 at Grotta di Fumane within this Aurignacian group—mainly on the basis of the presence of bone points—despite the fact that marginally retouched bladelets are the dominant artifact forms (and contrary to the opinions of the site's excavators) (Bartolomei et al. 1992).

Palma di Cesnola (1993:150–154) also recognizes a third Aurignacian variant, the so-called Uluzzo-Aurignacian, a possible candidate for a hybrid or transitional industry. The Uluzzo-Aurignacian has been found in stratigraphic context at only one site, Grotta di Serra Cicora in southern Puglia, where it overlies a "terminal" Uluzzian layer (Spennato 1981). All other examples of this group come from unstratified open-air localities.

Fortunately, a large number of absolute dates are available for the Italian Aurignacian, especially for the early assemblages with many retouched bladelets. Sites in the northern part of the country consistently provide earlier ages. At Grotta Fumane, Aurignacian levels have yielded AMS radiocarbon dates ranging from around 36,500 to about 32,000 B.P. in layers A1 and A2 (with one aberrantly old date of ca. 40,000 B.P.), and from $32,300\pm500$ to $31,700\pm1200/1100$ B.P. in layers D3–D6 (Bartolomei et al. 1992:156–161). For some reason, there is a marked discrepancy between dates from the "A" levels on the interior and exterior of the cave (table 1). A similar but poorer assemblage from layer 9 at nearby Paina cave provided two AMS radiocarbon determinations of $38,600\pm1400/1800$ and $37,900\pm800$ B.P. (Broglio 1994:43). Layer G at Riparo Mochi in Liguria yielded a series of AMS dates ranging from $33,400\pm750$ to $35,700\pm850$ (Kuhn and Stiner 1998:177; Hedges et al. 1994). An additional, unpublished date places the bottom of layer G at around 37,400 B.P. In contrast, ^{14}C ages for the earliest Aurignacian layers in southern Italy range from $31,950\pm650$ at Grotta di Castelcivita (layer gic) to $29,800\pm900$ at Grotta della Cala. Serino, one of a very few stratified open-air Aurignacian sites in Italy, yielded a single date of $31,200\pm650$ B.P. (Accorsi et al. 1979). On the Adriatic coast, there are two dates for the Aurignacian at Grotta Paglicci: $34,000\pm900/800$ B.P. from near the bottom of the layer and $29,300\pm600$ from the top (Gambassini et al. 1995:125). The "classic" Aurignacian is less well dated. A single sample from Riparo Mochi yielding an age of $32,280\pm580$ comes from a level close to or at the boundary between layers F and G.

Most of the human remains attributed at one time or another to the Aurignacian in Italy come from nineteenth-century excavations at the so-called Grimaldi caves (Balzo della Torre, Grotta del Caviglione, Barma Grande, Grotta dei Fanciulli, etc.) in Liguria, near the French-Italian border. Although the individuals represented are clearly anatomically modern humans, their chronological and cultural attributions are highly ambiguous, because of the lack of precise information on stratigraphic position and cultural associations. Two fragmentary specimens from Grotta del Fossellone (Mallegni and Segre-Naldini 1992) are probably associated with the Aurignacian. The human fossils from Fontana Nuova, which consist of two teeth, two cranial fragments, and a talus, are clearly attributable to the genus *Homo*, but are not diagnostic at the level of species or subspecies (Chilardi et al. 1996).

SYNTHESIS AND DISCUSSION

In order to facilitate synthetic discussions, relevant portions of some key stratigraphic sequences (with absolute dates marked) are provided in figure 12, and all dates discussed in the text are presented in table 1. Figures 13 and 14 show the distributions of late Mousterian, Aurignacian, and Uluzzian sites during two intervals, 40,000–35,000 B.P. and 35,000–30,000 B.P. In constructing these maps, we have erred on the side of caution. With the exception of two sites (S. Francesco and Serino), all of the sites shown are stratified caves or rockshelters. In addition, ages for most layers have been determined based on associations with radiometric dates. Assemblages for which ages are fairly secure but that lack absolute dates are rendered as open symbols on the maps. For the most part, age determinations based exclusively on stratigraphic evidence, faunal inventories, or worst of all, lithic typology are simply not sufficiently precise to assign sites to such narrow intervals of time; use of the third criterion also introduces a degree of circularity into the enterprise. One consequence of this conservative approach is that site distributions appear relatively sparse, especially in figure 14 (40,000–35,000 B.P.). Undoubtedly, the numerous unstratified open-air occurrences and currently undated levels in stratified sites would fill out these distributions considerably.

Although the number of absolute dates is not large, and only two sites (Castelcivita and Fabbrica) contain late Mousterian, Uluzzian, and Aurignacian in the same sequence, it is still possible to draw a number of conclusions about the stratigraphic and chronological relationships among the late Mousterian, Uluzzian, and Aurignacian.

1. The Uluzzian is always stratigraphically younger than the Mousterian (if the latter is present).
2. Aurignacian assemblages rich in retouched bladelets are always stratigraphically younger than Uluzzian or Mousterian layers when they occur in the same site.

RIPARO MOCHI
Gravettian
D
Aurignacian (classic)
F
Aurignacian with retouched bladelets
G   32,280
           33,400
           34,680
           35,700
           34,870
           37,400
mixed
H
Mousterian
I

RIPARO TAGLIENTE
Final Epigravettian
6-25a
Aurignacian with retouched bladelets
25b-25c-d
35-36
Mousterian
37

GROTTA DI FUMANE (INTERIOR)
Aurignacian with retouched bladelets?
D1-D7   31,700
            32,300
Aurignacian with retouched bladelets
A1-A3   34,200
            35,400
            36,500
            36,800
???
A4
Mousterian
A5-A13

GROTTA PAGLICCI
"archaic" Gravettian
22-23
Aurignacian with retouched bladelets
24a1-24b4   29,300
            34,000
Sterile (clay and stalagmite)
25
Mousterian ("archaic")
26

GROTTA DI CASTELCIVITA
Aurignacian with micropoints
ars
gic   32,930
Aurignacian with retouched bladelets
rsa (upper) 31,950
            32,930
Uluzzian
rsa (lower) 32,470
rpi   33,300
pie   33,200
rsi (upper)

GROTTA DEL CAVALLO
Final Epigravettian
Bia-Bii
Sterile layer
Ci
Ci
Dia
Evolved or Middle Uluzzian
Ei, Eii   >31,000
Early Uluzzian
Eii
Mousterian
Fa, Fi

GROTTA DELLA CALA
Gravettian
Q
Aurignacian with retouched bladelets
ß
R (upper)   29,800
Mousterian
R (lower through ∂)

GROTTA LA FABBRICA
Aurignacian
3-4
Uluzzian
2
Mousterian
1

Figure 12. Relevant portions of key stratigraphic sequences, with absolute dates marked.

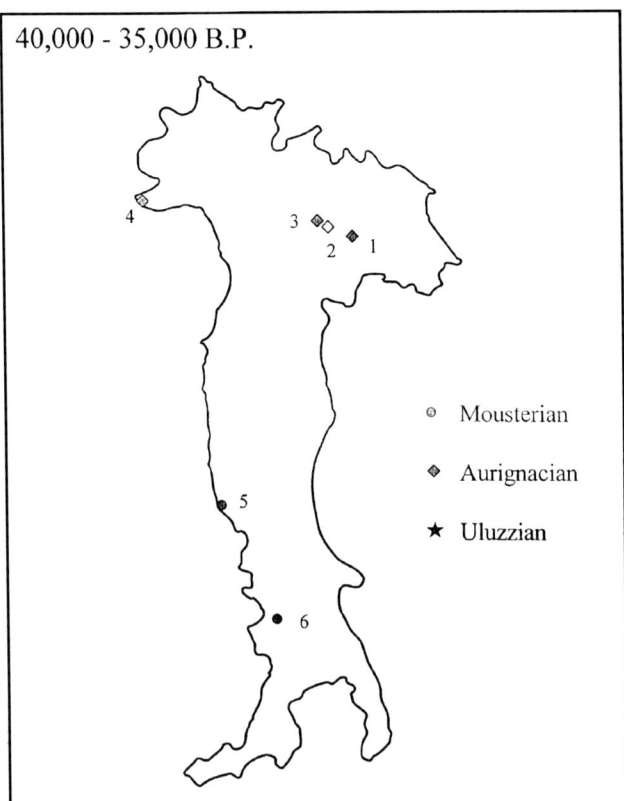

Figure 13. Distribution of late Mousterian, Aurignacian, and Uluzzian sites from 40–35 ka B.P. 1. Grotta di Paina, 2. Riparo Tagliente, 3. Grotta di Fumane, 4. Riparo Mochi, 5. Grotta Breuil (also Grotta Barbara?), 6. Grotta di Castelcivita. Filled symbols indicate radiometrically dated sites. Open symbols indicate undated sites.

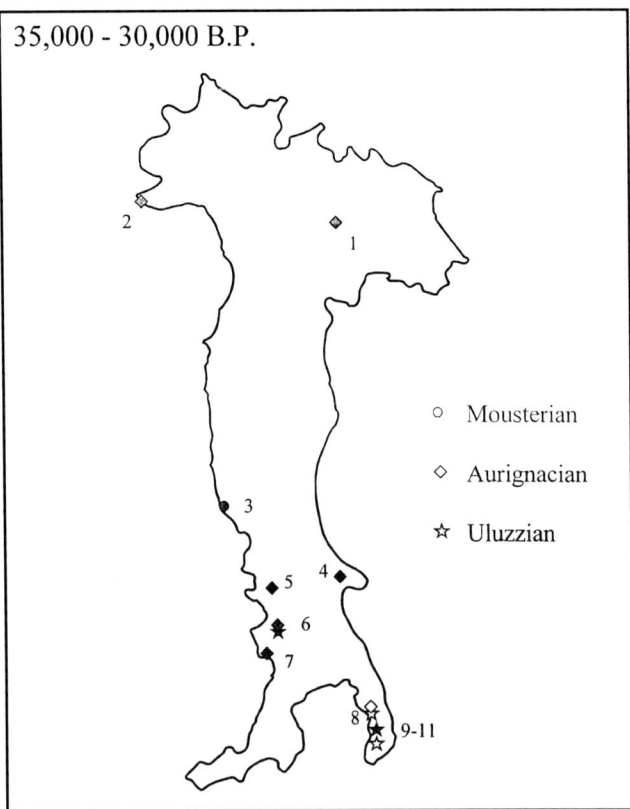

Figure 14. Distribution of late Mousterian, Aurignacian, and Uluzzian sites from 35–30 ka B.P. 1. Grotta di Fumane, 2. Riparo Mochi, 3. Grotta Breuil, 4. Grotta Paglicci, 5. Serino, 6. Grotta di Castelcivita, 7. Grotta della Cala, 8. Grotta della Serra Cicora, 9. Grotta del Cavallo, 10. Grotta di Uluzzo, 11. Grotta/Riparo Uluzzo C. Filled symbols indicate radiometrically dated sites. Open symbols indicate undated sites.

3. There is no interstratification of Mousterian, Aurignacian, and Uluzzian, as sometimes occurs for the Aurignacian and Chatelperronian in France (e.g., Bordes and Labrot 1967; Demars 1990).
4. The earliest Aurignacian occurrences are in the north of the country and date from as early as 37,000–38,000 B.P. to around 32,000 B.P.
5. The earliest Aurignacian in the north (Fumane, Mochi, Paina) appears to predate the Uluzzian in southern Italy by several thousand years. The early Aurignacian of northern Italy predates the Aurignacian in the south of the country by a somewhat greater margin.
6. Neither early Aurignacian nor Uluzzian is present in Latium, but Mousterian assemblages may have been produced in this area as late as 33,000 years B.P.

The chronological picture is complicated by the fact that there is no widely accepted calibration for radiocarbon ages greater than 20,000 years B.P. A recent attempt at calibration using variation in the strength of the earth's magnetic field indicates that radiocarbon dates between 30,000 and 40,000 B.P. underestimate the actual calendar age by 2000–3000 years (van Andel 1998). Another study, based on carbon dating of plant materials from varved lake sediments (Kitagawa and van der Plicht 1998) comes to roughly similar conclusions, except that it shows radiocarbon determinations of around 33,000 to 34,000 B.P. to be close to actual ages. If these findings are eventually replicated and confirmed, they would have two main implications for the argument at hand. Most important, they imply that the earliest Aurignacian in Veneto and Liguria could well have an actual age approaching 40,000 years, extending the temporal overlap with the late Mousterian at sites like Grotta Breuil, Buca della Iena, and Castelcivita (provided the ESR and U/Th dates are not consistently biased). The close correspondence between actual and ^{14}C ages between 33,000 and 34,000 years reported by Kitagawa and van der Plicht would also increase the degree of apparent chronological overlap between the Aurignacian and the Uluzzian.

Despite the chronostratigraphic ambiguities, it seems fairly clear that at least two different types of lithic assemblage were being produced in Italy at any particular point in time between 38,000 and 30,000 B.P. We say "at least" because it is possible that the Uluzzian actually subsumes more than one distinct type of industry. If the dates of around 33,000 B.P. from layer 6 at Grotta Breuil and cgr at Grotta di Castelcivita are approximately correct, then Mousterian industries continued to be produced for at least 4,000 years after the Aurignacian made its first appearance in Veneto and Liguria. Likewise, there seems to be almost complete overlap between the Uluzzian and the later Aurignacian between roughly 33,500 and perhaps 30,000 B.P. Whether the Uluzzian and Mousterian overlap significantly in time remains unanswerable at present given the level of precision of dating techniques. The few concrete data currently available suggest that if Mousterian and Uluzzian coexisted at all, it was not for long.

The chronological overlap between various assemblage types is tempered by their spatial complementarity. During the period of coexistence between Aurignacian, Mousterian, and Uluzzian, the former was confined to the northern part of the country. Between roughly 38,000 and 33,500 B.P., while early Aurignacian layers were being deposited at Riparo Mochi, Grotta di Fumane, and Grotta Paina, human groups living in southern and west-central Italy were using Middle Paleolithic toolkits and technologies. Sometime between 34,000 and 33,000 B.P., Uluzzian technologies replaced Mousterian ones in the southern part of the country. From the few available dates, it appears that the Uluzzian was a short-lived phenomenon in southern Italy: at Grotta di Castelcivita, all dates for Aurignacian and Uluzzian overlap at approximately one standard error. As there are no dates available for the Uluzzian of Tuscany, it is not clear when the Mousterian-Uluzzian transition might have occurred there. In Latium, the Uluzzian never developed or penetrated. The situation on the Adriatic coast is cloudy, in part because the number of sites is smaller, but it is interesting that the earliest date for the Aurignacian at Paglicci overlaps at one standard error with most of the dates on the Uluzzian from Castelcivita. Finally, by sometime after 32,500 B.P. or so, *all* of the inhabitants of Italy were utilizing some form of Aurignacian toolkit and technology, albeit with notable differences between regions.

Developing a scenario to account for this situation is complicated by the scarcity of hominid remains. *If* one wants to attach hominid species or subspecies to assemblage types—a risky endeavor in general, but especially where there are so few fossils—the following scenario would fit the data from Italy. Sometime around 37,000–38,000 radiocarbon years B.P., populations manufacturing proto-Aurignacian assemblages began to move into northern Italy. This event is just part of a phenomenon that extends beyond Italy, as similar assemblages rich in retouched bladelets and of equivalent or slightly earlier age are found at other sites in southern Europe, including Krems in Austria (Laplace 1970) and Abreda cave in Spain (Bischoff et al. 1989, Soler and Fullola 1996). There is broad agreement that the proto-Aurignacian is intrusive to Italy (e.g., Bietti 1997, Mussi 1990, Palma di Cesnola 1993). With their abundant bladelets, implying the use of complex composite tools, as well as bone technology and many ornaments, the assemblages from layers A1–A2 at Grotta di Fumane and layer G at Riparo Mochi certainly represent a profound departure from the local Mousterian. That this event represents an intrusion of populations rather than a diffusion of techniques is an inference that cannot be directly substantiated at present. However, in contrast to the Chatelperronian of southwest France, which bears many similarities with the Mousterian of Acheulean Tradition B (e.g., Pelegrin 1990), the proto-Aurignacian seems to contains so few elements of the local Mousterian that it would difficult to argue for technological continuity. Following the majority opinion in paleoanthropology (e.g., Gambier 1989; Stringer et al. 1984), we would have to assume that the carriers of the early Aurignacian were anatomically modern humans, although there is admittedly no direct proof of this supposition in the case of Italy.

Although they became established in the north of Italy by 37,000 years ago, the makers of the proto-Aurignacian did not then rapidly flood the peninsula. Existing populations utilizing Mousterian technologies—late Neandertals in all probability—remained firmly entrenched from Tuscany to Apulia. The behavior, in particular the technology, of the endemic groups continued to change as well. In Latium, the distinctive late Mousterian at Grotta Breuil seems to embody the culmination of trends in subsistence and technology that had begun as long as ago as 55,000 B.P. (Kuhn

1995; Stiner 1994; Stiner and Kuhn 1992). Because patterns such as a tendency toward laminar methods of blank production were first manifest in Latium more than 10,000 years before there is any clear evidence for an Aurignacian presence in Europe, it would be absurd to argue that the "bladey" late Mousterian of Grotta Breuil represents a borrowing of technological ideas from anatomically modern populations. Still, we cannot rule out the possibility that the appearance of new human groups in the north had some influence over the evolution of Neandertal behavior in central and southern Italy. If groups using Mousterian technology were displaced to the south by the spread of the Aurignacian, resulting changes in population/resource relationships could well have amplified any preexisting pressures on indigenous populations. Mousterian populations had been well established along the Tyrrhenian coast for tens of thousands of years. Subsistence changes, such as the appearance of prime-dominated mortality profiles, are evidence of increasingly intense exploitation of large game species during the later Mousterian (Stiner 1993, 1994). Any subsequent rise in regional population levels, brought on either by an influx of Upper Paleolithic human groups from outside or by the shifting of local populations toward the southern end of the peninsula, would certainly upset existing relationships between hominid foragers and their resource base. It is difficult to predict how demographic factors might affect the forms of stone tools, the aspect of behavior about which we know the most, but it is not unreasonable to think that demographic pressures could have helped to accelerate the pace of behavioral change among late Middle Paleolithic hominids.

The case of the Uluzzian is somewhat more difficult, yet also more intriguing. There is some disagreement as to the origins of the Uluzzian. Some authors argue that it developed in situ, possibly out of some variety of late Denticulate Mousterian (Geurreschi 1992:200), and perhaps with some influence from southeastern Europe (Palma di Cesnola 1996:217). Gioia (1988, 1990), in contrast, stresses the relationship between Uluzzian and Chatelperronian, considering the former a subset of the latter (e.g., Gioia 1990:244; see also D'Errico et al. 1998:16). In fact, aside from its general chrono-stratigraphic position and the presence of some elements with curved backs, the Uluzzian bears little resemblance to the French industry. For example, the heavy emphasis on blade production found in many Chatelperronian assemblages (Harrold 1989; Pelegrin 1995) is simply not replicated in the Uluzzian. Conversely, a high frequency of *pièces esquilées* is not usually considered typical of the Chatelperronian. In our opinion, while the Uluzzian may well represent a similar order of phenomenon to the Chatelperronian, it is not simply a southern variant.

It has been argued that the Chatelperronian of France represents a case of acculturation, of Neandertals borrowing elements of Upper Paleolithic culture from intrusive anatomically modern humans (e.g., Harrold 1989; Mellars 1989, 1996:414). This is not a very convincing scenario for the Chatelperronian (D'Errico et al. 1998), and it is even less likely for the Uluzzian. By definition, acculturation involves the adoption of culture traits. In the case of Italy, it is difficult to identify what exactly the local Mousterian groups borrowed from the newly arrived, Upper Paleolithic populations. The most distinctive features of the proto-Aurignacian—blade and especially bladelet production—are notably absent from the Uluzzian, while the novel characteristics of the Uluzzian, arched backed pieces and *pièces esquilées*, are not typical features of the early Aurignacian. The time lag between the appearance of the Aurignacian and the earliest Uluzzian is also difficult to account for. However, we currently have age estimates for the Uluzzian only in southern Italy. Absolute dates from Uluzzian sites in Tuscany, closest to the "Aurignacian front," might change the situation if they prove to be substantially earlier than in the south, although this would still amount to necessary but not sufficient support of an acculturation model.

To say that the Uluzzian does not represent a case of acculturation is not to assert that the hypothetical incursion of the carriers of the Aurignacian had no consequences for the behavior of indigenous human groups. Coevolution is a remarkably pervasive phenomenon in nature, and coevolving species or populations can interact in many ways. Even if intrusive Aurignacian groups did not interbreed or cooperate economically with indigenous populations, direct or indirect competition could still have stimulated relatively rapid behavioral change, especially near the "frontier." Shifts in demographic factors associated with the appearance of new foraging groups might also have had important implications for the locals. The fact that assemblages classified as Uluzzian are rather variable (Bietti 1997, Mussi 1998) lends some support the notion that the Uluzzian *sensu largo* represents an adaptive response to a set of synchronous but locally variable factors, such as resource stress associated with large-scale population displacements.

It is tempting to view the late appearance of the Aurignacian in southern Italy after 33,000 B.P. as part of the last stages of population expansion from the north. However, based on the data currently available, it is difficult to argue conclusively that this event represents displacement rather than diffusion. The current evidence is not especially convincing, but the so-called "Uluzzo-Aurignacian" remains as a possible candidate for some kind of hybrid of these two Early Upper Paleolithic traditions. Obviously, whether or not such a scenario might be entertained hinges in part on one's position as to the genetic relationships between Neandertals (the presumed makers of the Uluzzian) and anatomically modern Aurignacian populations. In the absence of definitive fossil evidence, the possibility of some kind of biological and cultural hybridization cannot be dismissed completely. Detailed analyses of the sedimentological contexts of the Uluzzo-Aurignacian (especially at Grotta di Serra Cicora, the only stratified occurrence) are called for to ascertain whether Pleistocene people or sedimentary processes have acted to combine traits of the two types of assemblage. Detailed analyses of technological features might also help to isolate the respective contributions—if any—of the Uluzzian and Aurignacian "traditions."

In many respects, the Uluzzian fits conventional expectations for an industry transitional between Middle and Upper Paleolithic. In light of the preceding discussion, it is interesting to consider whether or not the Uluzzian is truly "transitional." The central issue is the definition of the term. If "transitional" simply means the modification of a basic Mousterian pattern with the addition of a few generic Upper Paleolithic traits, then the Uluzzian would seem to fit the definition nicely. But this seems to be an unduly broad interpretation of the term. A narrower and more appropriate definition would require a demonstrable connection between one dynamic state and another. Thus, there are two questions to be answered:

a. whether the Uluzzian evolved out of the Mousterian, and
b. whether the Uluzzian in turn evolved into anything else.

Although many authors are comfortable with the notion of an autochthonous origin for the Uluzzian, this question has not been explored in great depth. Many of the supposed points of similarity between Uluzzian and Mousterian are either generic (i.e., the abundance of sidescrapers and denticulates) or negative (i.e., the absence of prismatic blade technology). As Gioia points out, the Uluzzian shows few technological similarities to most late Mousterian assemblages (1990). What remains to be demonstrated is which specific "derived" Middle Paleolithic traits—technological, typological, and economic features particular to the late Mousterian in a given area—carry over into the Uluzzian. Fixing the relationship between Uluzzian and Mousterian is just the first step, however. Evidence for marked shifts in behavior at the end of the Middle Paleolithic is certainly interesting, but we must recognize that every instance of change in the Middle Paleolithic did not necessarily lead to the Upper Paleolithic and all that followed. As is also the case with the Chatelperronian, the fate of the Uluzzian, the question of whether it contributed directly to later human cultural traditions or disappeared "without issue," remains to be answered. Given the chronological gap between Uluzzian and Gravettian, 4,000 years at an absolute minimum (see Skeates and Whitehouse 1994:151–152), as well as the ambiguous nature of the Uluzzo-Aurignacian, this would seem to be the more problematic end of the transition.

CONCLUSIONS

As in the rest of Europe, the interval between 40,000 and 30,000 B.P. was a dynamic and complex period in Italy. At least three distinct types of lithic assemblage were produced and, although hominid fossils are quite scarce, it is quite possible that two different species of hominid produced them. There is good evidence that the early Aurignacian, and by implication anatomically modern humans, arrived in the north of Italy by at least 37,000 (radiocarbon) years ago, if not earlier. On the other hand, it is apparent that indigenous producers of Mousterian and Uluzzian industries—probably Neandertals—persisted in central and southern Italy until 33,000 B.P., if not later, albeit with notable changes in lithic technology and other dimensions of behavior.

The situation in Italy is remarkably similar to that recently documented in Spain, although in Spain the late persistence of Neandertals is better supported by fossil evidence (Carbonell et al., this volume; Hublin et al. 1995). For this reason, southern Italy could be added to the list of late Pleistocene "refugia" for Neandertals and the Mousterian. However, the term "refugium" should be used with caution, as it implies that the older populations survived in isolation, preserved and protected by virtue of a lack of contact with competitors. Sparse as it is, the chronological evidence can also be interpreted to mean that Neandertals were able to "hold out" in Italy for a substantial period of time. Far from being quickly out-competed and overrun, they apparently prevented invasion in the central and southern parts of the peninsula for several thousand years. Moreover, the local hominids had more options than simply retreating before the advancing Aurignacian. The terminal Mousterian and Uluzzian may show us part of a broader set of adaptive responses to the new situation. Regardless of the fact that they eventually lost out, indigenous Mousterian populations showed a considerable degree of adaptive flexibility and demographic potential in the face of changing circumstances.

Emphasizing flexibility and demographic potential is neither an apology for the Neandertals nor an attempt to vindicate them as possible direct ancestors of modern humans. However, if we are to comprehend the spread of anatomically modern humans as well as the evolution of those traits said to define "modern behavior," we do ourselves a disservice by underestimating the capacities of the hominids and the cultures that were eventually superseded. Over the long term, the indigenous populations may have had nearly as profound an influence on new arrivals as the newcomers had on them, not so much as a font of fresh ideas but as a competitive stimulant. One could even speculate that the impressive artistic and technological developments of the European Upper Paleolithic may in part be a consequence of competition between modern humans and indigenous archaics. The data currently available for the Italian peninsula allow us to sketch out hypothetically the chronological and spatial dimensions of interactions between Neandertals and early anatomically moderns, but mutual influences between ancient populations will not be revealed through comparisons of coarse-grained typological categories such as Uluzzian or proto-Aurignacian. Evidence for such effects is more likely to come from future studies of foraging behavior (prey choice, hunting techniques), lithic raw material economies, mobility and land use patterns. For the time being, however, it is of some importance to recognize that that the first Upper Paleolithic humans in southern Europe did not occupy an empty landscape, and that if they had, the long-term trajectory of the Upper Paleolithic might have been very different.

Notes

1. Several important sites were excavated in the late nineteenth and early twentieth centuries, including many of the well-known "Grimaldi" caves. With a few exceptions, the quality of stratigraphic, chronological, and archaeological information available for these sites is quite limited. As for the bias towards caves, it is simply a case of there having been few excavations of stratified open-air late Pleistocene localities in Italy.

2. A thin layer between the Mousterian and early Aurignacian at Grotta di Fumane yielded a few artifacts reminiscent of the Uluzzian, but the size of the assemblage is insufficient for classification and comparison (Bartolomei et al. 1992).

BIBLIOGRAPHY

Accorsi, C., E. Aiello, C. Bartolini, L. Casteletti, G. Rodolfi, and A. Ronchitelli
   1979 "Il giacimento di Serino (Avellino): stratigrafia, ambienti, e paletnologia." *Atti della Società Toscana Scienze Naturali* Memorie Ser. A, 86:435–487.

Alessio, M., F. Bella, S. Impronta, G. Belluomini, C. Cortesi, and B. Turi
   1970 "University of Rome Carbon-14 Dates VIII." *Radiocarbon* 12:599–616.

Azzi, C., L. Bigliocca, and E. Piovan
   1977 "Florence Radiocarbon Dates III." *Radiocarbon* 19:165–169.

Azzi, C., and F. Gulisano
   1979 "Florence Radiocarbon Dates IV." *Radiocarbon* 21:353–357.

Bartolomei, G., A. Broglio, P. F. Cassoli, L. Castelletti, L. Cattani, M. Cremaschi, G. Giacobini, G. Malerba, A. Maspero, M. Presani, A. Sartorelli, and A. Tagliacozzo
   1992 "La Grotte de Fumane. Un site aurignacien au pied des Alpes." *Preistoria Alpina* 28:131–179.

Bartolomei, G., A. Broglio, L. Cattani, M. Cremaschi, A. Guerreschi, E. Mantovani, C. Peretto, and B. Sala
   1982 "Depot würmien a industrie protoaurignacienne a lamelles Dufour dans l'Abri Tagliente (Monts Lessini, Verona, Italie)." *Etudes et Recherches Archeologiques de l'Université de Liège* 13(2):45–63.

Bartolomei, G., P. Gambassini, and A. Palma di Cesnola
   1975 "Visita ai giacimenti del Poggio e della Cala a Marina di Camerota (Salerno)." *Atti dell' Istituto Italiano di Preistoria e Protostoria* 17:107–140.

Baumler, M.
   1988 "Core Reduction, Flake Production and the Middle Paleolithic of Zobiste (Yugoslavia), in *The Upper Pleistocene Prehistory of Western Eurasia*, H. Dibble and A. Montet-White, eds., pp. 255–274. University Museum Monograph 54. University of Pennsylvania Press, Philadelphia.

Bietti, A.
  1976–1977 "Analysis and Investigation of the Epigravettian Industry Collected during the 1955 Excavations at Palidoro (Rome, Italy)." *Quaternaria* 19:197–387.
  1997 "The Transition to Anatomically Modern Humans: The Case of Peninsular Italy," in *Conceptual Issues in Modern Human Origins Research*, G. A. Clark and C. Willermet, eds., pp. 132–150. Aldine de Gruyter, New York.

Bietti, A., and S. Grimaldi
  1995 "Levallois Debitage in Central Italy: Technical Achievements and Raw Material Procurement," in *The Definition and Interpretation of Levallois Technology*, H. Dibble and O. Bar-Yosef, eds., pp. 125–142. Monographs in World Archaeology 23. Prehistory Press, Madison, Wisconsin.

Bietti, A., S. Kuhn, A. Segre, and M. Stiner
  1990–1991 "Grotta Breuil: A General Introduction and Stratigraphy." *Quaternaria Nova* 1:305–323.

Bietti, A., and V. Mancini
  1990 "Industria Musteriana rinvenuta sul Monte Genzana (Scanno, L'Aquila). Risultati delle campagne di ricognizione 1984–1985." *Preistoria Alpina* 24:7–36.

Blanc, A. C., and A. Segre
  1953 "Le Quaternaire du Mont Circeo." IV Congrès INQUA, Guide à l'excursion au mont Circé. Roma.

Bischoff, J., N. Soler, J. Maroto, and R. Julia
  1989 "Abrupt Mousterian/Aurignacian Boundary at c. 40 ka B.P.: Accelerator ^{14}C Dates from L'Abreda Cave (Catalunya, Spain)." *Journal of Archaeological Science* 16:563–576.

Bordes, F., and J. Labrot
  1967 "Le stratigraphie du gisement de Roc de Combe (Lot) et ses implications." *Bulletin de la Société Préhistorique Française* 64:15–28.

Broglio, A.
  1964 "Le industrie musteriane della Grotta del Broion." *Memorie del'Museo Civico di Scienze Naturali di Verona* 12:369–390.
  1994 "Il Paleolitico superiore del Friuli-Venezia Giulia," in *Atti della XXIX Riunione Scientifica del Istituto Italiano di Preistoria e Protostoria*, pp. 36–56. IIPP, Firenze.

Chilardi, S., D. Frayer, P. Gioia, R. Macchiarelli, and M. Mussi
  1996 "Fontana Nuova di Ragusa (Sicily, Italy): Southernmost Aurignacian Site in Europe." *Antiquity* 70(269):553–564.

Demars, P.-Y.
  1990 "Les interstratifications entre Aurignacien et Châtelperronien à Roc-de-Combe et au Piage (Lot). Approvisionnement en matières premières et position chronologique," in *Paléolithique Moyen Récent et Paléolithique Supérieur Ancien en Europe*, C. Farizy, ed., pp. 235–249. A.P.R.A.I.F. Mémoirs du Musée de Préhistoire d'Ile de France no. 3, Nemours.

D'Errico, F., J. Zilhão, M. Julien, D. Baffier, and J. Pelegrin
  1998 "Neanderthal Acculturation in Western Europe? A Critical Review of the Evidence and Its Interpretations." *Current Anthropology* 39(supplement):1–44.

Gambassini, P., ed.
  1997 *Il Paleolitico di Castelcivita, Cultura e Ambiente*. Electa, Naples.

Gambassini, P., F. Martini, A. Palma di Cesnola, C. Peretto, M. Piperno, A. M. Ronchitelli, and L. Sarti
  1995 *Il Paleolitico dell'Italia centro-meridionale*. Guide Archaeologiche: Preistoria e Protostoria in Italia 1, UISPP and A.B.A.C.O. Edizioni, Forlì.

Gambier, D.
  1989 "Fossil Hominids of the Early Upper Paleolithic (Aurignacian) of France," in *The Human Revolution: Behavioural and Biological Perspectives on the Origins of Modern Humans*, P. Mellars and C. Stringer, eds., pp. 194–211. Edinburgh University Press, Edinburgh.

Gioia, P.
  1988 "Problems Related to the Origins of the Italian Upper Paleolithic: Uluzzian and Aurignacian," in *L'Homme de Neanderthal: La Mutation*, J. Kozlowski, ed., pp. 71–101. Etudes et Recherches Archeologiques de l'Université de Liège 35, Liège.
  1990 "An Aspect of the Transition between Middle and Upper Paleolithic in Italy: The Uluzzian," in *Paléolithique Moyen Récent et Paléolithique Supérieur Ancien en Europe*, C. Farizy, ed., pp. 241–250. A.P.R.A.I.F. Mémoirs du Musée de Préhistoire d'Ile de France no. 3, Nemours.

Guerreschi, A.
  1992 "La fine del Pleistocene e gli inizi dell'Olocene," in *Italia Preistorica*, A. Guidi and M. Piperno, eds., pp. 198–237. Editori Laterza, Bari.

Harrold, F.
  1989 "Mousterian, Châtelperronian, and Early Aurignacian in Western Europe: Continuity or Discontinuity?" in *The Human Revolution: Behavioural and Biological Perspectives on the Origins of Modern Humans*, P. Mellars and C. Stringer, eds., pp. 677–713. Edinburgh University Press, Edinburgh.

Hedges, R. E. M., R. A. Housley, C. Bronk Ramsey, and G. J. Van Klinken
  1994 "Radiocarbon Dates from the Oxford AMS System: Archaeometry Datelist 18." *Archaeometry* 36:337–374.

Hublin, J.-J., C. Ruiz, P. Lara, M. Fontugne, and J. Reyss
  1995 "The Mousterian Site of Zafarraya (Andalucia, Spain). Dating and Implications for the Paleolithic Peopling Processes of Western Europe (in French)." *Comptes Rendus de l'Academie des Sciences* Serie II fasc. A, Sciences de la Terre et des Planetes 321:931–31.

Kitagawa, H. and J. van der Plicht
  1998 "A 40,000-Year Varve Chronology from Lake Suigetsu, Japan: Extension of the ^{14}C Calibration Curve." *Radiocarbon* 40(2):505–516.

Kuhn, S. L.
  1995 *Mousterian Lithic Technology: An Ecological Perspective*. Princeton University Press, Princeton, New Jersey.

Kuhn, S. L., and M. C. Stiner
  1992 "New Research on Riparo Mochi, Balzi Rossi (Liguria): Preliminary Results." *Quaternaria Nova* 2:77–90.
  1998 "The Earliest Aurignacian of Riparo Mochi (Liguria, Italy)." *Current Anthropology* 39(supplement):S175–S189.

Lanzinger, M.
  1984 "Risultati preliminari delle ricerche nel sito aurignazione del Campon di Monte Avena (Alpi feltrine)." *Rivista di Scienze Preistoriche* 39(1–2):287–299.

Laplace, G.
  1961 "Recherches sur l'origine et l'evolution des complexes leptolithiques." *Quaternaria* 5:153–240.
  1966 *Recherches sur l'origine et l'evolution des complexes leptolithiques*. Ecole Française de Rome, Mélanges d'Archeologie et d'Histoire 4. E. de Boccard, Paris.
  1970 "L'industrie de Krems Hundssteig et le problème de l'origine des complexes aurignaciens," in *Frühe Menschheit und Umwelt*, pp. 242–297. Fundamenta, Monographien zur Urgeschichte, Reihe A, vol. 2. Wien, Bohlau, Köln.

Leonardi, P.
  1964 "Nuova stazione Musteriana con resti di leone speleo nella Grotta del Broion sui Colli Berici (Vicenza)." *Istituto Ferrarese de Paleontologia Umana*, Publicazioni 1962–1964 4:97–120.

Lucas, G.
  1997 "Les lamelles Dufour du Flageolet I (Bézenac, Dordogne) dans le context Aurignacien." *Paleo* 9:191–219.

Lumley, H. de
  1969 *Le Paléolithique Inférieur et Moyen di Midi Méditerranéen dans son Cadre Géologique*. Vol. 1, Ligurie-Provence. 5e Supplement à Gallia Préhistoire. Éditions du CNRS, Paris.

Lumley, H. de, and G. Isetti.
  1965 "Le Moustérien à denticulés tardif de la station de San Francesco (San Remo) et de la Grotte Turnal (Aude)." *Cahiers Ligures de Préhistoire de Archéologie* 14:5–30.

Mallegni, F.
  1992 "Quelques restes humaines immatures, des niveaux mousteriens de la Grotte du Fossellone (Monte Circeo, Italie): Fossellone 3 (olim Circeo IV)." *Bulletin de la Société Anthropologique du Paris* 4:21–32.
  1996 "L'homme du Paléolithique moyen en Italie," in *Le Paléolithique inférieur et moyen en Italie*, A. Palma di Cesnola, ed., pp. 205–210. Jérôme Millon, Grenoble.

Mallegni, F., and E. Segre-Naldini
  1992 "A Human Maxilla (Fossellone 1) and Scapula (Fossellone 2) Recovered from the Pleistocene Layers of Fossellone Cave, Mt. Circeo, Italy." *Quaternaria Nova* 2:211–255.

Manzi, G., and P. Passarello
  1990–1991 "The Human Remains from Grotta Breuil (M. Circeo, Italy): Comparative Analysis of the Parietal Fragment Breuil I." *Quaternaria Nova* 1:429–439.
  1995 "The Archaic/Modern Boundary of the Genus Homo: The Neandertals from Grotta Breuil." *Current Anthropology* 36:355–366.

Mellars, P.
  1989 "Major Issues in the Emergence of Modern Humans." *Current Anthropology* 30:349–385.
  1996. *The Neandertal Legacy*. Princeton University Press, Princeton, New Jersey.

Mussi, M.
  1990 "Le peuplement de l'Italie a la fin du Paléolithique moyen et au début du Paléolithique supérieur," in *Paléolithique Moyen Récent et Paléolithique Supérieur Ancien en Europe*, C. Farizy, ed., pp. 251–262. A.P.R.A.I.F. Mémoirs du Musée de Préhistoire d'Ile de France no. 3, Nemours.
  1998 "Comment on D'Errico et al." *Current Anthropology* 39(supplement):26–27.

Mussi, M., and D. Zampetti
1990–1991 "Le site Moustérien du Grotta Barbara." *Quaternaria Nova* 1:277–288.

Palma di Cesnola, A.
1986 "Panorama del Musteriano Italiano," in *I Neandertaliani*, D. Cocchi Genick, ed., pp. 139–174. Museo Preistorico e Archeologico "Alberto Carlo Blanc," Viareggio.
1991 "Gli scavi nella Grotta Paglicci durante il 1990," in *Atti del XI Convegno della Preistoria, Protostoria e Storia della Daunia*. S. Severo, Foggia.
1993 *Il Paleolitico Superiore in Italia: Introduzioni allo Studio*. Garlatti e Razzai Editori, Firenze.
1996 *Le Paléolithique Inférieur et Moyen en Italie*. Jérôme Millon, Grenoble.

Palma di Cesnola, A., and P. Messeri
1967 "Quatre dents humaines paléolithiques trouvées dans les cavernes de l'Italie méridionale." *L'Anthropologie* 71:3–4.

Pelegrin, J.
1990 "Observations technologiques sur qulques séries du Châtelperronien et du MTA B du sud-ouest de la France: Un hypothèse d'évolution," in *Paléolithique Moyen Récent et Paléolithique Supérieur Ancien en Europe*, C. Farizy, ed., pp. 39–42. A.P.R.A.I.F. Mémoirs du Musée de Préhistoire d'Ile de France no. 3, Nemours.
1995 *Technologie Lithique: Le Châtelperronian de Roc-du-Combe (Lot) et de La Côte (Dordogne)*. Cahiers du Quaternaire no. 20. CNRS, Paris.

Peretto, C.
1992 "Il Paleolitico medio," in *Italia Preistorica*, A. Guidi and M. Piperno, eds., pp. 170–197. Editori Laterza, Bari.

Pesce-Delfino, V., and E. Vacca
1994 "Report of an Archaic Human Skeleton Discovered at Altamura (Bari), in the "Lamalunga" District." *Human Evolution* 9(1):1–19.

Pitti, C., C. Sorrentino, and C. Tozzi
1976 "L'industria tipo Paleolitico superiore arcaico della Grotta la Fabbrica (Grosseto): nota preliminare." *Atti della Societá Toscana di Scienze Naturali* Serie A, 83:174–203.

Pitti, C., and C. Tozzi
1971 "La Grotta del Capriolo e la Buca della Iena presso Mommio (Camaiore). Sedimenti, fauna, industria litica." *Rivista di Scienze Preistoriche* 26:213–258.

Rossetti, P., and G. Zanzi
1990–1991 "Technological Approach to Reduction Sequences of the Lithic Industry of Grotta Breuil." *Quaternaria Nova* 1:351–365.

Schwarcz, H., W. Buhay, G. Grün, M. Stiner, S. Kuhn, and G. Miller
1990–91 "Absolute Dating of Sites in Coastal Lazio". *Quaternaria Nova* 1:51–68.

Skeates, R., and R. Whitehouse
1994 *Radiocarbon Dating and Italian Prehistory*. Archaeological Monographs of the British School at Rome, vol. 8. British School at Rome and Accordia Research Centre, London.

Soler, M., and J. M. Fullola
1996 "Cultural Change between Middle and Upper Paleolithic in Catalonia." in *The Last Neandertals, the First Anatomically Modern Humans*, E. Carbonell and M. Vaquero, eds., pp. 219–250. Fundacio Catalana per la Recerca, Tarragona.

Sonneville-Bordes, S. de, and J. Perrot
1954–1956 "Lexique typologique du Paléolithique supérieur. Outillage lithique." *Bulletin de la Société Préhistorique Française* 51:327–335; 52:76–79; 53:408–412, 547–559.

Spennato, A.
1981 "I livelli protoaurignaziani della grotta di Serra Cicora (Nardò, Lecce)." *Studi per l'Ecologia del Quaternario* 3:61–76.

Speth, J., and E. Tchernov
1998 "The Role of Hunting and Scavenging in Neanderthal Procurement Strategies: New Evidence from Kebara Cave (Israel)," in *Neandertals and Modern Humans in Western Asia*, T. Akazawa, K. Aoki, and O. Bar-Yosef, eds., pp. 223–239. Plenum Press, New York.

Stiner, M. C.
1990–1991 "Ungulate Exploitation in the Terminal Mousterian of Italy: The Case of Grotta Breuil." *Quaternaria Nova* 1:333–350.
1990 "The Uses of Mortality Patterns in Archaeological Studies of Hominid Predatory Adaptations." *Journal of Anthropological Archaeology* 9:305–351.
1993 "Modern Human Origins—Faunal Perspectives." *Annual Review of Anthropology* 22:55–82.
1994 *Honor among Thieves: A Zooarchaeological Study of Neandertal Ecology*. Princeton University Press, Princeton.

Stiner, M. C., and S. L. Kuhn
1992 "Subsistence, Technology, and Adaptive Variation in Middle Paleolithic Italy." *American Anthropologist* 94(2):306–339.

Stringer, C., J.-J. Hublin, and B. Vandermeersch
1984 "The Origin of Anatomically Modern Humans in Western Europe," in *The Origins of Modern*

Humans: A World Survey of the Fossil Evidence, F. Smith and F. Spencer, eds., pp. 51–135. Alan R. Liss, New York.

Taraborrelli, E.
    1969 "Nuovo contributo alla conoscenza del Paleolitico abruzzese di montagna." *Rivista di Scienze Preistoriche* 24:65–90.

Tavoso, A.
    1988 "L'outillage du gisement de San Francesco à San Remo (Ligurie, Italie): nouvel examen," in *L'homme de Neanderthal: La Mutation*, J. K. Kozlowski, ed., pp. 193–210. Etudes et Recherches Archeologiques de l'Université de Liège 35. Université de Liège, Liège.

Tozzi, C.
    1970 "La Grotta di S. Agostino (Gaeta)." *Rivista di Scienze Preistoriche* 25:3–87.

van Andel, T.
    1998 "Middle and Upper Paleolithic Environments and ^{14}C Dates beyond 10,000 B.P." *Antiquity* 72:26–33.

Vitagliano, S., and M. Piperno
    1990–1991 "Lithic Industry of Level 27 beta of the Fossellone Cave (S. Felice Circeo, Latina)." *Quaternaria Nova* 1:289–304.

Vogel, J., and H. Waterbolk
    1967 "Groningen radiocarbon dates VII." *Radiocarbon* 9:107–155.

CHAPTER 5

The Problem of Cultural Continuity between the Middle and the Upper Paleolithic in Central and Eastern Europe

Janusz K. Kozlowski

Institute of Archaeology, Jagellonian University

INTRODUCTION

The difference between the Aurignacian and the units in Europe that derived from a local Middle Paleolithic consists not only of the cultural and possibly also biological hiatus separating Aurignacian modern humans from Middle Paleolithic Neandertals but also of the surprising uniformity of the Aurignacian between the Atlantic and the Don. In contrast with this morphological and technological uniformity of the Aurignacian, the so-called transitional units (so-called due to the mixture of techno-typological attributes that are found in the Middle and Upper Paleolithic), which, it is assumed, developed from a local Middle Paleolithic base, are strongly diversified and form a cultural mosaic on the map of Europe in the period from 50 to 30 ka B.P. This mosaic is made up of "transitional units" whose technology and tool morphology has some bladey Upper Paleolithic elements and Middle Paleolithic characteristics that survived in some areas unchanged up to at least 35 ka B.P. in Central Europe (see fig. 1 and tables 1 and 2) and 28/30 ka B.P. in Eastern Europe.

The aim of this paper is to describe the processes of technological transformations in lithic raw materials processing that justify the separating of "transitional units" from their Middle Paleolithic base.

In terms of technology, we can generally distinguish "transitional units" connected with the evolution of the Levallois technique in the direction of Upper Paleolithic blade technology from units based on the exploitation of blade technology unrelated to any of the Levallois technique, as is often found in the context of Mousterian discoidal flake technology.

In terms of typology, we can distinguish units with only "ubiquitous" forms of Upper Paleolithic tools and units with the Upper Paleolithic diagnostic forms such as leaf points or backed blades. The correlation of technology and tool morphology and the precise classification of diagnostic forms provide the groundwork for the classification of "transitional units."

EVOLUTIONARY TRENDS IN TECHNOLOGY BASED ON LEVALLOIS CORES

In the penultimate glaciation, the evolution of local lithic industries began a period of technical oscillation. From Levallois technology, it passed through a major change in the volumetric concept of the cores by adopting a blade technology resembling those of the Upper Paleolithic. It then returned to the traditional Levallois techniques. Especially in northwestern Europe, this seems to have been an abortive episode, which did not leave a permanent imprint on the evolution of the Middle Paleolithic industries (Tuffreau 1983; Ameloot-Van der Heijden 1994).

In the period between 50 to 35 ka B.P., similar phenomena (i.e., the evolution of Levallois technologies toward blade technologies) are recorded in assemblages that contain some Upper Paleolithic elements, such as endscrapers and burins, but that cannot yet be considered as typical Upper Paleolithic contexts. The earliest instance of this type of "transitional assemblage" is the inventory of layer VI, trench TD–II in Temnata Cave in Bulgaria (Ginter et al. 1996). The

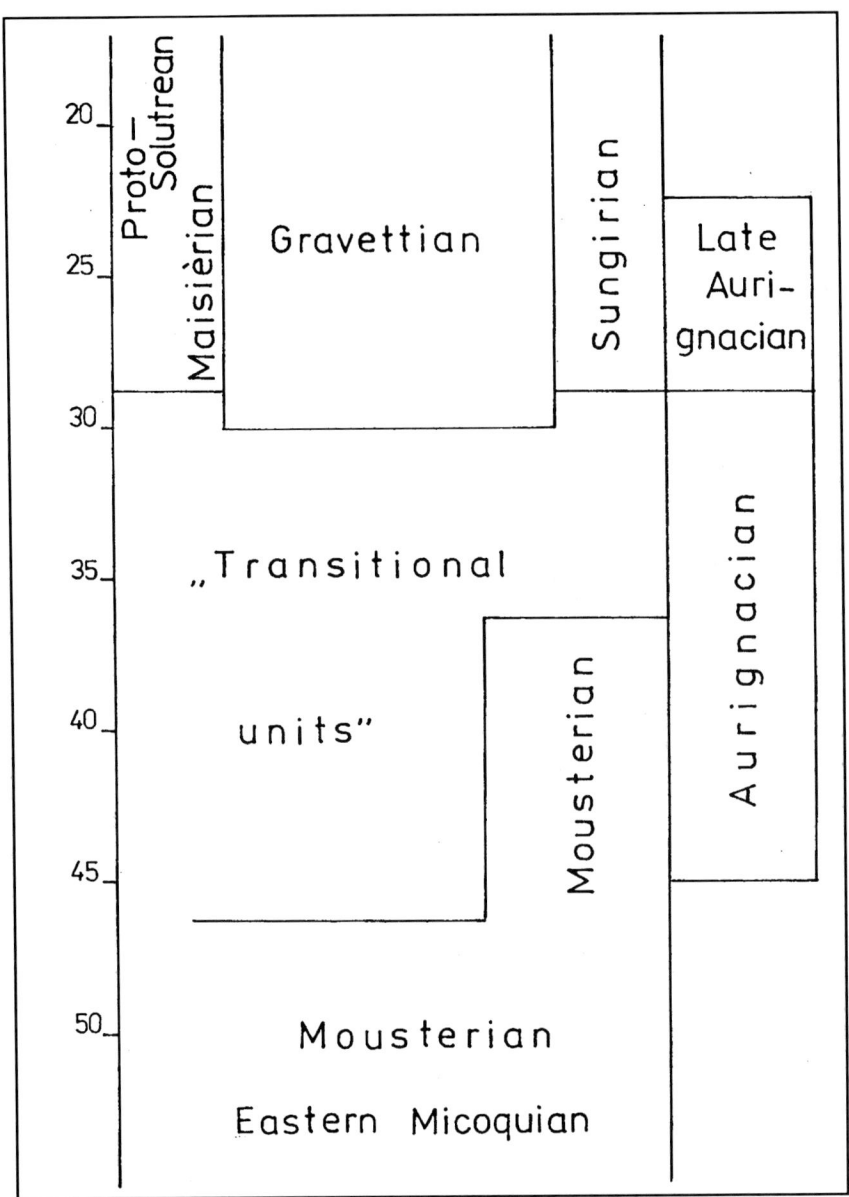

Figure 1. General scheme of Early and Middle Upper Paleolithic units in Europe.

stratigraphical position of layer VI places this inventory at about 50 to 45 ka B.P. Three basic core reduction strategies are seen:

1. Levallois core reduction with a centripetal flaking surface and back preparation. This allowed the detachment of blades from two opposite platforms, and flake exploitation of a recurrent type. In the final phase of reduction, the recurrent type cores could be transformed into discoidal cores.
2. Upper Paleolithic core reduction, where the flaking surface was prepared from the central crest, and blades were subsequently detached from two opposite platforms. Because the flaking surface extended onto the sides and, possibly, the core back, cores of this type could be transformed into cylindrical forms. During reduction, lateral trimming crests were rejuvenated. Where the blades obtained were less regular, they were replaced by flakes. At this stage, cores could have polyhedral-spherical shapes. Close examination of the *chaînes opératoires* reveals the transformation of some Levallois double-platform cores into dou-

TABLE 1
Most important sites dated to the period 50–40 ka B.P. See also figure 15.

SITE	LAYER	DATING TYPE	DATES (IN KA B.P.)
1. Temnata Cave, TD-II	VI	X	c. 50
TD-I	4	T	45.0±6.0
		T	46.0±7.0
2. Korolevo II	II	C	38.5±1.0
3. Kulichivka	Lower	C	>36.0
4. Brno-Bohunice	Kejbaly	C	40.173±1.2
		C	41.4+1.4-1.2
	Cihelna	C	42.9+1.7-1.4
5. Stranska skala IIIa	3	C	41.3+3.1-2.2
6. Ondratice			
7. Dzierzyslaw	Lower	T	>36.0
8. Jezerany			
9. Sajobabony and other sites near Miskolc			
10. Bacho Kiro	11, IV	C	>43.0
11. Istallosko	Lower	C	39.8±0.9
		C	44.3±1.9
		C	42.35±0.9
12. Willendorf II	2	C	41.7+3.7-2.5
		C	41.6+4.1-2.7
		C	39.5+1.5-1.2
13. Vedrovice II (?)			
14. Samoulitsa II		C	42.78±1.27
15. Borosteni	Cave Cioara	C	43.5+3.2/-1.1
		C	47.75+3.2/-1.1
16. Nandru, Curata Cave	1b		
	1c	X	40.0
17. Ripiceni-Izvor	III	C	46.0+4.7/-2.9
		C	45.0+1.4/-1.2
	IV	C	44.8+1.3/-1.1
		C	40.2±1.1
18. Molodova I	4	C	>44.0
19. Molodova V	11	C	>45.6
		C	>40.3
20. Korman IV	XI	C	44.4+2.05/-1.63
21. Kulna Cave	7b	C	45.66+2.85/-2.2
22. Penios valley in Thessaly		ESR	>50.0±5.0
		C	42.0±3.5
		C	38.0±1.5
23. Szeleta	lower	C	>41.7
24. Divje Babe	8	C	45.8+1.8/-2.4
			45.1+1.5/-1.8
	6	C	43.4+1.0/-1.4
25. Ohaba Ponor Cave	Bordu Mare	C	43.6+2.8/-2.1

Key to dating techniques: X–dated on the basis of geological sequences, C–radiocarbon-dated, T–Thermoluminescence dated, ESR–dated by Electron Spin Resonance.

TABLE 2
Most important sites dated to the period 40–35 ka B.P. See also figure 16.

SITE	LAYER	METHOD	DATES (IN KA B.P.)
1. Vedrovice	V	C	39.5±1.1
		C	37.65±0.55
		C	37.6±0.8
		C	35.15±0.65
2. Radosina	Certova Pec	C	38.4+2.8/-2.1
3. Dzierzyslaw I	Upper layer	T	36.5±5.5
4. Krakow-Zwierzyniec		X	38.0 - 32.0
5. Jerzmanovice, Nietoperzowa	6	C	38.16±1.1
6. Stranska skala III	5	C	38.2±1.1
		C	38.5+1.4/-1.2
7. Bacho Kiro	Layer 11, level I	C	34.8±1.15
		C	37.6±1.45
8. Temnata Cave, Sector TD-I and V	4	C	39.1±1.5
		C	38.8±1.7
		C	38.2±1.5
		C	38.3±1.8
		C	36.9±1.3
9. Willendorf II	3	C	38.8+1.53/-1.28
		C	37.93±0.75
10. Krems-Hundsteig		C	35.5±2.0
11. Pesko Cave		C	34.6±0.58
12. Budospest Cave		C	
13. Theopetra Cave	3.95–4.20m	C	39.415±3.914
		C	39.724±4.771
		C	38.079±1.942
		C	36.827±0.845
Kostenki 1 (outside figure 16 map area)	5	C	37.9+2.8/-2.1
Kostenki 12	3	C	36.28±0.36
Kostenki 17	2	C	36.4+1.7/-1.4

Key to dating techniques: X–dated on the basis of geological sequences, C–radiocarbon-dated, T–Thermoluminescence dated.

ble-platform Upper Paleolithic cores (fig. 2:1, 2). This is the result of edge retrimming, which forms a centrally located crest, with the subsequent displacement of the flaking surface.

3. On the other hand, an opposite transformation also occurs: from typical Upper Paleolithic double-platform cores with a narrow flaking face into flat cores with a broad flaking surface formed by intersecting scars from the opposite platform (fig. 3:1–3).

Besides typical Middle Paleolithic tools (mainly sidescrapers), the inventory from layer VI in Temnata Cave contains numerous endscrapers, endscrapers on blades, and some burins (fig. 4).

A similar trend in the technological evolution is represented by the inventory from layer II at the Korolevo II site and layer Ia at Korolevo I in Trans-Carpathian Ukraine (Gladilin and Demidenko 1989). These assemblages are not, unfortunately, associated with precise dates. As layer Ia is directly covered by

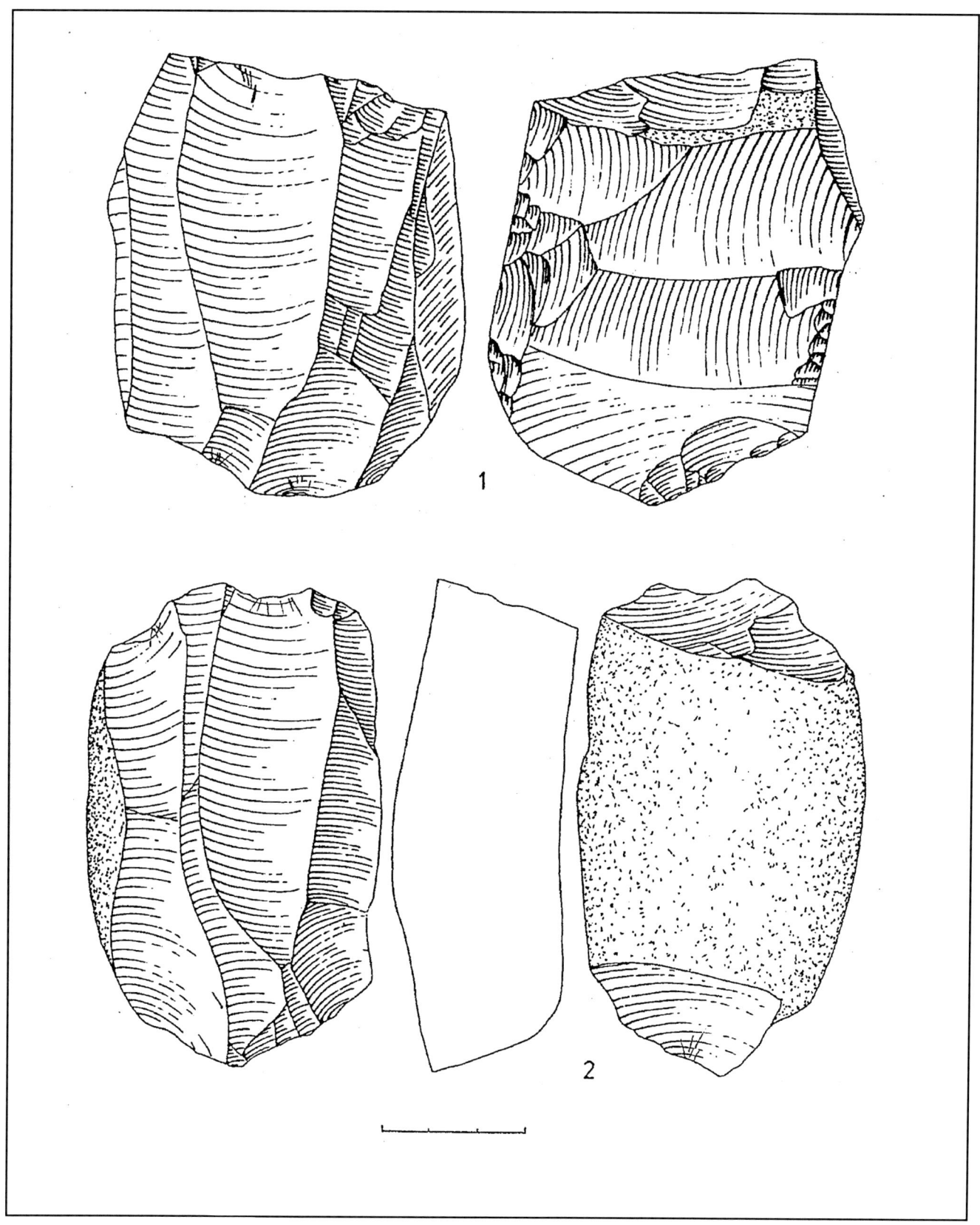

Figure 2. Temnata Cave, Bulgaria, sector TD-II, layer VI. Levallois double platform blade cores (1, 2). Scale in cm.

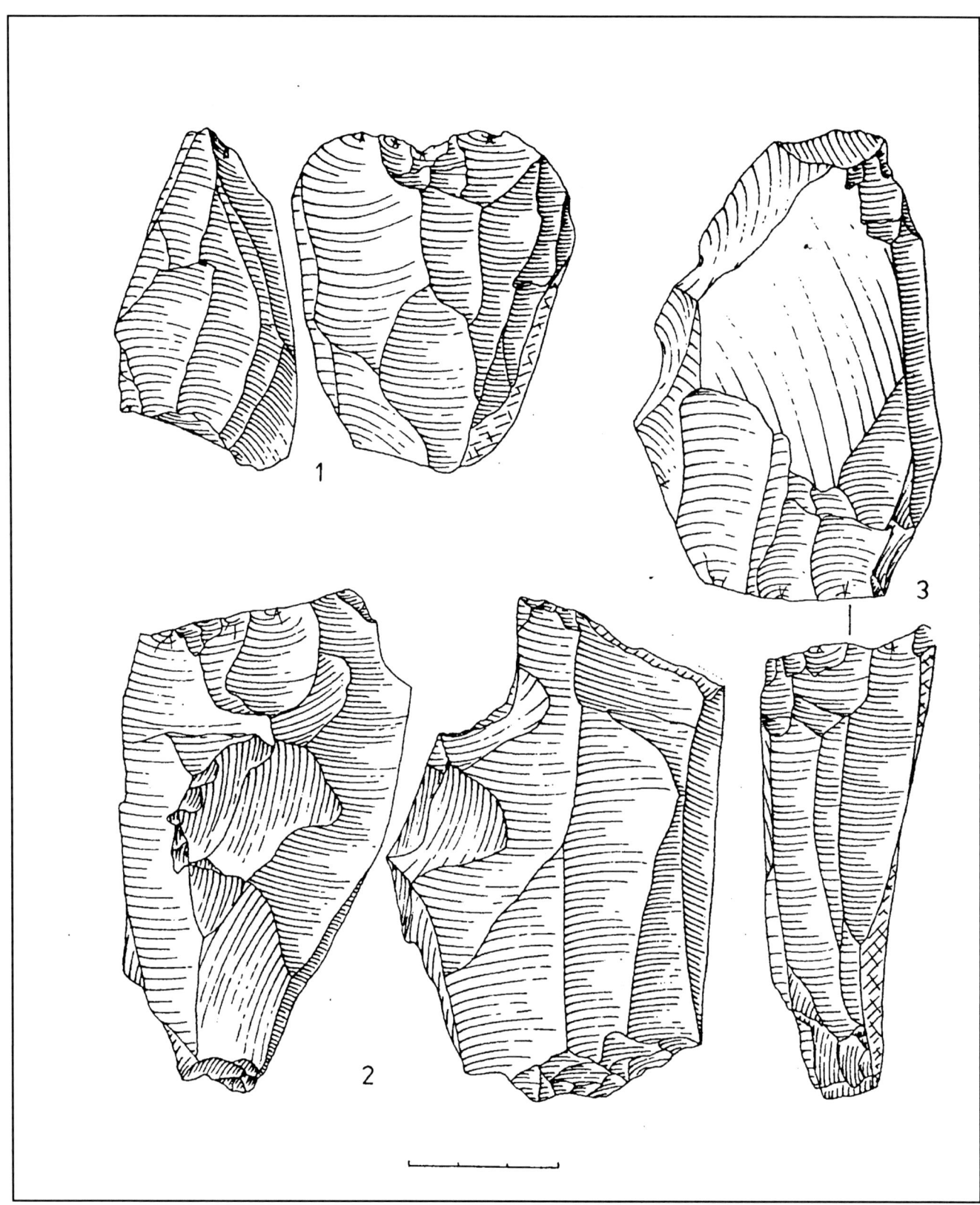

Figure 3. Temnata Cave, Bulgaria, sector TD-II, layer VI. Upper Paleolithic cores with narrow flaking face and lateral crests transformed into flat cores with broad flaking face (1–3). Scale in cm.

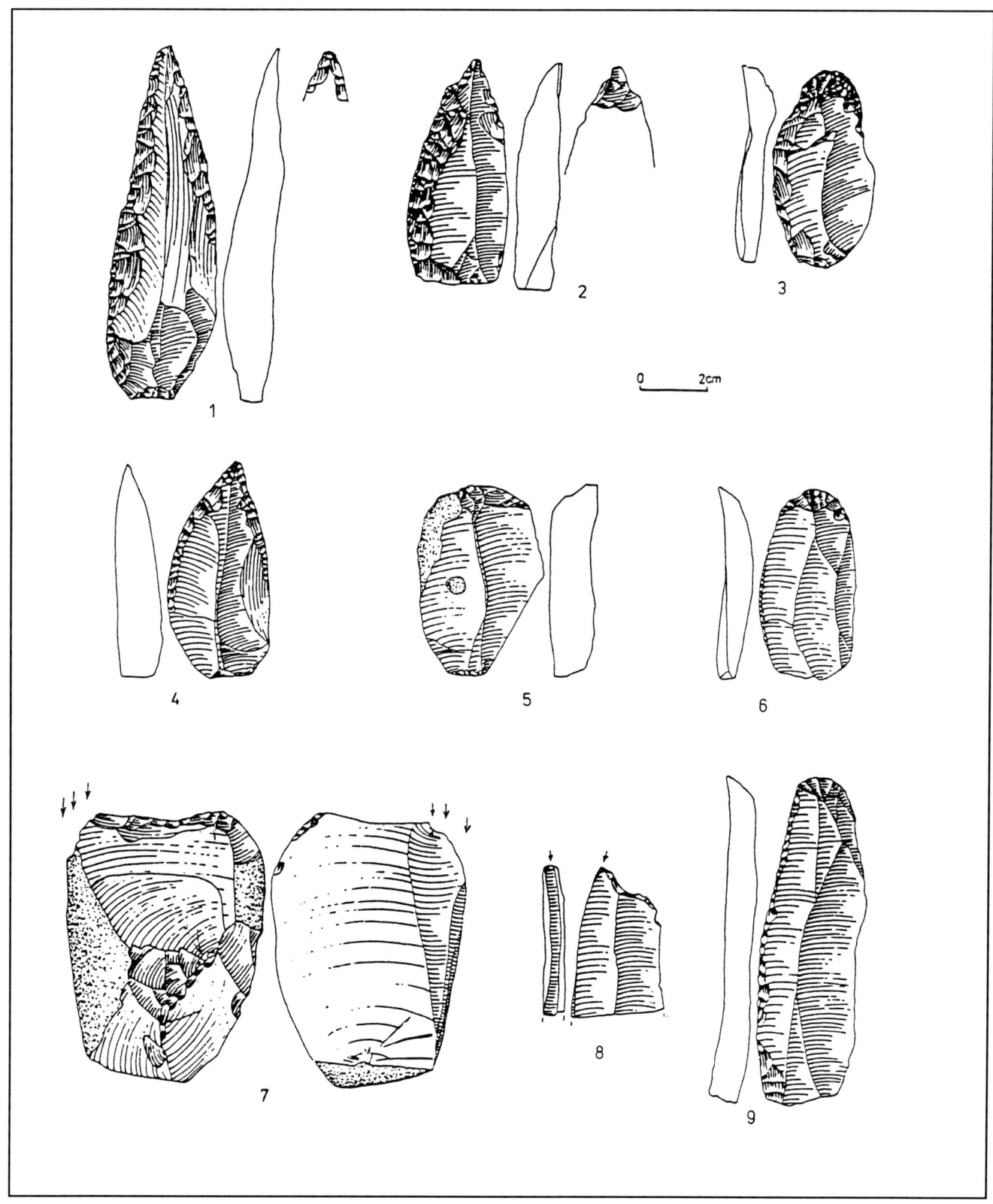

Figure 4. Temnata Cave, Bulgaria, sector TD-II, layer VI. Retouched tools: Mousterian points (1, 2, 4), side- and endscrapers (3), endscrapers (5, 6, 9), burins (7, 8).

interpleniglacial soil dated at between 38–36 (^{14}C) to 44 (paleomagnetism) ka B.P., it can be placed in the first half of the Interpleniglacial. Level II is younger than the TL date of about 60 ka (which is not very certain on loess grains). A ^{14}C date of about 38 ka B.P. defines the upper chronological boundary. It seems that the two assemblages can be placed in the first half of the Interpleniglacial rather than in the Early Glacial, as was suggested by V. N. Gladilin (1989).

The technology of these two assemblages has carefully been reconstructed by V. I. Usik (1989) based on the refitted pieces (fig. 5). Single- and double-platform blade cores play the most important role. Their reduction was initiated by the trimming of the flaking surface from the central crest (fig. 5:1). Consequently, blade exploitation began from the narrow side of the core, and the flaking surface was then extended (fig. 5:2), which leads to the hypothesis that flat Levallois-like cores are exhausted forms. The presence of Levallois cores for elongated points indicates links with layer IIb from Korolevo II.

A similar type of link between Upper Paleolithic and Levallois technologies has also been recorded in Moravian sites ascribed to the Bohunician. Reduction strategies derived from the Levallois concept are best demonstrated by flat, single- or double-platform cores with lateral crests, or crests round the entire circumference of a core. The Upper Paleolithic strategies are represented by blade cores with central crests, usually double-platform. The ratio of the two core categories in the Bohunician sites is usually 5:1. The only exception is the site at Brno-Lisen, where the proportion of Upper Paleolithic cores is higher than at other sites: almost 40 percent of Levallois cores. In between Levallois and Upper Paleolithic cores, there exists a large, intermediate group of cores in various stages of preparation (35–54 percent of all cores), including cores with parallel lateral trimming edges. Perpendicularly oriented flakes were detached from these cores, which were prepared on both the flaking surface and the core back (cores with upright preparation, cf. Svoboda 1987). The various core reduction strategies are not mutually exclusive, but can form a single *chaîne opératoire*—just as in Temnata Cave. It is interesting that refitted pieces (fig. 6) suggest that initially the Upper Paleolithic preparation and core reduction is used, and only in a later phase is the core flattened and reduced as a Levallois core of recurrent type (Svoboda and Skrdla 1996).

Bohunician assemblages contain approximately equal proportions of Middle Paleolithic tool types (sidescrapers, denticulated and notched tools, and slender Mousterian points) and Upper Paleolithic tools (endscrapers with retouched sides and, rarely, burins). Diagnostic forms—bifacial leaf points resembling Szeletian points or unifacial points similar to Jerzmanowice specimens—do not occur in all the assemblages (Svoboda 1988, Oliva 1984).

The Bohunician developed from about 45 to about 36 ka B.P., primarily in southern Moravia (Brno Basin, Drahany Plateau; Svoboda 1994), although single sites are known in Silesia (Dzierzyslaw, lower level; Kozlowski 1964) or even in Volhynia (Kulichivka, lower layer; Demidenko and Usik 1993).

None of the three industries we have mentioned (Temnata layer V, Korolevo, and Bohunician), deriving from the Moustero-Levalloisian substratum, survived past about 36 ka B.P.—as far as we know at present. In later industries of the Early Phase of the Upper Paleolithic, no distinct Levallois technological background was identified.

The bearers of the Levallois-based "transitional" industries in Central Europe occupied open landscapes of loess and karstic uplands. In the faunal assemblage of Temnata, layer VI, Equids dominate over Bovids, and in Bohunician sites, horse is also favorite game. From the point of view of symbolic expression, Temnata, layer VI yielded one stone slab with rhythmically repeated, parallel engraved lines. In Bohunice, one pebble with multiple but unstructured incisions was found. Interpretation of these objects in terms of symbolic expression remains questionable.

The Levallois-based, "transitional" industries are not a phenomenon restricted exclusively to the territories of the Balkans and Central Europe. It is important to emphasize that in the Near East, too, we can see continuation from the Moustero-Levalloisian industries to the Emiran and the Ahmarian (Marks 1993, Ferring 1988). In the territory of Central Asia, evolution from an industry using the Levallois technique to an Upper Paleolithic blade industry can not only be seen in the well-known Kara Bom sequence in the Altai between 45 and 30 ka B.P. (Derevianko et al. 1998), but also seems to constitute the dominant tendency in the technological development at the Middle/Upper Paleolithic boundary much farther to the east, as far distant as the territory of Mongolia.

There are a number of arguments in favor of interpreting the various centers with transition industries based on the evolution from Levallois to Upper Paleolithic technology as related to independent innovations. However, a hypothesis whereby the processes of the emergence of such centers are accounted for by diffusion from the territory of the Near East, via the Balkans to Central Europe, and via Iran and Afghanistan to the Altai cannot be excluded. On the

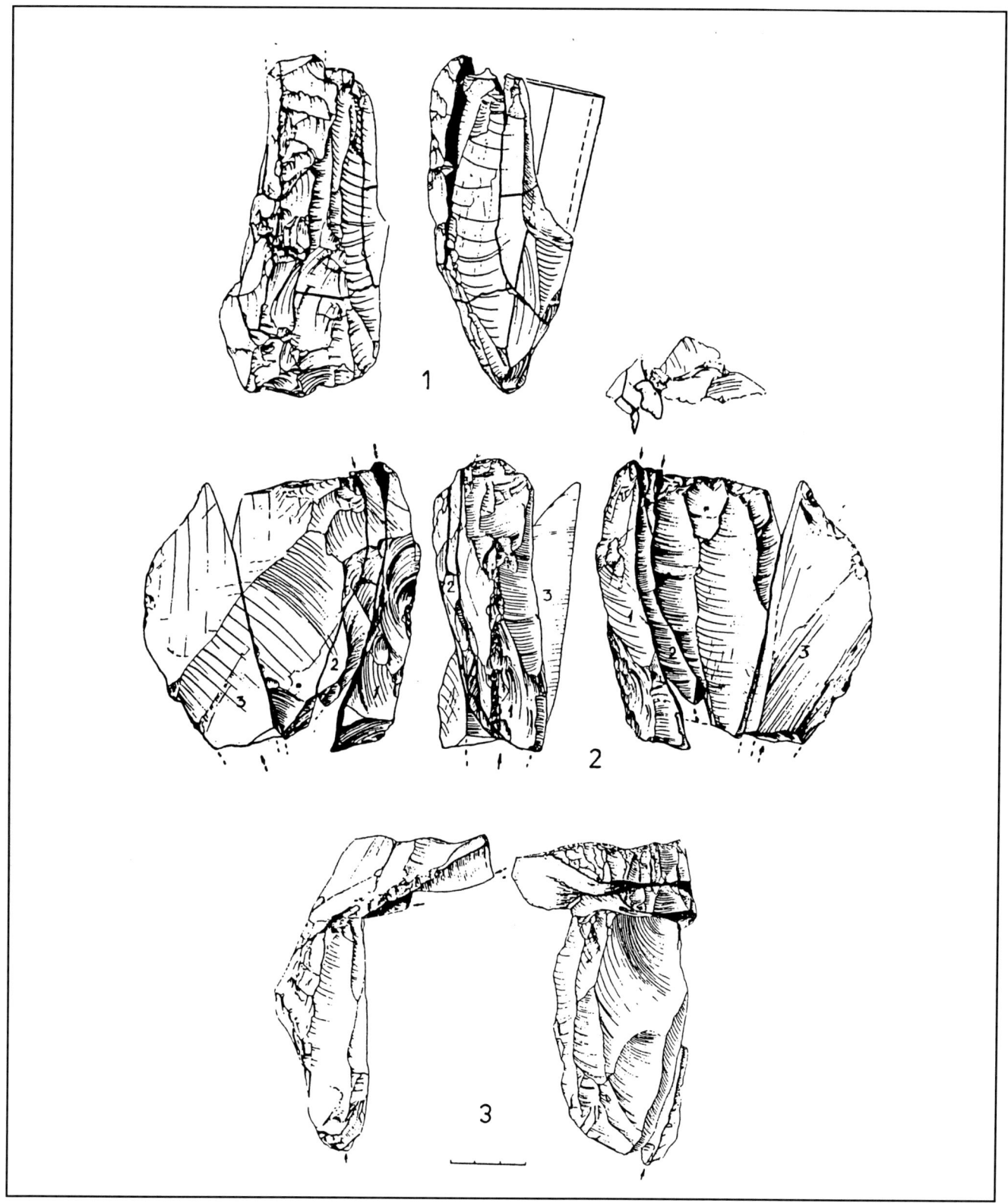

Figure 5. Korolevo II, complex II: Double platform blade core with central crest (1). Korolevo I, complex Ia: Volumetric blade core with crest on the narrow side (2); Volumetric residual blade core with sequence of detached tablets (3) (adapted from V. I. Usik 1989, figs. 3, 20, and 22). Scale in cm.

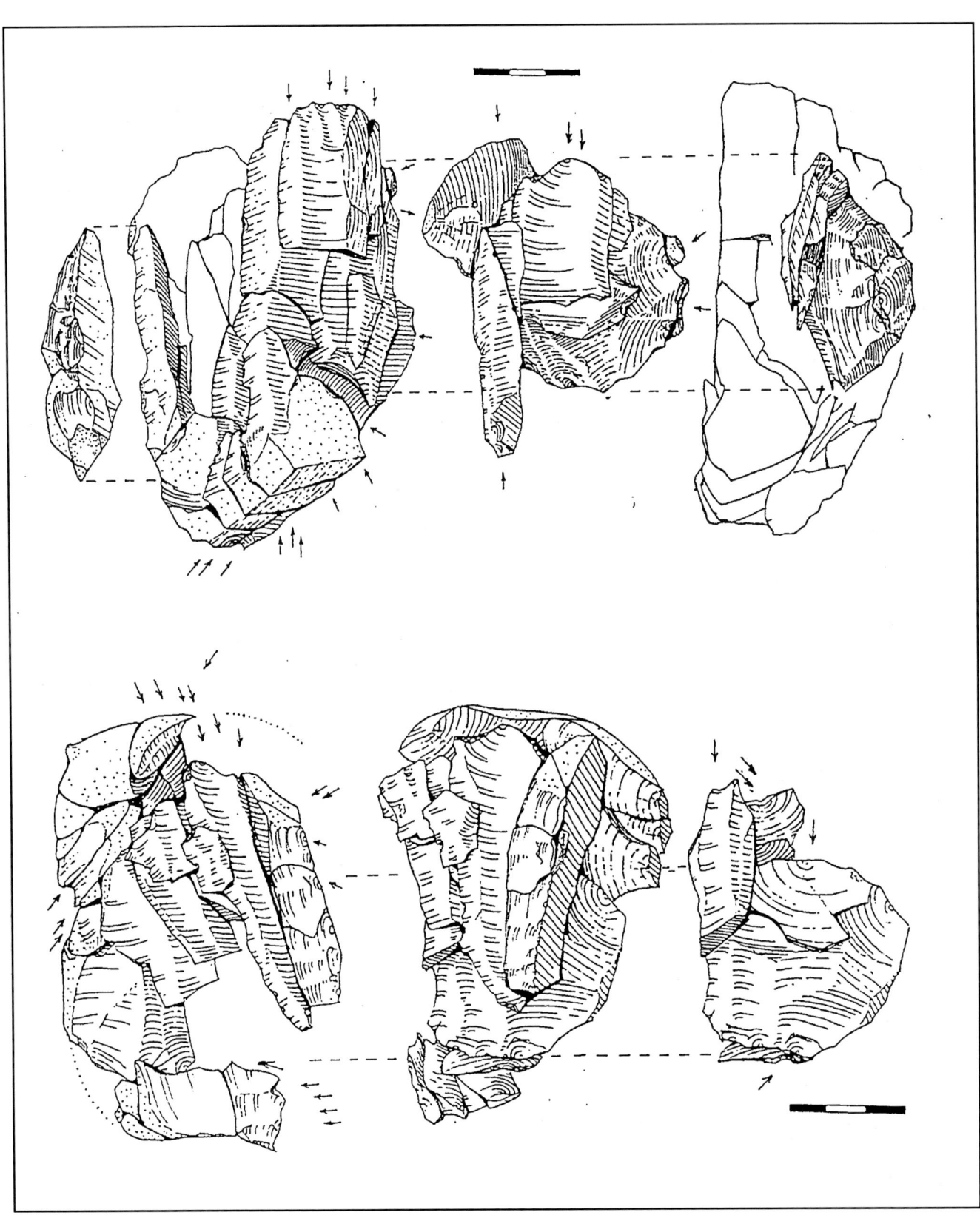

Figure 6. Stranska Skala, Moravia: Bohunician reconstructed cores (adapted from Svoboda and Skrdla 1996, figs. 29.3 and 29.5). Scales in cm.

other hand, diffusion like this does not seem probably, as the phenomenon of the transformation of Levallois technique into Upper Paleolithic technology is synchronous (at approximately 45 ka B.P.). Had this process begun earlier (e.g., 50 ka B.P.) in some territories, it would have been in the Balkans rather than in the Near East. An argument in support of the independent innovations hypothesis is the occurrence of Upper Paleolithic units with Levallois technology and Mousterian typology in all those listed territories with Middle Paleolithic units. The diffusion hypothesis, in turn, could be justified by certain stylistic features of tools with distinctly Near Eastern roots (e.g., points with a ventrally thinned base approximating the Emireh type) that are found—albeit rarely—both in Europe (e.g., in the Temnata cave layer VI) and in Central Asia (e.g., at Kara Tenesh in the Altai).

TECHNOLOGICAL EVOLUTION BASED ON BIFACIAL TOOL SHAPING

The bifacial tool shaping technique is dominant in several "transitional units." This technique is used in the manufacture of leaf points, while other tools are produced from flakes made using the Mousterian discoidal core technique, and from flakes and blades detached from mainly single-platform cores without preparation (except for platform preparation). Among these units belong three industries with leaf points, namely; the Szeletian, the Bryndzenian, and the Streletskian. It is difficult to trace the Middle Paleolithic roots and the dynamics of the internal evolution of these three units.

Szeletian

The Szeletian is interpreted in various ways: as the industry of the lower level in the Szeleta Cave in Hungary (Siman 1990); as Moravian-Silesian industries partially contemporaneous with the Bohunician but without the Levallois strategy of core reduction (Oliva 1995, Valoch 1990); and finally, as the industry of the upper level in the Szeleta Cave (Siman 1995, Siman and Svoboda 1989). This industry is much later, possibly related to the origins of backed-piece industries. All these assemblages can be interpreted either as a sequence bound by genetic links or as completely autonomous. In the light of radiocarbon determinations, the oldest assemblage is the lower level in the Szeleta Cave (>41,700 B.P.). This industry has a fairly small number of cores, blades, and flake tools. Nevertheless, flat, double-platform cores for blades with limited platform preparation do occur, and the number of blades compared with that of flakes is high (53.8 percent). For these reasons, I am inclined to interpret the lower level in the Szeleta Cave as a "transitional unit" with leptolithic features (Kozlowski 1988). This represents a view opposed to the interpretation of K. Siman (1990), who attempts to ascribe this industry to the Middle Paleolithic and stresses the hiatus between the lower and the upper Szeletian in the Szeleta Cave.

A more complex problem is the origin of the lower Szeletian. Although K. Valoch insists on the presence of Szeletian diagnostic features in association with the Micoquian in the inventories at Jezerany in Moravia, such an association is not yet certain, as the materials come from surface collections only (Valoch 1966). Similarly, the interesting typological structure of Babonyan sites in northeastern Hungary, where Micoquian asymmetrical knife-side scrapers occur in association with Szeletian points, poses the question: are asymmetrical bifacial forms perhaps simply half-products of Szeletian leaf points? If we assume that affinities existed between the Micoquian and Szeletian, then Micoquian characteristic features must have disappeared earlier than the lower level in Szeleta Cave. The Micoquian technological tradition could have continued in the special process of shaping bifacial points on tabular quartz-porphyry (Ringer 1983, 1990; Ringer et al. 1995).

It is interesting that the Early Moravian Szeletian from Vedrovice V, dated at about 40 ka B.P., still contains some asymmetrical half-products of leaf points (Valoch 1993:fig. 22:1, 4). At the same time, the Early Szeletian continues to use the Mousterian concept of a discoidal core (fig. 7.1). Numerous single-platform flake cores without preparation occur next to these cores (fig. 7.2), and are transformed during reduction into cores with changed orientation and polyhedral-spherical cores (fig. 7.3). Trimming edges on these cores are extremely rare, which suggests that the majority of trimming flakes (described by Valoch as "Kernkanten") came from a change of orientation, not from intentional core shaping. Blade production does not seem to be the effect of core preparation. The types of scars on cores indicate that blades were not obtained systematically (fig. 7.4, 5).

This same method of blank production without the Upper Paleolithic strategy of core preparation from the central crest (fig. 8) was typical of the younger phase of the Moravian-Silesian Szeletian (Kozlowski 1964).

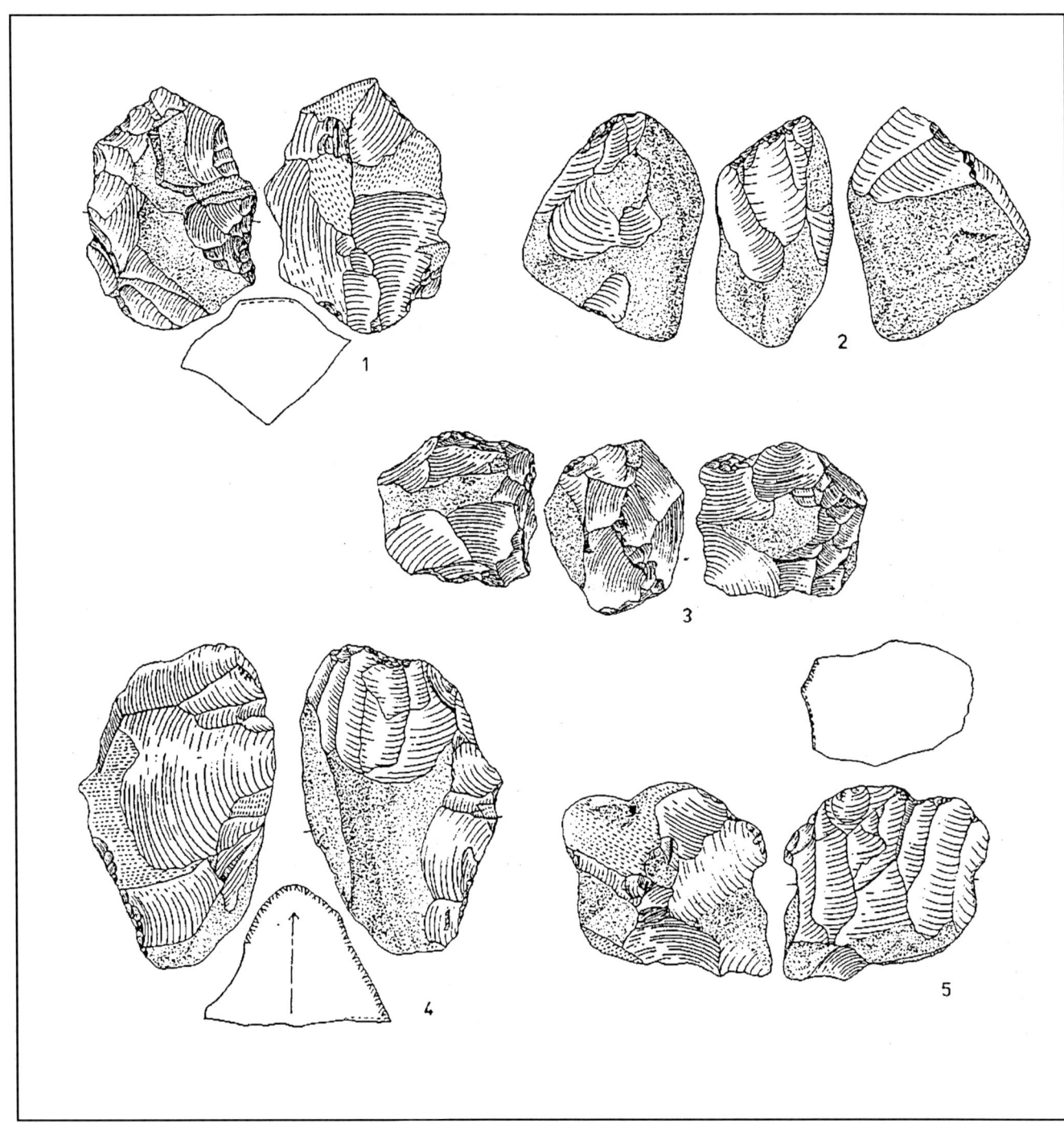

Figure 7. Vedrovice V, Moravia: Discoidal core (1), single platform unprepared core (2), polyhedral-spherical flake cores (3), unprepared blade cores (4, 5) (adapted from K. Valoch 1993).

Only in the youngest phase, represented by the upper level in Szeleta Cave (with a date of 32,580±420 B.P.), does a tendency appear to introduce the typical Upper Paleolithic concept of single-platform blade cores with two crests (Kozlowski 1988). These cores are carinoidal or flat in shape. The blade index increases considerably. In some early Moravian sites (Vedrovice V), it is about 5.9 percent, and in younger sites it reaches from 30 to 70 percent (Valoch 1990).

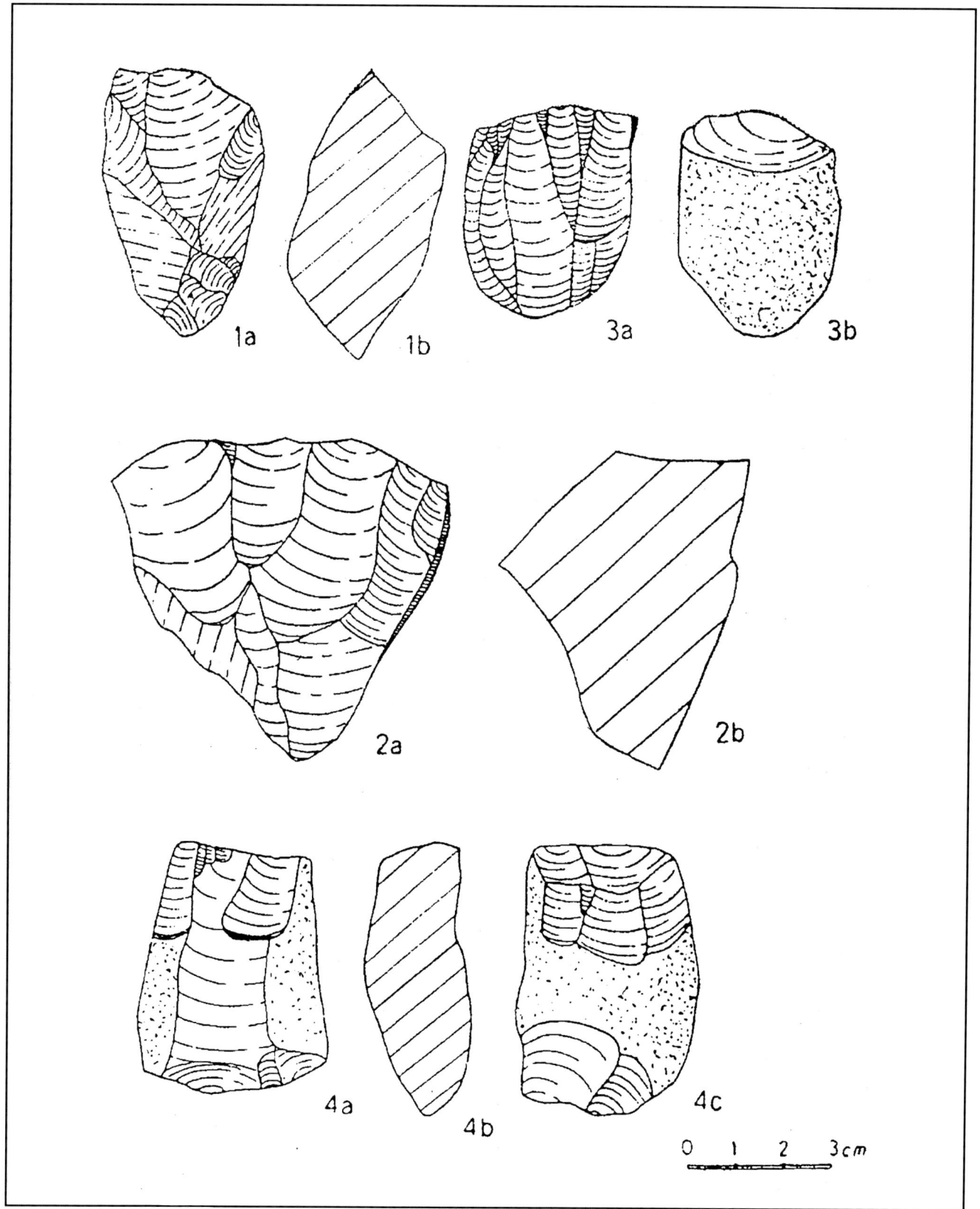

Figure 8. Dzierzyslaw, Poland: Szeletian single (1–3) and double (4) platform unprepared blade-flake cores.

Bryndzenian

The second territory in which Early Upper Paleolithic (EUP) leaf points appeared is Moldavia. East of the Carpathians, the presence of Middle Paleolithic industries with leaf points, with typical Levallois technology of leaf points and blade production (e.g., Ripiceni Izvor in the Prut valley), and industries with denticulated tools and leaf points, also using Levallois technology (Stinka) is recorded. These industries persisted certainly until about 40 ka B.P. at Level Xa in the Molodova V site on the Dnester. This site's assemblage, although it is not rich, suggests that a Levallois tradition continued until about 35 ka B.P., and what is more, that this tradition evolved in the direction of Upper Paleolithic core reduction strategies, just as happened in the Bohunician (Chernich 1987).

Viewed in this light, the appearance of a group of sites described as the Bryndzenian (from the Bryndzeny Cave) in the territory of the Republic of Moldova is puzzling because their technological context seems to be non-Levallois. Besides the Bryndzeny Cave, other sites have been registered, including Butechty, Bobuleshty, Chuntu, and others. Unfortunately, these sites were investigated in the sixties and seventies, when rigorous methods and excavation techniques were not observed (Borziak 1990). The sites yielded bifacial leaf points, resembling Szeletian points, in the context of flake technologies based on discoidal single-platform cores without preparation. On the other hand, the small number of blades used for the shaping of Upper Paleolithic type tools (endscrapers, burins) had been obtained from cores with suitable preliminary preparation. It is not certain whether Bryndzenian assemblages are homogeneous, or whether some more advanced Upper Paleolithic tools may not be intrusions from younger layers. The late dates obtained for the Bryndzenian (ranging from 26.6 to 14.7 ka B.P.) seem to provide evidence in support of the latter hypothesis (Otte et al. 1996).

Streletskian

The third and final group that can be ascribed to the category of inventories with bifacially shaped points are eastern European inventories of the early phase of the Upper Paleolithic consisting of triangular points of Streletskaya-Sungir type with a concave base (fig. 9). This group, notably its early phase, occupied the Middle and Lower Don Basin and the Crimea. In the Middle Paleolithic, these territories were inhabited by diverse east Micoquian and Mousterian groups assigned to the Western Crimean Mousterian (WCM). The controversial issue is the continuation of these units into the late phase of the Interpleniglacial. Chabai (1996) believes that the Micoquian did not survive after Pleniglacial I and that its development did not continue after 60 ka B.P. The WCM, on the other hand, could have lasted until about 30 to 31 ka B.P., which is in agreement with the AMS, U-series, and ESR determinations from Kabazi II/1 in Crimea (i.e., until the appearance of the first, fully developed Upper Paleolithic industries; Yanievich et al. 1996).

Recent results of investigations conducted in the Buran Kaya III rockshelter make the cultural evolution in the Crimea in the period from 35 to 28 ka B.P. even more complex. Above the relatively weakly defined blade industries (layer E) at Buran Kaya III, layer C contains industries with leaf points and short endscrapers, accompanied by bifacially retouched microlithic trapezoids that have no counterpart either in the Middle or the Upper Paleolithic. Layer C has been dated to about 32 ka, although one date is as early as 36.7 ka. In the overlying layer B, the Micoquian appears—the latest Micoquian so far-dated at 29.6 ka B.P. (Marks 1998, Marks and Monigal in press). Summing up, we can say that in the Crimea we are dealing with the parallel development of two Middle Paleolithic cultures (the WCM and the Micoquian) and—interstratified between these cultures—"transitional" units with leaf points that in term of typology and technology are closest to the Streletskian of the Russian Lowlands. To refer to the unit as the "Szeletian" (Marks 1999, Chabai 1999) raises objections, as there exist considerable differences in the technology of the production of the leaf points, their shape, and associated tools. Moreover, distinct discontinuity in the range of the Central European Szeletian and the Eastern European units with leaf points further justifies our objections. In the exceptionally high standard of the pressure technique used in the production of the its leaf points, the assemblage from Buran Kaya III layer C resembles the Streletskian, but this does not make the derivation of this unit from the Crimean Micoquian any less difficult. It is more likely, therefore, that the genesis of Eastern European assemblages with leaf points should rather be sought in the Russian Lowlands, and not in the Crimea. The stratigraphical sequence of the complex of open air sites—unfortunately of workshop character—in the region of Biriuchaya Balka in the Severski Donets River basin points to the affiliation of the Middle Paleolithic with asymmetrical knives-sidescrapers of the Micoquian type and the Upper Paleolithic with triangular leaf points and short endscrapers (Matioukhin 1990).

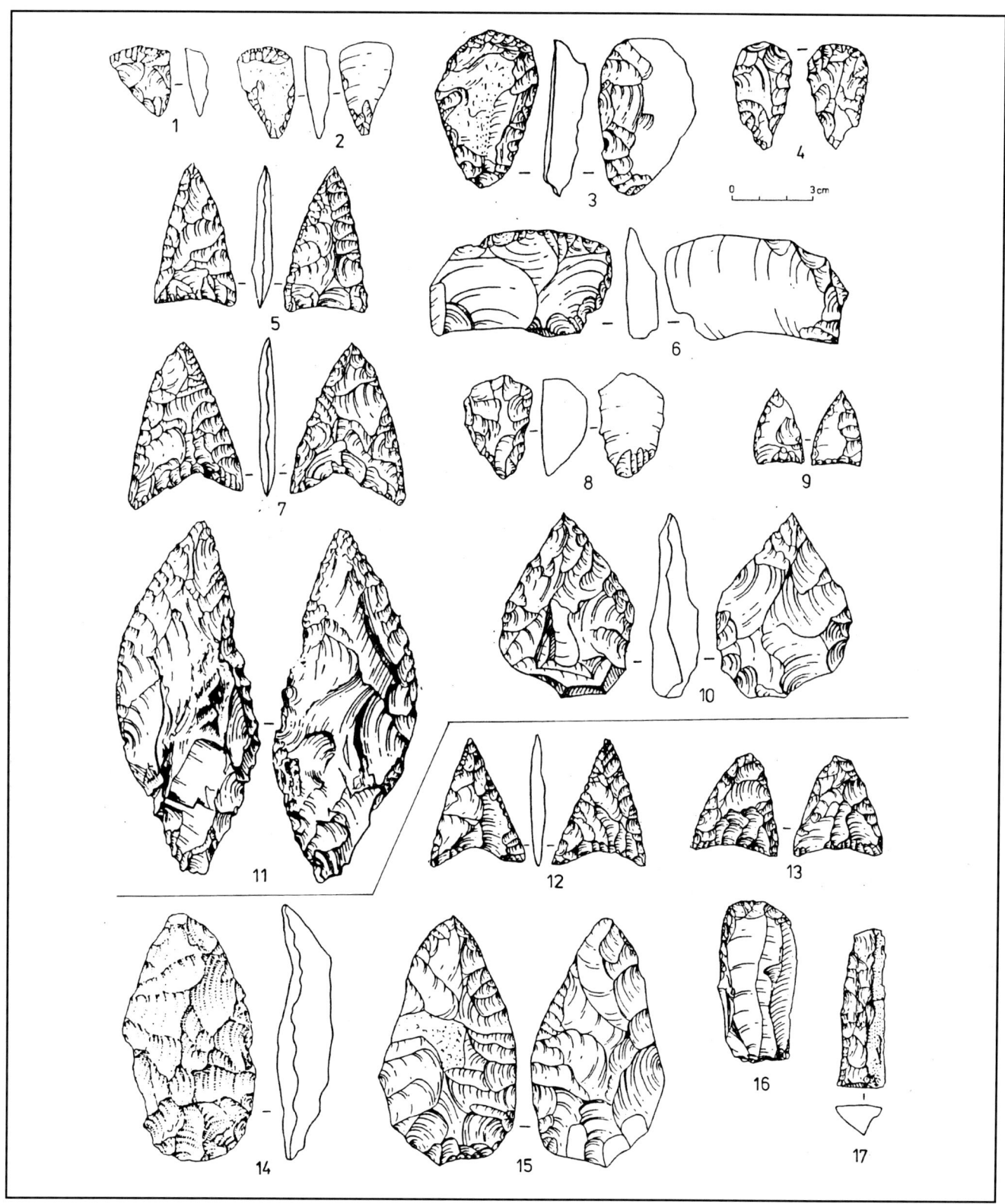

Figure 9. Streletskian tools: Kostenki I, Russian, layer V (1–11), Kostenki 6 (Streletskaya) (12–17). Endscrapers (1–4, 8, 16), triangular leaf-points with concave base (Sungir points) (5, 7, 9, 12, 13), sidescraper (6), blade with lateral retouch (17), unfinished foliates (10, 11, 14, 15).

If we assume that the Streletskian derived from the Crimean Micoquian and later expanded to the north into the Don Basin, then certain chronological problems arise. Some Streletskian inventories are known in the region of Kostenki (fig. 9). They are contained in the lower humic soil on the Don terrace, which — on the basis of tephrachronology and the only date from Kostenki XVII/2 (36,400±1700/1400) — some researchers place at the Hengelo oscillation (38–36 ka B.P.). Also, some of the Streletskian assemblages have been dated between 37,900±2800/2100 (Kostenki I/5) and 36,280±360 (Kostenki XII/3). We would then face a controversy between the dating of the "transitional" Middle Paleolithic-Upper Paleolithic phase in Crimea to about 33–31 ka B.P., and even earlier date for the beginning of the Streletskian on the Don. On the other hand, some of the dates for the Streletskian on the Don (Kostenki 6, Xii/1a) are younger than 32 ka B.P. In terms of technology, the sites on the Don do not provide evidence that would question their Micoquian roots.

This origin is also supported by the fact that Streletskian assemblages are mainly based on *façonnage* technique (the shaping of bifacial tools from chunks), while *débitage* (flake production from discoidal cores or single-platform cores without preparation, with flat flaking surfaces) was a fairly marginal method. At sites such as Kostenki 6 (Streletskaya) or Kostenki I level V, approximately ten cores occur per 1000–2000 artifacts. Similarly, at Buran Kaya III level C, with the exception of bifacial shaping, no other reduction strategy was present. On the other hand, the presence of typical Upper Paleolithic short endscrapers, produced more often on flakes than on blades, in conjunction with the occurrence of technologically the most advanced leaf points in Europe at that time, suggests that the Streletskian was the result of rapid changes in the local Middle Paleolithic base.

The second transitional unit known in the Don basin, namely the Gorodtsovian (the eponymous site of Kostenki 15 — Gorodtsovskaya, Praslov and Rogatchev 1982) is more conservative in terms of lithic technology. This unit has been dated to the period from 32 to 26 ka B.P., and suggests the reduction of polyhedral multiplatform flake cores. The fairly large component of Middle Paleolithic tools (e.g., sidescraper and asymmetrical, partially bifacial knives-sidescrapers) may indicate the Micoquian origins of the Gorodtsovian. In this industry, Upper Paleolithic forms are also represented, mainly by endscrapers, usually with lateral retouch and are sometimes fairly thick (fig. 10). As in the Streletskian, the splintered technique was used. However, it is bone artifacts that most convincingly endow this industry with its Upper Paleolithic nature, in particular the shovel-like objects, which are frequently richly ornamented, and are much more elaborate than the individual bone artifacts known from the Streletskian (also from its Crimean variety, *compare* d'Errico and Laroulandie 1999).

The Gorodtsovian is a single "transitional" unit in which two burials occur, discovered at Kostenki 14/3 (below a sample dated to 28,580±420) and at Kostenki 15 (dated at 25,700±250). Both graves contained remains of typical Cro-Magnoids, however, the skull from Kostenki 14/3 exhibits more alveolar prognathism than other skulls. The burial from Kostenki 15 was furnished with stone and bone implements and personal adornments.

EVOLUTION BASED ON BLADES USED AS BLANKS FOR LEAF POINTS

Between 40 and 30 ka B.P., industries with blade *pointes à face plane*, defined as the Lincombian-Ranisian-Jerzmanowician, appear in the European Lowlands, between the British Islands and Poland (fig. 11). Regrettably, points of this type are usually discovered as single finds, without the context of debitage or cores used for blade production. The findspots tend to be ephemeral hunting camps located in caves on plateaus surrounding the European Lowland in the south. Our knowledge of these sites is incomplete, although there are some indications of Middle Paleolithic affiliations for these industries. We should first consider the possibility that genetic links exist between the Ranisian and the industry with leaf point from the Weinberghöhle near Mauern, in the river Altmühl valley in southern Germany. I have tried to prove the existence of a relationship between bifacial points from Weinberghöhle and the bifacial points preserved in assemblages from older layers at Ranis and the Nietoperzowa Cave in Jerzmanowice. The presence at Weiberghöhle of blades from single- or double-platform cores (even triple-platform cores), mostly without preparation, indicates that the technological evolution of this industry is already close to the fully fledged Upper Paleolithic (Kozlowski 1990). The only prepared core at Weiberghöhle seems to be derivative of the Levallois cores, as it has centripetal preparation of the back. The links between southern Germany and the Ranisian are also confirmed by the presence of artifacts made from Bavarian "Plattensilex" at Ranis (Weber 1990).

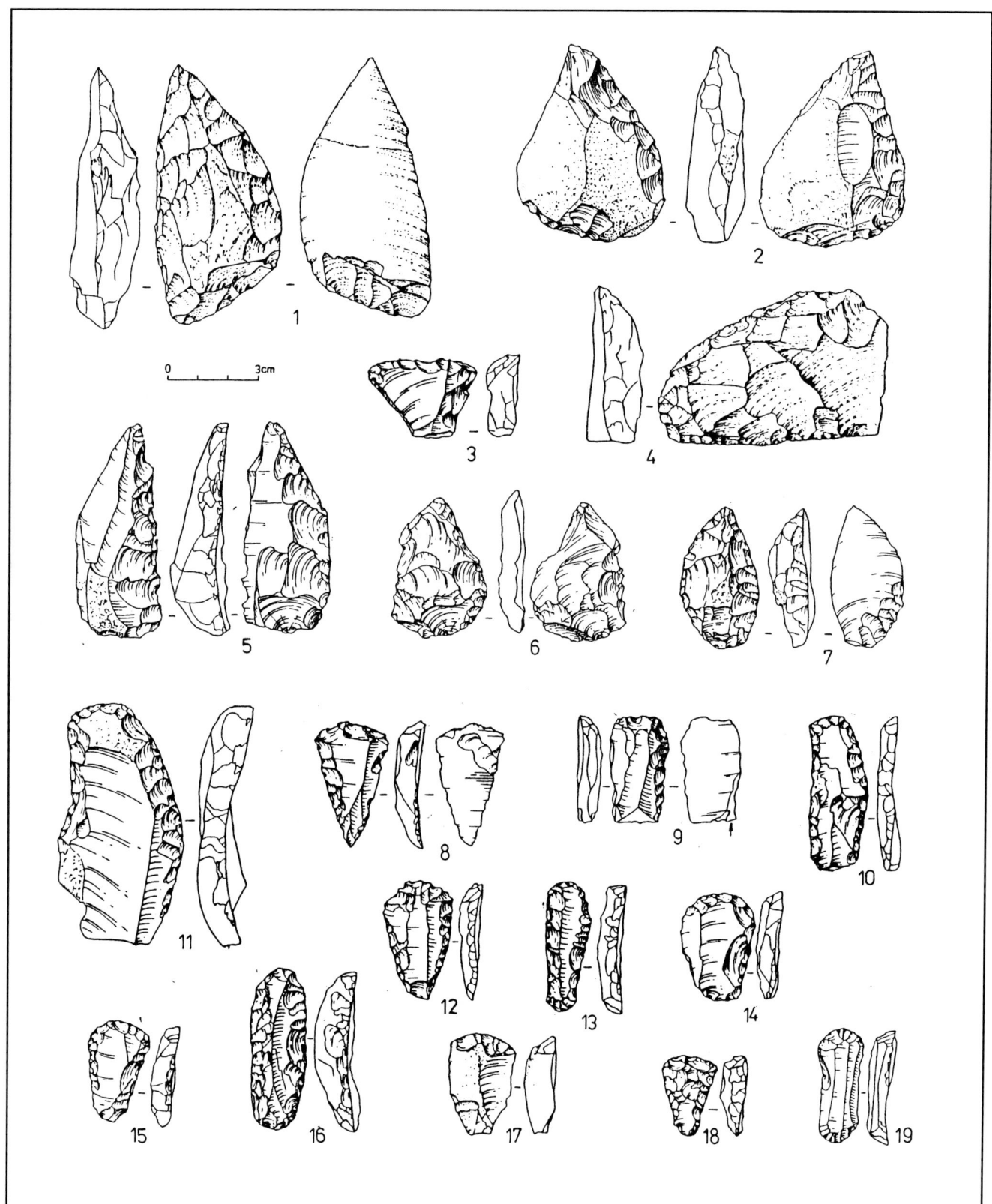

Figure 10. Gorodtsovian tools: Kostenki 15, Russia. Sidescrapers (1–7), endscrapers (8–19) (adapted from Praslov and Rogatchev 1982, figs. 57 and 58).

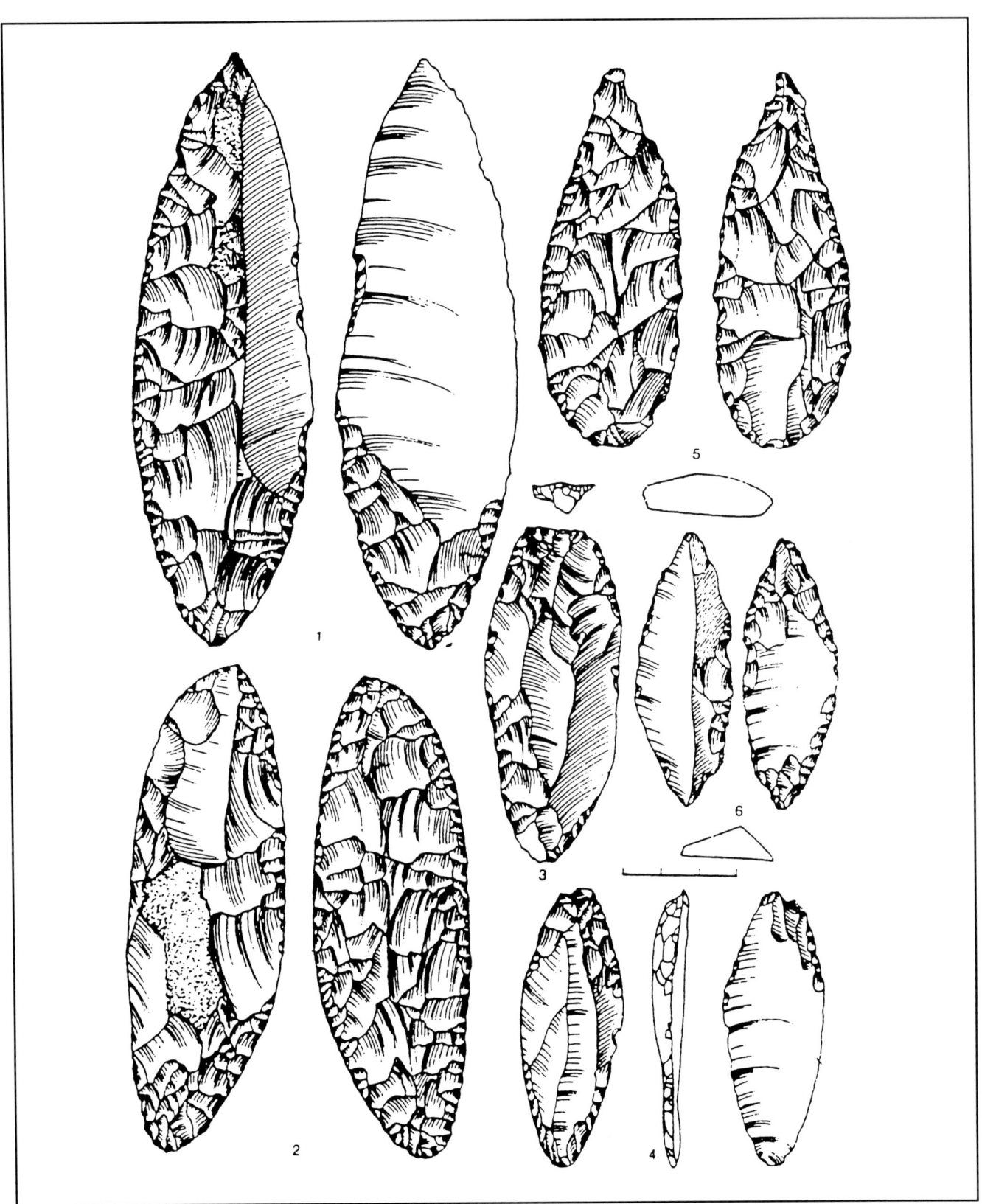

Figure 11. Jerzmanowician leaf points: Jerzmanowice, Nietoperzowa Cave, layer 6 (1–4); Wierzchowie, Poland, Mamutuwa Cave (5, 6). Leaf points on blades (*pointes à face plane*) (1, 3, 4, 6), bifacially worked foliates (2, 5). Scale in cm.

On the other hand, other industries in northwestern Europe, in the period from 50 to 40 ka B.P., could also be the antecedents of the Ranisian. These include, primarily, the industry from Couvain Cave in Belgium, where bifacial points co-occur with unifacial points, some of which resemble the later Lincombian-Ranisian points. The points in Couvain Cave are present in the context of a rich set of sidescrapers, mainly lateral and convergent, made on flakes detached from proto-prismatic or single-platform convergent cores. The final products are blade flakes and blades (Ulrix-Closset 1995), technologically "affiliated" to the Upper Paleolithic but not quite the "real" Upper Paleolithic.

The younger Lincombian-Ranisian inventories consist almost entirely of Upper Paleolithic type tools, for example the unique inventory of the Pulborough site in England, where *pointes à face plane* are present together with burins, retouched blades, and Kostenki knives. A similar tendency can be seen in the Nietoperzowa Cave in Poland (fig. 11). In this cave, the whole sequence of layers 6 to 4a is placed at between 38 and 30 ka B.P. The blade inventory, including blade leaf points and a few other tools, is fully Upper Paleolithic (Kozlowski and Kozlowski 1996).

EVOLUTIONARY TRENDS BASED ON BLADE TECHNOLOGY AND BACKED TOOLS

This type of evolution from the Middle to Upper Paleolithic is specific to western Europe, where it is represented by the Chatelperronian and the Uluzzian. In central-eastern Europe, this evolutionary direction is much less known. It is so far represented in individual sites that do not form sequences or clusters. Sites with arched backed blades (fig. 12) are known in the northern part of Central Europe (e.g., Kraków-Zwierzyniec in Poland; Kozlowski and Kozlowski 1996), in the Danube Basin (Vlckovce; Barta 1980) and in Moldavia (Korpatch; Borziak et al. 1981, Grigorieva 1983). The coexistence of arched backed blades and Szeletian leaf points in these sites suggests that some Szeletian or Bryndzenian groups may also have produced arched backed blades in the period from 35 to 26 ka B.P. (fig. 12). This is not certain, because electron microscope analyses of the state of preservation of artifacts from Kraków-Zwierzyniec have shown differing states of preservation of Szeletian points and arched backed blades. This means that although the specimens occur in the same layer, they were not deposited in the same period (Kozlowski and Kozlowski 1996). Our knowledge of these inventories does not allow us fully to support the hypothesis that autonomous units with arched backed blades existed in the Danube basin and in the northern part of central Europe at the end of the Interpleniglacial. An argument in favor of the existence of such units is, possibly, the discovery of sites with arched backed blades (Regensburg) in the Upper Danube basin (i.e., beyond the range of the western Chatelperronian). However, these sites gave a relatively late date (26 ka B.P.).

Recent discoveries in Klisoura Gorge in the eastern Peloponese in Greece (1997) are of great interest. Layer V contained a blade industry with arched backed blades, microlithic segments and truncations (fig. 13), short endscrapers, blades with marginal retouch, and burins. This industry will prove of essential importance in determining the existence of autonomous arched backed blade units in the Balkans below the Aurignacian, whose lower portion is dated at between 33 to 34 ka B.P. This industry is now under study. It differs from both the Uluzzian and the Chatelperronian, despite the fact that diagnostic forms are similar in all those units.

DISCUSSION

The four groups of "transitional" units (fig. 14) distinguished in the period from 50 to 30 ka B.P. stem in varying degrees from the Middle Paleolithic base, and their evolution in the Early Upper Paleolithic time period followed a different course. In their final manifestations, all are contemporary with the Aurignacian (considered to be the "real" Upper Paleolithic). The first group, whose links with the Levallois technology were strongest, realized most completely its transformation toward the classical Upper Paleolithic blade technology. On the other hand, the absence of diagnostic forms of Upper Paleolithic tools makes it impossible to associate the units in the first group with specific Upper Paleolithic cultures. It seems that units in the first group disappear about 35 ka B.P. with no continuation. Very little is known about them in terms of economy, life style, or camp structure. We know that, with the exception of Temnata Cave, all the others were open, mainly workshop-type sites, which processed high quality, local raw materials. These workshops represent tendencies similar to those in the sites of the late Balkan-Danubian Moustero-Levalloisian with leaf points.

The second group, hypothetically derived from different variants of the Micoquian, contains leaf

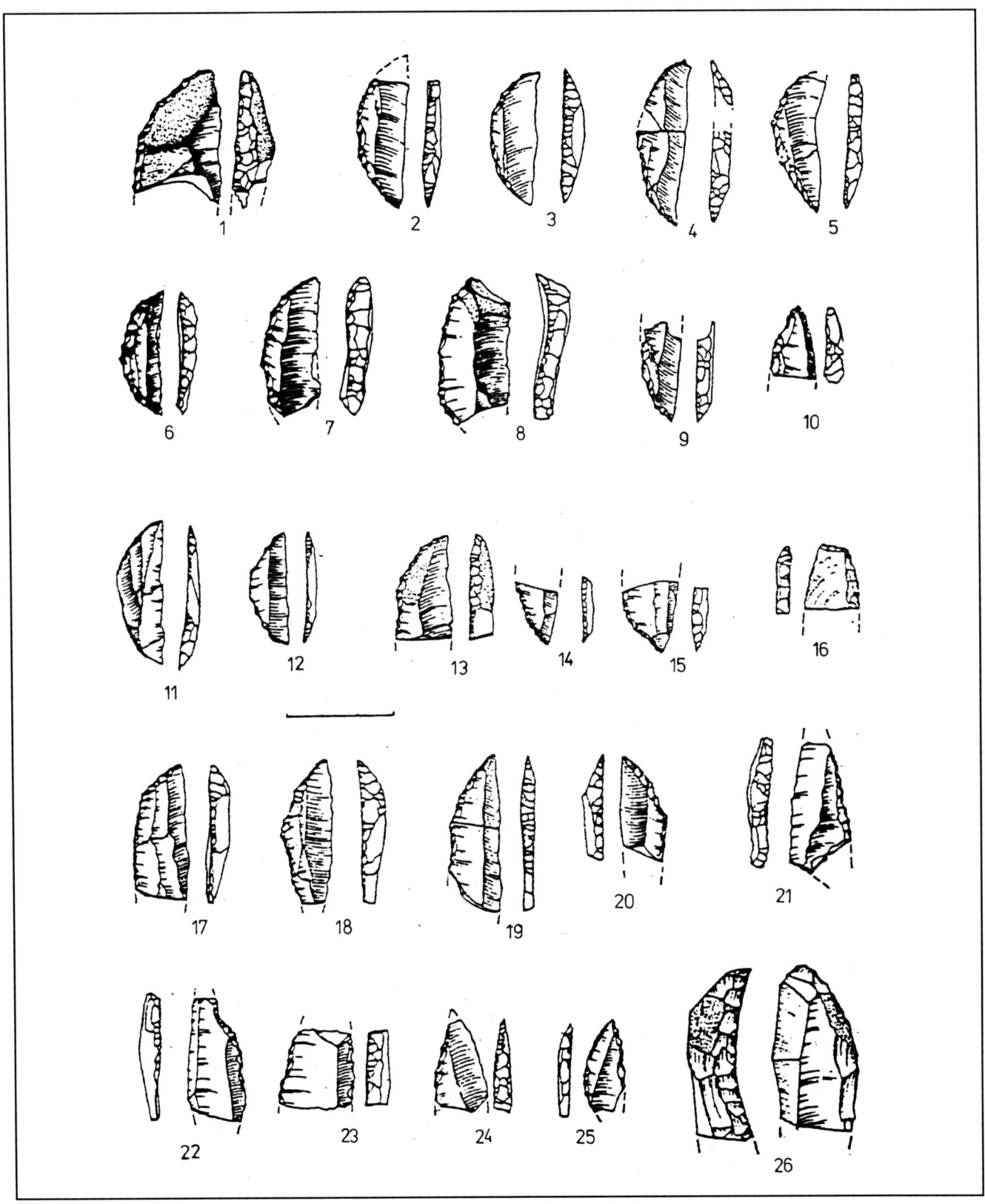

Figure 12. Arched backed blades from Kraków-Zwierzyniec I, Poland, layers 12–14, in sectors J3, 4a, and 4b. Scale in cm.

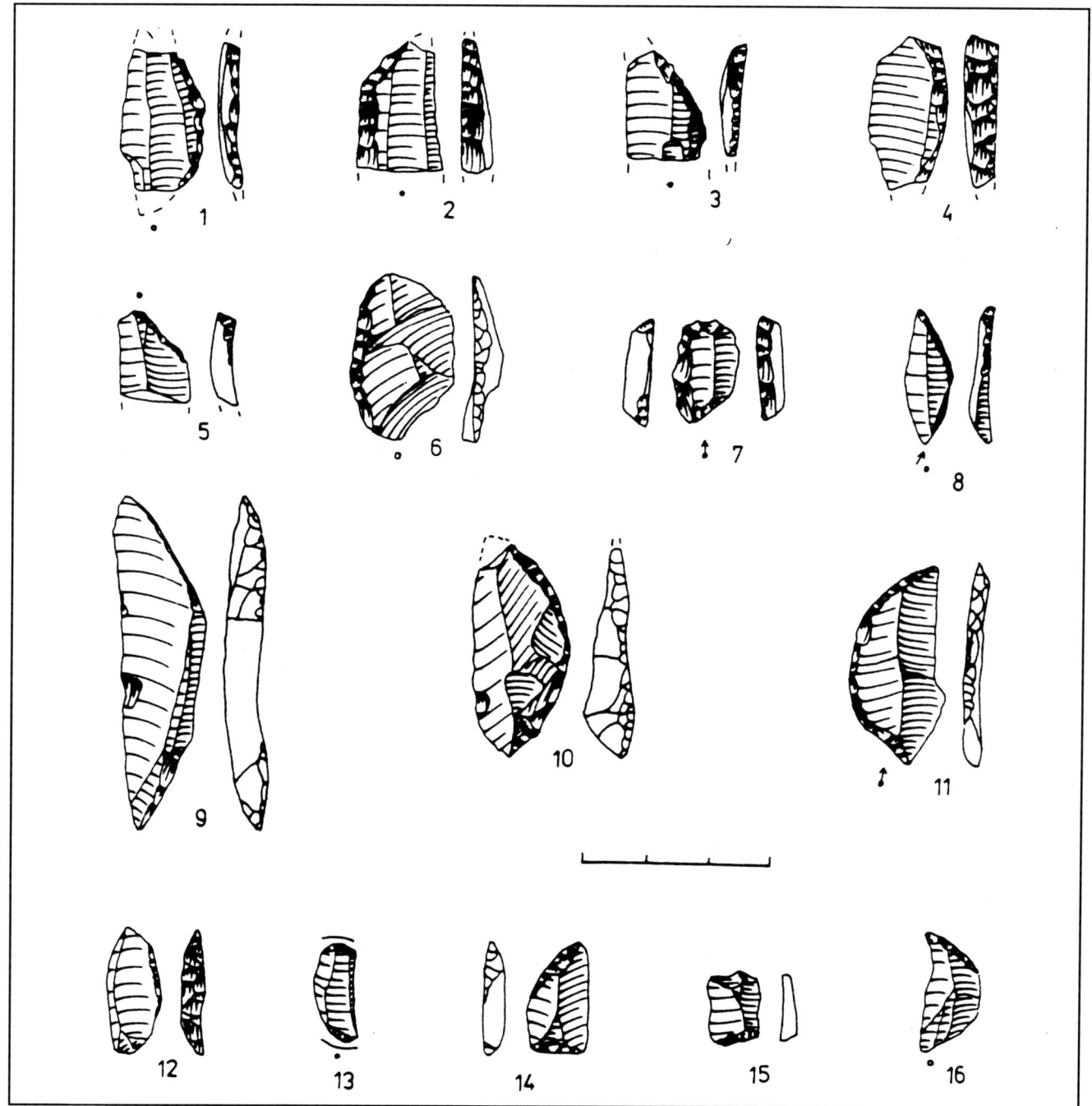

Figure 13. Arched backed blades (1–6, 9–12), microlithic truncations (7, 8, 13–16) from Klisoura Cave I, Greece, layer V. Scale in cm.

points, which persisted locally far into the Upper Paleolithic, even as far as the beginning of the maximum of Pleniglacial II. Good examples are Szeletian triangular points with a Moravany-Dlha-type convex base and Streletskian triangular points with a concave base. Streletskian points continued as Sungirian points. It should be remembered that Szeletian-type points occur in the Middle Danubian Gravettian (the Pavlovian), and gravettian backed points (if they are not intrusions) appear in the upper layer in Szeleta Cave.

The transformations in the technology of blade blank production in this group are more complex: the

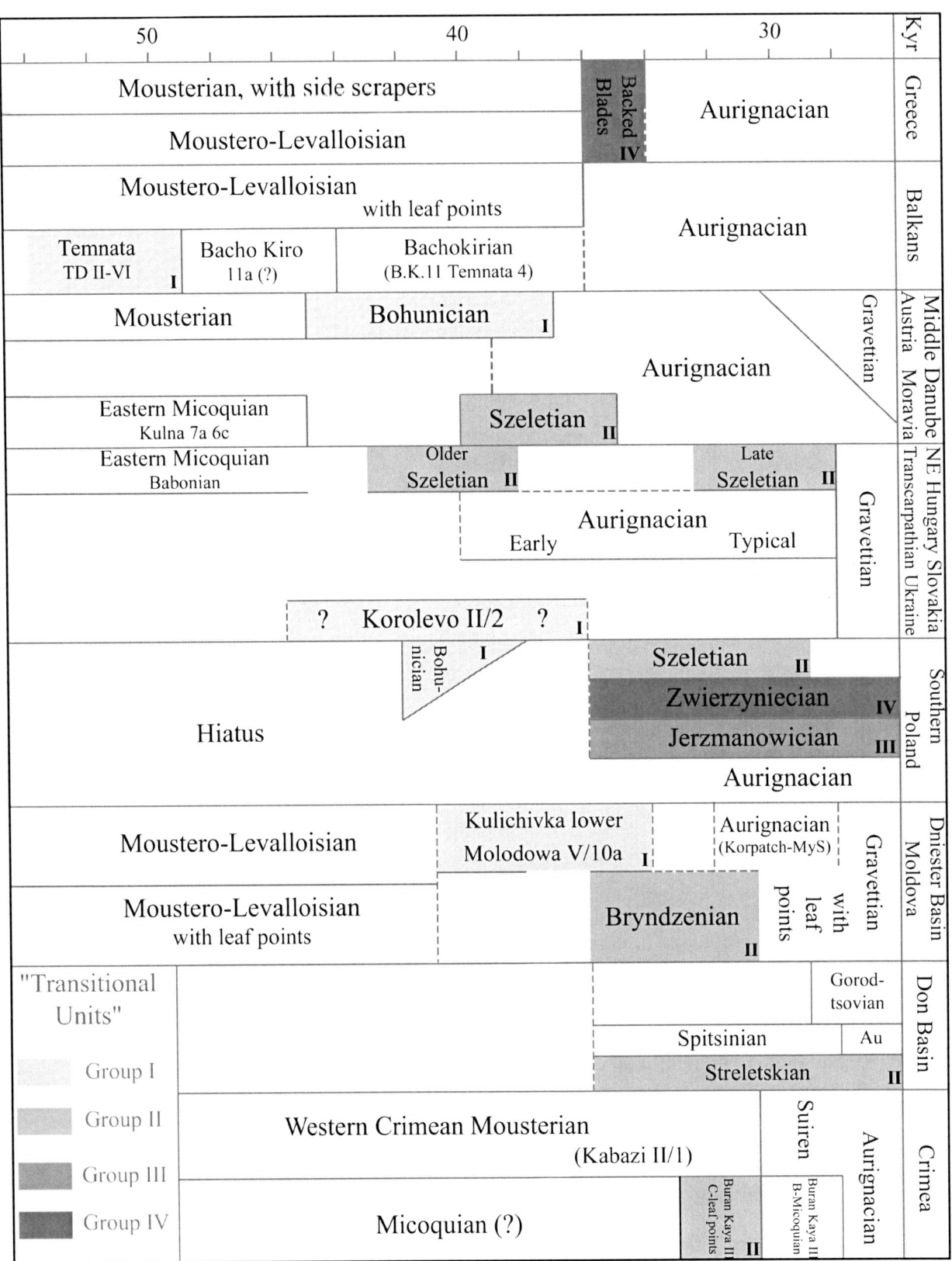

Figure 14. Chronological relationships between particular "transitional units" and the Aurignacian in Central and Eastern Europe.

Upper Paleolithic blade technology does not seem to have developed in this group as the result of internal dynamics of evolution of Middle Paleolithic technologies, but rather as the effect of independent innovations and/or human contacts with contemporaneous Upper Paleolithic communities, mainly Aurignacian groups. The ongoing interactions are evidenced by the exchange of special tools: a few Szeletian quartz-porphyry folates are found in Aurignacian sites in Eastern Slovakia (Banesz 1968, Kaminska 1995). In the Bryndzenian, endscrapers and carinoidal cores were found in layer 3 in Bryndzeny Cave (Otte et al. 1996), and in Crimea (Siuren) leaf points were made by the Aurignacians. In addition, Aurignacian bone points were found in Szeletian sites (Dzerava skala in Slovakia, and Oblazowa in Poland). A number of parameters, such as manner of terrain exploitation, site location, specialized hunting camps, and methods of building houses link the Szeletian and the Aurignacian. It should be added that an ornamented spade-shaped ivory object from Bryndzeny Cave, thought to represent a fish, resembles Aurignacian zoomorphic figurines in its decorative technique (Ketraru 1973).

The third group, whose deeper Middle Paleolithic roots are not known, may have derived from the Upper Danubian Altmühlian. From its very beginning, this group has a well-advanced blade technology. In this respect, units of this group differ strikingly from the Szeletian and Bryndzenian. In the period from 30 to 20 ka B.P., the continuation of the Lincombian-Ranisian-Jerzmanowician is recorded in western Europe (the industry from Maisières-Canal, Otte 1985; and possibly the north-French proto-Solutrean, Schmider 1995), as well as in eastern Europe (Kostenki–Telmanskaya (upper layer); Praslov and Rogatchev 1982).

The fourth group distinguished here, of industries with arched backed blades, has not been studied thoroughly enough to afford the formulation of conclusions as to its genesis and continuation in central Europe.

For the most part (although touching on the possibility of acculturation), I have left the Aurignacian out of my discussion. I believe this unit to be of an allochthonous nature over the whole European territory, unrelated to the local Middle Paleolithic. Nor have I mentioned the physical aspects of people who created these "transitional" units: the almost total absence of human bone remains in the sites of these units—with the exception of the Gorodtsovian—makes any speculations extremely tentative. Unquestionably, the human remains that so far have been associated with the Aurignacian in Central Europe belong to anatomically modern man.

CONCLUSIONS

There are not many reliable radiometric dates from the period between 50 to 40 ka B.P. that are in agreement with the lithostratigraphic data. Most radiocarbon determinations for this period indicate the minimum age of samples. Synchronization of these dates is also difficult, as the record of climatic cycles in the sediments is incomplete. Because of this, the map in figure 15 and the dates in table 1 indicate only a few sites, which, however, consist of distinctly different taxonomic units. During the period from 50 to 40 ka B.P., "transitional units" occur over the whole territory of Central Europe. They are derived from the Levallois technological tradition and developed Upper Paleolithic blade technology. However, typically Mousterian assemblages, with or without Levallois technology, are also present. Moreover, the evolution of Eastern Micoquian assemblages in the direction of Szeletian Leaf Point industries can be seen in the same period. This trend is, however, restricted to the Carpathian Basin and Moravia. At the end of the period in question, the earliest Aurignacian appears in the territory of the northeastern Balkans as a separate unit with no local predecessors. This unit is referred to as the Bachokirian.

The number of dates within the period from 40 to 35 ka B.P. is not large; these dates, too, frequently determine only the minimum age and have large standard errors. During that period, the territory of Central Europe is more clearly divided into the southern and northern parts. The southern part covers the Balkans and that part of the middle Danube Basin where the Early Aurignacian develops (partially with bone points with split bases). The northern part covers the territory of the western Carpathians, where the industries with leaf points (Szeletian and Bohunician) developed. Further to the north is the Jerzmanowician. Sites with a strong Mousterian tradition occur at that time mainly in Transylvania and Greece, although this picture may simply result from the random territorial scatter of the radiocarbon determinations obtained so far (fig. 16 and table 1).

The number of dates obtained for the period from 35 to 30 ka B.P. increases rapidly (fig. 17). These are, however, mainly dates from Aurignacian sites of the classical phase with Mladec points. During that period, the Aurignacian occupies almost the whole of Central Europe, first of all the loess plateaux and practically all mountain regions (the Alps, the Transylvanian Mountains, the Carpathians, and the Central Balkans). "Transitional units" with leaf points (Szeletian, Jerzmanowician and probably Bryndzenian) occur only locally, in the northern part of Central Europe.

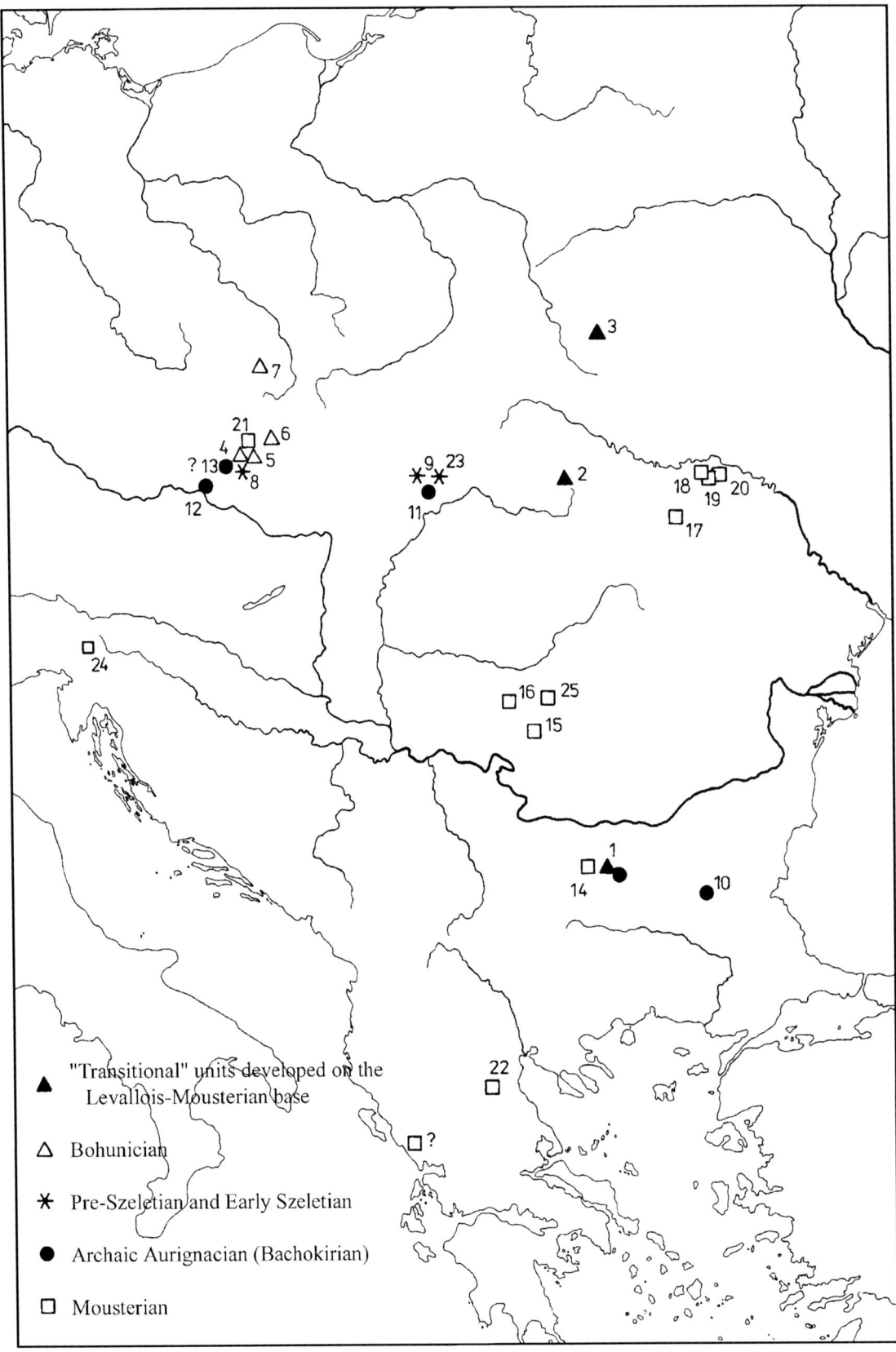

Figure 15. Most important sites dated to the period 50–40 ka B.P. For details of sites, see table 1.

The Problem of Cultural Continuity between Middle and Upper Paleolithic in Central and Eastern Europe

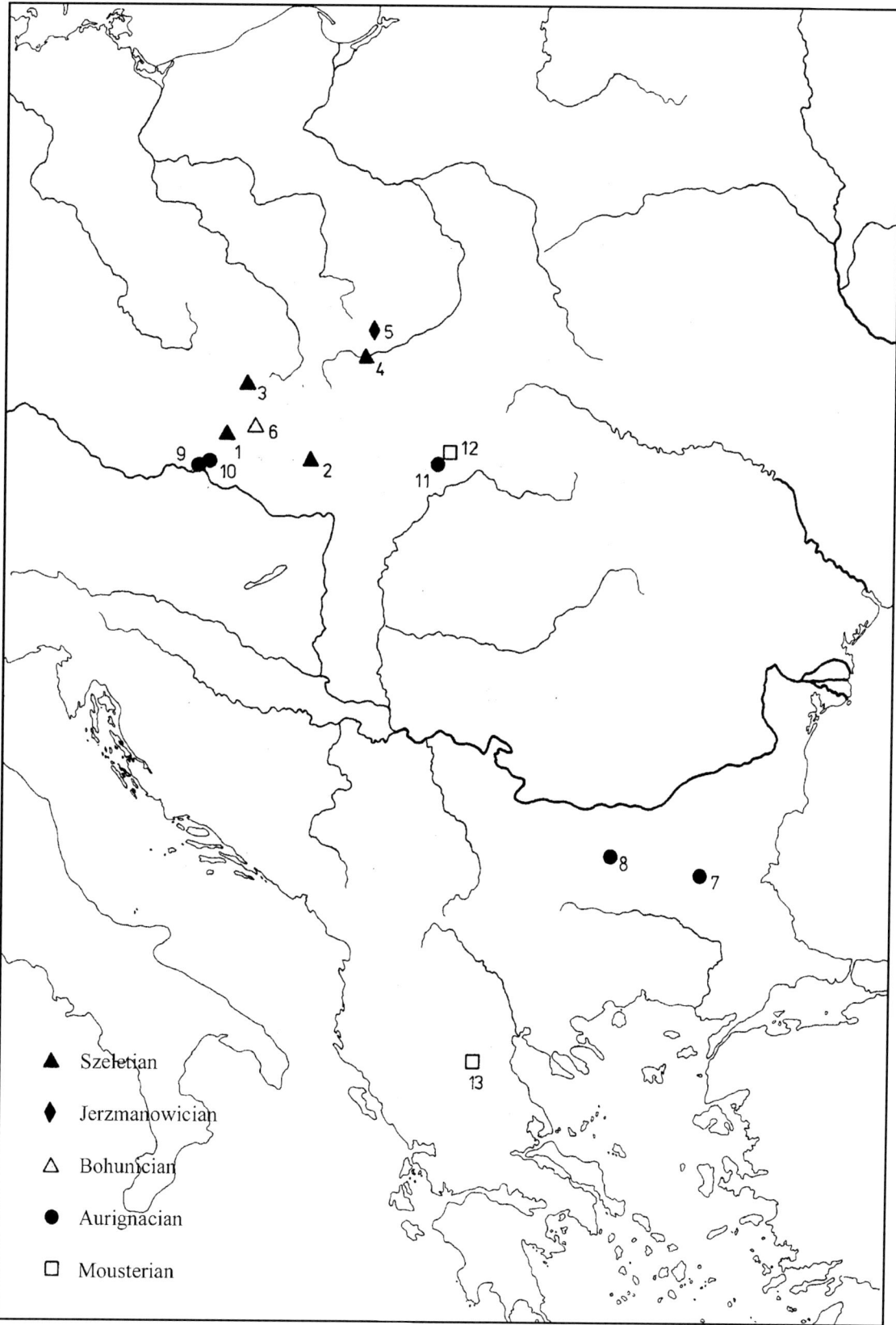

Figure 16. Most important dated sites to the period 40–35 ka B.P. For details of sites, see table 2.

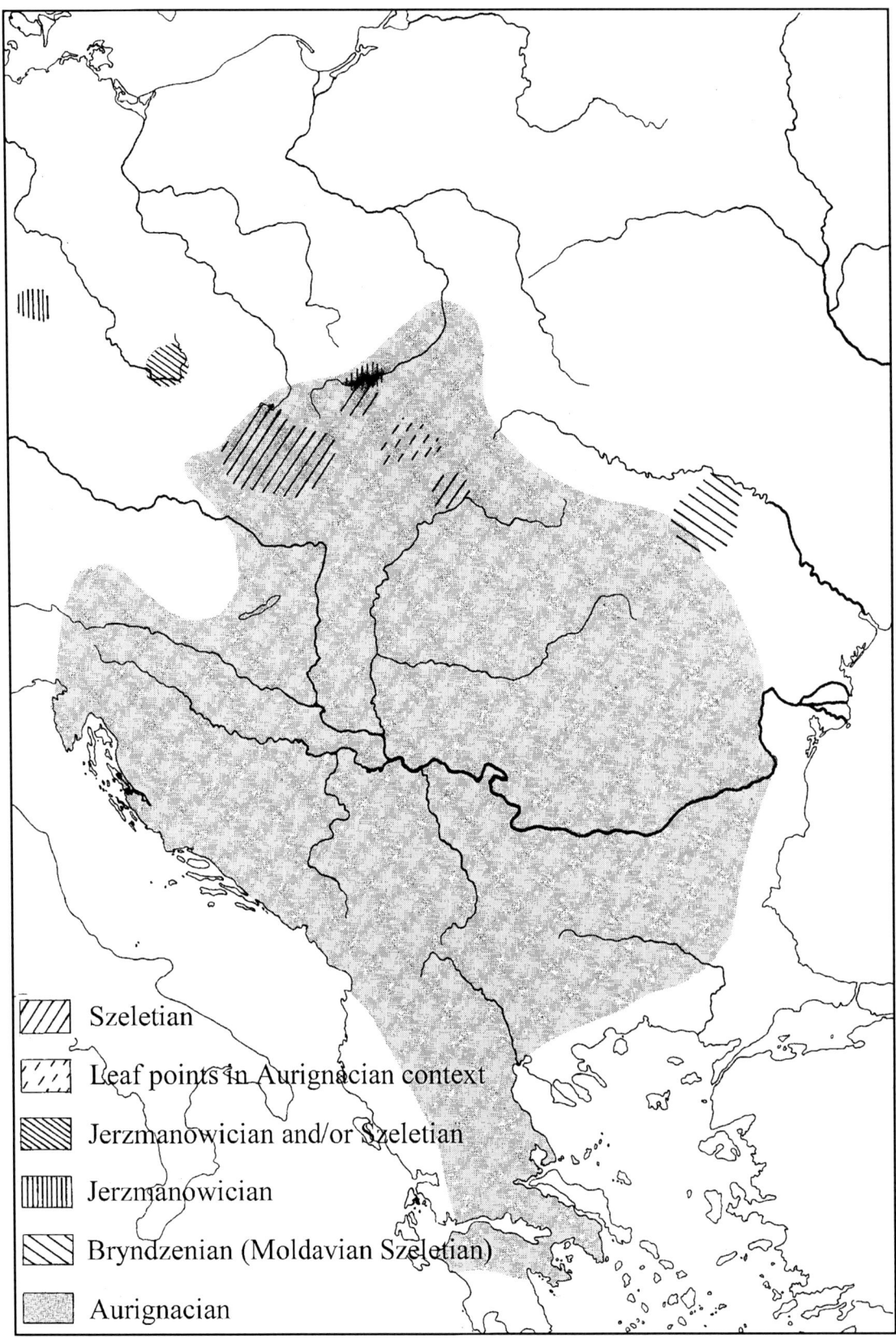

Figure 17. Most important regions of settlement in the period 35–30 ka B.P. .

BIBLIOGRAPHY

Ameloot-Van der Heijden, N.
1994 "L'ensemble lithique du niveau CA du gisement Riencourt-les-Bapaume (Pas de Calais)," in *Les industries laminaires au Paléolithique moyen*, S. Revillion and A. Tuffreau, eds., pp. 63–75. CNRS, Paris.

Banesz, L.
1968 *Barca bei Kosice, paläolithische Fundstelle*. SAV, Nitra.

Barta, J.
1980 *Importantes sites Paléolithiques de la Slovaquie centrale et orientale*. SAV, Nitra.

Borziak, I.
1990 "Bifacial Tools of Late Paleolithic in Dniester-Prut interfluve," in *Les Feuilles de Pierre*, J. K. Kozlowski, ed., pp. 125–136. Etudes et Recherches Archéologiques de l'Université de Liège 42, Liège.

Borziak, I., G. V. Grigorieva, and N. A. Ketraru
1981 *Stoyanki kamiennogo veka na severo-zapade Moldavii*. Shtiintsa, Kichinev.

Chabai, A.
1996 "Kabazi II in the Context of Crimean Middle Paleolithic." *Préhistoire Européenne* 9:31–48.
1999 "The Evolution of Western Crimean Mousterian Industry," in *Central and Eastern Europe from 50,000–30,000 B.P.* (abstracts), G. A. Wagner, ed., pp. 53–54. Neanderthal Museum, Düsseldorf.

Chernich, A. P.
1987 *Mnogosloynaya paleoliticheskaya stoyanka Molodova V*. Nauka, Moscow.

Demidenko, J., and V. Usik
1991 "On the Levallois Technique in the Upper Paleolithic," in *XII Congrès UISPP, Aurignacien en Europe et au Proche Orient*, L. Banesz and J. K. Kozlowski, eds., pp. 239–242. SAV, Bratislava.

Derevianko, A. P., V. T. Petrin, E. P. Rybin, and I. M. Chalkov
1998 *Paleoliticheskiye kompleksy stratifitsirovannoy chasti stoyanki Kara Bom*. The Institute of Archaeology and Ethnology Press, Novosibirsk.

d'Errico, F., and V. Laroulandie
1999 "Szeletian Worked Bones From Buran Kaya III site," in *Central and Eastern Europe from 50,000–30,000 B.P.* (abstracts), G. A. Wagner, ed., pp. 57–58. Neanderthal Museum, Düsseldorf.

Ginter, B., J. K. Kozlowski, H. Laville, N. Sirakov, and R. E. M. Hedges
1996 "Transition in the Balkans: News from the Temnata Cave, Bulgaria," in *The Last Neandertals, The First Anatomically Modern Humans*, E. Carbonell and M. Vaquero, eds., pp. 169–200. Universitat Rovira i Virgili, Tarragona.

Gladilin, V. N.
1989 "The Korolevo Paleolithic Site." *Anthropologie* 27(2–3):93–103.

Gladilin, V. N., and J. Demidenko
1989 "Upper Paleolithic Stone Tool Complexes from Korolevo." *Anthropologie* 27(2–3):143–178.

Grigorieva, G. V.
1983 "Korpatch—un gisement stratifié du Paléolithique supérieur en Moldavie." *L'Anthropologie* 87(2):212–232.

Kaminska, L.
1995 "La retouche plate paléolithique en Slovaquie orientale." *Paléo* supplement 1:79–82.

Ketraru, N. A.
1973 *Pamiatniki epokh paleolita i mezolita Moldavii*. Edited by N. K. Anisiutkin and G. V. Grigorieva. Shtiintsa, Kishinev.

Kozlowski, J. K.
1964 *Paleolit na Gornym Slasku*. Ossolineum, Wroclaw.
1988 "The Transition from the Middle to the Upper Paleolithic in Central Europe and the Balkans," in *The Early Upper Palaeolithic*, J. F. Hoffecker and C. A. Wolf, eds., pp. 193–236. British Archaeological Reports International Series 437, Oxford.
1990 "Certains aspects techno-morphologiques des pointes foliacées de la fin du paléolithique moyen et du debut du Paléolithique supérieur," in *Paléolithique moyen récent et Paléolithique supérieur ancien en Europe*, C. Farizy, ed., pp. 125–133. Mémoires du Musée de Préhistoire de l'Ile de France no. 3, Nemours.

Kozlowski, J. K., and S. K. Kozlowski
1996 *Le Paléolithique en Pologne*. Millon, Grenoble.

Marks, A. E.
1993 "The Early Upper Palaeolithic: The View From the Levant," in *Before Lascaux: The Complex Record of the Early Upper Palaeolithic*, H. Knecht, A. Pike-Tay, and R. White, eds., pp. 5–22. CRC Press, Boca Raton.
1998 "A New Middle to Upper Palaeolithic 'Transitional' Assemblage from Buran Kaya III level C: A Preliminary Report," in *Préhistoire d'Anatolie —*

génèse de deux mondes, M. Otte, ed., pp. 353–366. Etudes et Recherches Archéologique de l'Université de Liège 85, Liège.

Marks, A. E., and C. R. Ferring
1988 "The Early Upper Palaeolithic of the Levant," in *The Early Upper Palaeolithic Evidence from Europe and the Near East*, J. F. Hoffecker, and C. A. Wolf, eds., pp. 43–72. British Archaeological Reports International Series 437, Oxford.

Marks, A. E., and K. Monigal
in press "The Middle Paleolithic-Upper Paleolithic Interface at Buran Kaya III, Eastern Crimea," in *Central and Eastern Europe from 50,000–30,000 B.P.*, pp. 55–56. Neanderthal Museum, Düsseldorf.

Matioukhin, A. E.
1990 "Les formes bifaciales d'ateliers et les stations-ateliers," in *Feuilles en Pierre—Les industries à pointes foliacées du Paléolithique supérieur européen*, J. K. Kozlowski, ed., pp. 141–162. Etudes et Recherches Archéologiques de l'Université de Liège 42, Liège.

Oliva, M.
1984 "Le Bohunicien, un nouveau groupe culturel en Moravie: quelques aspects psycho-technologiques du développement des industries paléolithiques." *L'Anthropologie* 88(2):209–220.
1995 "Le Szélétien en Tchécoslovaquie: industries et repartition geographique." *Paléo* supplement 1:83–90.

Otte, M.
1985 "Les industries à pointes foliacées et à pointes pedoncuées dans le Nord-Ouest européen. Artefacts 2." *Éditions du Centre d'études et de documentation archéologiques*, Viroinval.

Otte, M., I. Lopez-Bayon, P. Noiret, I. Borziac, and V. Chirica
1996 "Recherches sur le Paléolithique supérieur de la Moldavie." *Anthropologie et Préhistoire* 107:45–80.

Praslov, N. D., and A. N. Rogatchev
1982 *Paleolit kostienkovsko-borchevskogo rayona na Donu*. Nauka, Leningrad.

Ringer, A.
1983 "Babonyen, eine mittelpaläolithische Blattwerkzeugindustrie in Nordostungarn." *Dissertationes Archaeologicae* Ser. 2, no. 11.
1990 "Le Szélétien dans les Bükk en Hongrie. Chronologie, origine et transition vers le Paléolithique supérieur," in *Paléolithique moyen récent et Paléolithique supérieur ancien en Europe*, C. Farizy, ed., pp. 107–109. Mémoires du Musée de l'Ile de France no. 3, Nemours.

Ringer, A., L. Kordos, L., and E. Krolopp
1995 "Le complexe Babonyen-Szélétien en Hongrie du Nord-Est dans son cadre chronologique et environmental." *Paléo* supplément 1:27–30.

Schmider, B.
1995 "Le Protosolutréen d'Arcy-sur-Cure." *Paléo* supplément 1:174–184.

Siman, K.
1990 "Considerations on the Szeletian Unity," in *Feuilles de Pierre*, J. K. Kozlowski, ed., pp. 189–198. Etudes et Recherches Archéologiques de l'Université de Liège 42, Liège.
1995 "La grotte Szeleta et le Szeletien." *Paléo* supplément 1:37–44.

Siman, K., and Svoboda, J.
1989 "The Middle–Upper Paleolithic Transition in Southeast Central Europe." *Journal of World Prehistory* 3(3):283–322.

Svoboda, J.,
1987 Stránska skála, Bohunicky typ v brnynské kotliny, Studie Moravskeho Muzea *SAV* 14/1. Academia, Prague.
1988 "Early Upper Paleolithic industries in Moravia: A Review of Recent Evidence," in *L'Homme de Neanderthal. Vol. 8 La Mutation*, M. Otte, ed., pp. 169–192. Etudes et Recherches Archeologiques de l'Université de Liège 35, Liege.
1994 *Paleolit Moravy a Slezska*. Institute of Archaeology, Brno.

Svoboda, J., and P. Skrdla
1996 "Bohunician technology," in *The Definition and Interpretation of Levallois Technology*, H. Dibble and O. Bar-Yosef, eds., pp. 432–438. Prehistory Press, Madison.

Tuffreau, A.
1983 "Les industries lithiques à debitage laminaire du paléolithique moyen de la France septentrionale." *Studia Praehistorica Belgica*, 3:30–39.

Ulrix-Closset, B.
1995 "Le Mousterien récent à pointes foliacées en Belgique." *Paléo* supplément 1:201–206.

Usik, V.
1989 "Korolevo—Transition from Lower to the Upper Paleolithic According to the Reconstruction Data." *Anthropologie* 27(2–3):179–212.

Valoch, K.
1966 "Die altertumlichen Blattspitzenindustrien von Jezerany (Südmähren)." *Casopis Moravského Musea, Sc. soc., Brno* 58:5–60.
1990 "Le Szeletien en Moravie," in *Feuilles de Pierre*, J. K. Kozlowski, ed., pp. 213–221. Etudes et Recherches Archéologiques de l'Université de Liège 42, Liège.
1993 "Vedrovice V, eine Siedlung des Szeletiens in Südmähren." *Quartar* 43/44:7–92.

Weber, M.
1990 "Some Remarks on Transportation Ways Represented in the Inventory Ranis 2 in the Cave Ilsenhöhle, Ranis," in *Feuilles de Pierre*, J. K. Kozlowski, ed., pp. 235–238. Etudes et Recherches Archeologiques de l'Université de Liège 42, Liège.

Yanievich, A. A., V. N. Stepanchuk, and V. Cohen
1996 "Burana Kaya III and Skalistyi Rockshelter: Two New Dated Late Pleistocene Sites in the Crimea." *Préhistoire Européenne* 9:315–324.

CHAPTER 6

The Middle and Early Upper Paleolithic in Southwest Asia and Neighboring Regions

Ofer Bar-Yosef
Peabody Museum, Harvard University

INTRODUCTION

The role of the Levantine Upper Pleistocene prehistoric entities and human fossils in interpreting the questions related to the origin of modern humans, and especially the emergence of Early Upper Paleolithic (EUP) cultural manifestations, has in recent years been at the center of lively debates. Disagreements concerning the classification of the Middle Paleolithic fossils continue to rage. No less debatable is what is sometimes known as the "capacity for modern culture," or in other words, whether the bearers of the Early Upper Paleolithic cultures, known as Cro-Magnons, were members of a behaviorally different human species or just a descendant population—unchanged in basic behavioral capabilities—of early *Homo sapiens*, for example, those from Skhul and Qafzeh. A separate argument is related to the nature of the transition; whether it was rapid and deserves the status of "revolution," or a long and gradual process. My position, as explained elsewhere (Bar-Yosef 1996a, 1998a, b), is that the process was rapid and therefore deserves the definition "revolution." It is expected that a revolution will be reflected archaeologically in economic shifts, cultural aspects (symbolic behavior such as mortuary practices, use of elements of body decoration and the like), site size, intensity of occupation, and settlement patterns.

In accordance with the basic aim of this symposium, I have tried to cover a wide geographic region primarily incorporating the Levant, for which more extensive data sets are available, and then, briefly, the neighboring regions of the Taurus-Zagros, the Nile Valley and Cyrenaica (fig. 1). As the number of dated Late Middle and Early Upper Paleolithic sites and assemblages in the Levant is larger than in Northeast Africa or the mountain ranges of the Taurus-Zagros, this first region is used as a temporary base-line for chronological correlations of prehistoric entities (fig. 2). For this purpose, TL, ESR, and ^{14}C determinations were employed (e.g., Bar-Yosef 1998a), while keeping in mind the potential errors caused by diagenesis and contamination of charcoal samples by relatively younger intrusions, uncertainties expressed recently in several cautionary notes (e.g., Millard and Pike 1999; Schwarcz and Rink 1998; Appendix A).

It is a common notion that the transition in the Levant from the Late Mousterian to the Earliest Upper Paleolithic demonstrates a rapid alteration in lithic knapping techniques, the slow appearance of bone industry and use of marine shells for body decoration, and changes in site distribution and intensity of occupation. This major cultural shift or revolution is cautiously dated to around 47–45 ka B.P. (e.g., Bar-Yosef et al. 1996; Marks 1993 and see the details below) in the Levant, based on the combined TL and ^{14}C readings. However, it is not certain that this was the core area of the technological and cultural revolution (Bar-Yosef 1998a). One option is that it all began in East Africa (Ambrose 1998a; Klein 1999), and so examining a larger geographic picture at the crossroads of Eurasia and Africa is important, despite the unsatisfactory chronological resolution and patchy information (e.g., Bar-Yosef 1987; Marks 1992a; McBurney 1967, 1975; van Peer 1998; Vermeersch et al. 1998).

It should be stressed that the main body of information is derived from the sites, their distribution, lithic assemblages, and estimated occupational inten-

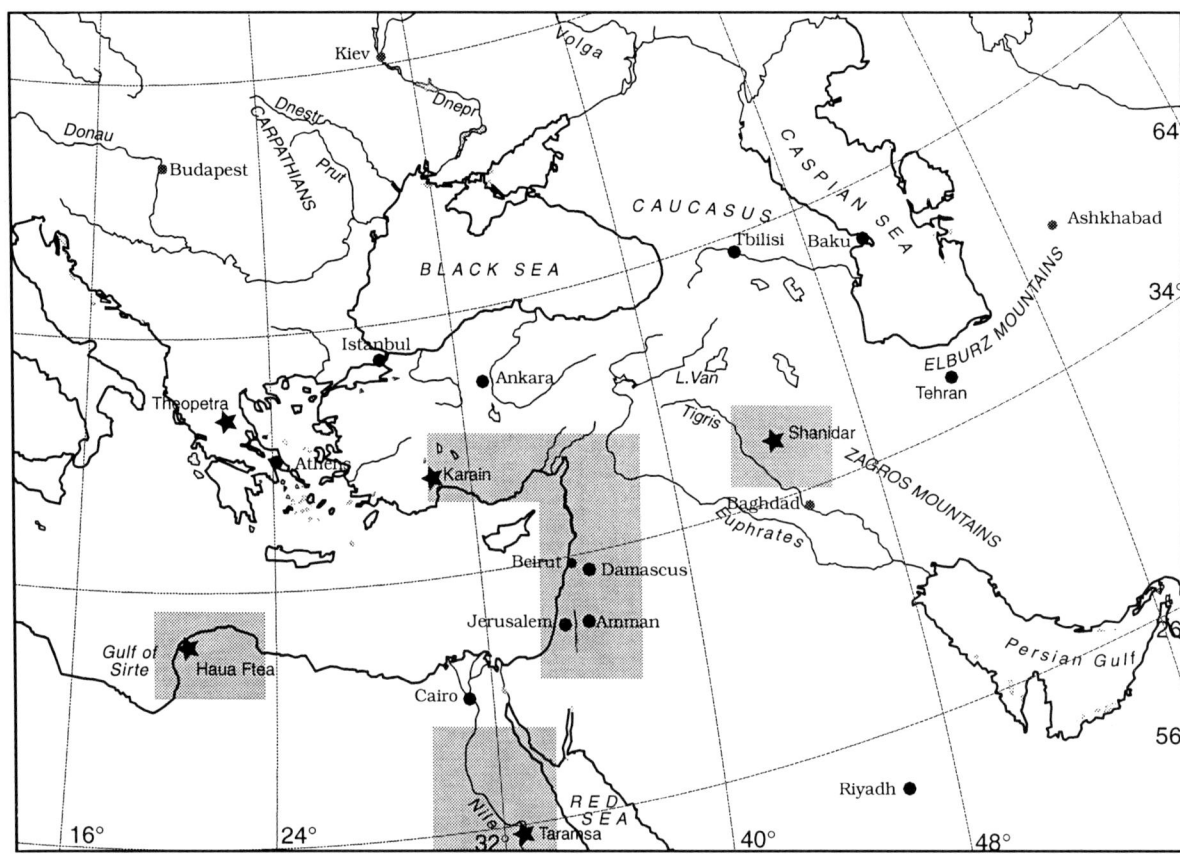

Figure 1. Map of the regions discussed in the text.

sity. The data for each of these aspects is based on site reports, which vary in quality. Notoriously, excavated sites or assemblages often do not constitute random samples. For example, palimpsests of occupational deposits result in averaging the variability within the lithic industries as well as the faunal assemblages. In addition, not all site reports provide the same types of data. However, the major differences between the Middle and the Early Upper Paleolithic assemblages in this vast region are already known and accepted by most scholars.

The study of this revolution or cultural transition began in Europe. Certain of the characteristics that became the common denominators in Europe are also noted in Western Asia and Northeast Africa. There are, to date, no bone and antler tools in the Late Mousterian assemblages, and these objects are rare even in EUP contexts. The same can be said concerning symbolic expressions, in which the EUP contexts of the Eastern Mediterranean are meager in comparison with the Franco-Cantabrian region, and are more in line with other neighboring regions such as North Africa and the Caucasus.

I concur with other scholars who consider the cluster of visible technological changes that took place across Eurasia from 47/45 ka through about 30 ka (and in Western Europe also the proliferation of symbolic expressions) as the cumulative signs of a major cultural transition. In an expressive term, the Middle to Upper Paleolithic transition was described as a "creative explosion" (Pfeiffer 1982). Most authors, but not all, would agree that this is a technological and cultural revolution, and that it can probably be attributed to the Cro-Magnons (e.g., Klein 1999 and references therein). Unfortunately, the paleobiological arguments to support this contention rely on rare EUP skeletal remains, which at best are dated to around 32/30–20 ka B.P.

THE PALEOCLIMATIC CONDITIONS

The Upper Pleistocene paleoclimatic sequence of Western Asia and Northeast Africa is based on studies of fluvial terraces, shorelines, lacustrine deposits and pollen cores in intermontane valleys, and speleothems

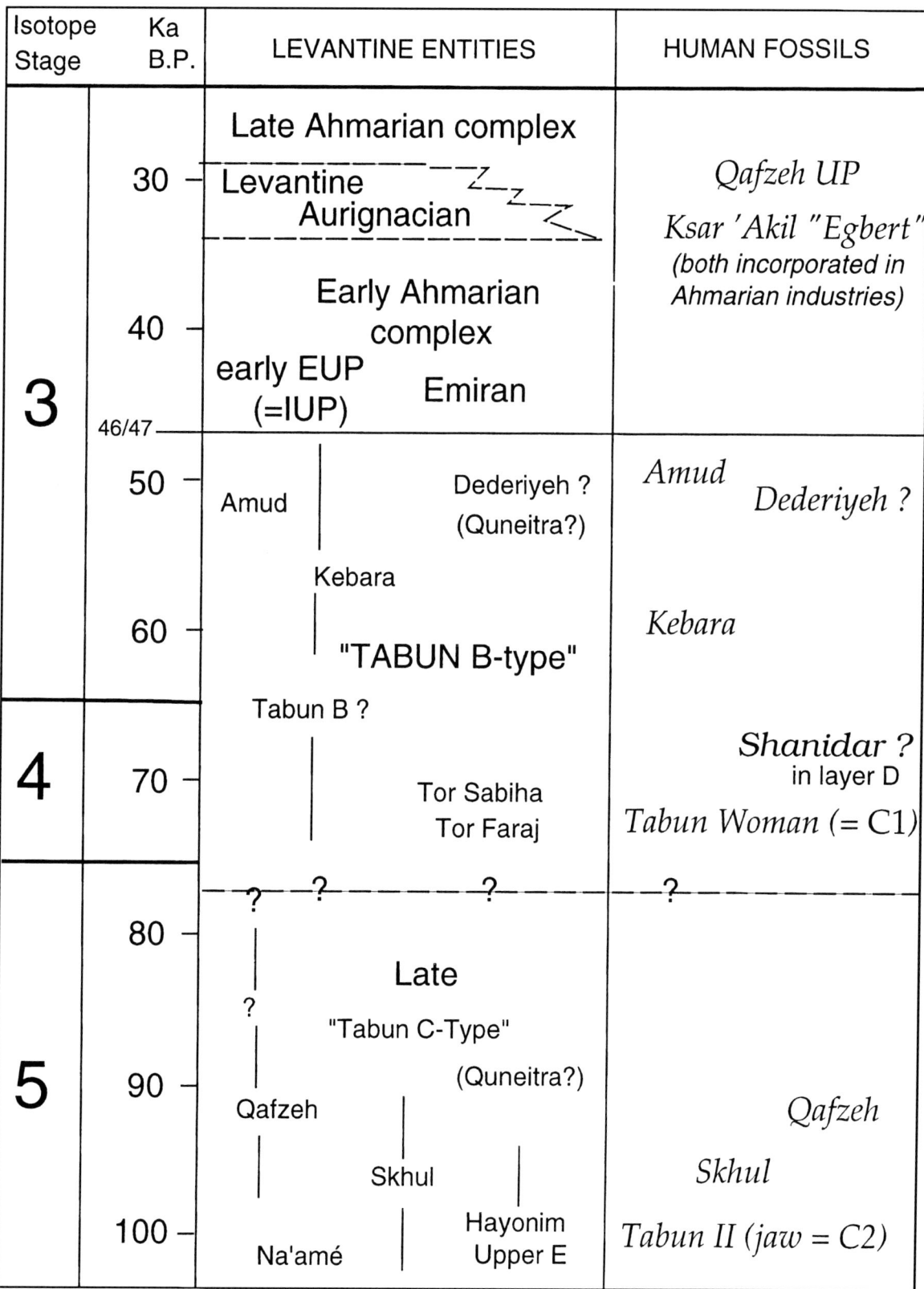

Figure 2. Generalized chronology of Middle and Upper Paleolithic sites in the Levant, based on TL, ESR, and uncalibrated radiocarbon measurements.

from karstic caves. The incorporation of data sets from both inland and coastal localities, together with marine and pollen cores, has been attempted more than once (e.g., Bar-Yosef 1989a; El-Moslimany 1994; Farrand 1979; Goldberg 1986; Henry 1986, 1995; Horowitz 1979, 1992; McBurney 1967, 1975; Paulissen et al. 1985; Sanlaville 1992; Tchernov 1997; van Zeist and Bottema 1991; Weinstein-Evron 1983, 1990; Wendorf et al. 1993). Interpretation of the evidence from the eastern Mediterranean, which lies over several atmospheric regimes, is not simple, and a couple of examples demonstrate this point.

The correlation between marine and terrestrial radiocarbon dated pollen cores of the Terminal Pleistocene and Holocene has recently been reviewed (Rossignol-Strick 1995, 1997). In her critical treatment, the researcher demonstrated that in several lakes, the effects of hard water on the radiometric readings caused major chronological discrepancies, which distorted the paleo-climatic interpretation. Thus, the established marine pollen zones (e.g., the Chenopodiaceae phase, which designates the Younger Dryas—a cold and dry period during the Terminal Pleistocene—and the Pistacia phase, which heralds the early Holocene in the terrestrial sequences), are chronologically misplaced.

In addition, correlating the detailed climatic record of the ice cores with the terrestrial sequence in the Near East is ambiguous, at least in part, as is demonstrated by the dating of the Younger Dryas. According to the ice cores, the Younger Dryas lasted 1300±70 years, from 12,900 to 11,600 years ago (Alley et al. 1993; Mayewski et al. 1996), while in the varve sequence of Lake Van in eastern Turkey (Lemcke and Sturm 1997) this cold and dry period is longer by some 800 years.

In brief, the depositional evidence for Upper Pleistocene inland lakes, such as Lake Lisan, Lake Palmyra, Lake Feiran, and others, together with the high frequencies of arboreal pollen in the known cores from the Levant, and the faunal spectra from the same environments, indicate that the same vegetation belts that characterize the region today existed in the past. The differences from today's base line are primarily the spatial distribution of the forests and parklands, which covered a wider area during wetter periods and a narrower during the drier intervals, in addition to some changes in the associated species. Illustrative is the dominance of Tabor Oak (*Quercus ithaburensis*) in the firewood remains of Kebara Cave (Baruch et al. 1992), when compared with the current, wider distribution of Common Oak (*Q. calliprinos*). As the Tabor Oak favors summer rains, this may lend support to a proposal based on the study of a series of speleothems in Jerusalem (Frumkin et al. 1999), that the climatic conditions during the Last Glacial period were generally colder and wetter than today. Stage 4 and the Last Glacial Maximum (LGM—Oxygen Isotope Stage [OIS] 2) were, however, drier, and caused a major shrinkage in the surface of Lake Lisan in the Jordan Valley, which was partially re-established following an increase in precipitation during the Terminal Pleistocene.

Under every climatic circumstance, the mountain ranges along the Eastern Mediterranean coast and those immediately east of the Orontes-Jordan-Dead Sea Rift Valley enjoyed winter and more ephemeral summer precipitation. The southern movement of the climatic belts during the Last Glacial cycle made survival on the Anatolian plateau more difficult, but during stadial phases populations could expand inland from the mountain ranges and the coastal areas. Similar observations can be made concerning the Zagros and Caucasus regions.

In Northeast Africa, where the boundary between the Sahara Desert and the habitable areas (depressions such as Kharga oasis, Bir Tarfawi, the Nile Valley, or the Gebel Akhdar in Libya, which borders the Mediterranean Sea), was even more marked, cold and arid periods meant ephemeral or no human exploitation of the deserts. This was also true for the Upper Paleolithic population in the arid belt of Western Asia. The archaeological evidence clearly demonstrates that before the LGM, from about 45 ka to 23/22 ka, desertic areas were occupied, perhaps seasonally, only during wetter periods. This does not include some of the inland oases, where copious water was depleted but did not dry out. Only after the LGM could humans occupy the deserts under all climatic conditions (Bar-Yosef 1996a). While this observation has interesting implications for both the technological aspects of human cultures and past demographies, the subject is beyond the scope of this paper.

In spite of the above caveats, there is a need to correlate the chronology of the Oxygen Isotope curve and/or the chronology based on proxy paleoclimatic data with the known TL, ESR, and ^{14}C chronology of the prehistoric entities of the Upper Pleistocene. The overlap between TL, ESR, and radiocarbon chronologies requires further study. It is assumed that TL dates provide calendrical ages while radiocarbon readings must be calibrated. However, the current disagreement concerning the calibration of the radiocarbon dates in the 30–40 ka interval (Kitagawa and van der Plicht 1998 and van der Plicht 1999 *contra* van Andel 1998) is not easily resolved.

In order to establish some long distance correlations, we begin with the Last Interglacial, the climatic details of which are poorly known for the terrestrial ecosystems of the Eastern Mediterranean. However, it does seem that the malacological shoreline assemblages are characterized by a warmth-loving suite of West African species, among which *Strombus bubonius* is the best known. The reanalysis of available dates indicates that these species reached the Eastern Mediterranean only at OIS 5e (Bar-Yosef 1989a). Earlier penetrations of this fauna into the Western Mediterranean may have occurred during previous warm interglacials (Hearty 1986). The presence of this malacological assemblage dates the Enfean II shoreline (Sanlaville 1981) in Lebanon, above which Middle Paleolithic assemblages of "Tabun C-type" industries, such as at Ras el-Kelb, Bezez, and Na'amé, have been recorded (Copeland 1998a; Copeland and Moloney 1998).

A great impact on human occupations in temperate Europe has been attributed to the dry and cold conditions of OIS 4, which effectively marks the onset of full glacial conditions in Eurasia (e.g., Bar-Yosef 1988). In the Eastern Mediterranean this may have been a time of reduced precipitation, expressed in the temporary shrinking of inland lakes.

In the wadi terraces of the semi-arid and arid belts of the Levant, OIS 4 is marked by the accumulation of gravely units (Goldberg 1986) dated to 75–65 ka. In Nahal Besor, in the northern Negev (fig. 3), the site of Farah II (Gilead 1988; Gilead and Grigson 1984) is embedded in silts, which suggests a return to somewhat wetter and possibly colder conditions (early Stage 3?). ESR dates for this site are 49.1±4.1 ka for EU (early uptake) and 62.2±7 ka for LU (linear uptake), while a single TIMS Uranium Series reading suggests 76.4±1.5 ka (Schwarcz and Rink 1998). The same paleoclimatic trend is also indicated by the deposits that underlie Boker Tachtit (Goldberg 1983), where the earliest Upper Paleolithic assemblage of Level 1 is radiocarbon dated at 47±9 to 46.9±2.4 ka B.P. (for details see Appendix A and Marks 1983).

Caves, as exemplified in the detailed studies of several Levantine sites, cannot serve as a source for proxy paleoclimatic information (Goldberg and Bar-Yosef 1998). Their deposits accumulated due to biogenic activities and therefore do not directly reflect climatic fluctuations. This situation may have been different in the caves of the Taurus and Zagros Ranges. Karain Cave, as it contains interchanged travertine and colluvial deposits, may indicate past climatic fluctuations (Otte et al. 1995).

During the Early Upper Paleolithic, conditions seem to have been variable, as is also reflected in the course of OIS 3. Major fluctuations between cold and dry, and warm and wet, spanning short periods of approximately 1000–1500 years characterized this period. It seems that wetter conditions facilitated the more intensive human exploitation of the semi-arid and arid zones (northern and southern Sinai), where Upper Paleolithic sites are dated to around 35–29 ka B.P. (Phillips 1994).

THE CHRONOLOGY OF THE LEVANTINE ENTITIES

In recent years, the chronology of the Levantine Mousterian has been the subject of major controversies. It is sufficient to compare the chronological assignments proposed since the early days of research at Mt. Carmel with the more recent efforts, which incorporate radiometric techniques, to realize that the picture has changed rapidly during the last decade (Bar-Yosef 1989a, 1992, 1994, 1998a; Bar-Yosef and Goren 1980; Bar-Yosef et al. 1996; Farrand 1979, 1994; Grün and Stringer 1991; Grün et al. 1991; Howell 1959; Mercier et al. 1995; Schwarcz and Rink 1998; Tchernov 1981, 1994, 1998; Valladas et al. 1987; Valladas et al. 1988; Valladas et al. 1998 and references therein; Zeuner 1946). At the time of writing, it seems that the TL based chronology is sound (fig. 2; Appendix A) with the support of ESR readings, with the exception of the non-invasive gamma spectroscopy technique, which inherently produces inaccurate results (Millard and Pike 1999).

On the whole, the radiometric dates, together with the stratigraphic evidence, indicate that the Levantine Mousterian lasted approximately from 270/250 to 48/47 ka B.P. (fig. 2; Appendix A). Radiocarbon dates from Upper Paleolithic layers in caves or open-air sites suggest that the earliest contexts could be about 47/45 ka B.P. and thus are among the oldest of known EUP sequences in Eurasia.

THE HOMINIDS

Relevant to our discussion, although I do not wish to take a stand on the debatable issues, are the human fossils; their type, cultural attributes and capacity for so-called "modern prehistoric culture" (e.g., Arensburg

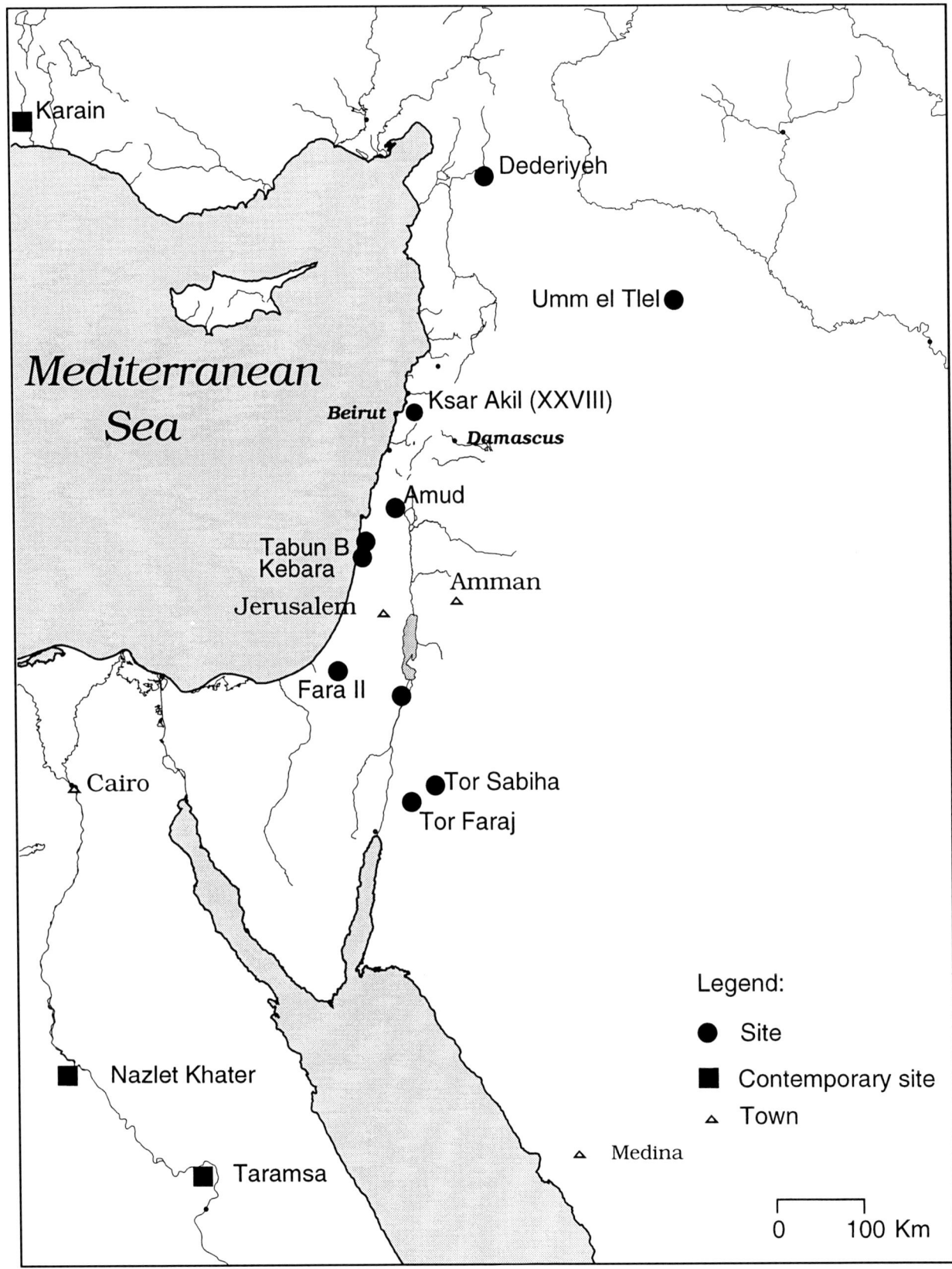

Figure 3. Map of Late Levantine Mousterian sites ("Tabun B-type").

and Belfer-Cohen 1998; Bar-Yosef 1998b; Goren-Inbar and Belfer-Cohen 1998; Howell 1998; Klein 1999; Meignen 1995, 1998; Stringer 1998). The Mousterian humans associated with "Tabun C-type" assemblages from Qafzeh and Skhul are dated to the period of the Last Interglacial and OIS 5d through 5a (fig. 2). It is noteworthy that the bearers of the "Tabun C-type" industry were present in the region at earlier times, as is indicated by the TL dates from Tabun C and Hayonim E, which are as old as 150/170 ka B.P. (Mercier et al. 1995; Schwarcz and Rink 1998; Valladas et al. 1998).

For clarity and brevity, it is worth mentioning the major remaining controversies, which are reminiscent of those of the past. Within a certain range of variability, one can find in the literature the two following, contradictory interpretations: (a) all Middle Paleolithic fossils in the coastal Levant were members of the same population (Arensburg and Belfer-Cohen 1998; McCown and Keith 1939; Wolpoff 1998); and (b) the fossils are the remains of two different populations, the Qafzeh-Skhul (or Modern Humans) one and the Western Asian Neandertals (Howell 1952, 1957, 1959, 1998; Howells 1976; Quam and Smith 1998; Rak 1998; Rak and Arensburg 1987; Tillier 1989, 1998, 1999; Trinkaus 1984, 1986, 1992; Trinkaus et al. 1998; Vandermeersch 1982, 1995). Some go further and claim that these populations represent two different species.

In particular cases scholars differ, and classify a particular fossil as a member of either of the two different populations. A current example of opposing interpretations was published in 1998. One (Stefan and Trinkaus 1998) suggests that the isolated jaw from Tabun (C2) has Neandertal affinities, while the other (Quam and Smith 1998; Rak 1998) proposes viewing it as representing a Modern Human. This disagreement echoes past debates concerning the stratigraphic position, classification, and time relationship between Tabun C1 (the woman) and C2.

By now, the comment of D. Garrod that she was not certain of the stratigraphic attribution of Tabun C1 (the Tabun woman) is well known (Garrod and Bate 1937:64). From a historical perspective, the reason Garrod suspected that Tabun C1 was actually a burial from layer B is resolved if earlier reports by her and by T. D. McCown are taken into account, together with the faunal observations of D. Bate (Bar-Yosef and Callander 1999). Garrod recognized the Neandertal characteristics of the woman when the skeleton was exposed at the top of layer C, where the reddish clayey deposit was inseparable from that of layer B. At the same time, she noticed the more modern features of the jaw (C2), which was found stratigraphically 0.90 meters below the woman, well within the ashy sediments typical of layer C. In her view, and according to McCown's original proposal (McCown 1934), this jaw closely resembled the Skhul group. In addition, according to Bate, and accepted by Garrod (Garrod and Bate 1937), there was a faunal break between layer C and layer B. This "faunal break" marked, according to Zeuner (1946, 1958), the transition from the drier Last Interglacial to the locally wetter Last Glacial conditions. Assuming that a Neandertal, as accepted in those days, could only be of Last Glacial age, Garrod thought it quite possible that the burial of the woman belonged to layer B. Her chronological interpretation was criticized vehemently by Vaufrey (1939), a position also adopted by R. Neuville (1951). In retrospect, the faunal collections published since the late 1930s demonstrate that a "faunal break" among the macromammals is not easy to trace; nevertheless, a major faunal turnover among the microvertebrate assemblages at the same general time has been identified by Tchernov (1984, 1994).

Human relics from the Levantine Upper Paleolithic are few. The oldest is probably the skull of "Egbert," a child 7–9 years old, which was found in layer XVII near the wall of Ksar 'Akil rockshelter, and is dated to about 35 ka B.P. (Bergman and Stringer 1989). The unpublished fragmentary crania of two adults uncovered in Qafzeh by R. Neuville are now attributed to about 30–28 ka B.P. on the basis of his as yet unpublished ^{14}C dates. All three specimens are considered modern humans.

THE STUDY OF LITHIC INDUSTRIES

The study of lithic industries is currently based on both in-depth recognition of the knapping techniques and the morphology of the secondarily trimmed pieces known as "retouched pieces" or tools. Traditionally, entities were defined only on the basis of the latter; currently, in accordance with the trend initiated by F. Bordes and J. Tixier, one examines the details of the knapping techniques, known in different schools of archaeology as "core reduction strategies" or *chaînes opératoires* (operational sequences). A brief treatment of this issue is required, as the last two decades have witnessed an increasing number of "archaeological cultures" characterized on the basis of their common (sometimes more than one) *chaîne opératoire* in both the Levant and the Nile Valley (Bar-Yosef and Meignen 1992; Boëda 1995; Hovers 1997; Marks 1983; Marks and Monigal 1995; Meignen 1995; Meignen and Bar-Yosef 1991; van Peer 1998).

The descriptive terminology for the study of *chaîne opératoire* is aimed at adequately identifying the phases along any technological sequence, but was adapted within French archaeology to the study of lithics (e.g., Boëda et al. 1990; Geneste 1990; Meignen 1995; Perlès 1992; Pigeot 1991; Schlanger 1996). It incorporates a detailed description of the various stages of production, from the initial procurement of raw material, through the shaping of the nodule into a core, and the systematic production of blanks (which involves intermittent reshaping of the detachment surface) to the secondary modification of selected blanks, their use, and discard.

The reconstruction of an individual core reduction sequence, when recognized as a repeated pattern within one or several assemblages, leads to the definition of a specific method such as "Levallois recurrent" or the different types of blade cores such as prismatic, uni-or bidirectional, narrow carinated, and the like (e.g., Bar-Yosef 1991; Baumler 1995; Boëda 1995; Dibble 1995; Inizan et al. 1992; Meignen 1995; Schlanger 1996).

In research into the history of technology, production technologies are considered within the social realm. The same is true for the prehistoric *chaînes opératoires* (operational sequences). Archaeologists are therefore challenged to decipher the setting in which a given technology was also a social production, but, unfortunately, the stones are silent. In addition, such a goal is more difficult to accomplish because, unlike the ethnographer, the archaeologist cannot observe the past operational sequences in action. It is has often been assumed that the reasons for adopting one particular manufacturing technique for stone artifacts over any other were related largely or entirely to constraints imposed by the available raw material, its mechanical and physical properties, and investments and energy expenditures in the course of procurement of nodules, in conjunction with the knowledge (*savoir faire*) of one or more knapping techniques. The possibility that the limitations imposed by the social system might be as, or more important than the natural constraints of a given environment, the functional needs, or the knowledge of the producer, are rarely discussed (but see Goren-Inbar and Belfer-Cohen 1998; Hovers 1998). That this aspect is of prime importance is shown by research among recent hunter-gatherers, for example, in Australia. These groups are commonly analogized with the foragers of Upper Paleolithic times, and their activities in the course of procurement of raw material, knapping, tool shaping and usage, carry symbolic meanings (e.g., Jones and White 1988). Unfortunately,

when one can only study the core reduction techniques and describe tool types, it is impossible to decipher the symbols conveyed by the social system from the mute stones. In reducing the interpretation of the artifacts solely to the measurable, such as the availability and nature of the raw material, the reconstructable reduction sequences, the incremental resharpening, and the microscopic microwear, we may lose the rare hints of past social systems, but we do retain insights into the *savoir faire* of the prehistoric artisans and their cultural templates.

Another limitation in the study of lithics is the number of percussion and pressure flaking techniques for obtaining blanks that could potentially have been applied to a given nodule. The constraints imposed by the physical properties of the various hard rocks are already reported in the literature (e.g., Andrefsky 1998), and in this domain—for most localities, and often within a relatively short distance (5–20 km)—the region under discussion is rich in good quality nodules of obsidian, flint (chert), and radiolarite. Therefore, this region can serve as a field laboratory for testing the relationship between *savoir faire*, cultural templates, and chronology. This notion is not always understood by prehistorians, perhaps particularly by those who work in regions where good raw material is rare. In addition, as mentioned above, paleoclimatic conditions were never so severe in terms of seasonal coverage by snow or sand dunes to prevent humans obtaining the required nodules.

Most researchers agree that the best method for tracing the different phases in core and blank exploitation is when blanks that have been refitted to cores are available. However, even without this time-consuming and expensive procedure, which is not always realizable, one can identify core reduction phases through detailed examination of blanks alone, as has been shown by recent studies (e.g., Hovers 1997, 1998; Marks and Monigal 1995; Meignen 1995, 1998).

As we try to get into the mind of the prehistoric knappers and visualize their basic goals, it seems that most informative are the initial phases of core reduction, when, following decortication (the removal of the natural cortex of the nodule), the first blanks are obtained by direct or indirect percussion. The series of usable blanks (determined by either their later subjection to secondary modification by retouch or through microwear analysis) reflect the initial aims of the artisan. The flaking of these blanks from the core was often interspersed with removals in order to maintain the shape (or volumetric concept) of the core and facilitate the flaking of additional desired products (for details see Meignen 1995; Schlanger 1996).

In classifying the operational sequences, especially in cases when refitting was not realized or was impossible to achieve, researchers attribute considerable importance to the study of the discarded cores. The scar pattern of an exhausted core, when compared with the primary post-decortication blanks, reflects the changes in the knapper's actions. For example, it may happen that a unidirectional recurrent Levallois core has been shifted to centripetal (also called "radial") exploitation. In the absence of contemporary observations, it is impossible to know whether this change in the organization of flake removals was implemented by the original knapper or by someone else. Identifying the individual knapper is a problem that is rarely addressed (e.g., Ploux 1991). Often, archaeologists assume that the same knapper used a particular core into its final, exhausted stage. One way of testing the option that more than one person was involved in the process of core reduction is when the evidence for the use of the core comes from refitted blanks that were collected from two or more spatially separated concentrations. When this kind of evidence is available, we may conclude either that a single person carried out spatially and temporally different knapping sessions, or that different knappers used the same core during its life history. In this context it is appropriate to raise the possibility that before cores became fully exhausted they were used in practice sessions, when one knapper taught another, especially for teaching younger members of the group. In addition, imitators, for example children, could have picked up the discarded cores and practiced without supervision.

In this paper, as in several previous ones, the rather schematic use of available studies of *chaîne opératoire* in Levantine Middle Paleolithic assemblages serves as the basis for clustering assemblages into industries (Bar-Yosef and Meignen 1992; Meignen 1995; Meignen and Bar-Yosef 1991). This is not to say that a certain amount of variability does not exist among these assemblages. A good example is the differences between units XII–IX and VIII–VII in Kebara (Meignen and Bar-Yosef 1991; Meignen et al. 1998), or the various layers at Qafzeh and Amud (e.g., Hovers 1997, 1998). However, the sources for the observable variability within each industry are not yet easily explained. Possible interpretations include individual differences in personal style and ability among flint knappers who were members of the same group; situations when the emergency need of fresh flakes/blades overtook systematic core reduction; a temporary shortage of raw material; or the training of children as future artisans using cores or thick flakes that adult knappers would consider to be unusable.

In sum, given the amount of intra-site and/or intra-assemblage variability, the identification of *chaîne opératoire* in my approach is based solely on the first series of blanks, and suggests assigning only a secondary value to the final shapes of the cores. The final forms of the cores could be regarded as simple cases of equifinality. For example, the proliferation of a centripetal pattern of scars on discarded cores in an assemblage where most larger and primary blanks indicate "recurrent Levallois" may simply mean that the cores were used for teaching or the expedient extraction of small flakes. Similar examples can be shown among Upper Paleolithic assemblages, where prismatic cores become in their final phase (sometimes after a change in the direction of blade removals which creates those types known as "crossed striking platforms" or "90 degrees") a source of small flakes or bladelets (e.g., Bar-Yosef and Belfer 1977).

In addition, we should not ignore the significance of the retouched pieces, traditionally called "tools." The operational sequences reveal the nature of the desired blanks that were selected for secondary retouch and used. Hence, the classification of retouched pieces is a critical aspect of archaeological investigation and, at least during the Upper Paleolithic, clearly demonstrates that while *chaînes opératoires* change very slowly through time, shifts in tool forms are much faster (e.g., Goring-Morris et al. 1998).

Chaîne opératoire is basically a system of technical skills learned by the user, and does not imply the use of language (although talking while knapping does help the student learner). On the basis of ethnographic observations, we assume that a certain *chaîne opératoire* employed in the manufacture of a product from one or more raw materials represents the technical tradition of a specific group of humans. The teaching of this skill, either through instructional sessions or by modeling the technique, ensures the passage of this knowledge from one generation to the next. Therefore, the time span during which a certain *chaîne opératoire* was practiced would indicate how long a particular technical tradition lasted. This information leads to the question of the biological and/or linguistic continuity of a given population in a particular region. Dates obtained by radiometric techniques may indicate this time depth and thus, by dating a stratigraphic sequence of archaeological assemblages we can investigate the history of a social group or close kin interaction sphere. Effectively, it is this kind of notion concerning *chaînes opératoires* and the forms of retouched types which has been employed by archaeologists studying the Upper Paleolithic to identify lithic and bone and antler industries with human populations and their spread over vast territories.

If the same approach does not apply to both Middle and Upper Paleolithic industries, then the study of *chaîne opératoire* is only of limited value in the analysis of a particular assemblage, as it does not supply the information required for inter-assemblage comparisons. Indeed, some researchers regard *chaîne opératoire* as a purely descriptive procedure and not as a valid measure that provides common cultural denominators for clustering assemblages into industries. Such an approach diminishes the value of this analytical tool. For those who justified the rejection of "guide fossils" as a tool for identifying industries or "cultures," it is perhaps neither pleasing nor appropriate to see *chaîne opératoire* as a replacement for the typologically-oriented *fossil directeur* (Sellet 1993).

THE LATE LEVANTINE MIDDLE PALEOLITHIC

The Definition of Lithic Industries

Employing the basic description of the lithic sequence of Tabun Cave as a rough scale for ordering the Middle Paleolithic industries in the Levant has been advocated by various scholars (e.g., Copeland 1975; Jelinek 1981, 1982a; Ronen 1979), and is an approach I support (Bar-Yosef 1989b, 1992, 1994, 1996b; Bar-Yosef and Meignen 1992).

Three major Middle Paleolithic entities are recognized today in the Levant (Bar-Yosef 1992, 1994, 1998b; Copeland 1975; and see fig. 2), but a cautious scholar will regard this as a temporary chrono-cultural scheme. As indicated by the current chronology, the early entities, namely the Abu Sifian or "Tabun D-type" and the Hummalian, as well as the early part of the "Tabun C-type," existed prior to the Last Interglacial, and are therefore beyond the scope of this paper.

The earliest entity discussed here is the "Tabun C-type" known today from the detailed study of Qafzeh (Boutié 1989; Hovers 1997). This industry is characterized by oval-rectangular blanks, and sometimes by large flakes, struck from Levallois cores after centripetal and/or bi-directional preparation. Triangular points appear in small numbers and in definite horizons, such as the top of Layer C in Tabun and layer XV in Qafzeh. Common tool types are side scrapers, mostly single sided, a few burins and borers, notches and denticulates (fig. 4). The Nahr Ibrahim technique (Solecki and Solecki 1970), originally named "truncated facetted" pieces (Schroeder 1969), is present, as it is in every Mousterian industry of the region. Similar assemblages include Skhul layer B (on the basis of the descriptions provided by D. Garrod in her publications), Ras el Kelb (Copeland 1998b), Na'amé (Fleisch 1970) as well as Ksar 'Akil XXVII and the upper layer E of Hayonim Cave (Meignen 1995, 1998). The presence of the later phase of this industry above the *Strombus* shoreline in Lebanon, along with the TL dates, supports a time range from OIS 5e through 5a (around 130–75 ka B.P. and see fig. 2).

The latest industry is the "Tabun B-type" currently known from Kebara (Bar-Yosef et al. 1992; Meignen 1995; Meignen and Bar-Yosef 1991), Amud (Hovers 1998; Hovers et al. 1991), Tor Faraj, and Tor Sabiha (Henry 1995, 1998). It is characterized by blanks removed mainly from unipolar convergent Levallois cores (fig. 5). Typical products are broad-based Levallois points, commonly with the typical *chapeau de gendarme* striking platform, and often having the special *concorde* tilted profile when viewed from the side. Blades do occur in this industry, and sometimes form up to 25% of the blanks. Similar "Tabun B-type" assemblages occur in Bezez B (Copeland 1975, 1983), Sefunim (Ronen 1984), which resembles unit V in Kebara, layer H at Erq el Ahmar (Neuville 1951), possibly in Dederiyeh (Akazawa et al. 1995), and in Ksar 'Akil XXVIII (Meignen 1995). The common tool types of this industry include side scrapers, Levallois points, rarely burins, some notches, and denticulates.

A later phase within this industry shows a tendency towards a slight increase in centripetal preparation exemplified in Kebara Units VIII–VII, and Ksar 'Akil XXVI (Meignen 1995; Meignen and Bar-Yosef 1991). The attribution of Quneitra to this phase is based on a single ESR date (Goren-Inbar 1990). If a technological transition to the Early Upper Paleolithic took place locally, it is difficult to argue that it emerged from centripetal core preparation, but it may have arisen from the convergent "recurrent Levallois," which was produced during the Latest Mousterian in several Levantine sites (see below for further discussion of this point). Earlier proposals to interpret the emergence of Upper Paleolithic laminar assemblages from the Early Mousterian ("Tabun D-type") are now untenable, as indicated by the TL dates of Tabun D and similar assemblages in Hayonim Cave (Valladas et al. 1998), and possibly at Ain Difla in Wadi Hassa (Clark et al. 1997).

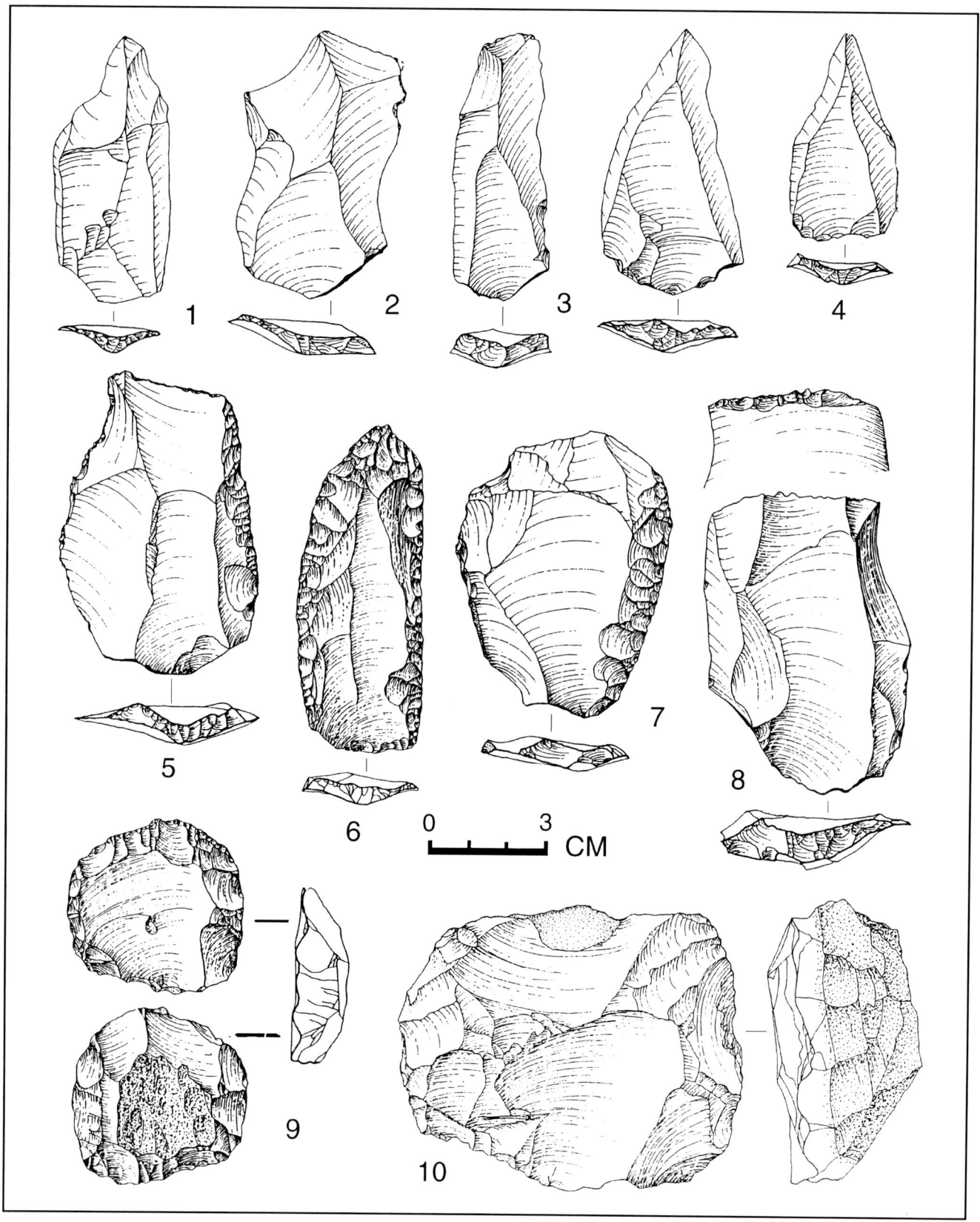

Figure 4. Middle Paleolithic artifacts from Qafzeh Cave (a "Tabun C-type" industry).

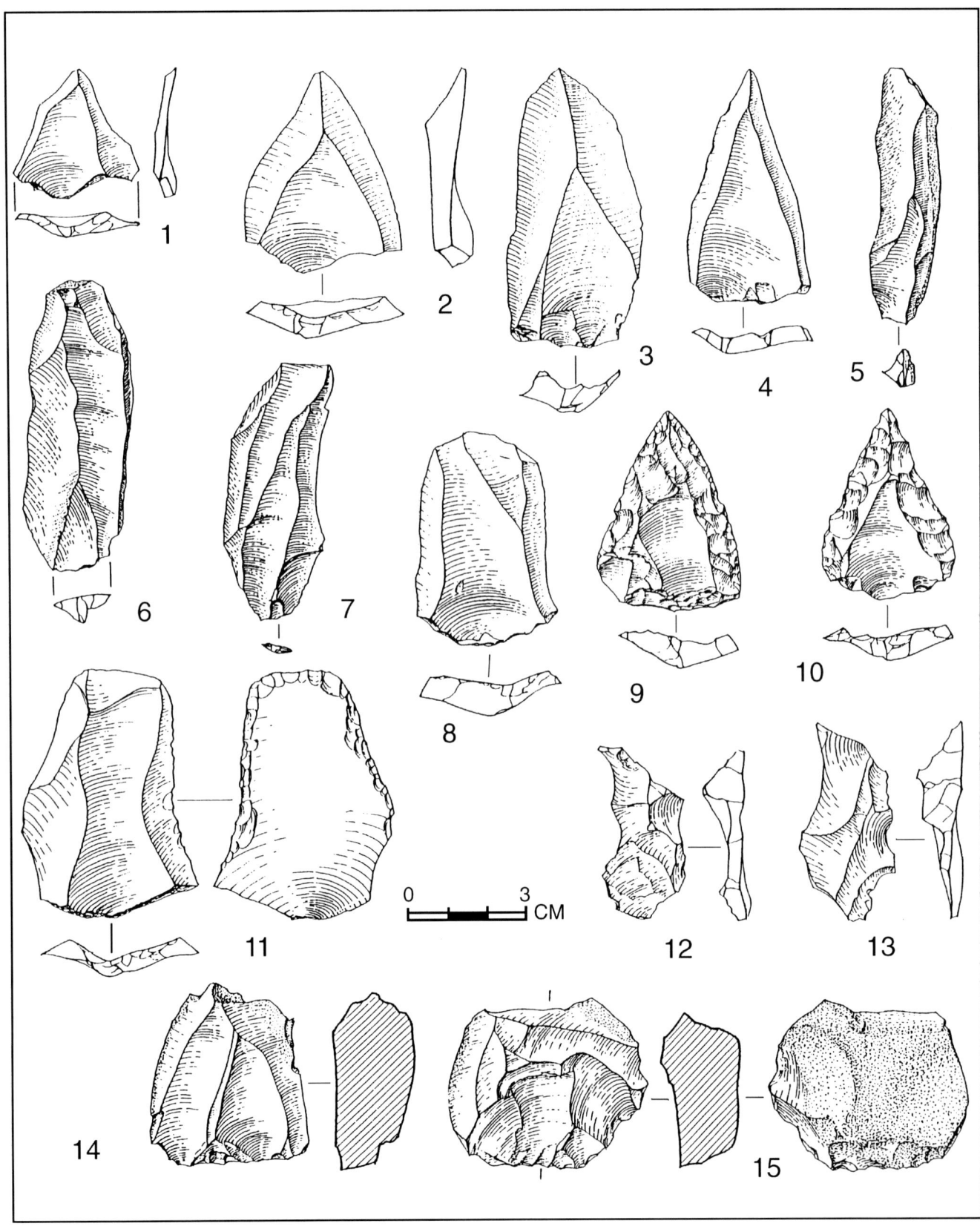

Figure 5. Middle Paleolithic artifacts from Kebara Cave (a "Tabun B-type" industry).

Mortuary Practices

The evidence for Middle Paleolithic burials—the use of red ochre, marine shells, and the incised flakes found in Quneitra (Goren-Inbar 1990; Marshack 1997) and Qafzeh (Hovers et al. 1996)—is often considered as reflecting symbolic behavior. Of the above, the Late Mousterian—the "Tabun B-type"—includes burials in the sites of Kebara, Amud, Tabun, and Dederiyeh (Akazawa et al. 1995; Bar-Yosef et al. 1992; Garrod and Bate 1937; Rak et al. 1994). The suggestion that Mousterian burials are simply depositional accidents (Gargett 1999) has already been refuted (Belfer-Cohen and Hovers 1992). Perhaps the most important observation to stress is that not one complete animal skeleton, even of a scavenger such as hyena, has been found in the excavations of the various cave sites. Moreover, the slow depositional rate, for example, a thickness of 1 m in 3,000 TL years in Kebara, and the same thickness in 10,000–15,000 TL years in Hayonim Cave (Bar-Yosef 1998a), indicates that for any large skeleton—whether animal or human—to have remained intact, it must have been placed inside a pit and covered. In addition, the intermittent occupations of humans and hyenas, evidenced by the presence of some hyena bones and coprolites in Kebara (e.g., Kolska Horwitz and Goldberg 1989), suggest that only well protected burials could have been preserved.

Finally, there are no demonstrable differences between the burials left by Middle Paleolithic, modern-looking hominids (Skhul and Qafzeh) and the local Mediterranean Neandertals in Tabun, Kebara, and Amud.

Subsistence

Our ideas about past subsistence strategies are derived from direct information such as plant and faunal remains, or indirectly from human bone chemistry (e.g., Ambrose 1998). Procurement and food preparation activities, such as hunting and butchery, or production and maintenance of equipment (e.g., wooden shafts, digging sticks), are also reflected in the forms and signs of utilization of stone tools. Reading these signs depends on replicatory experiments, the results of which are employed deciphering types of activities from the microscopic chips and polishes on the edges of artifacts (e.g., Beyries 1988; Boëda et al 1999; Meignen et al. 1998; Plisson and Beyries 1998; Shea 1989).

The bulk of direct evidence concerning the Middle Paleolithic diet still comes from the analyses of the preserved animal bones. Rare finds of plant remains, in sites such as Kebara and Douara Caves, indicate that we are missing information on this aspect of the daily menu. We assume that, as among other low to mid-latitude hunter-gatherers, Middle Paleolithic diets were based primarily on fruits, seeds, leaves, and some tubers. In Douara Cave, the fruits of *Celtis* sp. were found (Akazawa 1987). Legume seeds, mostly various species of *Vicia* sp., and lentils occur in all the Mousterian layers in Kebara, implying occupation of the cave in springtime, while *Pistacia* and acorn shells may indicate the presence of humans in the cave in the fall (Lev and Kislev 1993).

Animal remains from the various sites are summarized in table 1. However, this list includes only mammals of certain sizes and does not incorporate other elements of faunal food refuse such as reptiles and birds. Two other limitations are the grouping of bone assemblages by site and the reliance on NISP, which reduces the conclusions that can be drawn from this table.

A preliminary study of the fauna from layer E-Upper at Hayonim Cave, which chronologically precedes the Mousterian at Qafzeh, demonstrates the importance of small game such as large reptiles, birds, and hares, which form 5–19% of the total NISP (Stiner and Tchernov 1998). The small prey species, in evolutionary perspective, is considered to reflect a division of labor within a group of prehistoric foragers similar to that observed among modern groups. However, little is yet known about the role of the small–large game dichotomy from sites dated to the Late Mousterian.

The rich faunal assemblages from Kebara Cave was analyzed by Speth (Speth in Bar-Yosef et al. 1992; Speth and Tchernov 1998), who concluded that most ungulates at Kebara, including the large-bodied and dangerous species such as aurochs or wild boar, were hunted and not scavenged. Similar conclusions, concerning positive evidence for hunting, were reached in the study of the animal bones from Umm el Tlel, where the main large-bodied species were wild camels and horses (Boëda et al. 1998).

A controversial, although indirect source of information concerning hunting is culled from a major disagreement concerning the Levallois points, which were an important component of the "Tabun B-type" industry. Experimental and microscopic examinations are used to test rival hypotheses. Plisson and Beyries (1998) concluded from their investigations that the Levallois points in Kebara and Umm el Tlel were multifunctional and bear evidence for meat cutting, piercing and wood working. However, Shea (1988, 1995, 1998) suggests that the design of the Levallois points and the presence of impact fractures imply that they

TABLE 1. **Frequencies of large, medium, and small mammals from Mousterian and**

	Bos sp.	Alcelaphus	Gazelle	Capra sp.	Red deer	Fallow deer	Roe deer
Hayonim layer E upper	8		45		13	27	5
Tabun C	24.3	-	32.8	3.8	4.2	9.0	-
Skhul	89.4	+	+	+	+	+	0.2
Qafzeh XVII–XXII	20.0	-	21.8	8.2	16.4	12.7	-
Qafzeh XV–XII	16.8	-	3.8	13.6	36.4	5.0	-
Qafzeh V–XI	21.3	2.7	14.8	9.2	23.2	10.2	-
Tabun B	2.3	-	12.6	1.6	1.0	77.2	0.1
Tabun Chimney	-	-	0.4	-	0.4	98.5	-
Ras el-Kelb	11.8	0.5	4.2	3.6	0.7	64.3	1.0
Bezez B	2.8	-	22.5	0.7	0.7	46.6	-
Ksar 'Akil 29-26	19.8	-	0.5	4.7	0.3	73.1	1.5
Ksar 'Akil 36-30	2.7	-	2.9	20.6	-	70.7	3.1
Kebara Mousterian	2.0	+	62.0	1.0	4.0	28.0	+
Farah II	24.0	31.3	0.8	0.8			
Douara	-	0.4	24.0	29.8	-	-	-
Shanidar 10-8	+	-	+	98.0	+	-	1.0
Shanidar 8-7	-	-	-	99.0	0.5	-	-
Shanidar 7-	-	-	-	98.0	1.0	-	-
Upper Paleolithic sites							
Ksar 'Akil 25-19	5.0	-	2.0	29.0	-	56.0	4.0
Ksar 'Akil 18-10	2.0	+	4.0	22.0	-	49.0	23.0
Kebara UP	1.0	-	62.0	1.0	1.0	28.0	1.0
Hayonim D	+	1.0	89.0	2.0	2.0	5.0	1.0
El-Wad E	10.7	1.6	13.5	0.9	6.6	63.0	0.2
El-Wad D	6.9	1.7	56.3	1.8	4.2	24.1	0.2
Kebara E	11.4	5.4	21.1	-	4.9	48.8	3.0
Kebara D	11.2	3.3	20.9		3.3	58.5	1.4
Rakefet Aurignacian	5.2	-	64.4	-	7.8	18.4	0.3

After Hooijer 1961; Bouchud 1974; Davis 1977; Evins 1982; Garrard 1982, 1983; Payne 1983; Stiner and Tchernov 1998;

were made to serve as projectiles. The recent discovery of a broken point embedded in the cervical vertebra of a wild ass in Umm el Tlel, in the el-Kowm basin (Boëda et al. 1999) demonstrates that at least some of the points were originally made as hunting devices but were also, as with Neolithic arrowheads (Moss 1983), used in butchery activities.

Settlement Patterns

Studies of Mousterian (and for that matter EUP) settlement patterns, or degrees of mobility, take into account site size and intensity, and the nature of the occupation, as well as information concerning the exploitation of food resources and raw materials. Models for prehistoric mobility are drawn from the ethnographic records, which display great diversity (Kelly 1995). Procurement strategies were probably mixed, as subsistence depended on scheduling the exploitation of resources as well as division of labor. The accessibility, predictability, and reliability of dispersed animals and seasonal plants could fluctuate yearly, especially in the eastern Mediterranean, where the distribution of the rains depended on variable storm tracks. Winter storms could sometimes arrive via North Africa, making the southern Levant lusher, while in other years the rain mostly watered the northern Levant. If summer rains are included in the formula proposed for the Upper Pleistocene, areas in the coastal ranges and immediately east of the Levantine Rift Valley were covered by woodland. Under such circum-

Upper Paleolithic sites in Southwest Asia (excluding carnivores)

Wild boar	Hippo.	Equid	Rhino	*Camellus* sp.	Hyrax	Hare	Hedgehog/ Porcupine	n=
2								85
5.5	3.8	3.2	4.7	+	1.3	0.5	1.0	376
+	0.5	9.7	+	-	+		+	(668)
1.8	-	17.3	1.8	-	-	-	-	110
5.0	-	2.9	1.2	0.3	-	-	-	338
14.8	-	3.7	-	-	-	-	-	108
0.2	-	2.4	-	-	0.2	-	-	1723
-	-	-	-	-	-	-	-	1461
8.0	-	+	2.4	-	+	-	-	994
1.4	-	-	-	-	-	-	-	142
+	-	-	+	-	+	-	-	2719
+	-	-	-	-	-	-	-	451
2.0	-	1.0	+	-	-	-	-	2098
0.8	38.0		4.0				147	
-	-	4.1	-	7.2	1.0	25.0	8.1	650
+	-	-	-	-	-	-	-	319
0.5	-	-	-	-	-	-	-	602
1.0	-	-	-	-	-	-	-	169

Upper Paleolithic sites

+	-	-	-	-				1049
+	-	-	-	-				1393
+	-	+	-	-				2098
+	-	+	-	-				1730
1.2	-	0.2	-	-	0.2	1.1	0.2	964
2.2	-	0.7	-		-	1.3	0.7	597
0.6	-	4.8	-					166
-	-	1.4	-	-				215
3.9	-	-	-	-				309

Speth and Tchernov 1998.

stances, we may expect to find archaeological markers for reduced mobility. An important measure of the latter is intensity of site occupation.

Measuring the intensity of occupation of a site in order to determine whether it was an ephemeral hunting/gathering camp or some sort of a base camp is often based on the lithic assemblages and the seasonal interpretation of faunal remains. In addition, one can cautiously employ the numbers of lithics and animal bones in relation to the volume of deposits, and the relative abundance of microvertebrates that accumulated by non-human agencies, especially in sites where the main agency for accumulations was biogenic (Bar-Yosef 1998a; Goldberg and Bar-Yosef 1998). For example, in the central area of Kebara Cave, where most hearths were located, one cubic meter based on TL dates accumulated over approximately 3,000 years and contained about 1,000 lithic pieces larger than 2 cm. Areas near the cave wall provided similar amounts of lithics (with a distinct increase in the numbers of cortical elements and cores), with ash but no hearths. Further evidence for the intensive human use of Kebara is the rare occurrence of small-sized rodents, harvested by Barn Owls occupying the cave when humans were absent. In comparison, at Hayonim in Layer E, the same volume was deposited over 10,000–15,000 TL years and yielded only 300 lithic pieces and large amounts of microvertebrates, supporting the notion of slow accumulation and the ephemeral use of the site by humans. The differences between the two sites, which are separated chronologically by at about 60,000 years, are also reflected in the exploitation of small, sessile reptiles such as tortoises (Stiner et al. 1999). Due to the current absence of Early Mousterian ("Tabun D-type") sites, which would be comparable to the intensity of occupation in Kebara, it is difficult to test the hypothesis that these differences reflect a change in human population size per territory from the Early to the Late Mousterian. Thus, it seems, during OIS 7 and 6, population densities were low and groups were highly mobile. In contrast, during the Late Mousterian, probably with the onset of the glacial conditions of OIS 4, a population increase due to influxes of people from the Anatolian plateau is expressed in the more intensive use of the cave sites, and led to some degree of resource depletion.

Other human ephemeral occupations in cave sites such as layers 12 and 13 in Sefunim Cave contain a small collection of artifacts that could represent a hunter's shelter (Ronen 1984). Further examples include layer H in Erq el Ahmar rockshelter (Neuville 1951). Low densities of artifacts, a few hearths, human burials, and huge assemblages of rodent bones in the lower layers at the entrance of Qafzeh Cave suggest a period when the site was used only occasionally for special activities (Bar-Yosef 1989b).

Open-air sites dated to the Last Glacial are few, and in most cases bones have not been preserved. Farah II in the northern Negev and Quneitra in the Golan Heights appear to have been hunting stations. In the first site, most of the artifacts were produced locally

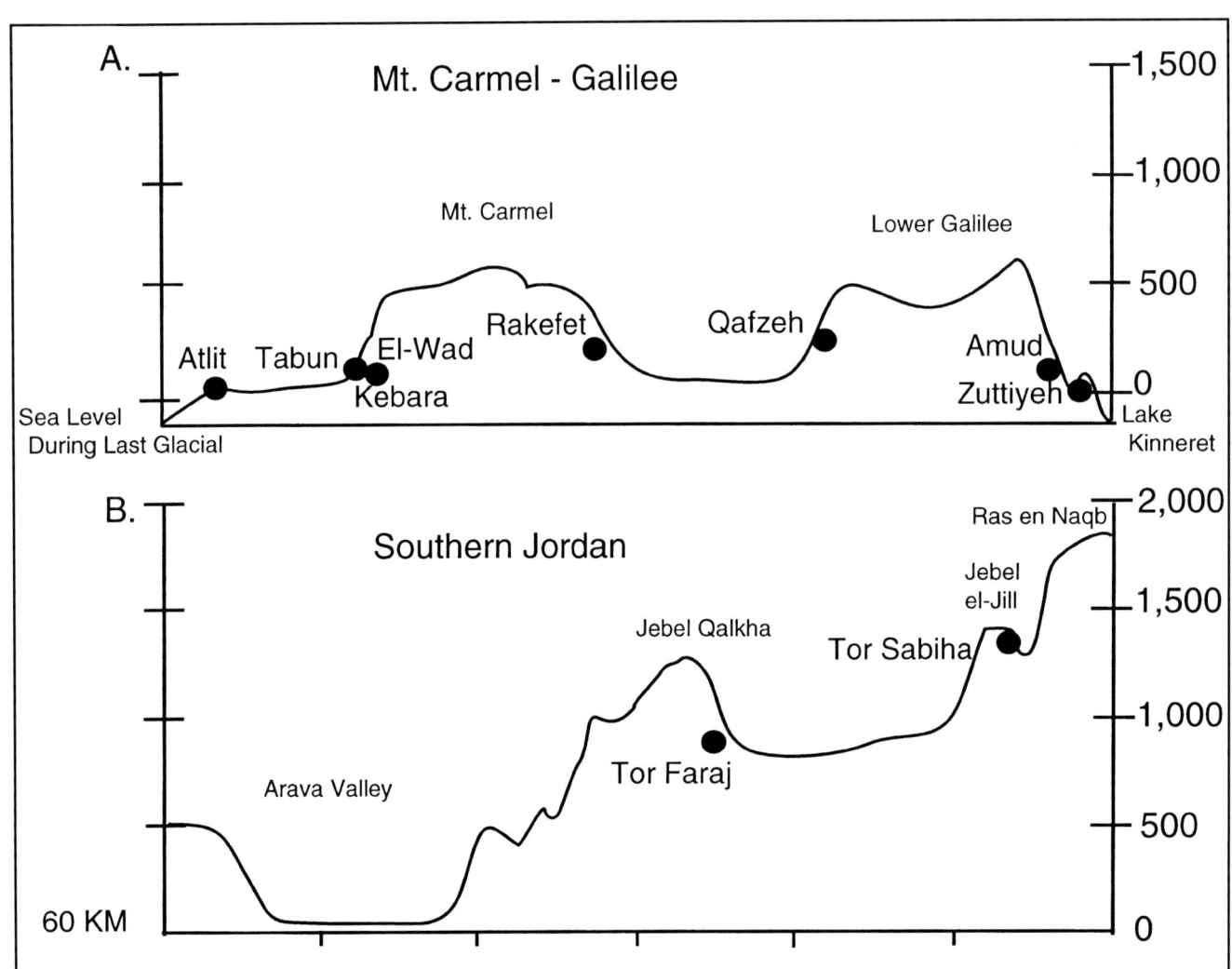

Figure 6. Middle Paleolithic settlement patterns: A. The Mt. Carmel/Galilee; B. Southern Jordan (model based on Henry 1995).

and many pieces were refitted to cores (Gilead 1988). In Quneitra, the raw material was brought in from a distance (Goren-Inbar 1990; Hovers 1990). Tirat Carmel, at the foot of Mt. Carmel was possibly a quarry site (Ronen 1974), but the lack of bones, due to poor preservation, does not allow further interpretation.

Seasonality, as mentioned above, is a major factor in figuring out mobility patterns. Through the study of tooth increments of gazelles, Lieberman (1993, 1998) was able to demonstrate that hunting in different sites took place during the summer, the winter, or all year round. Combining his observations with the microwear studies of Shea (1989, 1998), these two scholars interpret the differences between the Qafzeh and Skhul sites (Modern Humans) on one hand and the later Kebara and Tabun B (Neandertals) on the other as a reflection of two different mobility patterns. The Modern Humans, according to this interpretation, moved between summer and winter camps, while the Neandertals lingered all year round in the same site or its immediate environs (Lieberman and Shea 1994). Unfortunately, this study was limited to sites in Mt Carmel and the Galilee. Information gathered by Henry (1995, 1998) from the excavations of Tor Faraj and Tor Sabiha in the semi-arid region of southern Jordan demonstrates how "Tabun B-type" producers (local Neandertals?) moved seasonally between lowlands and highlands (fig 6). Within the stratified faunal assemblages at Kebara, J. D. Speth documented a shift in the occupation pattern of the cave (Meignen et al. 1998). In units IX–X, the animal remains are interpreted as the result of longer annual occupation, while in the upper units (VIII–VII) the use of the cave was probably limited to springtime. In this context, the presence of thicker Mousterian deposits in the cave-sites of the Mediterranean coastal belt and thinner ones in sites in the wadis descending to the Jordan Valley was noted by S. Binford (1968), who suggested that human groups moved across the countryside in a west-east direction, following the main wadi courses.

Finally, intra-site patterning is often examined in order to estimate the size of the social unit (Binford 1996). Information on hearth size, and the distribution of artifacts and bones is often sought after as a sound source. However, the situation in the Levantine caves, even in relatively well preserved contexts, is not easy to decipher. Small, round-oval hearths were uncovered in Qafzeh and Kebara. A large hearth, 5m in diameter, was reported from Douara Cave (Akazawa 1987). Hearth remains and ashes were recorded in Amud Cave (Hovers et al. 1991). However, it is almost impossible to identify the entire surface of "living floors" even in the best preserved cave deposits in the Levant.

Ashy deposits of Layer C in Tabun Cave (Garrod and Bate 1937; Jelinek 1981, 1982a, b) were interpreted as the results of brush fires, but have been shown through phytolith studies to be a series of overlapping hearths (Albert et al. 1999). Micromorphological evidence suggests that the main combustibles were different types of wood, and that the grass phytoliths were attached to the bark of this firewood (Albert et al. in press; Goldberg and Bar-Yosef 1998). Among the most common species brought into the cave were Common and Tabor oak (*Q. calliprinos* and *Q. ithaburensis*) (Baruch et al. 1992; Baruch personal communication).

In sum, Levantine Mousterian settlement patterns demonstrate the shifting exploitation of sites and territories during the Last Glacial, with higher mobility in the steppic and arid areas, and a more stable, centered pattern in the Mediterranean coastal ranges. On the whole, the number of sites and the intensity of occupation indicate a relative population increase during the later period around 60–48 ka B.P.

EARLY UPPER PALEOLITHIC ENTITIES IN THE LEVANT

Historically, the Early Upper Paleolithic (EUP) was first described on a stratigraphic basis in the excavations of el-Wad in Mt. Carmel (Garrod and Bate 1937) and in et-Tabban and Erq el-Ahmar in the Judean Desert (Neuville 1934, 1951; fig. 11). These earliest industries were then incorporated into a six-part subdivision of the Upper Paleolithic proposed by Neuville (1934), a scheme accepted by Garrod (1937), who originally preferred the common European terminology of a sequence of named entities.

From the early days it was obvious that the lithic assemblages contained both Middle and Upper Paleolithic elements (Garrod 1951–1952; Garrod and Bate 1937; Neuville 1934, 1951) such as Levallois points, side scrapers, blades, endscrapers, and burins. This admixture of technological and typological traits was interpreted as documenting cultural continuity (Copeland 1975).

Restoring her basic cultural approach, having re-studied the collections from Turville-Petre's excavations at Emireh cave in Wadi Amud, Garrod suggested labeling the earliest entity from el-Wad and Emireh caves as the "Emiran," the same culture as Neuville's Upper Paleolithic Phase I (Garrod 1955). It was only later that the combination of Middle and Upper Paleolithic traits of the lithic assemblages from these sites as well as from Ksar 'Akil led to the coining of the term "Transitional Industry," which has evolutionary connotations (Azoury 1986; Copeland 1975; Ohnuma 1988). This notion was reinforced when the site of Boker Tachtit in the Negev highlands was excavated and published (Marks 1983). The excavator suggested, on the basis of refitted cores and blanks from all four layers, that the lithic assemblages from Level 1 up through Level 4 represent the shift from the Middle Paleolithic technology to the blade-dominated one of the Upper Paleolithic.

Since then, the two terms—namely the Emiran and Transitional Industries—serve interchangeably in the various summaries of the Levantine Earliest Upper Paleolithic. Although the use of the second term implies *in situ* cultural transition, or in other words, that the Upper Paleolithic of the Levant emerged from a local Middle Paleolithic assemblage, this is also the contention of those who employ the first term (e.g., Bar-Yosef and Belfer-Cohen 1988; Belfer-Cohen and Bar-Yosef 1999; Gilead 1991; Marks 1993).

Two recent excavations add much needed data to the study of this period. The site of Umm el Tlel in the el-Kowm basin (northeast Syria), provided three horizons of what the excavators called an "Industrie Intermédiaire," on top of a long Mousterian sequence (Boëda and Muhesen 1993; Bourguignon 1998). In a detailed analysis, following the example of Boker Tachtit, two of these EUP levels are also called Late Mousterian (*Moustérien tardif*) (Bourguignon 1996).

Recently, Kuhn and associates (Kuhn et al. 1999), in reporting their finds from two sites in the northern Levant (near Antalya, south-central Turkey), proposed naming the entire array of Early Upper Paleolithic assemblages as Initial Upper Paleolithic (IUP), a neutral term that does not carry the connotation of cultural evolution.

The image of the pan-Levantine IUP industries is currently rather complex, mainly due to the paucity of sites, chronological ambiguities, and the presence of particular local tool types, such as the chamfered blades and flakes in Wadi Antelias (Ksar 'Akil and Abri Antelias), or the Emireh points in the southern Levant (fig. 7). For clarity, the survey of the known lithic assemblages begins in the south, followed by a discussion of the dating issue.

The lowermost layers (XXV–XXIV) at Ksar 'Akil were rather poor in lithic artifacts, but are characterized by opposed platform cores with parallel sides, one of the attributes of a major change in volumetric concept (Ohnuma 1988; Ohnuma and Bergman 1990; fig. 8). In layers XXIII–XXI/XX, the triangular shape of the cores caused the production of convergently shaped blades and Levallois points. However, Ohnuma and Bergman (1990:202) note that "the Levallois points in levels XXIII–XXI/XX are far more numerous than Levallois cores probably because many of them were detached from prismatic cores during continuous production of blades."

This conclusion could not have been reached without the previously published report from Boker Tachtit (Marks 1983, 1993; Volkman 1983; fig. 9), in which the refitted cores clearly demonstrated the change in how the knappers conceived the volume of the nodule. The non-Levallois points in these assemblages are shaped by bi-directional removals as documented by the scars (the Y-pattern), and thus differ from the Late Mousterian typical Levallois points (and should perhaps be renamed Boker Points?). This raises the question of why the artisans continued with the production of points that are morphologically similar to the Levallois, when other blanks could be reshaped. The answer lies perhaps in the continued use of hafting methods that facilitated the production of thrusting spears at the time when the first bows or spear throwers (e.g., atlatl) were invented.

While the retouched pieces in Boker Tachtit Levels 1 and 2 include many Emireh points—the "guide fossil" type for Emireh Cave—Ksar 'Akil manufacturers preferred the chamfered blanks for which a side blow, based on the retouched end of the piece, formed a rounded edge that is assumed to have served as a scraper (Newcomer 1970:fig. 7). Interestingly, the EUP of Haua Fteah Cave in Cyrenaica, named the Dabban culture, is also rich in *chanfreins* (McBurney 1967). I will return to this point in the Discussion.

At the site of Umm el Tlel, layers IIBase and III2A are characterized by what is described as a *chaîne opératoire* that follows the Levallois concept (Bourguignon 1996; fig. 10). Many of the cores are volumetrically flat, and are the source of numerous blades, many of which resemble narrow and elongated Levallois points, with uni-directional scar patterns. These points and pointed blades, which (to judge from the drawings) grade into regular blades, are named Umm el Tlel points. While this proposal is of interest, it would be more appropriate, given the grading of formal points (elongated triangles) into real blades, to name the *chaîne opératoire* as the Umm el Tlel technique. The similarity between the typical Umm el Tlel cores and those produced by the convergent Levallois method is striking. However, considering the full operational sequence (*chaîne opératoire*), which ended by retouching many blanks into many typical Upper Paleolithic tool types, reminds one of the observation of L.

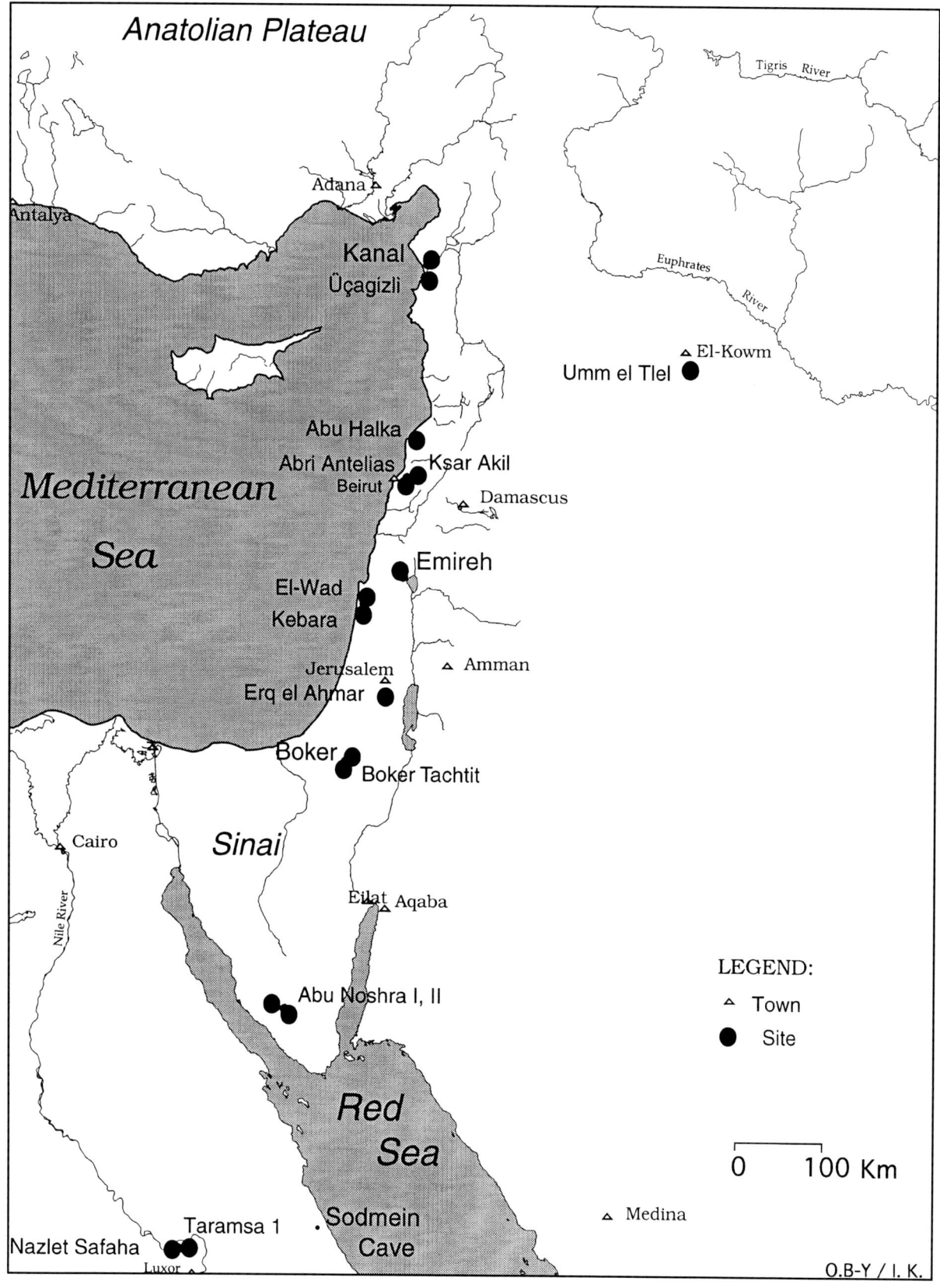

Figure 7. Map of the Levant with the earliest Upper Paleolithic sites.

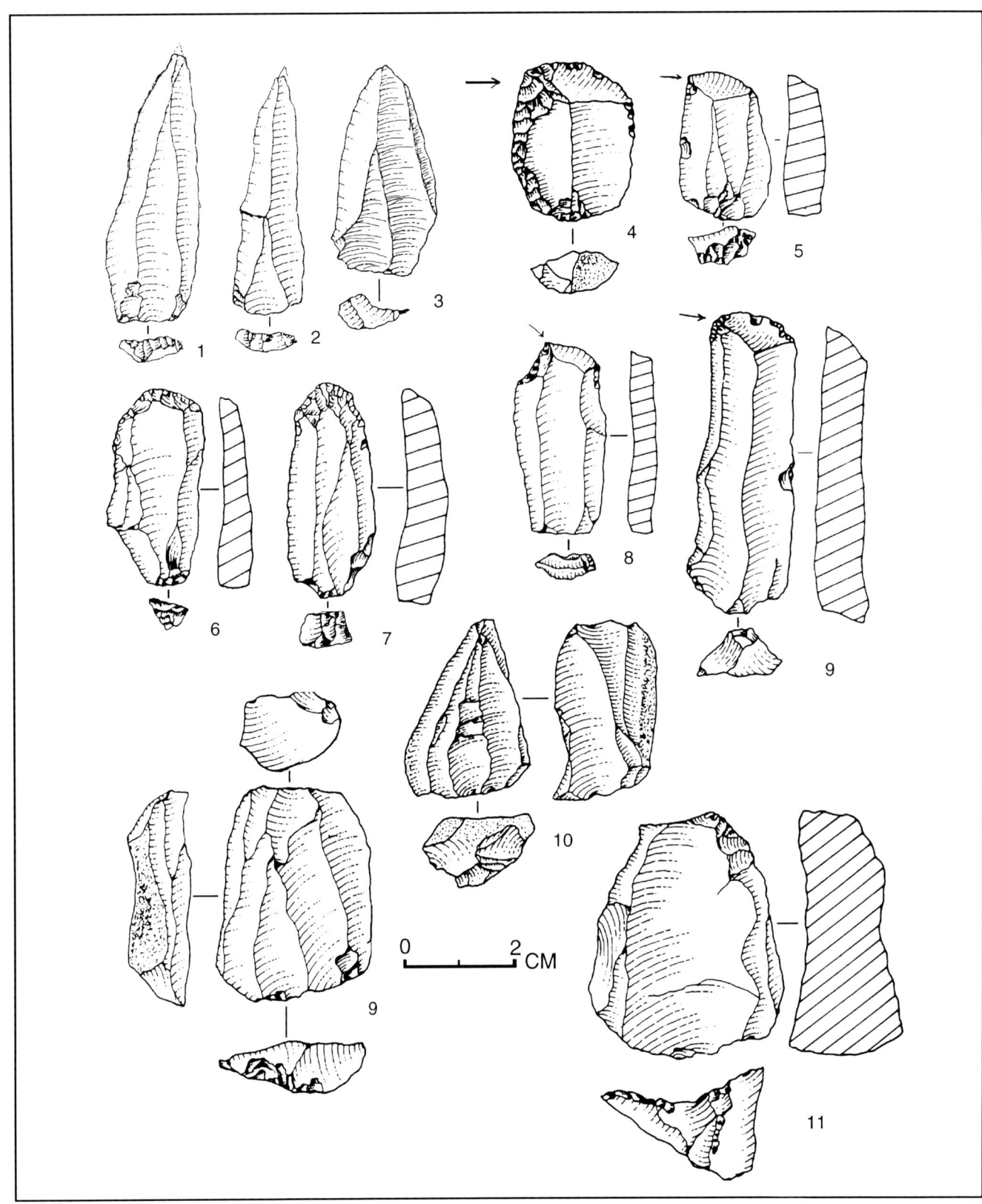

Figure 8. Early Upper Paleolithic artifacts from Ksar 'Akil and layers XXV–XXIV in Kebara (adapted from Azoury 1986): points (1–3), chamfered flakes and blades (*chanfreins*) (4, 5, 8, 9), endscrapers (6, 7), cores (10, 11).

Copeland concerning the Early Upper Paleolithic phase in Ksar 'Akil, which used to be called Ksar 'Akil Phase A:

> We are not dealing here with a mixture of Middle Paleolithic tools made by Middle Paleolithic technology, Upper Paleolithic tools made by Upper Paleolithic technology, but the characteristically Upper Paleolithic tool types are found on blanks made by a Middle Paleolithic tradition of flint knapping (direct percussion, on prepared cores, to produce Levallois blades or points). Thus, the transitional aspect occurs *on the same piece of flint* (Copeland 1975:337–339, italics in original).

Other products, in particular the retouched pieces, are definitely Upper Paleolithic, with numerous burins and end scrapers, as well as some Middle Paleolithic elements such as the Nahr Ibrahim technique, and notches and denticulates. An AMS date for III2A is 34,530±750 (GifA-93216) and a TL date 36±2.5 ka (GifA-93215).

Additional assemblages were uncovered in Üçagizli and Kanal Caves (Kuhn et al. 1999). The recent excavations in the first uncovered an assemblage, which, together with that previously excavated from Kanal, forms a blade-based industry, with faceted striking platforms and the presence of the so-called Umm el Tlel points with end scrapers, burins and retouched blades (Kuhn et al. 1999:fig 4:7). Noteworthy are the shell beads made of marine mollusks. Two AMS dates of 39,400±1,200 (AA-27994) and 38,900±1,100 (AA-27995) place the earliest assemblage from Üçagizli within the range of EUP industries (fig. 11).

Although the EUP assemblages are not rich in elements besides the lithic industries, it is worth noting one bone awl, found in layer XXIII in Ksar 'Akil (Newcomer, in Bergman 1987). In addition, over three hundred Mediterranean marine shells (small gastropods), some of which were intentionally perforated, were collected in layers XXIV–XIX (Altena 1962). Similar finds of shell beads were reported from Üçagizli (Kuhn et al. 1999). This means that the earliest Upper Paleolithic in the Levant incorporated one of the cultural components considered critical for characterizing modern behavior.

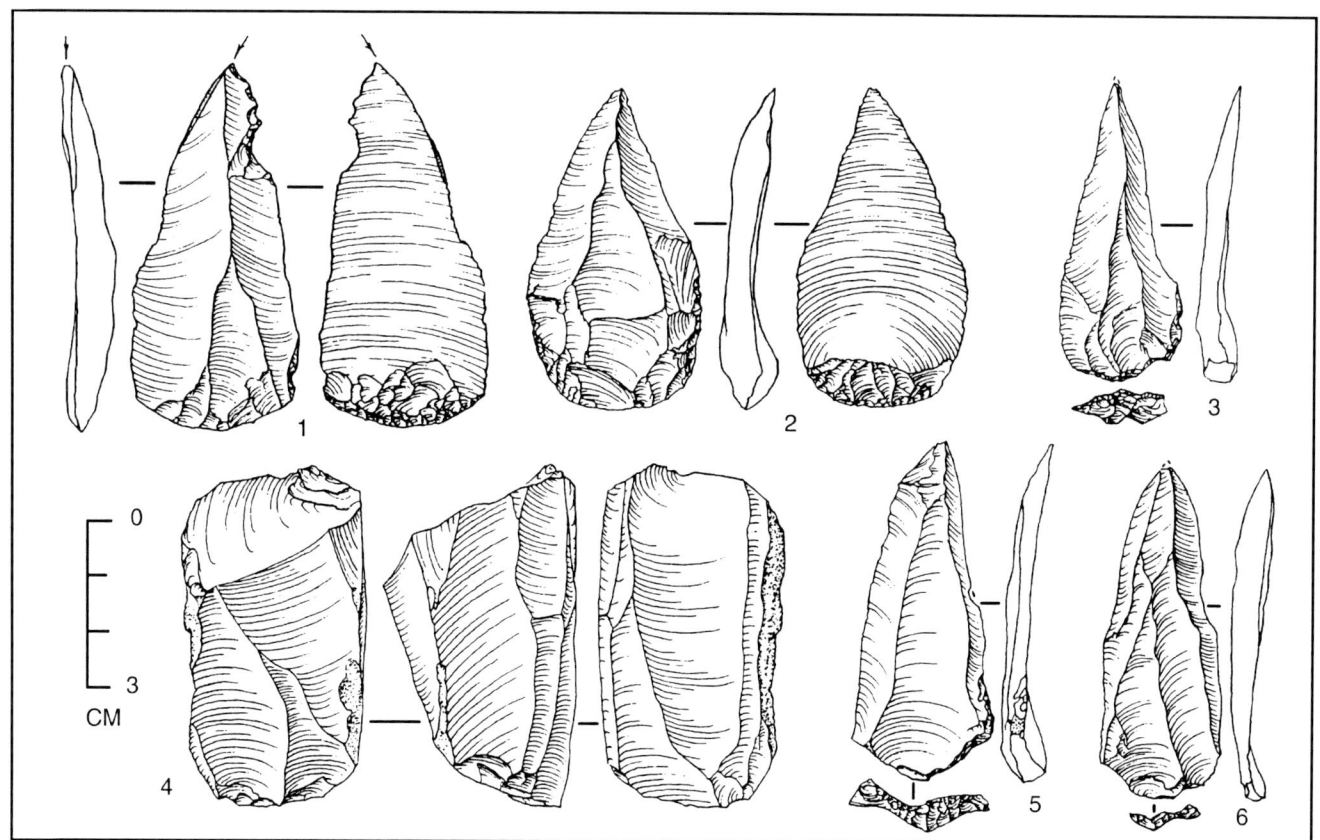

Figure 9. Early Upper Paleolithic tools from Boker Tachtit, levels 1 and 2 (adapted from Marks 1983): Emireh points (1, 2), Y-scar points (3, 5, 6), Core (4).

The Dating of the Levantine Early Upper Paleolithic

It is generally agreed that radiocarbon readings earlier than 30 ka should be considered as minimal ages (e.g., Mellars et al. 1999; van der Plicht 1999). Therefore none of the Mousterian charcoal dates for the coastal belt of the Eastern Mediterranean obtained in the past are accepted today. This rejection was assisted by the publication of TL and ESR dates for the Late Mousterian sites in the region. The calibration of ^{14}C dates is as yet uncertain. Van Andel (1998) claims that the dates older than approximately 40 ka B.P. are closer to the real ages and do not underestimate the true age, similar to readings younger than 30 ka. However, van der Plicht (1999) disagrees. Additional uncertainties arise from the involvement of different laboratories and the possible contamination of charcoal caused by bioturbation (in rodent-like burrows).

Advancements in dating techniques in recent years should allow us to synchronize TL and ^{14}C dates from Late Middle and Early Upper Paleolithic sites in the Levantine sequence. However, the range of differences between uncalibrated radiocarbon years and TL years must be clarified. Interestingly, the two samples from Umm el Tlel indicate a difference of about 2 ka, but there is an overlap if the TL standard deviation is taken into account. In Western Europe this discrepancy is considered as around 3 ka (Mellars, in Mellars et al. 1999).

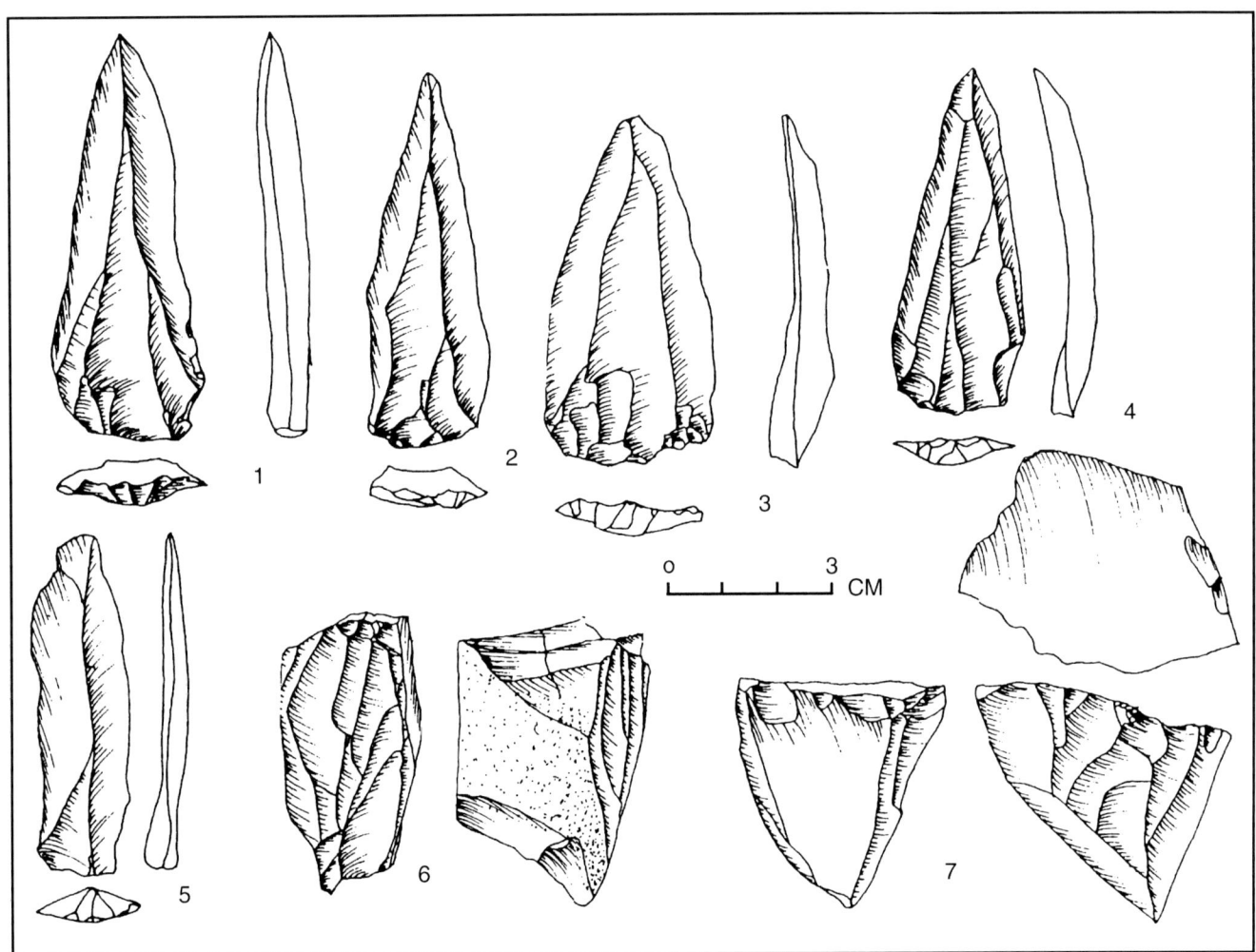

Figure 10. Early Upper Paleolithic tools from Umm el Tlel, layers IIIbase and III2a (adapted from Bourguignon 1996): Umm el Tlel points (1–4), blades (5), cores (6–7).

Appendix A shows the list of dates available at the time of writing, and demonstrates some of the difficulties in reaching an agreement concerning the time of the cultural transition and establishing temporal correlations between the sites mentioned above. The first proposal for combining the two dating techniques was attempted for Kebara Cave, where there is a stratigraphic gap between the Mousterian and the EUP assemblages (Bar-Yosef et al. 1996). The TL dates provide a sound chronological determination for the upper part of the Mousterian sequence (Valladas et al. 1987). The Late Mousterian Unit VI is dated at 48.3±3.5 ka, although there are no secure dates for Unit V, the very latest Mousterian assemblage in this site. The EUP assemblages, which appear to follow the phase with Emireh Points, date to 43/42 ka. It seems that the gap in the lithic sequence of Kebara lasted from about 46/45 ka to 43/42 ka and this observation lends credence to the ^{14}C dates of Boker Tachtit Level 1 (47 and 46 ka, Marks 1983). It was therefore suggested that the MP/UP transition occurred around 46/45 ka B.P.

Another option for dating the boundary between the Middle and the Upper Paleolithic is to employ the dates available for the Ksar 'Akil sequence. Mellars and Tixier (1989), in a manner similar to McBurney at Haua Fteah (see below), calculated a rough estimate of the rate of deposition. This estimation relied on 11 AMS radiocarbon readings, as well as three conventional dates for the Aurignacian assemblages and one for a Mousterian layer. According to the above, the

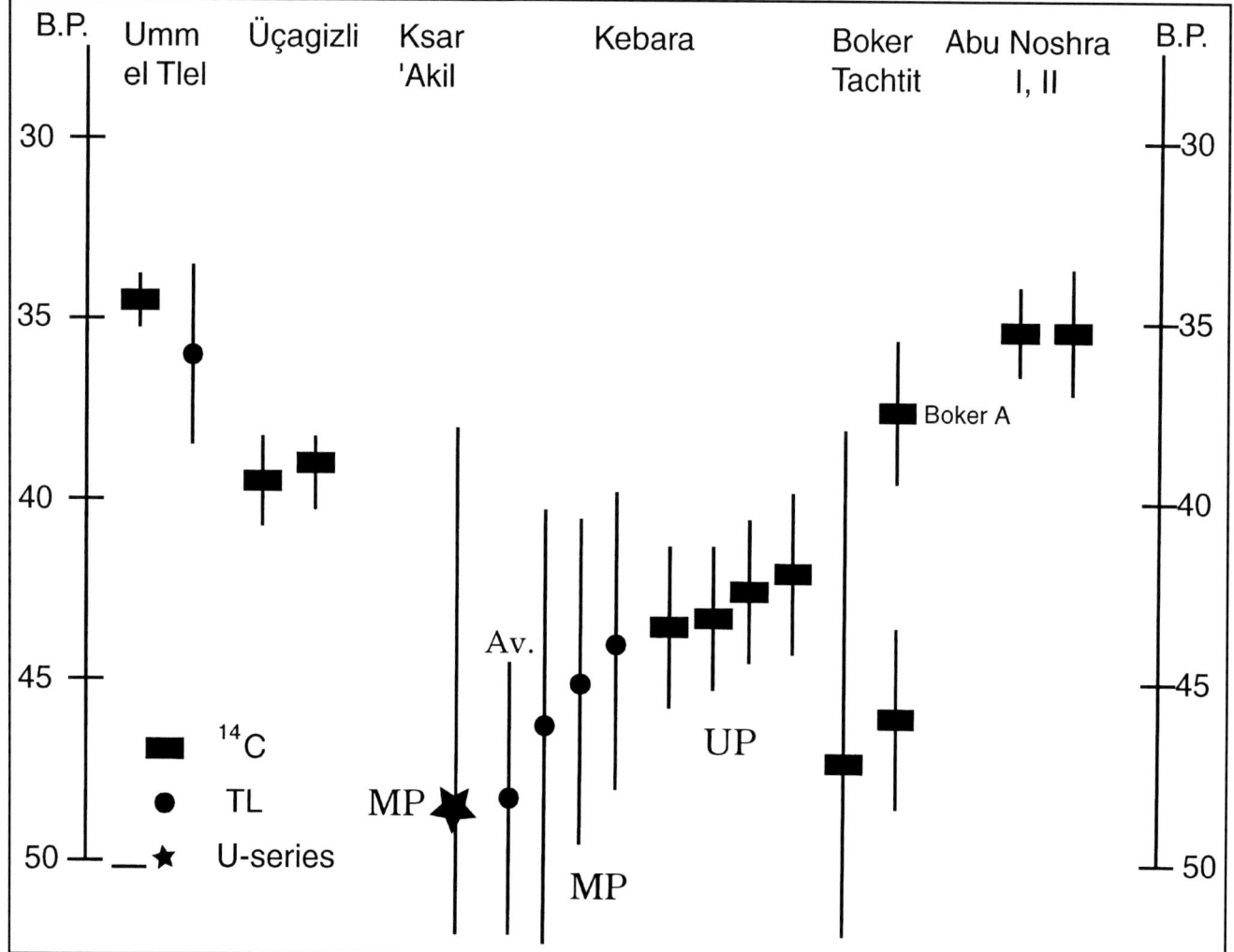

Figure 11. Dates of the Late Middle and Early Upper Paleolithic in the Levant.

cultural transition took place around 50 ka. Surprisingly, the U-series disequilibrium dates on two bone samples produced somewhat similar readings, although the scientists caution against accepting them without reservations (van der Plicht et al. 1989). The bone dates are given as "surface" and "bulk" material and are as follows: for layer XXVI (last Mousterian level) 47±9 ka (G-888174S) and 19±5 (G-88173B), and for layer XXXII (Mousterian) 51±4 ka (G-88177S) and 49±5 (G-88178B).

The earliest Levantine EUP is followed by a blade industry often called Ahmarian. It is represented in Kebara Units IV and III, Boker A, Boker Tachtit Level 4, and in Ksar 'Akil layers XXI–XVII. Figure 11 is a chronological chart based on the available dates. Given the cautionary notes above, the persistence of an older lithic tradition in Umm el Tlel fits the model that views the original inventions as emerging earlier in the core area and the subsequent adoption of the new modes of production by others.

The Ahmarian

The Ahmarian tradition was defined in 1981, following a decade of growing recognition that there are blade/bladelet dominated assemblages which differ from those defined as Levantine Aurignacian (Gilead 1981; Marks 1981). The term "Ahmarian" was adopted from the name of the Erq el-Ahmar ("Red Cliff") rockshelter in Wadi Khareitun (Judean Desert), excavated by Neuville (1951). In this site, a series of layers (B through F) were exposed overlying a sterile lens that separated them from a Mousterian layer (H). Although the excavator's description is rather short, and focuses mainly on the retouched items with no debitage counts, the impression is that in most cases the production of blades exceeded that of flakes. A later examination of the Erq el-Ahmar collections by L. Copeland (1976) confirmed the general observations as reported by Neuville (1951). Furthermore, Copeland noted the rarity or absence of elements that could be classified as typical Aurignacian, such as carinated and nosed scrapers.

Additional excavations by Neuville's Bedouin foreman in Mazaraq an-Naaj and el-Quseir, two small cave-sites in the lower reaches of the Judean Desert, furnished similar assemblages (Perrot 1952, 1955; Gilead 1981).

The proliferation of core reduction to obtain laminar blanks was uncovered in Qafzeh Cave, currently dated to 31–28 ka, as well as in numerous sites in the Negev, southern Jordan, and the Sinai peninsula (fig. 12; Baruch and Bar-Yosef 1986; Bar-Yosef and Belfer 1977; Becker 1999; Coinman and Henry 1995; Gilead 1981; Gilead and Bar-Yosef 1993; Henry 1995; Marks 1976, 1983; Phillips 1988, 1994). All these assemblages, often retrieved from systematic excavations, exhibit fully-fledged blade/bladelet core reduction strategies. Blank reduction was carried out by manipulating cores with one or two platforms.

The major tool-groups consist of retouched and backed blades and bladelets and include the El-Wad Points. Endscrapers are quite common, but burins are rare, given the length of time over which this generalized type of laminar tradition prevailed (from around 43/42 through 18 ka) and the actual continuity in core reduction strategies from the late Ahmarian during most of the Epi-Paleolithic industries. There are definitely changes through time and space, in the laminar technologies and methods, as well as in the typological variability. In several cases, regional variability was recorded from different environments, a fact that will necessitate further subdivision of the Ahmarian. One example is the sites from Gebel Maghara in northern Sinai, dated to 34/34–30 ka, which were named "Lagaman" (Bar-Yosef and Belfer 1977).

The early Ahmarian demonstrates a certain continuity with the EUP in the presence of some bone tools and the continuous exploitation of Mediterranean marine shells for body decorations, as in Ksar 'Akil layer XVII–XIV (Altena 1962), and in Kebara Cave, units III/IV (D. Bar-Yosef personal communication).

Subsistence information is limited to rather meager bone collections, in which the dominant species are generally the same as in the Mousterian. Forest and woodland species are somewhat more common in the hilly areas and northern Levant, and gazelle, aurochs, and equids in the drier areas (Davis 1982; Garrard 1982; Rabinovich 1998).

Other Archaeological Aspects of the Levantine Early Upper Paleolithic

Information on the subsistence of the EUP is rather limited. In most of the arid land sites, bones were not preserved. An exceptional case is the site of Abu Noshra in Wadi Feiran (southern Sinai), where the bones of wild oxen, ibex, gazelle, and onager, as well as the remains of a wolf and a fox were identified.

The occupational deposits of the steppic and desertic sites are often isolated horizons such as at Boker Tachtit, Kadesh Barnea, the Lagaman sites, and those in Wadi Feiran (Bar-Yosef and Belfer 1977; Becker 1999; Gilead and Bar-Yosef 1993; Marks 1983; Phillips 1988; Phillips and Gladfelter 1989).

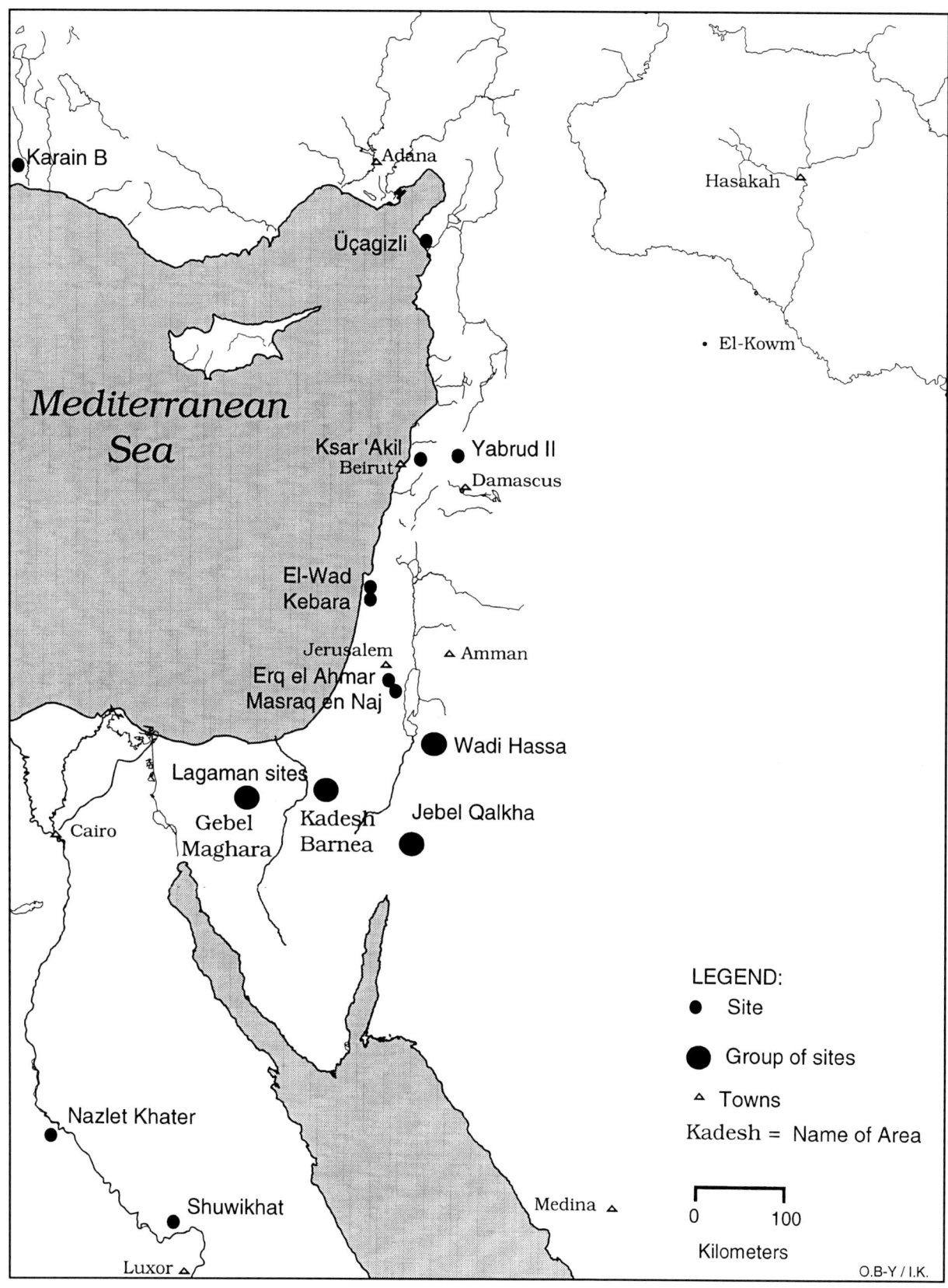

Figure 12. Map of the Ahmarian sites in the Levant and other related Upper Paleolithic sites.

The cave sites along the Levantine coast produced some counts of animal bones (see table 1), reflecting hunting in the general environment of each site. The situation in Yabrud II, on the drier slopes of the Anti-Lebanon Mountains, is similar. Somewhat deeper deposits representing palimpsests and more intensive use of caves were exposed in el-Wad and Kebara Caves, while Emireh, Rakefet, Hayonim, and Qafzeh Caves (the latter three of younger age) contained short EUP sequences. Exceptional is Ksar 'Akil, which, despite the incorporation of colluvial sediments, provided the longest and richest sequence in the Levant: 18 m deep, with assemblages representing almost every variety discovered to date. The possibility that this location served as some sort of an aggregation site, or had a special sacred status, cannot be ruled out.

In sum, the ephemeral nature of many of the EUP sites suggests that these mobile foragers were characterized by a social and economic cultural template different from that which had gone before. Their larger exploitable territory would have required changes in their communication system in order to maintain contact with other groups and to ensure that their mating networks remained viable.

THE LEVANTINE AURIGNACIAN

The Levantine Aurignacian was originally defined on the basis of typological criteria that followed the European example. Prominent among the lithic assemblages are the proliferation of nosed and carinated scrapers, which often outnumber the burins, and the presence of the now-called El-Wad Points (earlier known as Font Yves or Krems Points), which are partially or fully retouched pointed blades/bladelets (fig. 13). The wide range of morphological variability among the El-Wad Points certainly depends on the basic blade/bladelet blanks retouched. In some cases this retouch is fine and semi-abrupt, and is considered as "correcting" the shape of a given piece. This kind of shaping was probably necessary, since many points served as projectiles (Bergman and Ohnuma 1983). Another laminar form is the Dufour Bladelet, which is often inversely retouched (Lucas 1997; fig. 14). The presence of these bladelets was only noticed when careful sieving was practiced during fieldwork.

Since the 1970s, the definition of the Levantine Aurignacian has followed the Ksar 'Akil sequence, with the subdivision as follows (and see table 2): Levantine Aurignacian A (layers 13–11), B (layers 10–8), and C (layers 7–6) (e.g., Azoury 1986; Bergman 1987; Copeland 1975). The frequencies in table 2, especially those of artifacts classified as nosed/carinated elements, demonstrate why all three complexes were originally considered as belonging to the Aurignacian tradition. In addition, it was recognized that Aurignacian contexts such as cave and rockshelters, for example Ksar 'Akil, Hayonim, el-Wad, Kebara, Sefunim, and Yabrud II, contained bone and antler objects (Newcomer 1974), although these are not as numerous as in the Aurignacian assemblages of temperate Europe. The common type in the Eastern Mediterranean assemblages is the bi-point, but the unique presence of the split-base points emphasizes the similarity between the Levantine Aurignacian and that of Europe (fig. 15). The three known examples were recovered in Kebara, Hayonim, and el-Quseir (Bar-Yosef and Belfer-Cohen 1996)

Previous revisions by Gilead (1981, 1991) and Marks (1981) proposed abandoning the use of the term "Aurignacian" in reference to the entity of Levantine Aurignacian A, as similar assemblages had not been reported from sites other than Ksar 'Akil. Instead, they suggested that only those assemblages in which flake production dominates over blade production should be labeled as "Aurignacian." Typologically, the proliferation of flake blanks was linked to the high frequencies of nosed and carinated scrapers (mainly in the Levantine Aurignacian B), as well as to the elevated percentages of simple flake scrapers and burins that characterized the so-called Levantine Aurignacian C assemblages, especially in the arid belt (Bergman and Goring-Morris 1987). In sum, it was undoubtedly the dichotomy between flake-dominated and blade-dominated assemblages within the Levantine Upper Paleolithic that led Gilead (1981) and Marks (1981) to recognize two lithic traditions. This view was held until recently by most scholars in the Near East, and was supported by the proliferation of reports on the various blade industries from Sinai and southern Jordan (e.g., Bar-Yosef and Belfer 1977; Coinman 1997, 1998; Coinman and Henry 1995; Gilead and Bar-Yosef 1993; Phillips 1988).

However, as the overall picture broadens geographically, it demands the return to the more basic definitions of the known assemblages, not only in terms of the *chaînes opératoires* practiced, but also taking into account the typological variability as well as the presence of bone and antler artifacts.

New data sets were provided by the excavations at Kebara Cave (Bar-Yosef et al. 1996; and see table 2), and at Umm el Tlel (Boëda and Muheisen 1993), as well as by additional studies of the Negev, southern

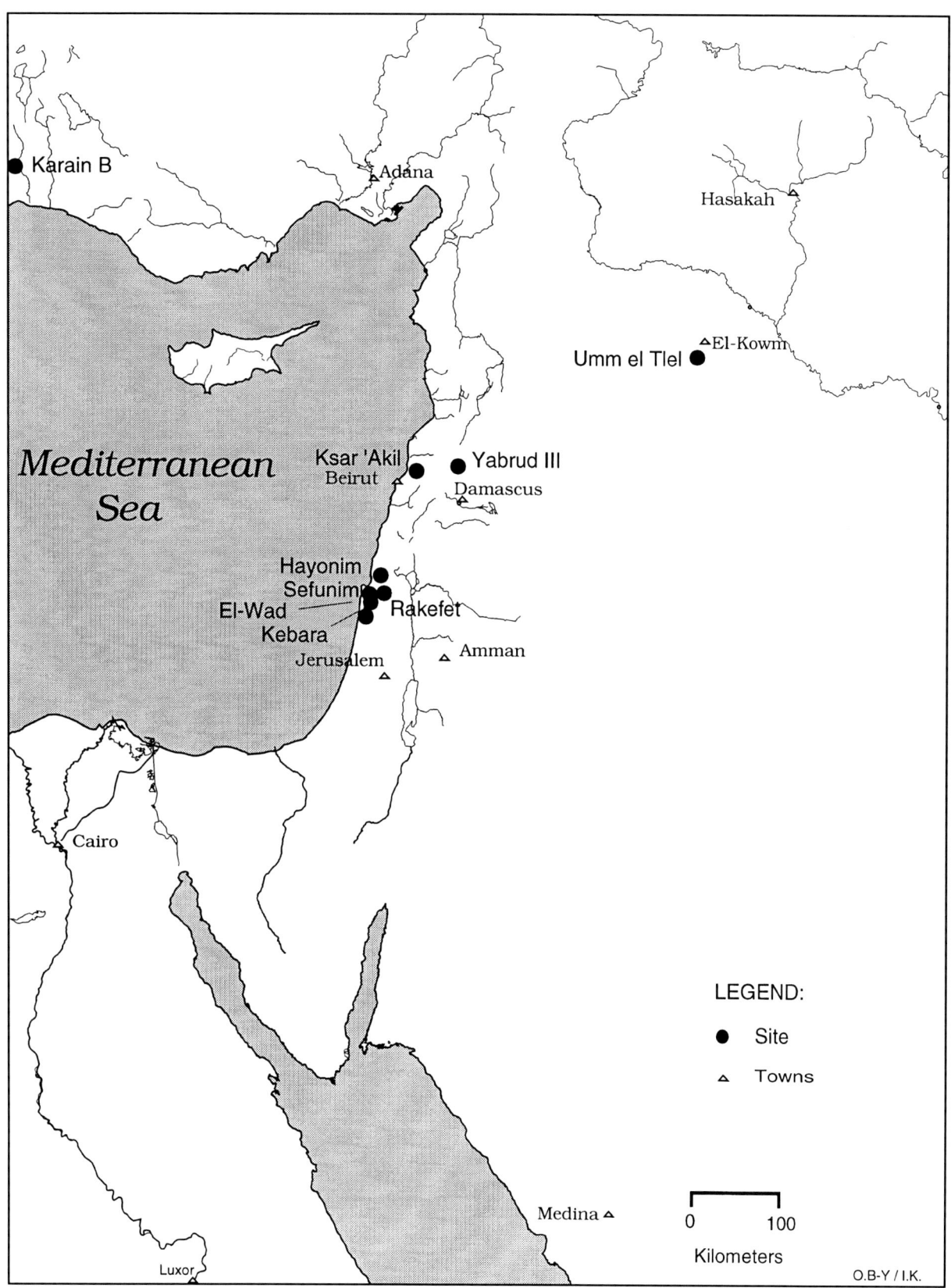

Figure 13. Map of the Aurignacian sites in the Eastern Mediterranean.

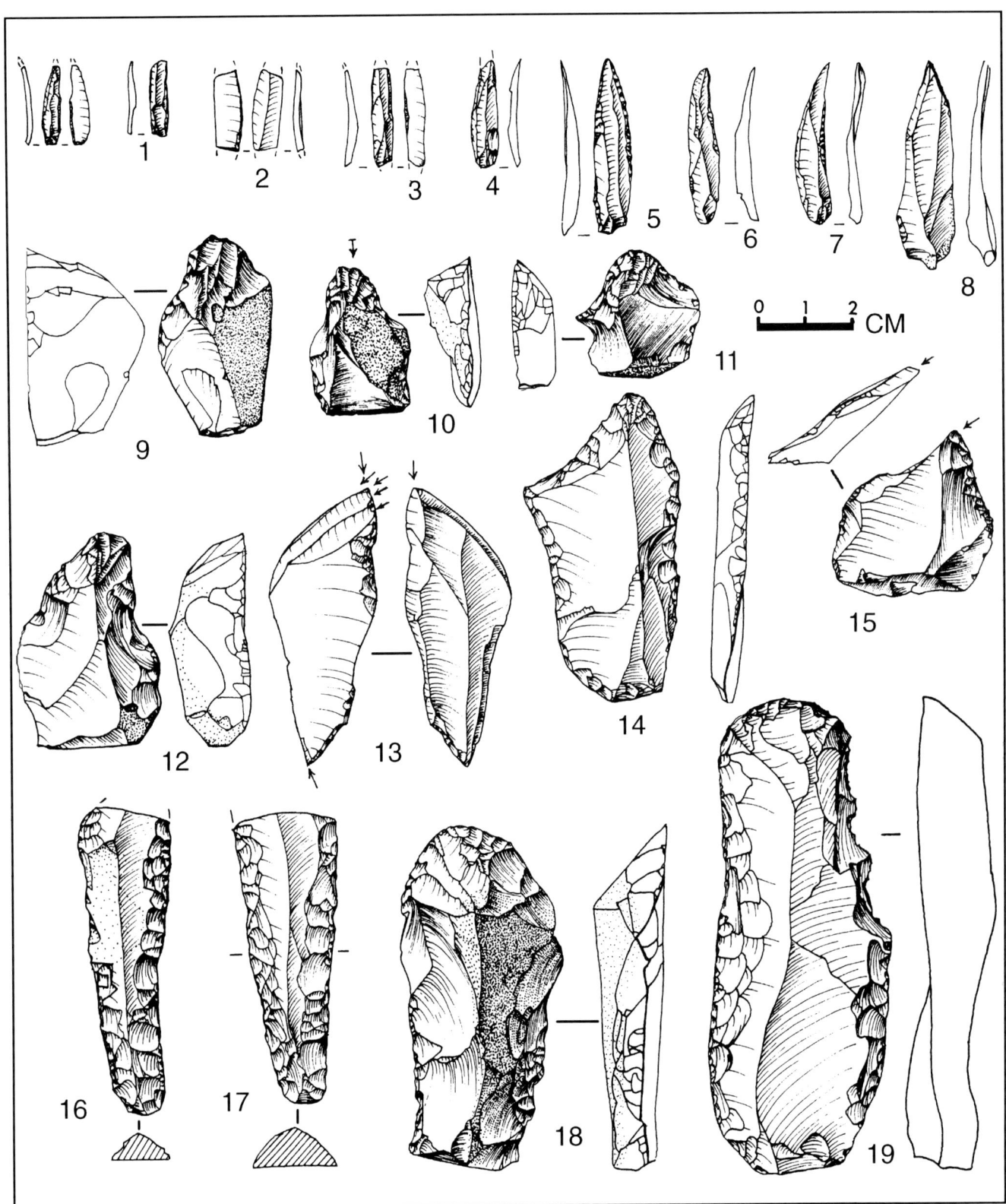

Figure 14. Levantine Aurignacian stone artifacts from Hayonim Cave (adapted from Belfer-Cohen and Bar-Yosef 1981): Dufour and retouched bladelets (1–8), carinated and nosed scrapers (9–12, 14), carinated burin (13), burin on truncation (15), Aurignacian blades (16–17), endscrapers on retouched blades (18–19).

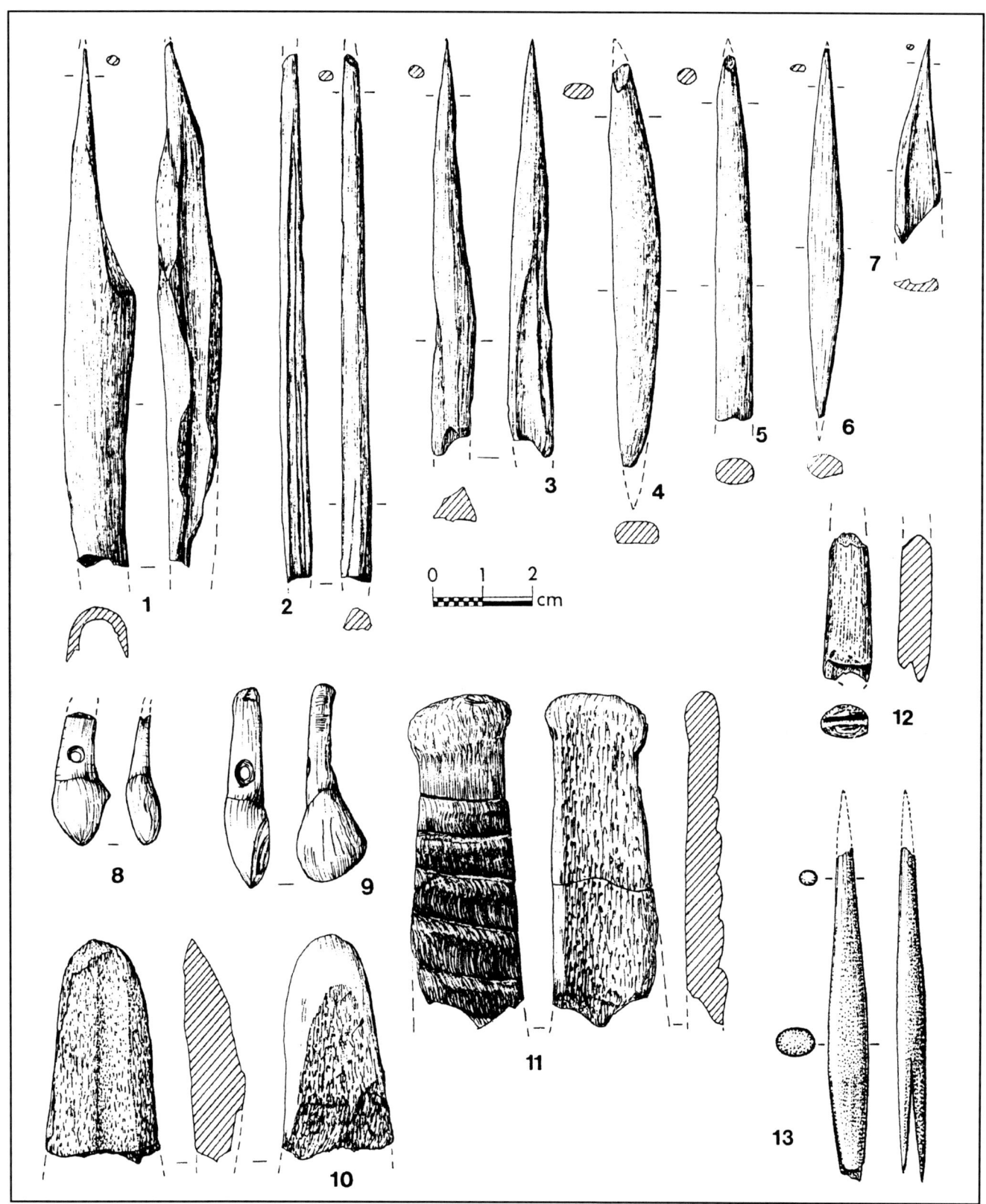

Figure 15. Levantine Aurignacian bone, tooth, and antler artifacts (adapted from Bar-Yosef and Belfer-Cohen 1996) from Hayonim Cave (1–12) and Kebara Cave (13). Note that 12 and 13 are split-based points.

TABLE 2
Percentages of tool types by Level (XII–VI) from Ksar 'Akil 1937–1938 (recalculated from Bergman 1987)

Type	Lev. Aurig. A		Lev. Aurig. B			Lev. Aurig. C	
	XII	XI	X	IX	VIII	VII	VI
Scrapers	8.8	17.7	24.2	31.6	31.6	28.3	18.7
Burins	42.5	22.3	17.4	10.1	7.4	11.2	42.5
Nosed/carinated	16.1	30.6	15.2	25.7	38	42.2	12.2
Aurignacian blades	0.2	0.3	0.3	0.1	0.1	0.2	0
El Wad forms	6.7	13.3	15.6	5.4	1.2	0.3	0.9
Backed and retouched blades	5.8	1.7	1.7	0.5	0.3	0.8	1.7
Retouched bladelets	3.3	2.3	15.7	15.1	5.4	2.1	9.9
Various retouched pieces	16.6	11.8	9.9	11.5	16.0	14.9	14.1
N=	657	1199	1734	3668	3697	2973	1193

Cultural designations follow Copeland 1975

Jordan, and Sinai sites (Coinman 1997; Coinman and Henry 1995; Henry 1995; Phillips 1988, 1994).

In Kebara Cave, an assemblage similar to the original Levantine Aurignacian A of Ksar 'Akil was identified in Units I–II (Bar-Yosef et al. 1996; Bar-Yosef and Belfer-Cohen 1996), namely, a blade industry with carinated and nosed scrapers, and retouched bladelets. This new sample is also very similar to that published earlier by Ziffer (1978) from M. Stekelis's excavations at Kebara in the 1950s. In addition, the bone and antler assemblages from several sites are taken into account, together with the typical Aurignacian pendants identical to European examples (White 1989), found only at Hayonim Cave. Deer, equid, and carnivore teeth were polished after the removal of the enamel (Belfer-Cohen and Bar-Yosef 1981; see fig. 15). In addition, the use of marine shells as beads is recorded at Yabrud II (Rust 1950), Ksar 'Akil (Altena 1962), and Hayonim Cave.

The other factor that caused a re-evaluation of the previous model was the reanalysis of assemblages collected or excavated in open-air sites in the Negev and Sinai. This research demonstrated that although the dominant core reduction strategy was flake-oriented, the resulting flake scrapers and burins do not exhibit any of the Aurignacian attributes mentioned above (Belfer-Cohen 1996; Belfer-Cohen and Bar-Yosef 1999), and thus, the entity previously called Levantine Aurignacian C should be redefined.

Finally, among the rare Levantine Aurignacian objects, two limestone slabs from layer D at Hayonim Cave should be mentioned. One bears a series of fine, intentional incisions and the other an incised ungulate, perhaps a horse (Belfer-Cohen and Bar-Yosef 1981:fig. 8; Marshack 1997).

The information on Levantine subsistence is rather limited. The main sources are the faunal assemblages from Ksar 'Akil, Hayonim, el-Wad, and Kebara (Davis 1982; Garrard 1982; Garrod and Bate 1937; Hooijer 1961; Rabinovich 1998). The dominant game species in the forested and craggy landscape of Ksar 'Akil were the Fallow Deer, Red Deer, and wild goat. The Western Galilee–Mt. Carmel area, with its wider coastal plain and more moderate hilly features, provided more gazelle remains than Fallow Deer, with lower frequencies of Red Deer, Roe Deer, aurochs, and equids.

The map of figure 13 incorporates all the known Aurignacian sites in the Levant, and their dates—as detailed in Appendix A—indicate the presence of their bearers in this region from around 36/34–28/27 ka. In comparison with the persistence of laminar industries in the region, mostly grouped under the term Ahmarian (46/45–18 ka), the Levantine Aurignacian is a short-lived archaeological phenomenon. The current radiocarbon and TL dates from western Europe (Richter et al. 2000) support the proposal to see the Aurignacian as a cultural manifestation that developed in Europe and not in the eastern Mediterranean. The recent discovery of an Aurignacian assemblage in Karain B (I. Yalçinkaya and M. Otte, personal communication), although not yet dated, may justify earlier proposals (e.g., Kozlowski 1992) to interpret the presence of the Levantine Aurignacian as evidence for population movement from southeast Europe into the Near East. This issue will be further discussed below.

THE MIDDLE AND UPPER PALEOLITHIC OF THE TAURUS-ZAGROS REGION

The Mousterian sequence in both the Taurus and the Zagros regions is very likely as long as the Levantine one, but it is as yet poorly dated. The lesser known sequence is that of the Taurus and Anatolia (e.g., Kozlowski 1998; Yalçinkaya 1988, 1995; Yalçinkaya et al. 1993). The main source of information is the excavation of Karain Cave, where a Mousterian industry dates back to at least 200 ka (Valladas, personal communication).

A series of ESR dates (Çetin et al. 1994; Appendix A) from the top layers at Karain suggest that the assemblages are rich in well-retouched pieces, many of which fall into the various categories of side and convergent scrapers, sometimes heavily reduced, as well as retouched points (fig. 16). The amount of debitage present in the site cannot account for all the blanks that were used to modify the retouched pieces, and therefore one should expect this site to be a seasonal camp into which stone tools were brought, often in already shaped form. It is as yet unknown whether this site represents a highland or lowland station within the mobile trajectory of a group.

Other sites from Anatolia (excluding southeast Turkey, which is part of the northern Levant) contain Levallois dominated assemblages (e.g., Yalçinkaya 1995).

Several cave sites were excavated in the Zagros Mountains (Dibble 1984, 1993; Dibble and Holdaway 1993; Solecki 1963, 1964; Solecki and Solecki 1993) including Shanidar, Hazar Merd, Bisitun, Warwasi, Houamian, and Kunji. The best known are Shanidar, where Neandertal burials were found in the 6m deep occupational sequence; Warwasi, where the thickness of the Middle Paleolithic layers reached about 2.5m; Bisitun; and Kunji. The latter is the southernmost site, with a little over one meter of deposits. To exemplify the paucity of information, it is worth mentioning that the distance from Shanidar to Kunji is about 800 km—only slightly less than the distance between el-Kowm in northeast Syria and Tor Faraj in southern Jordan (approximately 1200 km), an area in which around 20 cave and open-air sites have been reported in detail.

Shanidar and Warwasi are located in relatively low altitudes (about 350 m above sea level), while Kunji Cave is situated at about 1300 m above sea level. The first two seem to have served as base camps, while Kunji was probably an ephemeral camp into which artifacts were brought from lowland sites. The difference is indicated by the rarity of cores in Kunji relative to the great abundance of retouched pieces (fig. 17).

Based solely on bone counts (Evins 1982; Turnbull and Reed 1974), the subsistence behavior, as in the Levant, involved foraging in the vicinity of the sites—as shown in Shanidar, where wild goats and sheep dominate the assemblage (table 1).

Only a few radiocarbon dates are available for this region, and my suggestion is therefore tentative. The key is the uppermost portion of layer D in Shanidar, where Neandertal remains were found associated with an industry that compares reasonably well with the upper Karain sequence, admittedly 1600 km away. This heavily retouched, non-Levalloisian, Mousterian assemblage resembles others of the "Charentian" facies (due to the preponderance of scrapers) in other regions (e.g., Kozlowski 1998, this volume; Yalçinkaya et al. 1993; fig. 16), and seems to be of mid-Upper Pleistocene age. Even if the radiocarbon readings of 46 and 50 ka from upper layer D (Appendix A) are interpreted simply as minimal dates, they could at the same time indicate the Late Mousterian age of Shanidar. Such a correlation, if sustained by future TL and ESR dates, would support the proposal that the Neandertals reached this part of Western Asia during or immediately after OIS 4 (approximately 75–64 ka B.P.) and endured through the earliest manifestations of the Levantine EUP.

The scarcity of field research in this region does not allow one to claim the existence or absence of the EUP in the known sites. The lithic assemblages of layer C in Shanidar served as the basis for the definition of the Baradostian, a laminar Upper Paleolithic industry dated to 34–28 ka. Similar assemblages were recovered from Warwasi, Gar Arjeneh, and Yafteh Caves (Olszewski 1993, 1994; Solecki 1958). The radiocarbon dates, even if considered as minimal readings, do not support a temporal correlation between the Baradostian and the EUP of the Levant. Based on the available counts and drawings, it seems that the lithic assemblage from Shanidar would correlate at best with the Ahmarian, while Warwasi contains Aurignacian tool forms (Olszewski and Dibble 1994). Therefore, additional studies describing and dating the Upper Paleolithic in the Zagros are crucial, providing the necessary clarification of the situation before further hypotheses can be tested.

In sum, the scarcity of Early Upper Paleolithic stratified and dated assemblages from the Taurus-Zagros region, and the rather limited amount of known Late Mousterian sites from this vast region make any far reaching conclusions merely speculation based on long distance interpolations. The emerging picture of what appears to be the patchy survival of Neandertals and of the so-called Late Mousterian

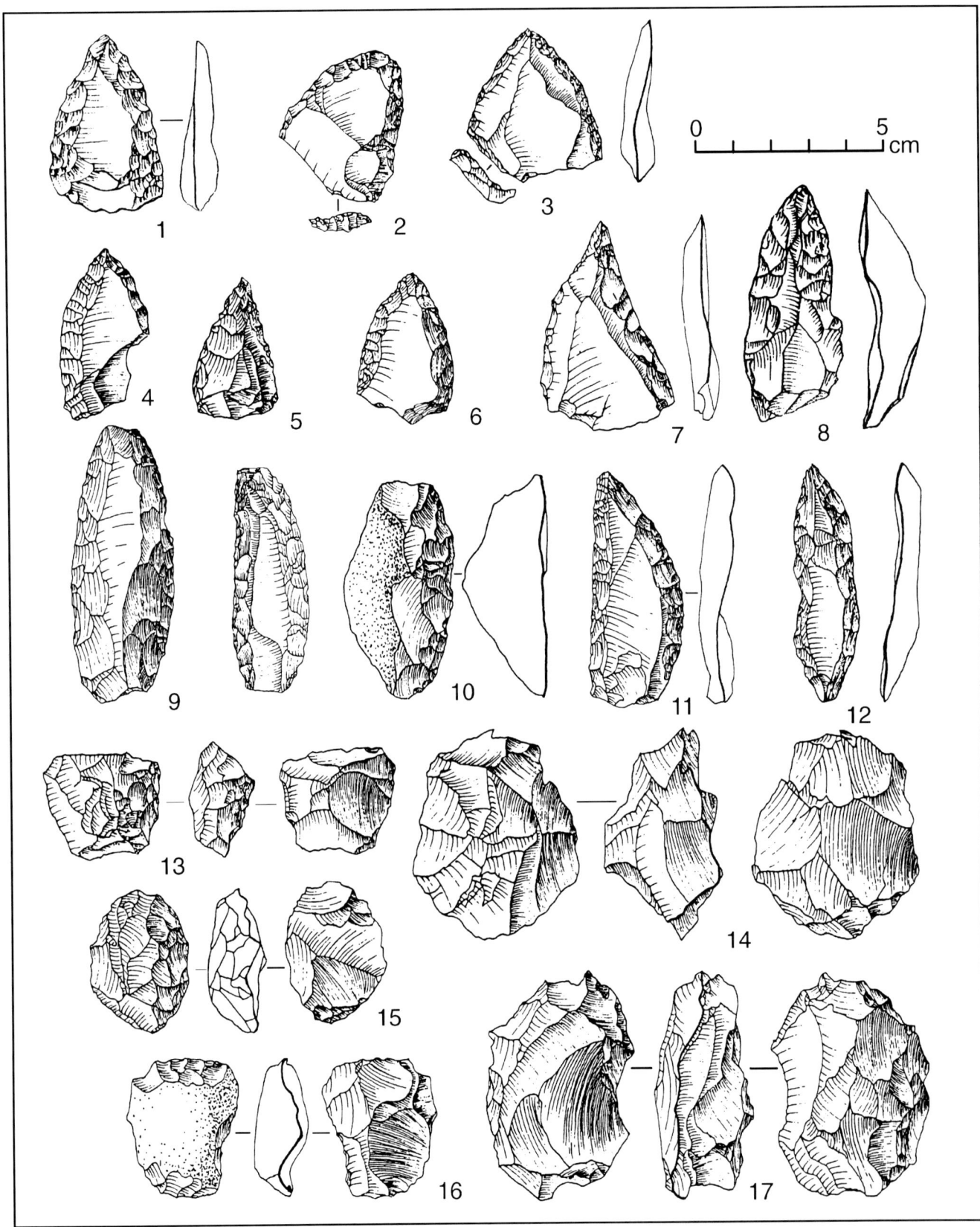

Figure 16. Middle Paleolithic artifacts from Karain Cave (adapted from Yalçinkaya 1991).

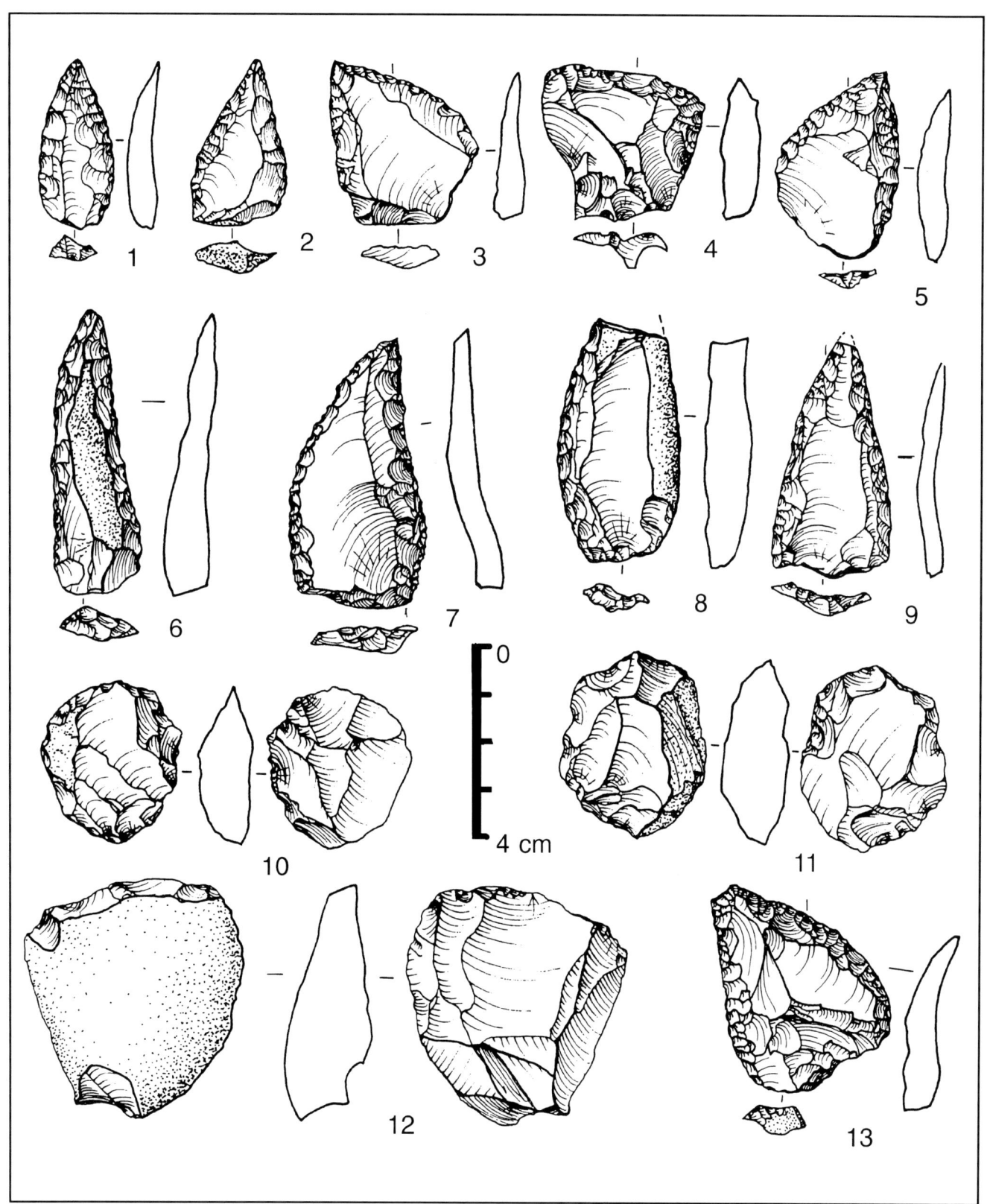

Figure 17. Middle Paleolithic artifacts from Kunji Cave in the Zagros (adapted from Baumler and Speth 1993, figs. 1.11–1.22).

industries across the European continent makes it quite possible that the beginning of the Upper Paleolithic in the Zagros was relatively late when compared to adjacent regions such as the Levant, a situation similar to that in the Caucasus (e.g., Golovanova et al. 1999; Kozlowski 1998).

THE MIDDLE AND UPPER PALEOLITHIC OF NORTHEAST AFRICA

In a recent summary, van Peer (1998 and references therein) reviewed the evidence from the Late Middle to the Upper Paleolithic in the Nile Valley. He describes two major cultural Middle Paleolithic components—the Nubian and the Lower Nile Valley complexes. The Nubian complex is present in the Red Sea hills, east of the Nile Valley, in Sodmein Cave, where it is dated to around 118 ka (Mercier et al. 1999). The same industry is found in the eastern Sahara, where it was replaced by the Aterian during the mid-Upper Pleistocene (Tillet 1993). In the region of the lower Nile Valley itself, van Peer suggests, on the basis of a few dated assemblages, that the Nubian complex demonstrates an overall contemporaneity with the Lower Nile Valley complex (van Peer 1998:fig. 1; Wendorf et al. 1993).

Through the analysis of core reduction strategies, taking into account the chronological position of each industry, van Peer proposes a change in the knapping techniques within the Lower Nile Valley complex. Excavations at the site of Taramsa 1, where successive periods of exploitation of chert nodules took place during the Middle Paleolithic, also produced a laminar assemblage stratigraphically above the latter. The refitting of blanks to cores in this assemblage demonstrated that the predominant production of blades was achieved due to a technological change that "consists of increasing the exploitable core volume by changing the core organization" (van Peer 1998:126). This type of "transitional technique" is considered similar to that uncovered at Boker Tachtit (Marks 1983, 1990; Vermeersch et al. 1998). The dating of the site is therefore of great importance. A radiocarbon date of 38,100±400 (OxA-2602) was obtained from charcoal specks collected from the deposits with the so-called transitional industry. Another site that produced a similar industry, Nazlet Safaha, provided a somewhat similar charcoal radiocarbon date of 37,200±1,300 (OxA-2601), but both dates are considered as minimal (Vermeersch et al. 1998).

The site of Taramsa 1 has recently produced a Middle Paleolithic burial, which, following a preliminary study, is considered to be the skeletal remains of an anatomically modern child (Vermeersch et al. 1998). A series of nine OSL dates of the aeolian infill of the extraction pit where the human relics were found *in situ* range from the lowermost one of 80.4±19.0 ka to the youngest of 49.8±12.2 ka. It seems that sometime around 48–40 ka, the transition to an Upper Paleolithic mode of blade production took place in the Nile Valley. Additional dates are needed, as well as excavated assemblages that would cover the time span from 50 to 30 ka, in order to conclude that the technological origin of this type of Upper Paleolithic industry was in this area. Unfortunately evidence concerning other aspects of behavior, such as subsistence, is still missing from the record.

Further west, in Cyrenaica (Libya), the site of Haua Fteah produced a sequence of Middle and Upper Paleolithic assemblages (McBurney 1967). The long sequence of this huge cave, exposed in the 1950s excavations, comprises (from bottom to top) the "Pre-Aurignacian," the Mousterian, the first Upper Paleolithic Dabban, the Epi-Paleolithic Oranian, the Capsian, and the Neolithic.

The lower Mousterian utilized the Levallois technique, and included, according to McBurney (1967:131), some foliates and prototypes of tanged Aterian points and scrapers. It was overlain by an assemblage the excavator named "Levalloiso-Mousterian," following Garrod's original terminology for the Levant. The two dates of 47,000±3,200 (GrN-2023) and 43,400±1,300 (GrN-2564) for the uppermost Mousterian layers are considered as minimal dates. In this sense they are no different from any of the radiocarbon dates available in Levantine caves before TL and ESR were introduced (see Appendix A). However, Crew (1975) disagreed with McBurney concerning the affinities of the Libyan Mousterian to the Levant, and found closer similarities with the Nubian Mousterian.

The main technological and typological characteristics of the Dabban, known from both Haua Fteah and Hagfet et Dabba (McBurney 1967) are as follows: it is a blade based industry with a preponderance of backed blades, a distinctive presence of chamfered blades, and an increasing number of burins and end scrapers. The earliest dates for the Dabban from Haua Fteah (McBurney 1967:Table III.1) were 33,100±400 B.P. (Grn-2550) and 28,500±800 B.P. (W-86). Using all the ^{14}C dates in the sequence of Haua Fteah, McBurney calculated the emergence of the Dabban as around 40,000±2,000. He found support for his estimate in a radiocarbon date of 40,500±2000 B.P. from the early layers at Hagfet ed Dabba (McBurney 1975: 419).

DISCUSSION

It appears that almost no one is seeking the origins of the Middle/Upper Paleolithic revolution in Western Europe, although everyone, including the media, uses the archaeological record from this region to characterize the differences between Neandertals and Cro-Magnons, the supposed bearers, respectively, of these industries. The majority of the scholars who have written about this transition consider it to be a revolution (e.g., Gamble 1986; Gilman 1984; Marshack 1997; Mellars 1996, this volume; Mellars and Gibson 1996; Mellars and Stringer 1989; Mellars et al. 1999; Mithen 1996; White 1989, 1997). However, there are others (e.g., Clark 1997; Straus 1997) who view the transition as a slow and gradual change that occurred on a regional scale. Some suggest that the last Neandertals had already changed their lifeways (including their symbolic behavior) before they encountered the incoming Cro-Magnons (d'Errico et al. 1998; Zilhão and d'Errico 1999; and see Mellars this volume).

I have suggested elsewhere (Bar-Yosef 1992, 1994, 1998b) that by employing recent models to explain the Neolithic revolution we may gain comparable insights into a techno-cultural revolution that occurred some 40,000 to 30,000 years earlier. This analytical procedure would be analogous to employing studies of the Industrial Revolution as sources for testing various aspects of the Neolithic revolution.

There are several common denominators for all these three revolutions. First is the emergence of new technology in a "core area." Second, the dispersal of the new technology with or without cultural baggage, either by the migration of overflow populations, or by diffusion. The study of these issues conforms to the goal of many archaeological projects, which try to tell the story of "where" and "when" human societies changed, and then speculate on "why" they did so. In the analytical process, we are seeking information concerning the similarities and differences among prehistoric societies in terms of their social structure and organization, subsistence strategies, perception of the landscape, and cultural constructs such as cosmology. Identifying the particular society occupying the "core area" may bring us closer to understanding "how" and perhaps "why" the techno-cultural revolution began there.

In a nutshell, I view the Middle to Upper Paleolithic transition in Western Asia and Europe as a technological and cultural revolution. A relevant lesson can be learned from the Neolithic Revolution (for details see Bar-Yosef 1998b; Bar-Yosef and Meadow 1995; Harris 1998). As it originates from a "core area" located in the Levant, comparing the West European Neolithic to the local Mesolithic provides no insights into "why" or "when" the Neolithic revolution began. Most researchers agree that no specific region in Europe should be considered as the core area for the Middle/Upper Paleolithic revolution. Therefore, the debate revolving around the assumed inter- and intra-relationships between Neandertals and Cro-Magnons, and the presence or absence of artistic manifestations in the local Mousterian, as opposed to the elaborate artistic manifestations of the Franco-Cantabrian Upper Paleolithic, is not relevant to the issue of the Middle/Upper Paleolithic revolution.

These comparisons inform us only of the differences that evolved since the appearance of the Upper Paleolithic traditions in Western Europe. Thus in seeking to answer the questions "why" and "when" for the beginning of the Upper Paleolithic Revolution, we should be looking for a "core area" somewhere else.

The archaeology of the very late European Mousterian in fact reflects the various ways in which the competition between the two populations developed. The record indicates that the final winners in the competition were the Cro-Magnons, and, therefore, the detailed examination of the technological and cultural attributes of Cro-Magnon populations may reveal their advantages over the local Neandertals. However, uncovering the reasons for the successful colonization of Europe will not explain how the revolution began, or where.

Currently, flimsy indications point to East Africa (Ambrose 1998a, b; Klein 1999), to the Nile Valley (van Peer 1998), or to the Levant (Stringer 1989) as the original homeland of the Upper Paleolithic. There are even suggestions that point in the direction of central Asia or Anatolia (e.g., Otte 1998). Considering models that view the revolution as emanating either from a biological change sometime around 50 ka (Klein 1995), or from techno-cultural inventions and innovations, it seems that currently the latter best fits the archaeological evidence (e.g., Bar-Yosef 1998b; Zilhão and d'Errico 1999). However, the paucity of field data in East Africa and dated sites in the Nile Valley cautions leaving all options open.

Accepting the notion of a "core area," the spread of the new technology among prehistoric societies (by migrating groups or group interactions) might be explained by their keeping the tradition of using the same *chaînes opératoires* (for the production of stone objects or shaping other raw materials) in their new homelands. Given the regional variability in the properties of raw materials and the time that it took for individuals and their descendants to colonize new territories (perhaps as much as 15–10 ka), a certain amount of variability within the overall systems of the *chaînes opératoires* can be expected. Thus, if the transition from the Middle Paleolithic technological behavior to the Upper Paleolithic occurred in the Nile Valley, there is no point in seeking the origins of the Levantine EUP industries in the local Late Mousterian. The historically known case of the early Iron Age Philistines provides a good example. Mycenean IIIC:1b pottery found in Philistine sites in Israel was once considered as a product imported from the Aegean. Neutron Activation Analysis revealed these pots to have been made locally by a migrant potter, who moved in as a member of a larger community (Gunneweg et al. 1991). This discovery is perhaps not so surprising, as other cultural aspects of the Philistine culture stemming from Aegean migrants had already been documented (for details see Stager 1995).

In light of these comments, we need to examine the archaeological record. Most Late Middle Paleolithic sites in the Levant and Northeast Africa contain Levallois-dominated industries, but there are some sites in which a different *chaîne opératoire* is present (e.g., Boëda 1995; Caton-Thompson 1952; Garrod and Bate 1937; Gilead 1995; Marks 1992b; Meignen 1995, 1998; Neuville 1951; Rust 1950; Schick and Stekelis 1977; van Peer 1998 and references therein). The non-Levallois methods are more common in the Nile Valley and its environs (van Peer 1998), as well as in the Zagros mountain ranges (e.g., Baumler and Speth 1993; Dibble and Holdaway 1993). The situation in the Taurus and the Anatolian plateau is poorly known; certain sites have produced evidence for the extensive use of the Levallois centripetal method, while in other sites, such as Karain, it seems that non-Levallois operational sequences are more frequent (Kozlowski 1998; Yalçinkaya 1995; Yalçinkaya et al. 1993).

The end of the Levantine Middle Paleolithic is marked everywhere by the appearance of Early Upper Paleolithic assemblages. When assemblages of both periods are compared across the chronological boundary, the transition seems to be a technological revolu-

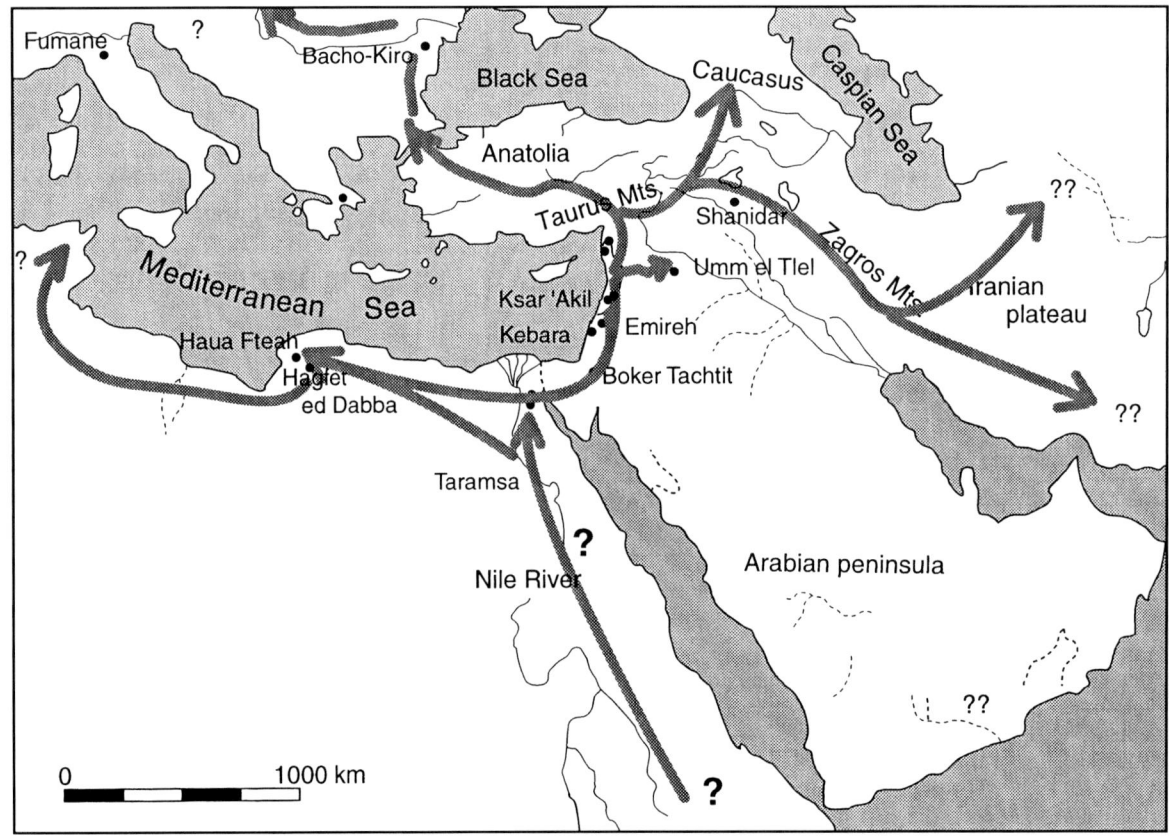

Figure 18. Hypothetical colonization routes in the eastern Mediterranean.

tion (e.g., Bar-Yosef 1998b). Unfortunately, the rarity of bone and antler objects, and the occurrence of marine shell beads in only two sites (Ksar 'Akil and Üçagizli), has made the lithic assemblages the main source of information. The presence of Levallois points, even when removed from bi-directional cores—beautifully demonstrated by the refitted cores from Boker Tachtit—or the well-studied Umm el Tlel technique, as well as the presence of some side scrapers, led to the labeling of these EUP industries as "Transitional." This implied that the technological transition took place locally.

Hypothetically, if the core area of the revolution was, for example, in the Nile Valley or East Africa, then the presence of "transitional" characteristics such as Levallois points with the Y scar pattern, Emireh points and *chanfriens* in sites such as Boker Tachtit, el-Wad, et-Tabun, Ksar 'Akil, and the like, can better be understood as attributes of the newly introduced lithic industry, conceived and originally manufactured elsewhere, in its homeland. Thus, for example, the presence of the new *chaîne opératoire* in Boker Tachtit level 1, and of the Emireh point as a new tool type could be interpreted as the physical evidence for colonizing foragers, who brought in the knowledge of a new core reduction strategy and, while employing it in the new land, invented an item that was not part and parcel of the original package (fig. 18). As Emireh points are not known from the northeast African contexts, but chanfreins were found in Egypt and Libya (McBurney 1955, 1967; Vignard 1920) as well as in the Levant, we may speculate that the bearers of this industry were the first EUP producers and by entering into the Levant, caused a cultural impact that is expressed in local inventions such as the Emireh point.

There is no doubt today that the rapid cultural changes through the Upper Paleolithic times reflect the results of a major revolution. The significance of the technological and social changes is sometimes dimmed, due to the grosgrain of the chronological resolution. However, even before further improvements to the radiocarbon technology for the 45–30 ka period are achieved, the nature of the change is obvious when we compare the latest Mousterian to the Early Upper Paleolithic. As with other revolutions, changes are better documented after a certain lapse of time, when the new cultural expressions stand in contrast to the pre-revolution times. In the case of the European sequence, the proliferation of antler and bone tools, mobile art objects, and cave art in the Franco-Cantabrian region supplies good examples. In the Near East, it is more the ephemeral character of the Upper Paleolithic sites indicating higher mobility, the evolved blade technology and the various types of points (e.g., Ksar 'Akil and El-Wad Points), the appearance of grinding tools, and the modest use of bone and antler that mark the cultural shift. The change was rapid, as is demonstrated by the radiometric dates. Mousterian industries are dominant until 48–46 ka B.P., while by 45–42 ka B.P., Upper Paleolithic manifestations are documented in the coastal ranges of the Eastern Mediterranean. The dates calculated for the Dabban in Cyrenaica are somewhat later (about 40 ka), but a faster change is witnessed in the eastern Balkans (43–30 ka; Kozlowski this volume). The Caucasus region was occupied even later, followed by the appearance of the Upper Paleolithic in Crimea. Indeed, the broader geographic picture seems to be complex, and therefore additional efforts to clarify the chronology and cultural changes of the Early Upper Paleolithic in the Levant may have a major impact on our understanding of the Middle to Upper Paleolithic transition.

Note

All radiocarbon dates are given in B.P. uncalibrated dates. To readings mentioned by the author as B.C. dates (e.g., McBurney 1967), 1950 years were added.

Acknowledgments

I am grateful to Janusz Kozlowski, Steve Kuhn, Paul Mellars, Jiri Svoboda, I. Yalçinkaya, Marcel Otte, Anna Belfer-Cohen, Liliane Meignen, and Erella Hovers for numerous discussions. ABC and LM made many useful comments on previous versions of the manuscript. I am solely responsible for the shortcomings of this version.

BIBLIOGRAPHY

Akazawa, T.
    1987 "The Ecology of the Middle Paleolithic Occupation at Douara Cave, Syria." *Bulletin of the University Museum, University of Tokyo* 29:155–166.

Akazawa, T., S. Muhesen, Y. Dodo, O. Kondo, Y. Mizoguchi, Y. Abe, Y. Nishiaki, S. Ohta, T. Oguchi, and J. Haydal
    1995 "Neanderthal Infant Burial from the Dederiyeh Cave in Syria." *Paléorient* 21(2):77–86.

Albert, R. M., O. Lavi, L. Estroff, S. Weiner, A. Tsatskin, A. Ronen, and S. Lev-Yadun
> 1999 "Mode of Occupation of Tabun Cave, Mt. Carmel, Israel During the Mousterian Period: A Study of the Sediments and Phytoliths." *Journal of Archaeological Science* 26(10):1249–1260.

Albert, R. M., S. Weiner, O. Bar-Yosef, and L. Meignen
> in press "Phytoliths in Kebara Cave, Israel: Study of the Plant Materials Used for Fuel and Other Purposes." *Journal of Archaeological Science*.

Alley, R. B., D. A. Meese, C. A. Shuman, A. J. Gow, K. C. Taylor, P. M. Grootes, J. W. C. White, M. Ram, E. D. Waddington, and P. A. Mayewski
> 1993 "Abrupt Increase in Greenland Snow Accumulation at the End of the Younger Dryas Event." *Nature* 362:527–529.

Altena, C. O. van Regteren
> 1962 "Molluscs and Evhinoderms from Palaeolithic Deposits in the Rock Shelter of Ksar 'Akil, Lebanon." *Zoologische Mededelingen* 38(5):87–99.

Ambrose, S. H.
> 1998a "Chronology of the Later Stone Age and Food Production in East Africa." *Journal of Archaeological Science* 25:377–392.
> 1998b "Late Pleistocene Human Population Bottlenecks, Volcanic Winter, and Differentiation of Modern Humans." *Journal of Human Evolution* 34(6):623–651.

Andrefsky Jr., W.
> 1998 *Lithics: Macroscopic Approaches to Analysis*. Cambridge University Press, Cambridge.

Arensburg, B., and A. Belfer-Cohen
> 1998 "Sapiens and Neandertals: Rethinking the Levantine Middle Paleolithic Hominids," in *Neandertals and Modern Humans in Western Asia*, T. Akazawa, K. Aoki, and O. Bar-Yosef, eds., pp. 311–322. Plenum Press, New York.

Azoury, I.
> 1986 *Ksar Akil, Lebanon: A Technological and Typological Analysis of the Transitional and Early Upper Palaeolithic Levels of Ksar Akil and Abu Halka*. British Archaeological Reports International Series 289. Oxford.

Bar-Yosef, O.
> 1987 "Pleistocene Connexions Between Africa and Southwest Asia: An Archaeological Perspective." *The African Archaeological Review* 5:29–38.
> 1988 "The Date of Southwest Asian Neanderthals," in *L'Homme de Néandertal*, M. Otte, ed., pp. 31–38. Etudes et Recherches Archeologiques de l'Université de Liège, Service de Préhistoire, Liège.
> 1989a "Geochronology of the Levantine Middle Palaeolithic," in *The Human Revolution: Behavioural and Biological Perspectives on the Origins of Modern Humans*, P. Mellars and C. Stringer, eds., pp. 589–610. Edinburgh University Press, Edinburgh.
> 1989b "Upper Pleistocene Cultural Stratigraphy in Southwest Asia," in *Patterns and Processes in Later Pleistocene Human Emergence*, E. Trinkaus, ed., pp. 154–179. Cambridge University Press, Cambridge.
> 1991 "The Search for Lithic Variability among Levantine Epi-Palaeolithic Industries," in *25 Ans d'Études Technologiques en Préhistoire. Bilan et perspectives. XI Rencontres Internationales d'Archéologie et d'Histoire d'Antibes*, C. d. R. A. d. CNRS, eds., pp. 319–336. Éditions APDCA, Ville d'Antibes.
> 1992 "The Role of Western Asia in Modern Human Origins." *Philosophical Transactions of the Royal Society*, B (London) 337:193–200.
> 1994 "The Contributions of Southwest Asia to the Study of the Origin of Modern Humans," in *Origins of Anatomically Modern Humans*, M. H. Nitecki and D. V. Nitecki, eds., pp. 23–66. Plenum Press, New York.
> 1996a "The impact of Late Pleistocene-Early Holocene Climatic Changes on Humans in Southwest Asia," in *Humans at the End of the Ice Age: The Archaeology of the Pleistocene-Holocene Transition*, L. G. Straus, B. V. Eriksen, J. M. Erlandson, and D. R. Yesner, eds., pp. 61–76. Plenum Press, New York.
> 1996b "The Middle/Upper Palaeolithic Transition: A View from the Eastern Mediterranean," in *The Last Neandertals, the First Anatomically Modern Humans*, E. Carbonell and M. Vaquero, eds., pp. 79–94. Universitat Rovira i Virgili, Tarragona.
> 1998a "The Chronology of the Middle Paleolithic of the Levant," in *Neandertals and Modern Humans in Western Asia*, T. Akazawa, K. Aoki, and O. Bar-Yosef, eds., pp. 39–56. Plenum Press, New York.
> 1998b "On the Nature of Transitions: The Middle to Upper Palaeolithic and the Neolithic Revolution." *Cambridge Archaeological Journal* 8(2):141–63.

Bar-Yosef, O., M. Arnold, A. Belfer-Cohen, P. Goldberg, R. Housley, H. Laville, L. Meignen, N. Mercier, J. C. Vogel, and B. Vandermeersch
> 1996 "The Dating of the Upper Paleolithic Layers in Kebara Cave, Mount Carmel." *Journal of Archaeological Science* 23:297–306.

Bar-Yosef, O., and A. Belfer
> 1977 "The Lagaman Industry," in *Prehistoric Investigations in Gebel Maghara, Northern Sinai*, O. Bar-Yosef and J. L. Phillips, eds., pp. 42–84. Institute of Archaeology, Hebrew University, Jerusalem.

Bar-Yosef, O., and A. Belfer-Cohen
1996 "Another Look at the Levantine Aurignacian," in *Colloquium XI - The Late Aurignacian*, A. Montet-White and A. Palma di Cesnola, eds., pp. 139–150. A.B.A.C.O. Edizioni, Forlí, Italy.

Bar-Yosef, O., and J. Callander
1999 "The Woman from Tabun—Garrod's Doubts in Historical Perspective." *Journal of Human Evolution* 37:887–885.

Bar-Yosef, O., and N. Goren
1980 "Afterthoughts Following Prehistoric Surveys in the Levant." *Israel Exploration Journal* 30:1–16.

Bar-Yosef, O., and R. H. Meadow
1995 "The Origins of Agriculture in the Near East," in *Last Hunters, First Farmers: New Perspectives on the Prehistoric Transition to Agriculture*, T. D. Price and A. B. Gebauer, eds., pp. 39–94. School of American Research Press, Santa Fe.

Bar-Yosef, O., and L. Meignen
1992 "Insights into Levantine Middle Paleolithic Cultural Variability," in *The Middle Paleolithic: Adaptation, Behavior, and Variability*, H. L. Dibble and P. Mellars, eds., pp. 163–182. The University Museum, University of Pennsylvania, Philadelphia.

Bar-Yosef, O., B. Vandermeersch, B. Arensburg, A. Belfer-Cohen, P. Goldberg, H. Laville, L. Meignen, Y. Rak, J. D. Speth, and E. Tchernov
1992 "The Excavations in Kebara Cave, Mount Carmel." *Current Anthropology* 33(5):497–550.

Baruch, U., and O. Bar-Yosef
1986 "Upper Palaeolithic Assemblages from Wadi Sudr, Western Sinai." *Paléorient* 12(2):69–83.

Baruch, U., E. Werker, and O. Bar-Yosef
1992 "Charred Wood Remains from Kebara Cave, Israel: Preliminary Results." *Bulletin de la Société Botanique de France* 139:531–538.

Baumler, M.
1995 "Principles and Properties of Lithic Core Reduction: Implications for Levallois Technology," in *The Definition and Interpretation of Levallois Technology*, H. Dibble and O. Bar-Yosef, eds., pp. 11–24. Prehistory Press, Madison.

Baumler, M. F., and J. D. Speth
1993 "A Middle Paleolithic Assemblage from Kunji Cave, Iran," in *The Paleolithic Prehistory of the Zagros-Taurus*, D. I. Olszewski and H. L. Dibble, eds., pp. 1–74. The University Museum, University of Pennsylvania, Philadelphia.

Becker, M. S.
1999 "Reconstructing Prehistoric Hunter-Gatherer Mobility Patterns and the Implications for the Shift to Sedentism: A Perspective from the Near East." Ph.D. Thesis, Department of Anthropology. University of Colorado, Boulder.

Belfer-Cohen, A., and O. Bar-Yosef
1999 "The Levantine Aurignacian: 60 Years of Research," in *Dorothy Garrod and the Progress of the Palaeolithic: Studies in the Prehistoric Archaeology of the Near East and Europe*, W. Davies and R. Charles, eds., pp. 118–134. Oxbow Books, Oxford.

Belfer-Cohen, A., and E. Hovers
1992 "In the Eye of the Beholder: Mousterian and Natufian Burials in the Levant." *Current Anthropology* 33(4):463–471.

Bergman, C. A.
1987 *Ksar Akil, Lebanon: A Technological and Typological Analysis of the Later Palaeolithic Levels of Ksar Akil*. British Archaeological Reports International Series 329, Oxford.

Bergman, C. A., and C. B. Stringer
1989 "Fifty Years After: Egbert, An Early Upper Paleolithic Juvenile from Ksar Akil, Lebanon." *Paléorient* 15(2):99–112.

Beyries, S.
1988 "Functional Variability of Lithic Sets in the Middle Paleolithic," in *Upper Pleistocene Prehistory of Western Eurasia*, H. L. Dibble and A. Montet-White, eds., pp. 213–224. The University Museum, University of Pennsylvania, Philadelphia.

Binford, L. R.
1996 "Hearth and Home: The Spatial Analysis of Ethnographically Documented Rock Shelter Occupations as a Template for Distinguishing Between Human and Hominid Use of Sheltered Space," in *Middle Palaeolithic and Middle Stone Age Settlement Systems*, N. J. Conard and F. Wendorf, eds., pp. 229–240. A.B.A.C.O. Edizioni, Forlí.

Binford, S. R.
1968 "Early Upper Pleistocene Adaptations in the Levant." *American Anthropologist* 70(4):707–717.

Boëda, E.
1995 "Levallois: A Volumetric Construction, Methods, a Technique," in *The Definition and Interpretation of Levallois Technology*, H. L. Dibble and O. Bar-Yosef, eds., pp. 41–68. Prehistory Press, Madison.

Boëda, E., J. M. Geneste, C. Griggo, N. Mercier, S. Muhesen, J. L. Reyss, A. Taha, and H. Valladas
    1999 "A Levallois Point Embedded in the Vertebra of a Wild Ass (*Equus africanus*): Hafting, Projectiles and Mousterian Hunting Weapons." *Antiquity* 73(280):394–402.

Boëda, E., J. M. Geneste, and L. Meignen
    1990 "Identification de chaînes opératoires lithiques du Paléolithique ancien et moyen." *Paléo* 2:43–80.

Boëda, E., and S. Muhesen
    1993 "Umm El Tlel (El Kowm, Syrie): Etude préliminaire des industries lithiques du Paléolithique moyen et supérieur 1991–1992," in *Cahiers de l'Euphrate*, J. Cauvin, ed., pp. 47–92. Editions Recherche sur les Civilisations, Paris.

Bouchud, J.
    1974 "Étude préliminaire de la faune provenant de la grotte du Djebel Qafzeh, pres Nazareth, Israël." *Paléorient* 2:87–102.

Bourguignon, L.
    1996 "Un Mousterien tardif sur le site d'Umm el Tlel (Bassin d'El Khowm, Syrie)? Exemples des niveaux IIBase' et III2A'," in *The Last Neandertals, the First Anatomically Modern Humans*, E. Carbonell and M. Vaquero, eds., pp. 317–336. Universitat Rovira i Virgili, Tarragona.
    1998 "Les industries du Paléolithique intermédiaire d'Umm dl Tlell: nouveaux éléments pour le passage entre Paléolithique moyen et supérieur dans le Bassin d'El Khown," in *Préhistoire d'Anatolie: Génèse de deux mondes*, M. Otte, ed., pp. 709–730. Etudes et Recherches de l'Université de Liège 85, Liège.

Boutié, P.
    1989 "Etude technologique de l'industrie Moustérienne de la grotte de Qafzeh (près de Nazareth, Israël)," in *Investigations in South Levantine Prehistory: Préhistoire du Sud-Levant*, O. Bar-Yosef and B. Vandermeersch, eds., pp. 213–229. British Archaeological Reports International Series 497, Oxford.

Caton-Thompson, G.
    1952 *Kharga Oasis in Prehistory*. Athlone Press, London.

Çetin, O., A. M. Özer, and A. Wieser
    1994 "ESR Dating of Tooth Enamel from Karain Excavation (Antalya, Turkey)." *Quaternary Geochronology (Quaternary Science Reviews)* 13:661–669.

Clark, G. A.
    1997 "The Middle-Upper Paleolithic Transition in Europe: An American Perspective." *Norwegian Archaeological Review* 30:25–53.

Clark, G. A., J. Schuldenrein, M. L. Donaldson, H. P. Schwarcz, W. J. Rink, and S. K. Fish
    1997 "Chronostratigraphic Contexts of Middle Paleolithic Horizons at the 'Ain Difla Rockshelter (WHS 634), West-Central Jordan," in *The Prehistory of Jordan, II. Perspectives from 1997*, H.-G. Gebel, Z. Kafafi, and G. O. Rollefson, eds., pp. 77–100. ex oriente, Berlin.

Coinman, N. R.
    1997 "Upper Paleolithic Technologies: Core Reduction Strategies," in *The Prehistory of Jordan, II. Perspectives from 1997*, H. G. Gebel, Z. Kafafi, and G. O. Rollefson, eds., pp. 125–136. ex oriente, Berlin.
    1998 "The Upper Paleolithic of Jordan," in *The Prehistoric Archaeology of Jordan*, D. O. Henry, ed., pp. 39–63. British Archaeological Reports International Series 705. Archaeopress, Oxford.

Coinman, N. R., and D. O. Henry
    1995 "The Upper Paleolithic Sites," in *Prehistoric Cultural Ecology and Evolution. Insights from Southern Jordan*, D. O. Henry, ed., pp. 133–214. Plenum Press, New York.

Copeland, L.
    1975 "The Middle and Upper Palaeolithic of Lebanon and Syria in the Light of Recent Research," in *Problems in Prehistory: North Africa and the Levant*, F. Wendorf and A. E. Marks, eds., pp. 317–350. Southern Methodist University Press, Dallas.
    1976 "Terminological Correlations in the Early Upper Paleolithic of Lebanon and Syria," in *Deuxième Colloque sur la Terminologie de la Préhistoire au Proche Orient*, F. Wendorf, ed., pp. 35–48. IXe Congrès UISPP, Nice.
    1983 "Levallois/non-Levallois Determinations in the Early Levant Mousterian: Problems and Questions for 1983." *Paléorient* 9:21–38.
    1998a "The Lower Paleolithic of Jordan," in *The Prehistoric Archaeology of Jordan*, D. O. Henry, ed., pp. 5–22. British Archaeological Reports International Series 705. Archaeopress, Oxford.
    1998b "The Middle Palaeolithic Flint Industry of Ras el-Kelb," in *The Mousterian Site of Ras el-Kelb, Lebanon*, L. Copeland and N. Moloney, eds., pp. 73–175. British Archaeological Reports International Series 706. Archaeopress, Oxford.

Copeland, L., and N. Moloney (eds.)
    1998 *The Mousterian Site of Ras el-Kelb, Lebanon*. British Archaeological Reports International Series 706. Archaeopress, Oxford.

Crew, H.
1975 "An Evaluation of the Relationship between the Mousterian Complexes of the Eastern Mediterranean: A Technological Approach.," in *Problems in Prehistory: North Africa and the Levant*, F. Wendorf and A. E. Marks, eds., pp. 427–437. Southern Methodist University Press, Dallas.

Davis, S. J. M.
1977 "The Ungulate Remains from Kebara Cave." *Eretz Israel* (Stekelis Memorial Volume) 13:150–163.
1982 "Climatic Change and the Advent of Domestication of Ruminant Artiodactyls in the Late Pleistocene–Holocene Period in the Israel Region." *Paléorient* 8(2):5–16.

d'Errico, F., J. Zilhão, M. Julien, D. Baffier, and J. Pelegrin
1998 "Neanderthal Acculturation in Western Europe? A Critical Review of the Evidence and its Interpretation." *Current Anthropology* 39 (Supplement): 1–44.

Dibble, H. L.
1984 "The Mousterian Industry from Bisitun Cave (Iran)." *Paléorient* 10(2):23–34.
1993 "Le Paléolithique moyen récent du Zagros." *Bulletin de la Société Préhistorique Française* 90(4):307–312.
1995 "Middle Paleolithic Scraper Reduction: Background, Clarification, and Review of the Evidence to Date." *Journal of Archaeological Method and Theory* 2(4):299–368.

Dibble, H. L., and S. J. Holdaway
1993 "The Middle Paleolithic Industries of Warwasi," in *The Paleolithic Prehistory of the Zagros-Taurus*, D. I. Olszewski and H. L. Dibble, eds., pp. 75–100. The University Museum, University of Pennsylvania, Philadelphia.

El-Moslimany, A. P.
1994 "Evidence of Early Holocene Summer Precipitation in the Continental Middle East," in *Late Quaternary Chronology and Paleoclimates of the Eastern Mediterranean*, O. Bar-Yosef and R. Kra, eds., pp. 121–130. Radiocarbon and the American School of Prehistoric Research, Tucson and Cambridge.

Evins, M. A.
1982 "The Fauna from Shanidar Cave: A Mousterian Goat Exploitation in Northeastern Iraq." *Paléorient* 8(1):37–58.

Farrand, W. R.
1979 "Chronology and Paleoenvironment of Levantine Prehistoric Sites as seen from Sediment Studies." *Journal of Archaeological Science* 6:369–392.

1994 "Confrontation of Geological Stratigraphy and Radiometric Dates from Upper Pleistocene Sites in the Levant," in *Late Quaternary Chronology and Paleoclimates of the Eastern Mediterranean*, O. Bar-Yosef and R. Kra, eds., pp. 21–31. Radiocarbon and the American School of Prehistoric Research, Tucson and Cambridge.

Fleisch, S. J.
1970 "Les habitats du Paléolithique moyen à Naamé, (Liban)." *Bulletin du Museé de Beyrouth* 23:25–98.

Frumkin, A., D. C. Ford, and H. P. Schwarcz
1999 "Continental Oxygen Isotopic Record of the Last 170,000 Years in Jerusalem." *Quaternary Research* 51:317–327.

Gamble, C.
1986 *The Palaeolithic Settlement of Europe*. Cambridge University Press, Cambridge.

Gargett, R. H.
1999 "Middle Palaeolithic Burial is Not a Dead Issue: The View from Qafzeh, Saint-Césaire, Kebara, Amud, and Dederiyeh." *Journal of Human Evolution* 37(1):27–90.

Garrard, A. N.
1982 "The Environmental Implications of a Re-analysis of the Large Mammal Fauna from Wadi el-Mughara Caves, Palestine," in *Palaeoclimates, Palaeoenvironments and Human Communities in the Eastern Mediterranean Region in Later Prehistory*, J. T. Bintliff and W. Van Zeist, eds., pp. 165–187. British Archaeological Reports International Series 133, Oxford.
1983 "The Palaeolithic Faunal Remains from Adlun and Their Ecological Context," in *Adlun in the Stone Age: The Excavations of D. A. E. Garrod in the Lebanon, 1958–1963*, D. A. Roe, ed., pp. 397–413. British Archaeological Reports International Series 159, Oxford.

Garrod, D. A. E.
1937 "Notes on Some Decorated Skeletons from the Mesolithic of Palestine." *Annual Report of the British School at Athens* 37:123–127.
1951–1952 "A Transitional Industry from the Base of the Upper Palaeolithic in Palestine and Syria." *Journal of the Royal Anthropological Institute* 81–82:121–130.
1955 "The Mugharet el Emireh in Lower Galilee: Type Station of the Emiran Industry." *Journal of the Royal Anthropological Institute* 85:141–162.

Garrod, D. A. E., and D. M. Bate
1937 *The Stone Age of Mount Carmel*. Clarendon Press, Oxford.

Geneste, J. M.
1990 "Dévelopment des systèmes de production lithique au cours du paléolithique moyen en Aquitaine septentrionale," in *Paleolithique moyen recent et Paleolithique superieur ancien en Europe: Ruptures et transitions*, C. Farizy, ed., pp. 203–213. APRAIF, Nemours.

Gilead, I.
1981 "Upper Palaeolithic Tool Assemblages from the Negev and Sinai," in *Préhistoire du Levant*, J. Cauvin and P. Sanlaville, eds., pp. 331–342. Centre National de la Recherche Scientifique, Paris.
1988 "Le site Moustérien de Fara II (Néguev septentrional, Israel) et le remontage de son industrie." *L'Anthropologie* 92:797–808.
1991 "The Upper Paleolithic in the Levant." *Journal of World Prehistory* 5(2):105–154.
1995 "Problems and Prospects in the Study of Levallois Technology in the Levant. The Case of Fara II, Israel," in *The Definition and Interpretation of Levallois Technology*, H. Dibble and O. Bar-Yosef, eds., pp. 79–92. Prehistory Press, Madison.

Gilead, I., and O. Bar-Yosef
1993 "Early Upper Paleolithic Sites in the Qadesch Barnea Area, Northeast Sinai." *Journal of Field Archaeology* 20:265–280.

Gilead, I., and C. Grigson
1984 "Farah II: A Middle Palaeolithic Open Air Site in the Northern Negev, Israel." *Proceedings of the Prehistoric Society* 50:71–97.

Gilman, A.
1984 "Explaining the Upper Palaeolithic Revolution," in *Marxist Perspectives in Archaeology*, E. Springs, ed., pp. 115–126. Cambridge University Press, Cambridge.

Goldberg, P.
1983 "The Geology of Boker Tachtit, Boker, and Their Surroundings," in *Prehistory and Paleoenvironments in the Central Negev, Israel*, A. E. Marks, ed., pp. 39–62. Southern Methodist University Press, Dallas.
1986 "Late Quaternary Environmental History of the Southern Levant." *Geoarchaeology* 1:225–244.

Goldberg, P., and O. Bar-Yosef
1998 "Site Formation Processes in Kebara and Hayonim Caves and Their Significance in Levantine Prehistoric Caves," in *Neandertals and Modern Humans in Western Asia*, T. Akazawa, K. Aoki, and O. Bar-Yosef, eds., pp. 107–125. Plenum Press, New York.

Golovanova, L. V., J. F. Hoffecker, V. M. Kharitonov, and G. P. Romanova
1999 "Mezmaiskaya Cave: A Neanderthal Occupation in the Northern Caucasus." *Current Anthropology* 40(1):77–86.

Goren-Inbar, N.
1990 *Quneitra: A Mousterian Site on the Golan Heights*. Hebrew University, Jerusalem.

Goren-Inbar, N., and A. Belfer-Cohen
1998 "The Technological Abilities of the Levantine Mousterians: Cultural and Mental Capacities," in *Neandertals and Modern Humans in Western Asia*, T. Akazawa, K. Aoki, and O. Bar-Yosef, eds., pp. 205–221. Plenum Press, New York.

Goring-Morris, N., O. Marder, A. Davidzon, and F. Ibrahim
1998 "Putting Humpty Together Again: Preliminary Observations on Refitting Studies in the Eastern Mediterranean," in *The Organization of Lithic Technology in Late Glacial and Early Postglacial Europe*, S. Milliken, ed., pp. 149–182. British Archaeological Reports International Series 700, Oxford.

Grün, R., H. P. Schwarcz, and C. B. Stringer
1991 "ESR Dating of Teeth from Garrod's Tabun Cave Collection." *Journal of Human Evolution* 20(3):231–248.

Grün, R., and C. B. Stringer
1991 "Electron Spin Resonance Dating and the Evolution of Modern Humans." *Archaeometry* 33(2):153–199.

Gunneweg, J., T. Beier, U. Diehl, D. Lambrecht, and H. Mommsen
1991 "'Edomite', 'Negbite' and 'Midianite' Pottery from the Negev Desert and Jordan: Instrumental Neutron Activation Analysis Results." *Archaeometry* 33(2):239–253.

Harris, D. R.
1998 "The Origins of Agriculture in Southwest Asia." *The Review of Archaeology* 19(2):5–12.

Hearty, P. J.
1986 "An Inventory of Last Interglacial (*sensu lato*) Age Deposits from the Mediterranean Basin: A Study of Isoleucine Epimerization and U-Series Dating." *Zeitschrift für Geomorphologie* 62:51–69.

Henry, D. O.
1986 "The Prehistory and Palaeoenvironments of Jordan: An Overview." *Paléorient* 12(2):5–26.
1995 *Prehistoric Cultural Ecology and Evolution*. Plenum Press, New York.
1998 "Intrasite Spatial Patterns and Behavioral Modernity: Indications from the Late Levantine Mousterian Rockshelter of Tor Faraj, Southern Jordan," in *Neandertals and Modern Humans in Western Asia*, T. Akazawa, K. Aoki, and O. Bar-Yosef, eds., pp. 127–142. Plenum Press, New York.

Hooijer, D.
1961 "The Fossil Vertebrates of Ksar Akil, a Paleolithic Rockshelter in Lebanon." *Zoologische Verhandelingen* 49:4–65.

Horowitz, A.
1979 *The Quaternary of Israel*. Academic Press, New York.
1992 *Palynology of Arid Lands*. Elsevier Science Publishers, Amsterdam.

Hovers, E.
1990 "The Exploitation of Raw Material at the Mousterian Site of Quneitra," in *Quneitra: A Mousterian Site on the Golan Heights*, N. Goren-Inbar, ed., pp. 150–167. Qedem 31. Institute of Archaeology, Jerusalem.
1997 "Variability of Levantine Mousterian Assemblages and Settlement Patterns: Implications for the Development of Human Behavior." Ph.D. Dissertation. Hebrew University, Jerusalem.
1998 "The Lithic Assemblages of Amud Cave: Implications for Understanding the End of the Mousterian in the Levant," in *Neandertals and Modern Humans in Western Asia*, T. Akazawa, K. Aoki, and O. Bar-Yosef, eds., pp. 143–163. Plenum Press, New York.

Hovers, E., Y. Rak, and W. Kimbel
1991 "Amud Cave—1991 Season." *Mitekufat Haeven, Journal of The Israel Prehistoric Society* 24:152–157.
1996 "Neandertals of the Levant." *Archaeology* Jan/Feb:49–50.

Howell, F. C.
1952 "Pleistocene Glacial Ecology and the Evolution of "classic Neandertal" Man." *Southwest Journal of Anthropology* 8:377–410.
1957 "The Evolutionary Significance of Variation and Varieties of "Neanderthal" Man." *The Quarterly Review of Biology* 32:330–347.
1959 "Upper Pleistocene Stratigraphy and Early Man in the Levant." *Proceedings of the American Philosophical Society* 103:1–65.
1998 "Evolutionary Implications of Altered Perspectives on Hominine Demes and Populations in the Later Pleistocene of Western Eurasia," in *Neandertals and Modern Humans in Western Asia*, T. Akazawa, K. Aoki, and O. Bar-Yosef, eds., pp. 5–27. Plenum Press, New York.

Howells, W. W.
1976 "Explaining Modern Man: Evolutionists Versus Migrationists." *Journal of Human Evolution* 5:477–495.

Inizan, M. L., M. Lechevallier, and P. Plumet
1992 "A Technological Marker of the Penetration into North America: Pressure Microblade Debitage. Its Origin in the Paleolithic of North Asia and its Diffusion," in *Materials Issues in Art and Archaeology III*, P. M. Vandiver, J. R. Druzik, G. S. Wheller, and I. C. Freestone, eds., pp. 661–681. Materials Research Society, Pittsburgh.

Jelinek, A. J.
1981 "The Middle Palaeolithic in the Southern Levant from the Perspective of the Tabun Cave," in *Préhistoire du Levant*, J. Cauvin and P. Sanlaville, eds., pp. 265–280. Centre National de la Recherche Scientifique, Paris.
1982a "The Middle Paleolithic of the Levant: Synthesis," in *Préhistoire du Levant*, J. Cauvin and P. Sanlaville, eds., pp. 299–302. Centre National de la Recherche Scientifique, Paris.
1982b "The Tabun Cave and Paleolithic Man in the Levant." *Science* 216:1369–1375.

Jones, R., and N. White
1988 "Point Blank: Stone Tool Manufacture at the Ngiliptji Quarry, Arnhem Land, 1981," in *Archaeology with Ethnography: An Australian Perspective*, B. Meehan and R. Jones, eds., pp. 51–87. Department of Prehistory, Research School of Pacific Studies, The Australian National University, Canberra.

Kelly, R.
1995 *The Foraging Spectrum: Diversity in Hunter-Gatherer Lifeways*. Smithsonian Institution Press, Washington, D.C.

Kitagawa, H., and J. van der Plicht
1998 "A 40,000-Year Varve Chronology from Lake Suigetsu, Japan: Extension of the ^{14}C Calibration Curve." *Radiocarbon* 40(2):505–516.

Klein, R. G.
1995 "Anatomy, Behavior, and Modern Human Origins." *Journal of World Prehistory* 9(2):167–198.
1999 *The Human Career: Human Biological and Cultural Origins* [2nd Edition]. University of Chicago Press, Chicago.

Kolska Horwitz, L., and P. Goldberg
   1989 "A Study of Pleistocene and Holocene Hyaena Coprolites." *Journal of Archaeological Science* 16:71–94.

Kozlowski, J. K.
   1992 "The Balkans in the Middle and Upper Palaeolithic: The Gate to Europe or a Cul de Sac?" *Proceedings of the Prehistoric Society* 58:1–20.
   1998 "The Middle and the Early Upper Paleolithic around the Black Sea," in *Neandertals and Modern Humans in Western Asia*, T. Akazawa, K. Aoki, and O. Bar-Yosef, eds., pp. 461–482. Plenum Press, New York.

Kuhn, S. L., M. C. Stiner, and E. Güleç
   1999 "Initial Upper Palaeolithic in South-Central Turkey and its Regional Context: A Preliminary Report." *Antiquity* 73(281):505–517.

Lemcke, G., and M. Sturm
   1997 "$\partial 18O$ and Trace Element Measurements as Proxy for the Reconstructions of Climate Changes at Lake Van (Turkey): Preliminary Results," in *Third Millennium BC Climate Change and Old World Collapse*, H. N. Dalfes, G. Kukla, and H. Weiss, eds., pp. 653–678. Springer-Verlag, Berlin.

Lev, E., and M. E. Kislev
   1993 The Subsistence and the Diet of the "Neanderthal" Man in Kebara Cave, Mt. Carmel. Society for the Protection of Nature, Tel Aviv.

Lieberman, D. E.
   1993 "Mobility and Strain: The Biology of Cementogenesis and its Application to the Evolution of Hunter-Gatherer Seasonal Mobility in the Southern Levant during the Quaternary." Ph.D. Dissertation. Harvard University. University Microfilms, Ann Arbor.
   1998 "Neandertal and Early Modern Human Mobility Patterns: Comparing Archaeological and Anatomical Evidence," in *Neandertals and Modern Humans in Western Asia*, T. Akazawa, K. Aoki, and O. Bar-Yosef, eds., pp. 263–275. Plenum Press, New York.

Lieberman, D. E., and J. J. Shea
   1994 "Behavioral Differences between Archaic and Modern Humans in the Levantine Mousterian." *American Anthropologist* 96(2):300–332.

Lucas, G.
   1997 "Les lamelles Dufour du Flageolet I (Bézenac, Dordogne) dans le contexte aurignacien." *Paléo* 9:191–219.

Marks, A. E. (ed.)
   1976 *Prehistory and Palaeoenvironments in the Central Negev, Israel*. Volume I. Southern Methodist University Press, Dallas.
   1983 *Prehistory and Paleoenvironments in the Central Negev, Israel*. Volume III. Southern Methodist University Press, Dallas.

Marks, A. E.
   1981 "The Upper Paleolithic of the Negev," in *Préhistoire du Levant*, J. Cauvin and P. Sanlaville, eds., pp. 299–304. Centre National de la Recherche Scientifique, Paris.
   1990 "The Middle and Upper Palaeolithic of the Near East and the Nile Valley: The Problem of Cultural Transformations," in *The Emergence of Modern Humans*, P. Mellars, ed., pp. 56–80. Cornell University Press, Ithaca.
   1992a "Upper Pleistocene Archaeology and the Origins of Modern Man: A View from the Levant and Adjacent Areas," in *The Evolution and Dispersal of Modern Humans in Asia*, T. Akazawa, K. Aoki, and T. Kimura, eds., pp. 229–252. Hokusen-Sha, Tokyo.
   1992b "Typological Variability in the Levantine Middle Paleolithic," in *The Middle Paleolithic: Adaptation, Behavior, and Variability*, H. L. Dibble and P. Mellars, eds., pp. 127–142. The University Museum, University of Pennsylvania, Philadelphia.
   1993 "The Early Upper Paleolithic: The View from the Levant," in *Before Lascaux: The Complete Record of the Early Upper Paleolithic*, H. Knecht, A. Pike-Tay, and R. White, eds., pp. 5–22. CRC Press, Boca Raton.

Marks, A., and K. Monigal
   1995 "Modeling the Production of Elongated Blanks from the Early Levantine Mousterian at Rosh Ein Mor," in *The Definition and Interpretation of Levallois Technology*, H. Dibble and O. Bar-Yosef, eds., pp. 267–278. Prehistory Press, Madison.

Marshack, A.
   1997 "Paleolithic Image Making and Symboling in Europe and the Middle East: A Comparative Review," in *Beyond Art: Pleistocene Image and Symbol*, M. Conkey, O. Soffer, D. Stratmann, and N. G. Jablonski, eds., pp. 53–91. Memoirs of the California Academy of Sciences, San Francisco.

Mayewski, P. A., M. S. Twickler, S. I. Whitlow, L. D. Meeker, Q. Yang, J. Thomas, K. Kreutz, P. M. Grootes, D. L. Morse, and E. J. Steig
   1996 "Climate Change During the Last Deglaciation in Antarctica." *Science* 272:1636–1638.

McBurney, C. B. M.
1967 *The Haua Fteah (Cyrenaica) and the Stone Age of the South-East Mediterranean.* Cambridge University Press, Cambridge.
1975 "Current Status of the Lower and Middle Paleolithic of the Entire Region from the Levant through North Africa," in *Problems in Prehistory: North Africa and the Levant,* F. Wendorf and A. E. Marks, eds., pp. 411–426. Southern Methodist University Press, Dallas.

McBurney, C. B. M., and R. W. Hey
1955 *Prehistory and Pleistocene Geology in Cyrenaican Libya.* Cambridge University Press, Cambridge.

McCown, T. D.
1934 "The Oldest Complete Skeletons of Man." *Bulletin of the American School of Prehistoric Research* 10:13–18.

McCown, T. D., and A. Keith
1939 *The Stone Age of Mount Carmel II: The Fossil Human Remains from the Levalloiso-Mousterian.* Clarendon Press, Oxford.

Meignen, L.
1995 "Levallois Lithic Production Systems in the Middle Paleolithic of the Near East: The Case of the Unidirectional Method," in *The Definition and Interpretation of Levallois Technology,* H. Dibble and O. Bar-Yosef, eds., pp. 361–380. Prehistory Press, Madison.
1998 "Hayonim Cave Lithic Assemblages in the Context of the Near Eastern Middle Paleolithic: A Preliminary Report," in *Neandertals and Modern Humans in Western Asia,* T. Akazawa, K. Aoki, and O. Bar-Yosef, eds., pp. 165–180. Plenum Press, New York.

Meignen, L., and O. Bar-Yosef
1991 "Les outillages lithiques moustériens de Kébara," in *Le Squelette Moustérien de Kebara 2, Mt. Carmel, Israël,* O. Bar-Yosef and B. Vandermeersch, eds., pp. 49–76. Centre National de la Recherche Scientifique, Paris.

Meignen, L., S. Beyries, J. Speth, and O. Bar-Yosef
1998 "Acquisition, traitement des matières animales et fonction du site au Paléolithique moyen dans la grotte de Kébara (Israël): Approche interdisciplinaire," in *Economie Préhistorique: Les Comportements de Subsistance au Paléolithique,* J.-P. Brugal, L. Meignen, and M. Patou-Matis, eds., pp. 227–242. Editions APDCA, Sophia Antipolis.

Mellars, P.
1996 *The Neanderthal Legacy: An Archaeological Perspective from Western Europe.* Princeton University Press, Princeton.

Mellars, P., and K. Gibson (eds.)
1996 *Modelling the Early Human Mind.* McDonald Institute of Archaeological Research, Cambridge.

Mellars, P., M. Otte, L. Straus, J. Zilhão, and F. d'Errico
1999 "The Neanderthal Problem Continued. CA Forum on Theory in Anthropology." *Current Anthropology* 40(3):341–364.

Mellars, P., and C. Stringer (eds.)
1989 *The Human Revolution: Behavioral and Biological Perspectives on the Origins of Modern Humans.* Edinburgh University Press, Edinburgh.

Mellars, P., and J. Tixier
1989 "Radiocarbon Accelerator Dating of Ksar Aqil (Lebanon) and the Chronology of the Upper Paleolithic Sequence in the Middle East." *Antiquity* 63:761–768.

Mercier, N., H. Valladas, G. Valladas, J. L. Reyss, A. Jelinek, L. Meignen, and J. L. Joron
1995 "TL Dates of Burnt Flints from Jelinek's Excavations at Tabun and Their Implications." *Journal of Archaeological Science* 22(4):495–510.

Mercier, N., H. Valladas, L. Froget, J.-L. Joron, P. M. Vermeersch, P. Van Peer, and J. Moeyersons
1999 "Thermoluminescence Dating of a Middle Palaeolithic Occupation at Sodmein Cave, Red Sea Mountains (Egypt)." *Journal of Archaeological Science* 26(11):1339–1346.

Millard, A. R., and A. W. G. Pike
1999 "Uranium-series Dating of the Tabun Neanderthal: A Cautionary Note." *Journal of Human Evolution* 36(5):581–586.

Mithen, S.
1996 *The Prehistory of the Mind: A Search for the Origins of Art, Religion, and Science.* Thames and Hudson, London.

Moss, E. H.
1983 "A Microwear Analysis of Burins and Points from Tell Abu Hureyra, Syria," in *Traces d'utilisation sur les outils Néolithiques du Proche Orient,* D. Stordeur, ed., pp. 143–161. Centre National de la Recherche Scientifique, Lyon.

Neuville, R.
1934 "Le préhistoire de Palestine." *Revue Biblique* 43:237–259.
1951 *Le Paléolithique et le Mésolithique de Désert de Judée.* Masson et Cie, Editeurs, Paris.

Newcomer, M. H.
  1970 "The Chamfered Pieces from Ksar Akil." *Bulletin of the Institute of Archaeology* 8, 9:177–191.
  1974 "Study and Replication of Bone Tools from Ksar Akil." *World Archaeology* 6(2):138–153.

Ohnuma, K.
  1988 *Ksar Akil, Lebanon: A Technological Study of the Earlier Upper Palaeolithic Levels at Ksar Akil*. Vol. 3, *Levels XXV–XIV*. British Archaeological Reports International Series 426, Oxford.

Ohnuma, K., and C. A. Bergman
  1990 "A Technological Analysis of the Upper Palaeolithic Levels (XXV–VI) of Ksar Akil, Lebanon," in *The Emergence of Modern Humans*, P. Mellars, ed., pp. 91–138. Edinburgh University Press, Edinburgh.

Olszewski, D. I.
  1993 "The Late Baradostian Occupation in Warwasi Rockshelter, Iran," in *The Paleolithic Prehistory of the Zagros–Taurus*, D. I. Olszewski and H. L. Dibble, eds., pp. 187–206. The University Museum, University of Pennsylvania, Philadelphia.
  1994 "The Late Epipalaeolithic Chipped Stone 'Heritage' in Early Aceramic Neolithic Assemblages in the Northern Fertile Crescent," in *Neolithic Chipped Stone Industries of the Fertile Crescent: Proceedings of the First Workshop on PPN Chipped Lithic Industries*, H. G. Gebel and S. K. Kozlowski, eds., pp. 83–90. ex oriente, Berlin.

Olszewski, D. I., and N. R. Coinman
  1998 "Settlement Patterning During the Late Pleistocene in the Wadi al-Hasa, West-Central Jordan," in *The Archaeology of the Wadi al-Hasa, West-Central Jordan, Volume 1: Surveys, Settlement Patterns and Paleoenvironment*, N. R. Coinman, ed., pp. 177–204. Arizona State University, Tempe, Arizona.

Olszewski, D. I., and H. L. Dibble
  1994 "The Zagros Aurignacian." *Current Anthropology* 35(1):68–75.

Otte, M.
  1998 "Turkey as a Key," in *Neandertals and Modern Humans in Western Asia*, T. Akazawa, K. Aoki, and O. Bar-Yosef, eds., pp. 483–492. Plenum Press, New York.

Otte, M., I. Yalçinkaya, J. M. Léotard, M. Kartal, O. Bar-Yosef, J. Kozlowski, I. López-Bayón, and A. Marshack
  1995 "The Epi-Palaeolithic of Öküzini Cave (SW Anatolia) and its Mobiliary Art." *Antiquity* 69:931–944.

Paulissen, E., P. M. Vermeersch, and W. Van Neer
  1985 "Progress Report on the Late Palaeolithic Shuwikhat Sites." *Nyame Akuma* 26):7–14.

Payne, S.
  1983 "The Animal Bones from the Excavations at Douara Cave," in *The Paleolithic Site of Douara Cave and Paleogeography of Palmyra Basin in Syria. Part III*, K Hanihara and T. Akazawa, eds., pp. 1–133. University Museum Bulletin 21. University Museum of Tokyo, Tokyo.

Perlès, C.
  1992 "In Search of Lithic Strategies: A Cognitive Approach to Prehistoric Chipped Stone Assemblages," in *Representations in Archaeology*, J. C. Gardin and C. S. Peebles, eds., pp. 223–247. Indiana University Press, Bloomington.

Perrot, J. J. F.
  1952 "Les industries lithiques palestiniennes de la fin du Mesolithique a l'Age du Bronze." *Israel Exploration Journal* 2(2):73–81.
  1956 "Le Paléolithique supérieur d'El Quseir et de Masaraq an Na'aj (Palestine): inventaire de la collection Rene Neuville I et II." *Bulletin de Société Préhistorique Française* 52:493–506.

Pfeiffer, J. E.
  1982 *The Creative Explosion: An Inquiry into the Origins of Art and Religion*. Harper and Row, New York.

Phillips, J. L.
  1988 "The Upper Paleolithic of the Wadi Feiran, Southern Sinai." *Paléorient* 14(2):183–200.
  1994 "The Upper Paleolithic Chronology of the Levant and the Nile Valley," in *Late Quaternary Chronology and Paleoclimates of the Eastern Mediterranean*, O. Bar-Yosef and R. Kra, eds., pp. 169–176. Radiocarbon and the American School of Prehistoric Research, Tucson and Cambridge.

Phillips, J. L., and B. G. Gladfelter
  1989 "A Survey in the Upper Wadi Feiran Basin, Southern Sinai." *Paléorient* 15:113–122.

Pigeot, N.
  1991 "Reflexions sur l'histoire technique de l'homme: De l'evolution cognitive a l'evolution culturelle." *Paléo* 3:167–200.

Plisson, H., and S. Beyries
  1998 "Pointes ou outils triangulaires? Données fonctionnelles dans le Moustérien levantin." *Paléorient* 24(1):5–24.

Ploux, S.
  1991 "Technologie, technicité, techniciens: méthode de détermination d'auteurs et comportements techniques individuels," in *25 Ans d'Études Technologiques en Préhistoire. Bilan et perspectives. XI Rencontres Internationales d'Archéologie et d'Histoire d'Antibes*, C. d. R. A. d. CNRS, eds., pp. 201–214. Éditions APDCA, Ville d'Antibes.

Quam, R. M., and F. H. Smith
  1998 "A Reassessment of the Tabun C2 Mandible," in *Neandertals and Modern Humans in Western Asia*, T. Akazawa, K. Aoki, and O. Bar-Yosef, eds., pp. 405–421. Plenum Press, New York.

Rabinovich, R.
  1998 "Patterns of Animal Exploitation and Subsistence in Israel, During the Upper Palaeolithic and Epi-Palaeolithic (40,000–12,500 B.P.), Based Upon Selected Case Studies." Ph.D. Dissertation. The Hebrew University, Jerusalem.

Rak, Y.
  1998 "Does any Mousterian Cave Present Evidence of Two Hominid Species?," in *Neandertals and Modern Humans in Western Asia*, T. Akazawa, K. Aoki, and O. Bar-Yosef, eds., pp. 353–366. Plenum Press, New York.

Rak, Y., and B. Arensburg
  1987 "Kebara 2 Neanderthal Pelvis: First Look at a Complete Inlet." *American Journal of Physical Anthropology* 73:227–231.

Rak, Y., W. H. Kimbel, and E. Hovers
  1994 "A Neandertal Infant from Amud Cave, Israel." *Journal of Human Evolution* 26:313–324.

Richter, D., F. Waiblinger, W. J. Rink, and G. A Wagner
  2000 "Thermoluminescence, Electron Spin Resonance and ^{14}C-Dating of the Late Middle and Early Upper Palaeolithic Site of Geißenklösterle Cave in Southern Germany." *Journal of Archaeological Science* 27(1):71–89.

Ronen, A.
  1974 *Tirat Carmel: A Mousterian Open Air Site in Israel*. Institute of Archaeology, Tel Aviv University, Tel Aviv.
  1979 "Paleolithic Industries," in *The Quaternary of Israel*, A. Horowitz, ed., pp. 296–307. Academic Press, New York.
  1984 *Sefunim Prehistoric Sites, Mount Carmel, Israel*. British Archaeological Reports International Series 230, Oxford.

Rossignol-Strick, M.
  1995 "Sea-Land Correlation of Pollen Records in the Eastern Mediterranean for the Glacial-Interglacial Transition: Biostratigraphy versus Radiometric Time-scale." *Quaternary Science Reviews* 14:893–915.
  1997 "Paléoclimat de la Méditerranée orientale et de l'Asie du Sud-Ouest de 15 000 à 6 000 B.P." *Paléorient* 23(2):175–186.

Rust, A.
  1950 *Die Höhlenfunde von Jabrud (Syrien)*. Karl Wacholtz Verlag, Neumünster.

Sanlaville, P.
  1981 "Stratigraphie et chronologie du Quaternaire continental du Proche Orient," in *Préhistoire du Levant*, P. Sanlaville and J. Cauvin, eds., pp. 21–32. Centre National de la Recherche Scientifique, Paris.
  1992 "Changements climatiques dans la péninsule arabique durant le Pléistocène supérieur et l'Holocène." *Paléorient* 18(1):5–26.

Schick, T., and M. Stekelis
  1977 "Mousterian Assemblages in Kebara Cave, Mount Carmel." *Eretz Israel* 13 (M. Stekelis Memorial Volume):97–150.

Schlanger, N.
  1996 "Understanding Levallois: Lithic Technology and Cognitive Archaeology." *Cambridge Archaeological Journal* 6(2):231–254.

Schroeder, B.
  1969 "The Lithic Industries from Jerf Ajla and their Bearing on the Problem of the Middle to Upper Paleolithic Transition." Ph.D. Dissertation. Columbia University, New York.

Schwarcz, H. P., and W. J. Rink
  1998 "Progress in ESR and U-Series Chronology of the Levantine Paleolithic," in *Neandertals and Modern Humans in Western Asia*, T. Akazawa, K. Aoki, and O. Bar-Yosef, eds., pp. 57–67. Plenum Press, New York.

Sellet, F.
  1993 "*Chaine Operatoire*: The Concept and its Applications." *Lithic Technology* 18(1 and 2):106–112.

Shea, J. J.
  1989 "A Functional Study of the Lithic Industries Associated with Hominid Fossils in the Kebara and Qafzeh Caves, Israel," in *The Human Revolution*, P. Mellars and C. Stringer, eds., pp. 611–625. Edinburgh University Press, Edinburgh.

1995 "Behavioral Factors Affecting the Production of Levallois Points in the Levantine Mousterian," in *The Definition and Interpretation of Levallois Technology*, H. Dibble and O. Bar-Yosef, eds., pp. 279–292. Prehistory Press, Madison.

1988 "Spear Points from the Middle Paleolithic of the Levant." *Journal of Field Archaeology* 15:441–450.

1998 "Neandertal and Early Modern Human Behavioral Variability: A Regional-Scale Approach to Lithic Evidence for Hunting in the Levantine Mousterian." *Current Anthropology* 39 (Supplement):S45–S78.

Sherratt, A.
1997 "Climatic Cycles and Behavioural Revolutions: The Emergence of Modern Humans and the Beginning of Farming." *Antiquity* 71:271–287.

Solecki, R. L., and R. S. Solecki
1970 "A New Secondary Flaking Technique at the Nahr Ibrahim Cave Site (Lebanon)." *Bulletin du Musée de Beyrouth* 23:137–142.

Solecki, R. S.
1958 "The Baradostian Industry and the Upper Palaeolithic in the Near East." Ph.D. Dissertation. Columbia University, New York.
1963 "Prehistory in Shanidar Valley, Northern Iraq." *Science* 139:179–193.
1964 "Shanidar Cave, A Late Pleistocene site in Northern Iraq." *Report of the VIth International Congress on the Quaternary, Warsaw, 1961* 413–423.

Solecki, R. S., and R. L. Solecki
1993 "The Pointed Tools from the Mousterian Occupations of Shanidar Cave, Northern Iraq," in *The Paleolithic Prehistory of the Zagros–Taurus*, D. I. Olszewski and H. L. Dibble, eds., pp. 119–146. The University Museum, University of Pennsylvania, Philadelphia.

Stager, L.
1995 "The Impact of the Sea Peoples in Canaan (1185–1050 BCE)," in *The Archaeology of Society in the Holy Land*, T. Levy, ed., pp. 332–348. Leicester University Press, London.

Stefan, V. H., and E. Trinkaus
1998 "Discrete Trait and Morphometric Affinities of the Tabun 2 Mandible (hu970210)." *Journal of Human Evolution* 34(5):443–468.

Stiner, M. C., N. D. Munro, T. A. Surovell, E. Tchernov, and O. Bar-Yosef
1999 "Paleolithic Population Growth Pulses Evidenced by Small Animal Exploitation." *Science* 283:190–194.

Straus, L. G.
1997 "The Iberian Situation Between 40,000 and 30,000 B.P. in Light of European Models of Migration and Convergence," in *Conceptual Issues in Modern Humans Origins Research*, G. A. Clark and C. M. Willermet, eds., pp. 235–252. Aldine de Gruyter, New York.

Stringer, C.
1998 "Chronological and Biogeographic Perspectives on Later Human Evolution," in *Neandertals and Modern Humans in Western Asia*, T. Akazawa, K. Aoki, and O. Bar-Yosef, eds., pp. 29–37. Plenum Press, New York.

Tchernov, E.
1981 "The Biostratigraphy of the Levant," in *Préhistoire du Levant. Chronologie et Organisation de l'Espace depuis les Origines jusqu'au VIe Millénaire*, J. Cauvin and P. Sanlaville, eds., pp. 67–97. Centre National de la Recherche Scientifique, Paris.
1984 *Faunal Turnover and Extinction Rate in the Levant*. The University of Arizona Press, Tucson.
1994 "New Comments on the Biostratigraphy of the Middle and Upper Pleistocene of the Southern Levant," in *Late Quaternary Chronology and Paleoclimates of the Eastern Mediterranean*, O. Bar-Yosef and R. S. Kra, eds., pp. 333–350. Radiocarbon and the American School of Prehistoric Research, Tucson and Cambridge.
1997 "Are Late Pleistocene Environmental Factors, Faunal Changes and Cultural Transformations Causally Connected? The Case of the Southern Levant." *Paléorient* 23(2):209–228.
1998 "The Faunal Sequence of the Southwest Asian Middle Paleolithic in Relation to Hominid Dispersal Events," in *Neandertals and Modern Humans in Western Asia*, T. Akazawa, K. Aoki, and O. Bar-Yosef, eds., pp. 77–90. Plenum Press, New York.

Tillet, T.
1993 "L'Atérien du Sahara méridional." Ph.D. Dissertation. Université di Provence Aix-Marseille I, France.

Tillier, A.-M.
1998 "Ontogenetic Variation in Late Pleistocene *Homo Sapiens* from the Near East: Implications for Methodological Bias in Reconstructing Evolutionary Biology," in *Neandertals and Modern Humans in Western Asia*, T. Akazawa, K. Aoki, and O. Bar-Yosef, eds., pp. 381–389. Plenum Press, New York.
1989 "The Evolution of Modern Humans: Evidence from Young Mousterian Individuals," in *The Human Revolution: Behavioural and Biological Perspectives in the Origins of Modern Humans*, P. Mellars and C. Stringer, eds., pp. 286–297. Edinburgh University Press, Edinburgh.

1999 *Les enfants moustériens de Qafzeh. Interprétations phylogénétique et paléoauxologique.* Centre National de la Recherche Scientifique, Paris.

Trinkaus, E.
1984 "Western Asia," in *The Origins of Modern Humans: A World Survey of the Fossil Evidence of Modern Humans*, F. H. Smith and F. Spencer, eds., pp. 251–293. Alan R. Liss, Inc., New York.
1986 "The Neandertals and Modern Human Origins." *Annual Review of Anthropology* 15:193–218.
1992 "Morphological Contrasts Between the Near Eastern Qafzeh-Skhul and Late Archaic Human Samples: Grounds for a Behavioral Difference?," in *The Evolution and Dispersal of Modern Humans in Asia*, T. Akazawa, K. Aoki, and T. Kimura, eds., pp. 277–294. Hokusen-Sha, Tokyo.

Trinkaus, E., C. B. Ruff, and S. E. Churchill
1998 "Upper Limb versus Lower Limb Loading Patterns among Near Eastern Middle Paleolithic Hominids," in *Neandertals and Modern Humans in Western Asia*, T. Akazawa, K. Aoki, and O. Bar-Yosef, eds., pp. 391–404. Plenum Press, New York.

Turnbull, P. F., and C. A. Reed
1974 "The Fauna from the Terminal Pleistocene of the Pelegawra Cave, a Zarzian Occupation Site in North-western Iraq." *Fieldiana Anthropology* 63(3):81–146.

Valladas, H., J. L. Joron, G. Valladas, B. Arensburg, O. Bar-Yosef, A. Belfer-Cohen, P. Goldberg, H. Laville, L. Meignen, and Y. Rak
1987 "Thermoluminescence Dates for the Neanderthal Burial Site at Kebara in Israel." *Nature* 330:159–160.

Valladas, H., N. Mercier, J.-L. Joron, and J.-L. Reyss
1998 "GIF Laboratory Dates for Middle Paleolithic Levant," in *Neandertals and Modern Humans in Western Asia*, T. Akazawa, K. Aoki, and O. Bar-Yosef, eds., pp. 69–75. Plenum Press, New York.

Valladas, H., J. L. Reyss, J. L. Joron, G. Valladas, O. Bar-Yosef, and B. Vandermeersch
1988 "Thermoluminescence Dating of Mousterian 'Proto-Cro-Magnon' Remains from Israel and the Origin of Modern Man." *Nature* 331:614–615.

van Andel, T. H.
1998 "Middle and Upper Palaeolithic Environments and the Calibration of ^{14}C Dates Beyond 10,000 B.P." *Antiquity* 72(275):26–33.

van der Plicht, J.
1999 "Radiocarbon Calibration for the Middle/Upper Palaeolithic: A Comment." *Antiquity* 73(279):119–123.

van der Plicht, J., A. van der Wijk, and G. J. Bartstra
1989 "Uranium and Thorium in Fossil Bones: Activity Ratios and Dating." *Applied Geochemistry* 4:339–342.

Van Peer, P.
1998 "The Nile Corridor and the Out-of-Africa Model: An Examination of the Archaeological Record." *Current Anthropology* 39:

van Zeist, W., and S. Bottema
1991 *Late Quaternary Vegetation of the Near East.* Dr. Ludwig Reichert Verlag, Weisbaden.

Vandermeersch, B.
1982 "The First *Homo sapiens sapiens* in the Near East," in *The Transition from the Lower to the Middle Palaeolithic and the Origin of Modern Man*, A. Ronen, ed., pp. 297–300. British Archaeological Reports International Series 151, Oxford.
1995 "Le role du Levant dans l'évolution de l'humanité au Pléistocene supérieur." *Paléorient* 21(2):25–34.

Vaufrey, R.
1939 "Paléolithique et Mésolithique palestiniens." *Revue scientifique* 79:390–406.

Vignard, A. E.
1920 "Station Aurignacienne à Nag Hamadi (Haute Egypte)." *Bulletin Institut Français d'Archéologie Orientale* 18:1–20.

Vermeersch, P. M., E. Paulissen, S. Stokes, C. Charlier, P. van Peer, C. Stringer, and W. Lindsay
1998 "A Middle Palaeolithic Burial of a Modern Human at Taramsa Hill, Egypt." *Antiquity* 72(277):475–484.

Vermeersch, P. M., E. Paulissen, S. Stokes, P. van Peer, M. De Bie, F. Steenhoudt, and S. Missotten
n.d. "Middle Palaeolithic Chert Mining in Egypt," in The Fourth International Flint Symposium, Madrid.

Volkman, P.
1983 "Boker Tachtit: Core Reconstructions," in *Prehistory and Paleoenvironments in the Central Negev, Israel*, A. E. Marks, ed., pp. 127–190. Southern Methodist University Press, Dallas.

Weinstein-Evron, M.
1983 "The Paleoecology of the Early Würm in the Hula Basin, Israel." *Paléorient* 9(1):5–19.

1990 Palynological History of the Last Pleniglacial in the Levant. *Etudes et Recherches Archeologiques de l'Université de Liège* 42:9–25.

Wendorf, F., R. Schild, and A. E. Close (eds.)
1993 *Egypt During the Last Interglacial: The Middle Paleolithic of Bir Tarfawi and Bir Sahara East.* Plenum Press, New York.

White, R.
1989 "Production Complexity and Standardization in Early Aurignacian Bead and Pendant Manufacture: Evolutionary Implications," in *The Human Revolution: Behavioural and Biological Perspectives on the Origins of Modern Humans*, P. Mellars and C. Stringer, eds., pp. 366–390. Edinburgh University Press, Edinburgh.
1997 "Substantial Acts: From Materials to Meaning in Upper Paleolithic Representation," in *Beyond Art: Pleistocene Image and Symbol*, M. W. Conkey, O. Soffer, D. Stratmann, and N. G. Jablonski, eds., pp. 93–121. Memoirs of the California Academy of Sciences, San Francisco.

Wolpoff, M. H.
1998 "Concocting a Divisive Theory." *Evolutionary Anthropology* 7(1):1–3.

Yalçinkaya, I.
1988 "Resultats recents des fouilles à Karain en Anatolie." *L'Homme de Néandertal*, M. Otte, ed., vol. 8, pp. 257–271. Etudes et Recherches Archeologiques de l'Université de Liège 32, Service de Préhistoire, Liège.
1991 "1990 Yili Karain Kazilari," in *XIII Kazi Sonuçlari Toplantisi I*, 27–31 Mayis 1991 Çanakkale, Ayri Basim, pp. 33–54. Ankara Üniversitesi Basimevi, Ankara.
1995 "Thoughts on Levallois Technique in Anatolia," in *The Definition and Interpretation of Levallois Technology*, H. Dibble and O. Bar-Yosef, eds., pp. 399–412. Prehistory Press, Madison.

Yalçinkaya, I., M. Otte, O. Bar-Yosef, J. Kozlowski, J. M. Léotard, and H. Taskiran
1993 "The Excavations at Karain Cave, South-Western Turkey: An Interim Report," in *The Paleolithic Prehistory of the Zagros-Taurus*, D. I. Olszewski and H. L. Dibble, eds., pp. 100–106. The University Museum of the University of Pennsylvania, Philadelphia.

Zeuner, F. E.
1946 *Dating the Past: An Introduction to Geochronology* 1st Edition. Hafner Publishing, Darien, Conn.
1958 *Dating the Past: An Introduction to Geochronology* 4th Edition. Hafner Publishing, Darien, Conn.

Ziffer, D. A.
1978 "A Re-evaluation of the Upper Palaeolithic Industries at Kebara Cave and Their Place in the Aurignacian Culture of the Levant." *Paléorient* 4:273–293.

Zilhão, J., and F. d'Errico
1999 "Reply in Mellars et al. The Neanderthal Problem Continued. CA Forum on Theory in Anthropology." *Current Anthropology* 40(3):355–364.

CHAPTER 7

Modern–Nonmodern Hominid Interactions: A Mediterranean Perspective

Jean-Jacques Hublin
Centre National de Recherche Scientifique, France

INTRODUCTION

Addressing the question of the interactions between Middle and Upper Paleolithic populations from a paleoanthropological perspective results in a discussion on the possible interactions between "archaic" (not anatomically modern) and anatomically modern humans. In the Mediterranean area, these groups of fossil hominids are contemporaneous for most of the Upper Pleistocene, possibly until as late as 30 ka B.P. It is thus difficult to restrict the discussion to the period of time strictly corresponding to the transition of the Middle to Upper Paleolithic. Addressing this question also results in an attempt to clarify the relations between biological groups of hominids and technocomplexes and/or cultural entities. These relations have been vigorously debated during the past decades. In the 1960s, it was still rather widely accepted that simple correspondence could exist between groups of fossil hominids and lithic assemblages. Then both were often considered as belonging to a succession of "stages," evolving more or less in parallel. This was most often assumed when considering the Middle and Upper Paleolithic. The views outlined by R. Foley and M. M. Lahr (1997) represent a continuation of this perspective. However, better chronological resolution, the emergence of more complex phylogenetic trees, and discoveries of unexpected associations between hominids and lithic assemblages gradually led to the abandoning of this view. Specifically, the evidence in favor of associating anatomically modern humans with Mousterian industries in Israel (Vandermeersch 1981), and late Neandertals with early Upper Paleolithic industries (Lévêque and Vandermeersch 1980) broke the equations Neandertal=Mousterian and anatomically modern humans=Upper Paleolithic.

A new wisdom, in accordance with which "culture" and "biological groups" had no direct relation and could be analyzed separately developed, and became especially influential among some European archaeologists. According to this approach, "Culture" is indeed a production of "Humans" but, by its flexible nature, it escapes the phylogenetic determinism that can be applied to biological entities (see for example Straus 1994). Thus, dividing humans into different biological entities certainly introduces more complexity into the picture of the Paleolithic, but it is not really relevant when sorting out the succession of Paleolithic "cultures." Furthermore, questioning the mental and technical abilities of different groups of hominids somehow became a burning topic, as expressed by the recent controversy over the transition from Middle to Upper Paleolithic in Europe and the possible interactions between Neandertals and contemporary modern humans (d'Errico et al. 1998).

Clearly, major cultural changes can occur without any perceptible biological change, as exemplified by the emergence of Upper Paleolithic behavior in modern populations. However, it is very unlikely that events such as the total replacement of one biological group by another would leave no cultural trace, unless the two belonged to exactly the same technocomplex. This point is crucial in understanding the process of replacement or evolution substituting modern for archaic humans throughout the Old World. However, discussions about these problems have been also obscured by the confusion sometimes surrounding the significance of the Paleolithic assemblages. Many of the Upper Paleolithic "lithic industries" likely match extinct ethnocultural entities which produced a number of stereotyped objects. Their geographical and chronological distributions follow a consistent pattern. This does not mean that different successive assemblages resulted from different biological groups. Nevertheless, in this situation, it is highly improbable that distinct biological populations could *independently* have produced the same stereotyped assemblages. The status of Middle Paleolithic assemblages is likely quite different and more complex. In some cases, local traditions may have played a role in the emergence of the different "Mousterian industries." However, raw material availability, local activities, and technological convergence included in the development of the "*chaînes opératoires*" also influenced the characteristics of these assemblages. As a result of these processes, the definitions of "cultures" are rarely sharply chiseled, and their exact significance often remains unclear. As a whole, "Mousterian" should be considered more as a technical stage, independently crossed by several groups of hominids. Under these conditions, pure parallelisms could occur between distinct groups, sometimes separated by significant geographical or chronological gaps. Probably this is why, so far, the attempts to match biological entities (e.g. anatomically modern humans and Neandertals) to specific Upper Paleolithic assemblages have been more successful than their match to Middle Paleolithic assemblages.

Geographical Presentation

Classically, three main geographical domains have been considered by the scholars dealing with the Paleolithic peopling of the Mediterranean areas: Europe, the Near East, and North Africa. Until the middle of the Lower Pleistocene, Europe seems to have remained essentially outside the expansion range of hominids. So far it is only toward the end of this period that clearly dated archaeological sites and fossil human remains are documented in the south of the continent (Turq et al. 1996; Carbonell et al. 1995; Ascenzi et al. 1996). Relatively isolated from neighboring areas by the Mediterranean, the Black Sea and the Caucasus, Europe is connected to the Near East by the corridors of the Bosphorus and the Dardanells. It is structured by the development of the Alpine arch extending from West to East and separating two main latitudinal eco-geographical bands. To the South, the Mediterranean areas represent a series of peninsulas and littoral plains clustered by mountain chains. To the North, a large plain runs from the northern shore of the Black Sea to the Atlantic. This structure favored the expansion of the humans from the southeast along two different routes. However, in reference to the climatic conditions, the southern route may have offered more favorable conditions for the greater part of the Pleistocene. The earliest human settlements were discovered in the south of the continent and it seems that, until the middle of the Middle Pleistocene, the Northern Plain was only sporadically penetrated (Roebroeks and Kolfschoten 1994). Indeed, European geography and landscapes were strongly affected by the alternation of glacial and interglacial periods that developed after 900 ka B.P. During the peaks of the former, the Northern plain was mostly covered by glaciers and permafrost, and was not suitable for extensive human occupation. In fact the adaptation of human groups to the peri-arctic environment is clearly demonstrated only by Upper Paleolithic populations. During the coldest phases, the geographical outline of Europe was significantly changed by lowered sea levels. The emersion of the continental plateau mainly extended the European territory to the west, but also widened littoral plains in the Mediterranean area, especially in the Tyrrhenian. The extension of the Caspian Sea and the development of glaciers on the Caucasus during cold episodes contributed to the isolation of western Eurasia. For most of the Paleolithic, human settlements in Europe were discontinuous in time and in space except for a few favorable areas (Bocquet-Appel and Demars 2000).

Human evolution in North Africa is best documented in the western part of the Maghreb. There, during most of the Pleistocene, the environment was mainly characterized by aridity, particularly marked at a distance from the coastlines. Aridity increased during the second half of the Middle Pleistocene ("Tensiftian" stage) and even more during the period corresponding to the European "Würm" ("Soltanian" stage). The studies of the large fauna (Arambourg 1960) and micromammals (Jaeger 1975) suggest the existence of two biogeographic provinces. The internal province was characterized by an open environment more xerophytic than that of the littoral province. The border between the two domains seems to have moved into the littoral zone during the Pleistocene. During the late Middle and the Upper Pleistocene, the pattern of human peopling likely depended on the periodic extension of the Sahara. These extensions were driven by global climatic changes. However, it seems difficult to establish a simple correspondence between the oxygen isotopic curves, the alternation of glacial and interglacial stages in Europe, and the variation in size of the African deserts. Contradicting a traditional view (see Lahr and Foley 1998 for example), the extensions of the Sahara did not simply match the peak of the cold and dry stages well documented in Europe. In the lower latitudes, the periodical extensions of African deserts are driven by a cycle corresponding to that of the equinoctial precession, modulated by eccentricity (see Rognon 1996). During OIS 5, a period of 23,000 years separates successive rainy periods. As a result of this phenomenon, major and simultaneous extensions of the African deserts occurred during OIS 5b and OIS 5d. In North Western Africa, hyper-arid phases signed by the development of calcareous and gypseous crusts are documented during "Tensiftian II" (in Texier et al. 1985 terminology) and "Soltanian" (Texier et al. 1986). The end of the "Tensiftian II" corresponds to the OIS 6 and is marked by a crisis leading to the extinction of the rodent genera *Ellobius*, *Arvicanthis*, and *Praomys* (Jaeger 1975; 1981). For the "Soltanian," the site of Doukkalla II yielded a fauna of very dry savanna (Laquay and Cheddadi 1986) and at the end of the "Soltanian" (OIS 2) the fauna of El Haroura cave corresponds to a semi-desert (Beckouche, quoted by Texier et al. 1986). During OIS 2, the South African deserts extended somewhat earlier (circa 23 ka B.P.) than the Sahara (circa 19–18 ka B.P.), corresponding to a discrepancy in the extension of glacial caps of the two hemispheres. In contrast, the near disappearance of the Sahara Desert occurred during intermediate stages such as OIS 3 (Rognon 1996).

The Mediterranean fringes of the Near East constitute a geographically complex area. Their northern part belongs to the Palearctic biogeographic domain. The Anatolian Plateau is delimited in the south by the Taurus-Zagros mountain chain, which represents a major biogeographic barrier. Further to the south, the southern Levant represents a corridor between the Syrian-Transjordanian plateau in the east and the Mediterranean in the west. Faunal exchanges between Africa and Eurasia occurred through this corridor. But, as a whole, the area remained rather isolated for most of the Pleistocene and more often played the role of a barrier between the Palearctic and Ethiopian biogeographic domains (Tchernov 1998). This region, like the Maghreb, is characterized by an increase in aridity during the Pleistocene. Climatic cycles resulted in fluctuations of the palearctic domain, which sometimes extending into the southern Levant during cold stages, and in intrusions of African faunal elements in the same area during the development of interglacial conditions. As pointed out by Tchernov (1992), while African elements could disperse south to north if the Zagros-Taurus could be surmounted, Palearctic elements could hardly expend further south than the Southern Levant cul-de-sac at the time of largest expansion of the Sahara. As in the Maghreb, part of OIS 3 seems to represent a period of reduction of aridity with the development of evergreen woodland and the extension of human occupations (Marks 1983; Goring-Morris 1987; Van Andel and Tzedakis 1996; Tchernov 1998)

North Africa

During the second half of the Middle Pleistocene, a phenomenon of accretion occurred in Africa, leading to the emergence of "primitive modern humans." In North Africa they are known in Jebel Irhoud associated with a Mousterian industry reminiscent of the La Ferrassie type in southwestern France. This series of human fossils is composed of one adult skull (Irhoud 1), one adult brain case (Irhoud 2), one juvenile mandible (Irhoud 3), one juvenile humerus (Irhoud 4), and one juvenile pelvis (Irhoud 5). Paleontological evidence (Biberson 1964; Thomas 1981; Amani and Geraads 1993) suggests an age greater than the Soltanian, possibly OIS 5. Attempts to determine the age of the deposit by ESR indicated EU age estimates ranging from 90 to 125 ka, and LU estimates between 105 and 190 ka (Grün and Stringer 1991). These last authors conclude that the site has a long depositional history covering at least OIS 5 and 6, and they favor an age within OIS 6 (130–190 ka) for the hominids, assuming that they were low in the stratigraphic sequence. The faunal assemblage, including a lot of Gerbillidae, indicates quite dry conditions that could represent the maximum extension of the Sahara during OIS 5d or some arid episodes of OIS 6.

The Irhoud specimens have been repeatedly allocated to the Neandertals or designated as bearing Neandertal features. However, there is no evidence of any Neandertal apomorphy in these hominids, in particular not in the anatomical areas such as the face or the occipital, which are most characteristic of the Neandertals. In contrast, clear synapomorphies with modern man are observed. On the Irhoud 3 mandible, a bony chin is well developed, the condyles are small and the *corpus mandibulae* displays modern proportions. On the skulls, one observes a convex and steep frontal squama, and well-defined and highly positioned *tuber parietale*. On Irhoud 2, there is a clear dissociation of the supraorbitory elements. The specimens also display some plesiomorphies (general robusticity, macrodonty, features related to a moderate platycephaly, strong supraorbital reliefs). However, this does not preclude an ancestor-descendant relationship with late Upper Pleistocene modern humans.

The Irhoud hominids should definitely be excluded from the Neandertal clade. They show affinities with the Skhul and Qafzeh samples, and represent a slightly more primitive (and older?) grade than the early modern humans of the Levant (Hublin et al. 1987; Hublin and Tillier 1988; Hublin 1993).

In the Maghreb, only two other specimens are assigned to Mousterian assemblages. In Haua Fteah (Libya), two fragmentary mandibles were unearthed in a "Levalloiso-Mousterian context." The archeological level that yielded the human remains was initially assigned to a period of time between 45 and 60 ka B.P. (McBurney 1967). It could, however, be significantly older and may even approach the age of the Irhoud specimens. It underlies Aterian layers and overlays pre-Aurignacian layers. The age of the latter was estimated by McBurney (1967) as between 80 and 65 ka B.P. on the basis of sedimentological and paleoclimatic considerations. However, similar blade industries in Southwestern Asia are now assigned to OIS 6 or older (Meignen 1998).

Haua Fteah 1 is represented by a young adult fragment composed of the left ramus and the posterior portion of the left corpus bearing M2 and M3. Haua Fteah 2 is represented by almost the same parts but bears only a non erupted M3 and belonged to a 12 to 14 year old individual (Tobias 1967). Although these specimens are quite fragmentary, they contrast strikingly with the European and southwestern Neandertals in the lack of frequently observed features in these groups. There is no strongly developed retromolar space, no oval-horizontal shape of the mandibular foramen, no development of the condyle lateral to the crest of the mandibular notch, and no hyper-development of the coronoid part of the ramus relative to the condylar part.

When the Jebel Irhoud and Haua Fteah examples are considered, Northwestern Africa appears well separated from Europe during the Late Middle Pleistocene and/or the Early Upper Pleistocene. Indeed, the Mediterranean Sea then played the role of a major biogeographic barrier. Although some possible technical exchanges may have occurred earlier or later through the Straits of Gibraltar during low sea level periods (Alimen 1975, but see also Otte 1996), paleontological evidence demonstrates that for most of this period, biological exchanges were very limited or non existent. While Neandertals were evolving in relative isolation in Western Europe (and this is now particularly well documented in the Iberian Peninsula), North Africa witnessed the emergence of pre-modern humans. Another conclusion can be drawn from analysis of the North African fossil record. The rise of anatomically modern features cannot be restricted to the sub-Saharan or East African area, as was initially assumed by the strict "out of Africa" genetic model, which emphasized the role of the sub-Saharan area (Cann et al. 1987; Cavalli-Sforza et al. 1988; Vigilant et al. 1989) nor does it strictly fit the initial "Afro-European hypothesis" (Bräuer 1984) which also allocated the origin of modern European to a southeastern part of Africa. Whatever the fate of these North African populations, they demonstrate that the development of modern morphology encompassed the African continent from south to north. This evidence could be used to support a genetic scenario in which large and subdivided African (and Southwestern Asian?) populations, as opposed to small and isolated East African populations, were involved in the development of fully modern *Homo sapiens* (Harris and Hey 1999).

In North Africa, one observes a continuum from Mousterian to Aterian assemblages, and a similar continuity seems to be observed with associated fossil hominids. In Morocco, the two assemblages seem to evolve one from the other without any discontinuity. In the Grotte des Pigeons at Taforalt (Roche 1952), at Temara (Debénath et al. 1986) and at Rhafas (near Oujda) (Wengler 1986) the two industries are observed. In the two last sites, typological transition is also observed. At the Rhafas cave, where a "proto-Aterian" lies between the final Mousterian and the Aterian, the series displays a regular evolution with a development of tanged artifacts and end-scrapers and a reduction in frequency of side-scrapers (Wengler 1990). The same strategies in raw materials procurement and debitage techniques were adopted in both the Mousterian and the Aterian, emphasizing their cultural likeness. In the eastern Maghreb it has been reported that Mousterian and Aterian may even widely overlap (Wendorf et al. 1990).

Contradictory opinions exist on the antiquity of the oldest Aterian assemblages. According to Debénath et al. (1986) and Texier et al. (1988), the Aterian in northwestern Africa is a rather recent industry, developing between 40 and 20 ka B.P. An even later development to the south, in North Chad and Niger, is supported by Tillet (1984). However, the oldest tentatively dated levels in Morocco are beyond the reach of the ^{14}C method. In Temara, three dates of >40 ka B.P. were obtained from levels 23 to 19 (Gif 2279, Gif 2588 and Gif 2589) (Debénath et al. 1986). In the Rhafas cave, overlaying a "proto-Aterian," the first genuine Aterian level still belongs to the "Lower Soltanian," identified with the "Lower Würm" in the local chronostratigraphy. TL dating BOR56: 41,160±3500 B.P. was obtained in the Aterian Level 1 of El Haroura, whereas in this site, as well as in Dar-es-Sultan, only the upper Aterian seems to be represented (Debénath et al. 1986). In Algeria, Aterian assemblages are documented in beach deposits of the last interglacial (Roubet 1969). Similar views have been supported on the Aterian assemblages of Libya and Egypt (Wendorf et al. 1990, 1994). The transition between the Mousterian and Aterian could then lie within OIS 5, a view supported by the fact that, especially in the Sahara, sedimentological and paleontological associations suggest an extension of the Aterian corresponding to the development of remarkably moist conditions. However, supporters of a recent history for the Aterian would argue that these conditions could be those of OIS 3, which witnessed a quasi disappearance of the Sahara (Rognon 1996). Finally, one can also assume a possible East to West cline for the final dates of the Aterian.

All the human remains assigned to the Aterian were discovered in Morocco, within rather late deposits. A fragment of a juvenile left maxilla and 3 isolated teeth were discovered at Mugharet el Aliya (Tangier). The specimen consists of an isolated and heavily worn left upper second molar and a fragment of a juvenile left maxilla bearing two unerupted premolars and an unerupted canine. These remains were compared with Neandertals and the juvenile maxilla was said to lack a canine fossa (Senyurek 1940), although a clear *incurvatio inframalaris frontalis* is observed on the specimen. Two other teeth discovered in 1947 remain undescribed. In 1959 the Temara mandible, a more complete specimen, was discovered by J. Roche near Rabat, and initially assigned to the Acheulean. New excavations at the site later demonstrated that the Temara mandible belonged to the Upper Aterian levels of the site (Roche and Texier 1976). These levels also yielded a fragmentary occipital squama with part of the adjacent parietals and a piece of the frontal from the same individual. In 1975, Upper Aterian deposits yielded at least 3 individuals, including a partial skull with the upper face and an associated hemimandible (Dar-es-Sultan 5), an adolescent mandible missing its ramus, and a juvenile calvaria (Debénath 1975; Ferembach 1976b; Debénath et al. 1982; Debénath et al. 1986). The Zouhra cave (El Haroura) also yielded an Aterian mandible and an isolated canine in 1978 (Debénath et al. 1982).

The morphology of the Aterian hominids is modern (Ferembach 1976a, b; Hublin 1993). In Temara, the occipital as well as the supraorbital areas do not display significant morphological or metrical differences from modern series such as those from Afalou or Taforalt. Dar-es-Sultan 5 is a very robust specimen, assigned to a mature male individual. The dimensions are large, especially the transversal ones (bizygomatic, bijugal, interorbital, orbital and nasal breadths). The vault is high but still wide. The mastoid process is robust and projecting, with a marked mastoid crest. The supraorbital area is of modern structure, but extremely developed and projecting. The Dar-es-Sultan 5 mandible is also very robust, but within modern variation. The Aterian people always display a very robust masticatory apparatus, and a pronounced megadonty. These features could explain why the Temara mandible was considered more primitive than it actually is. Interestingly, general robusticity, development of a modern-like but very strong supraorbital superstructure, wide transverse dimensions, and megadonty were primitive retentions differentiating the Irhoud specimens from recent modern humans. Together with the cultural evidence, the current biological evidence supports the hypothesis of a continuity of population from the Mousterian to the late Aterian in North Western Africa. Continuity with later modern populations (i.e., Iberomaurusian) is more debatable, as a possible hiatus in the occupation of the area, or at least a dramatic decrease of the population, may have occurred between the Aterian and Iberomaurusian (Roche 1976), related to the climatic crisis of OIS 2.

Southwestern Asia

Following Howell (1957, 1958), an increasing number of scholars have supported the view that Southwestern Asian hominids represent two distinct populations, rather than one variable one (Suzuki and Takaï 1970; Stringer 1974; Tillier 1974, 1984, 1991; Howells 1975; Trinkaus 1976, 1981, 1984, 1992; Vandermeersch and Tillier 1977; Hublin 1978a; Santa Luca 1978; Stringer and Trinkaus 1981; Vandermeersch 1981; Rak 1990; Condemi 1992). They assigned the specimens of Qafzeh and Skhul and possibly Tabun II to a group of "Proto-Cro-Magnons" or "early modern humans," and specimens from Shanidar, Amud, Kebara, Tabun I, and Dederiyeh to a group of "Near Eastern Neandertals" or "late archaic humans." Despite some attempts to resuscitate the "one population" view (Arensburg and Belfer-Cohen 1998) most of the discussion now focuses on the interpretation of a fragmentary specimen (Tabun II; Quam and Smith 1998; Rak 1998); the chronology of the sites (Bar-Yosef 1998; Valladas et al. 1998; Schwarcz and Rink 1998); the possible interactions between the two groups; and the relation of Near Eastern and European Neandertals (Condemi 1992).

To the present, only the presence of non-Neandertal hominids is demonstrated in southwestern Asia during OIS 6 and 5. Fossil hominids from Qafzeh and Skhul represent early modern humans displaying a mosaic of derived modern features and some plesiomorphies but no Neandertal apomorphies (Vandermeersch 1981; Trinkaus 1984, 1992; Tillier 1999). To these samples could be added the Tabun II mandible, which also displays a similar combination of features (Rak 1998). The Qafzeh-Skhul samples cannot simply be considered as a part of the range of variation of extant humans (Corruccini 1992). However, they display strong affinities with Upper Paleolithic anatomically modern populations, even if the term "Proto-Cro-Magnon" once ascribed to them is no longer used by their promoters (Bar-Yosef and Vandermeersch, in Tillier 1999). The Qafzeh hominids were first assigned to OIS 5 on sedimentological and paleontological evidence (Haas 1972; Bar-Yosef and Vandermeersch 1981; Tchernov 1981). This was later confirmed by radiometric methods, which dated both the Qafzeh and Skhul samples between 90 and 100 ka (Schwarcz et al. 1988; Valladas et al. 1988; Stringer et al. 1989). This date contradicts the former interpretation of the Qafzeh-Skhul material as being intermediate in age (Trinkaus 1983) and/or morphologically "transitional" between Southwestern Asian Neandertals and Upper Paleolithic populations (Smith 1985).

In interpreting the occurrence of early modern humans in the area, several points should be emphasized. As already mentioned, the Qafzeh and Skhul samples display affinities with older African specimens. Their body proportions, contrasting with those observed in later Southwestern Asian Neandertals, are reminiscent of recent inter-tropical African populations (Trinkaus 1981; Holliday 1995). This suggests that they originated in hot regions of the world. Furthermore, they are associated with a suite of rodents and large vertebrates appearing as African immigrants in the South Levant during OIS 5 (Tchernov 1998). The early modern humans associated with Mousterian industries (type C Mousterian in the local denomination) are so far confined to the Southern part of the Levant, and no other example of this association is known further north in Eurasia. The Staroselye (Crimea) child, once believed to represent a similar (and rather confusing) case, is in fact a recent individual, intrusive into Middle Paleolithic layers (Marks et al. 1997). All together, these observations strongly support the view that the early modern humans of the Levant represent a wave of immigrants coming from the south, during OIS 5, along with a northern extension of the Afro-arabian faunas. It seems probable that this extension did not encompass the northern Levant (Tchernov 1998). It has been proposed that this "out of Africa" event could be related to a major extension of savanna areas resulting from the pluvial conditions during OIS 5 (Lahr and Foley 1998). However, it could be equally well supported that, on the contrary, it was one of the arid phases of OIS 5 (5d) that provoked the extension of the desert areas in Africa (Rognon 1996), which would have pushed some of the northeast African population further North.

One issue concerning the early modern humans in the Near East is the question of their fate and relations with Upper Paleolithic modern Europeans. Vandermeersch (1981) emphasized their affinities with the Aurignacian (Cro-Magnon) and Gravettian (Predmosti) hominids. However, a hiatus of maybe 70 ka separates the two groups. No immediate modern descendants of these populations are known in the Levant, only the Neandertal populations (see below). No modern human remains are documented in the area earlier than the occurrence of Upper Paleolithic assemblages. The oldest Upper Paleolithic hominids in the Levant may be found in Qafzeh. The age of layers 7–9 is estimated at circa 35 ka B.P., on the basis of inter-site comparisons (Belfer-Cohen and Bar-Yosef 1981). The Ksar 'Akil child associated with Aurignacian industries is dated to around 29 ka (Mellars and Tixier 1989; Bergman 1989; Tillier and Tixier 1991), and the Ohalo specimen to only 19 ka (Hershkovitz et al. 1995). One can assume that the penetration of early modern humans in the Levant during OIS 5 results from a very limited "Out-of-Africa" event, and that it is not until the development of genuine Upper Paleolithic technologies than modern humans could outdo their contemporaries in Eurasia (Klein 1998). Alternatively, a more complex process than the simple "Out-of-Africa 2" model could be supported if Chinese "archaic *Homo sapiens*" did not emerge from a parallel evolution of local Homo erectus and/or if the peopling of Australia is demonstrated to have occurred at 60 ka or earlier (Roberts et al. 1990; Roberts et al. 1994; Thorne et al. 1999). Further archeological exploration of Southern Asia will prove crucial in demonstrating the possible occurrence outside Africa of any Qafzeh/Skhul related populations during OIS 4.

The securely dated Neandertals in the Near East are all OIS 4. In the Southern Levant, they appear as late immigrants associated with palearctic faunas. The Zuttiyeh skull, possibly as old as OIS 8 or 7 (Bar-Yosef 1995; Vandermeersch 1995) does not display clear Neandertal affinities (see Sohn and Wolpoff 1993 for discussion and references), at a time when Neandertal derived features are already well developed in European hominids.

The Tabun C1 hominid is another candidate for an early Neandertal in the Southern Levant. Its chronological position has been highly debated. An assignment of the specimen to late stage 7 or early stage 6, predating the Skhul/Qafzeh sample has been supported by TL dating of the C layer of Tabun (Mercier et al. 1995). However, although Tabun "C1" is certainly "1" it might not be "C" but represent an intrusive burial into the top of layer C (see Bar-Yosef 1995 and Bar-Yosef and Callander 1999 for further comments). Yet, among the Near East Neandertals, Tabun 1 displays one of the most derived morphologies of the occipito-mastoidian area. This feature might support the later age of Tabun 1 (Hublin 1998a). This view is also reinforced by the direct dating of the specimen by gamma ray spectrometry (Schwarcz, Simpson, and Stringer 1998)

In contrast to the local early modern humans of stage 5, Levant Neandertals display body proportions reminiscent of those of the western Neandertals (Trinkaus 1981; Holliday 1995). If these body proportions really result mainly from adaptation to a colder environment, this is also consistent with an origin in higher latitudes. As documented in the European Upper Paleolithic record, a short period of time (less than 20 ka) is enough to allow significant changes in the climatic adaptation of body proportions (Holliday 1995). This also supports the view that the wave of Neandertals in the South Levant was of rather short duration.

This movement could have been related to environmental pressure resulting from the glacial OIS 4 reducing available territories in Europe and extending the palearctic domain further south (Bar-Yosef 1988). This hypothesis could explain some of the similarities between Near Eastern Neandertals and European Neandertals from OIS 5 (Condemi 1992). However, Eastern European Neandertals potentially ancestral to the Levant Neandertals are almost unknown. One may also wonder why such a movement did not happen during earlier cold stages, such as OIS 6. A related question concerns the nature of the Mousterian peopling of the northern Levant. Was the southern boundary of the palearctic province peopled by Neandertals in the late Middle Pleistocene along the paths between the Anatolian plateau and the Balkans, or along the Taurus-Zagros line? Supporting the second hypothesis is the evidence for cultural affinities between the interglacial Middle Paleolithic industries of the Balkans and the northern Middle East (Zagros Group, Kozlowski 1992). The only fossil evidence in the northern part of the Near East comes from the sites of Shanidar (Iraq) and Karain (Turkey). The Shanidar layer D hominid sample is assigned to OIS 5 by some authors (Trinkaus 1995). However, the exact chronology of this site remains uncertain. In Karain, a series of fragmentary remains has been yielded by layers assigned to a period between 200 and 250 ka ago (Otte et al. 1998). If their Neandertal status is supported by further analysis, this would constitute an early occurrence of the Neandertals in the northern part of the Near East. Morphological differences observed between Neandertals of the southern Levant and the European Neandertals would then be explained by an older geographical differentiation.

Another issue is the eastern extension of the Neandertals in middle latitudes. The exceptionally warm OIS 5e allowed Neandertals to expand into the Ukrainian and Russian plain, and probably to a greater extent to the east. Neandertal adaptations allowed their expansion beyond the northern shores of the Caspian Sea which, in contrast with the Mediterranean and Black seas, underwent regression and was much reduced during the interglacial. The occurrence of Neandertals further east at Teshik-Tash (Uzbekistan) could have resulted from the use of the northern and shortest route from Eastern Europe to Central Asia. This situation would also explain a later major southern movement into the Near East during the succeeding cold stage (OIS 4). Dental remains from southern Siberia at Denisova and Okladnikov have been tentatively assigned to the Neandertals (Turner 1990), but only future discoveries will tell us how far east the Neandertal extension continued in middle latitudes.

Europe

Europe witnessed the emergence of the Neandertals from the middle of the Middle Pleistocene. Clearly Neandertal-derived features are already observed on specimens from Arago, Swanscombe, Sima de los Huesos, and may also have been present on the Mauer mandible (Rosas and Bermudez de Castro 1998). Considering the specificity of some of these features, it seems unlikely that they could have developed independently in later European populations as proposed by Lahr and Foley (1998). More probably, European and African populations remained isolated for most of the last half million years. The evolution of the Neandertal lineage results from an accretion process in which it is difficult to posit clear-cut steps. Genetic isolation and periodic demographic crashes may have played a major role in its individualization and evolution (Hublin 1998a).

Regarding the Neandertal peopling of Europe, several points have to be emphasized.

Neandertals represent large-bodied, archaic humans adapted to cool to cold environments (Ruff, Trinkaus, and Holliday 1997; Holliday 1997b). They differ markedly from contemporary African populations and specifically from the early anatomically modern humans. However, they do not simply display primitive conditions relative to the latter. Instead, they are highly derived in several of their features (Hublin 1978b, 1988a; Santa Luca 1978; Rak 1986, 1998; Trinkaus 1987; Condemi 1988; Hublin et al. 1996). This rejects the possibility of a Neandertal ancestry for the first anatomically modern humans in Europe. It supports the view claiming that Neandertals represent a distinct sub-species of *Homo sapiens* or a close but distinct species of *Homo* (*Homo neanderthalensis*).

The oldest Neandertals are found in Western Europe as well as the most recent. Neandertals found outside Europe (in Central and Southwestern Asia) are essentially late Neandertals. In Europe, there is a west to east and a north to south cline in the number of Neandertal remains discovered. This may result only partly from the history of archeological research in different countries, but may also reflect the distribution of Neandertal populations. Very likely, in relation to its particular environmental history, Europe represents the area of origin of this group of extinct hominids.

Until OIS 3, no modern or pre-modern human remains are known in Europe. The so-called "European pre-sapiens" are either ill dated and/or highly fragmentary specimens, or are preneandertals sharing some primitive features with anatomically modern humans (Hublin 1988b). Together with the two previous points, this supports the view of the genetic isolation of the European population from their African contemporaries.

Archaeological, paleontological, and geological data provide us with the picture of a land occupation by the Neandertals discontinuous in space and fluctuating with climatic oscillations. In the late Middle and early Upper Pleistocene, the most numerous and richest sites belong to interglacial, interstadial or early glacial periods. Glacial peaks resulted in major contractions of the available European territory. As demonstrated for OIS 2, the extreme conditions of previous cold stages could have had a major impact on the occupation of areas located on the northwestern plain (Tuffreau 1984; Hublin 1990). OIS 6 witnessed less extreme conditions than OIS 2, but was much longer (Jouzel et al. 1993). Although some sites in the middle latitudes are assigned to this stage (Achenheim, Ariendorf 2, La Cotte St. Brelade), none of these rare sites can be securely assigned to the peak of the pleniglacial conditions. During the cold conditions of OIS 4, very few human occupations are reported in northern France (Auguste 1995). In addition to a north to south cline, the pattern of raw material transports also suggests quite a different interpretation for the Middle Paleolithic land occupation between Western and Central/Eastern European regions exposed to more continental conditions (Féblot-Augustins 1993).

One of the main advances of the last two decades has been the demonstration of the persistence of Neandertals in Europe after 40 ka B.P., and their coexistence with the first modern humans in the same area. This demonstration was based on paleontological and archeological evidence. In Europe, the latest Neandertals remains (post-dating 40 ka B.P. in the ^{14}C calendar) are found in association either with late Mousterian industries at Zafarraya (Spain, Barroso Ruiz and Hublin 1994; Hublin et al. 1995; Hublin and Trinkaus 1998) or with Chatelperronian assemblages in Saint-Césaire (France, Lévêque and Vandermeersch 1980), and Arcy sur Cure (France, Leroi-Gourhan 1959; Hublin et al. 1996). This observation is consistent with the rooting of the Chatelperronian assemblages within the local Mousterian of Acheulean tradition type B, which seems to represent the terminal phase of the evolution of the Mousterian in western Europe (Bordes 1968; Mellars 1986; Pelegrin 1990). So far, there is no evidence of any hominids other than Neandertals in the European Mousterian, nor in its continuation into the Early Upper Paleolithic. The identity of the toolmakers of the other "transitional industries" that continued into the European Middle Paleolithic (such as the Szeletian, Uluzzian, Lincombian, etc.) remains obscure, as these assemblages have not so far yielded diagnostic human remains. However, comparisons have often been established with the Chatelperronian of France and Northern Spain which has provided some Neandertal remains, and on which attention has been concentrated. Recent dates were also provided by direct dating of two specimens assigned to the Neandertals from the layer G1 of Vindija (Smith et al. 1999). This layer yielded a split-base point that could not be dated directly, but also a leaf-shaped bifacial piece. The cultural association of the two dated human specimens remains is debatable, and the G1 layer seems to display the features of a deposit possibly disturbed by carnivore activities (Zilhão and d'Errico 1999a).

The occurrence of anatomically modern humans in Western Europe is clearly related to the spread of Aurignacian industries in this area. Numerous and quite complete specimens have been found in Aurignacian sites, and so far, all the identifiable remains discovered in an undisturbed Aurignacian context are of a modern nature. As far as these industries represent a genuine ethno-cultural entity, the most economical and likely hypothesis is that it was entirely produced by anatomically modern humans (but see Straus et al. 1993). Only the oldest specimens will be commented on in the following discussion.

Eastern sites (Istallosko and Bacho Kiro) yielded only very fragmentary remains (Malan 1955; Kozlowski 1982). In Bacho Kiro, a fragment of juvenile mandible associated with a "Bachokirian" assemblage and dated at greater than 43 ka B.P. is reported from layer 11. It is "unquestionably" modern according to Kozlowski (1992) but "nondiagnostic" according to Zilhão and d'Errico (1999a). However, in Central and Western Europe, much more complete, if later specimens have been unearthed. In the northwestern plain, an isolated frontal bone, anatomically modern but bearing strong supraorbital structures, was found at Hannofersand (Germany), out of archeological context. It was dated by R. Protsch and associates at the University of Frankfurt by ^{14}C to 36.3±0.6 ka, and by amino acid racemization at 36.0 ka (Braüer 1980). On the basis of these measurements, it is the oldest modern human known in Western Europe. Younger specimens, ca 32–30 ka B.P., displaying fully modern morphology have been dated directly or indirectly. An age of 31.9±1.1 ka B.P. has been established for the Middle Aurignacian assemblages of Stetten (Volgeherd, Germany; Hahn 1983) to which a calvarium and mandible (Stetten 1) discovered in 1931 are assigned. One adult calvarium from Kelsterbach (Germany), without archeological association, is dated by ^{14}C to 31.2±0.6 ka B.P., and by amino acid racemization to 32.0 ka B.P. (Protsch and Semmel 1978). A maxilla from Kent's Cavern (England) was directly dated by AMS ^{14}C technique, giving an age of 30.9±0.9 ka B.P. (Stringer 1990). In this case, the archeological association is not quite clear. The Velika Pecina (Croatia) frontal bone, which has been considered for many years as one of the oldest modern remains in Europe, proved recently to be quite recent, with a direct dating by AMS at 5,045±40 B.P. (Smith et al. 1999).

Other specimens were not dated by radiometric methods but are likely to belong to the same range of time. In the two caves of Mladec (Moravia), a large series of human remains was unearthed in an interstadial context in association with Aurignacian industries. Most of the specimens were destroyed in 1945 and today only one adult skull (Mladec 1), 4 skullcaps (Mladec 2, 4, 5, 6), an isolated maxilla, some post-cranial bones, and some fragmentary juvenile remains survive. Inferences to their possible age come mainly from the geological evidence, as they are assigned to the Podhradem interstadial stage and would therefore belong to a range of time between 33 and 28 ka (Allsworth-Jones 1982). They are considered as ca 32 ka by Jelinek (1976) and Vlcek (1995). Some of the specimens display a marked robusticity, developed supraorbital relief (Mladec 5 and 6), incipient occipital torus (Mladec 5 and 6), and "bun-shape" of the rear skull (Mladec 1, 5, 6), all features that can occur in modern humans. Attempts to demonstrate the persistence of derived Neandertal features (Frayer 1986) are refuted by close re-examination of the material (Gambier 1992; Braüer and Broeg 1998). Three other Moravian specimens: the Zlaty Kun and Svitavka partial skeletons and the Svaty Prokop mandible, are allocated to a range of time between 30 and 32 ka by Vlcek (1995). The exact age of these specimens is not known. Zlaty Kun is reminiscent of some aspects of the Mladec series (Smith 1984) and, like the other two specimens, does not display any Neandertal retention (Braüer and Broeg 1998).

In 1868, the site of Cro-Magnon (near Les Eyzies, France) yielded the first human remains found in an Upper Paleolithic context. The series includes at least 4 adults including the famous "vieillard" ("old man") Cro-Magnon 1, and one juvenile. Comparison with the nearby site of Abri Pataud led Movius (Movius 1995) to assign the Aurignacian layer G and burials of the Cro-Magnon shelter an age of ca. 30 ka B.P. (^{14}C calendar). In 1995, AMS ^{14}C dating of the human remains themselves was attempted in the laboratory of Gif-sur-Yvette, but it proved unsuccessful due to the lack of sufficient collagen from which to extract a viable amount of carbon.

In France, more fragmentary specimens were discovered in Aurignacian layers, notably in Arcy-sur-Cure, Abri Castanet, La Chaise, La Combe, La Ferrassie, Le Flageolet, Font-de-Gaume, Fontéchevade, Chez Leix, Gourdan, Montmaurin, La Quina, Le Piage, Les Roches. More than 40 sites were listed by Gambier (1993). Three sites yielded specimens clearly associated with early Aurignacian industries and are probably therefore older than the Cro-Magnon specimens, found with a more evolved Aurignacian: La Crouzade (Aude), La Grotte des Rois (Charente) and Brassempouy (Landes). In La Crouzade, an adult frontal bone and a juvenile fragmentary maxillary are fully modern (Gambier and Sacchi 1991). In Les Rois, two juvenile mandibles (from individuals 9 and 12 years of age) and a large series of isolated teeth display some archaic features and a great robusticity, but no Neandertal features. In Brassempouy, a series of teeth and skeletal fragments from early Aurignacian layers are dated between 33.5 and 31.0 ka (Bon et al. 1998; Gambier, in press). A precise assignment to the Aurignacian 1 is more arguable for the Les Cottés human remains (Gambier 1989), and for one mandible from Isturitz (Gambier 1993).

The assumptions of the contemporaneity of the last Neandertals and Upper Paleolithic Modern humans are based essentially on archaeological evidence. Two main arguments support this view: 1) the early dating of the oldest Aurignacian layers (ca. 40 ka or earlier in ^{14}C), predating the end of the Mousterian Chatelperronian; and 2) the occurrence of interstratifications of Chatelperronian and Aurignacian deposits. These interstratifications were described in southern France at Roc de Combe (Bordes and Labrot 1967) and Le Piage (Champagne and Espitalie 1981), possibly at Châtelperron (White 1998), and in Spain at El Pendo (González 1980). The fact that the latest Neandertals, associated with Chatelperronian assemblages, developed "Upper Paleolithic behaviors"—including the production and use of personal ornaments—virtually at the moment of (or perhaps slightly after) the arrival in western Europe of modern humans bearing Aurignacian industries, has been interpreted by several authors as resulting from an acculturation process (Demars and Hublin 1989; Harrold 1989; Hublin 1990; Mellars 1991, 1996; Djindjian 1993; Stringer and Gamble 1993; Hublin et al. 1996). This process of cultural interaction between the modern invaders and the local population has also been employed to explain the emergence of the Szeletian and other leaf-point industries in Central Europe (Allsworth-Jones 1986, 1990; Kozlowski 1990, 1996; Valoch 1990) and of the Italian Uluzzian (Gioia 1990; Mussi 1990; Kuhn and Bietti this volume).

The dates of the earliest Aurignacian are highly debated, however. European sites that have produced ^{14}C dates of around 40 ka for the earliest Aurignacian occupations include Abric Romaní (Bischoff et al. 1994), El Castillo (Cabrera and Bischoff 1989), L'Arbreda (Bischoff et al. 1989), and Reclau Viver (Maroto 1994) in Northern Spain; Fumane (Bartolomei et al. 1994) and Grotta di Paina (Broglio and Importa 1995) in Northern Italy; Trou Magrite (Straus and Otte 1996) in Belgium; Keilberg-Kirche (Uthmeier 1996) and Geissenklösterle (Hahn 1995, 1996) in Germany; and Willendorf II (Damblon et al. 1996) in Austria. Further east, dates in excess of 40 ka B.P. have been obtained for Bachokirian layers in Bacho Kiro and Temnata (Bulgaria, Hedges et al. 1994; Ginter et al. 1996, Kozlowski 1992) and for early Aurignacian in Istallosko (Hungary), the dating of the latter more debatable (Svoboda et al. 1996). In a recent review of the available data, Zilhão and d'Errico (1999a) criticized the earliest dating, which, in their view, results either from contamination from underlying Mousterian, Chatelperronian or Uluzzian layers, or from a misinterpretation of the assemblages related to the dated samples. In conclusion of their review, these authors claim that the oldest Aurignacian in Europe is to be set around 36,500 B.P. in the ^{14}C calendar. Zilhão and d'Errico (1999a) also reject observations of interstratifications of Aurignacian and Chatelperronian as the resulting from redeposition or from some misinterpretation of stratigraphy by the excavators. They emphasize the fact that, if these interstratifications are not taken into consideration, the Chatelperronian always stratigraphically underlies the Aurignacian. Their conclusion is that the Chatelperronian predates the earliest occurrence of the Aurignacian in Europe, and that it cannot be interpreted as resulting from an acculturation process, but as the local and independent invention of Upper Paleolithic behavior by the Neandertals before the arrival of modern humans.

It should be noted that these authors do not really challenge the view that dating obtained in Aurignacian sites widely overlaps in time the final Mousterian and Chatelperronian (Zilhão and d'Errico 1999a:50). Nor do they reject the modern nature of the Aurignacian populations and Neandertal nature of the Chatelperronian toolmakers. Certainly, one of the crucial problems one frequently faces in dealing with dates provided by the C14 method in the range of time between 40 and 35 ka is the limit of the application of the technique itself. Contamination and calibration problems may make the establishment of any accurately detailed chronology an almost impossible task. However, in this situation, demonstrating from the radiometric evidence that the Chatelperronian emergence possibly predates the earliest Aurignacian by 1.5 ka (Zilhão and d'Errico 1999a:47) seems an even more challenging task. According to these authors "... the earliest Aurignacian of Northern Spain and Southwestern France must lie somewhere between ca. 36,000 and ca. 37,000 B.P. at the earliest—that is, later than ca. 38,000 B.P. AMS results obtained on bone for several French Châtelperronian sites." (Zilhão and d'Errico 1999a:31). Still, the standard deviation for the dates considered most reliable lies in the range of 610 to 1000 years. The stratigraphic arguments according to which the Chatelperronian always underlies the Aurignacian could support exactly the opposite view to that defended by Zilhão and d'Errico (1999b). As already pointed out by some authors (Hublin 1999; Mellars 1999; Otte 1999), if, on a broad geographical scale, the two industries show a significant chronological overlap, the expansion of the Aurignacian at the expense of neighboring acculturated Chatelperronian Neandertal populations would inevitably always result *locally* in the superposition of the Aurignacian on the Chatelperronian. This is the classical geological problem of a diachronic transgressive deposit: a beach layer always antedates the fully marine deposits of an extending sea. It does not mean a beach ever preexisted the sea itself.

Finally, even if one follows the criticisms by Zilhão and d'Errico (1999a) on the interstratification of Aurignacian and Chatelperronian, and accepts their chronology for the development of early Aurignacian in Europe, it remains very difficult to accept their final and most important conclusion: the simultaneous and independent invention of the Upper Paleolithic suite of behaviors by the Neandertals. In their view, after more than 400,000 years of separate evolution on each side of the Mediterranean, Neandertals and Modern Humans reached the elaboration of the same body ornaments virtually at the same time but through totally separate and parallel processes! The comparison made with the separate emergence of agriculture in Eurasia and in America is not really relevant. The development of corn agriculture in Americas and cereals in the Near East was not simultaneous and moreover, so far, there is no evidence of any population movement in the early Holocene between the Near East and pre-Columbian Mexico.

A puzzling aspect of the replacement process in Europe is the estimated duration of coexistence between modern humans developing the Aurignacian industries and the late Neandertals associated with either Chatelperronian or Mousterian assemblages. One would expect that on a local scale, coexistence between the two groups of hominids was very brief. However, on the scale of Western Europe, the picture looks very different, even if one accepts the minimalist position of Zilhão and d'Errico (1999b), that Aurignacian assemblages are documented in Western Europe only 36.5 ka ago (^{14}C). Neandertal remains are known in Saint-Césaire ca. 36 ka (TL), in Zafarraya (Southern Spain) and Arcy-sur-Cure[1] (south of the Parisian basin) ca. 33–34 ka (^{14}C). The direct AMS dating obtained at Vindija on human remains displaying arguably diagnostic Neandertal features[2] at ca 29–28 ka may provide more biological evidence of a late survival of Neandertals (Smith et al. 1999). However late dates are also provided by archeological deposits that can hardly be assigned to any other hominids than Neandertals. In Western Europe, a number of C14 dates of Mousterian layers post-date 30 ka (see for example Combier 1990). The majority of them most likely result from contamination. However, in the south of the Iberian Peninsula,

several authors (Villaverde and Fumanal 1990; Vega Toscano 1990; Zilhão 1993; Hublin et al. 1995; Raposo 1995; Zilhão, in press) have pointed out the consistency between the occurrence of late Mousterian assemblages assigned to a range of time between 35 and at least 30 ka (C14) and the absence of early Upper Paleolithic industries in the domain located south of the Ebro River. In Zafarraya (southern Spain), U/Th dates range, in agreement with stratigraphy and with C14 dates, between 33.4±2 ka and 25.1±1.3 ka (Hublin et al. 1995). In Portugal, several dates support the survival of the local Mousterians until ca. 28 ka ago (Zilhão 1993, in press). The top of level K at Gruta do Caldeirao is dated by AMS ^{14}C at 27.6±0.60. At Gruta Nova (Columbeira, Bombarral) a Mousterian level was dated on earth rich in charcoal (Delibrias 1972, unpublished) at 26.4±0.75 ka (GIF-2703). Although this type of material is not of high quality, the possibility of contamination in situ seems slight. In addition, according to the laboratory, the samples were submitted to rigorous chemical treatment. The Iberian Peninsula is indeed at the bottom of the European cul-de-sac and its southern region was a refuge for archaic mammalian faunas throughout the Pleistocene. However, it is still unclear why Neandertals survived specifically in this area millennia after modern humans were already settled in southern France and northern Spain. In any case, it reinforces the view that modern invaders did not demonstrate overwhelming superiority over the autochthonous populations (Hublin et al. 1995). The Catalonian and Cantabrian areas still represent ecogeographical zones related to the Pyrénées and southwestern France, and are distinct from the rest of the Iberian Peninsula. This also reinforces the hypothesis of a sharing of the European territory between Neandertals and Modern Humans according to some ecogeographical differentiation. Furthermore, in most of the Iberian Peninsula, Neandertals did not follow a process of acculturation similar to that of their contemporaries living in higher latitudes. This likely resulted from the greater degree of isolation of most of the Iberian Peninsula. In the model supported by Zilhão and d'Errico (1999a), that European Neandertals underwent evolution toward the Upper Paleolithic, some degree of geographical and adaptive differentiation of the Iberian Neandertals has also to be assumed in order to explain why Iberian Neandertals remained excluded from this process (Zilhão, in press).

In France, the longest Chatelperronian stratigraphy was excavated in the "Grande Roche" in Quinçay (Vienne). It develops from an "archaic" to "evolved" and even "regressive" Châtelperronian. Attempts to correlate the stratigraphies of Quinçay and Saint-

Césaire (Charentes Maritimes), located some 120 km further to the south, on sedimentological and palynological grounds, led Lévêque and Miskovsky (1983) and Leroyer (1986) to correlate the terminal layers of Quinçay to layers of Saint-Cesaire that yielded an "evolved" Aurignacian, and were contemporary with the Arcy oscillation. At least partly similar situations may have occurred elsewhere in Europe. Leaf-point industries, rooted in the local middle Paleolithic and tentatively assigned to late Neandertals, have been dated to younger than 30 ka in northwestern and central Europe, where they may have co-existed with Aurignacian industries during the development of the latter (Kozlowski, this volume).

In 1999, the Iberian Paleolithic landscape has given rise to an even more complex situation with the discovery in Lagar Velho (Portugal) of an intentionally buried, modern human child claimed to display possible inherited Neandertal features (Duarte Cidalia et al. 1999). The specimen is dated to ca. 25 ka by the AMS dating of charcoals found inside the burial, and has been related to the Gravettian techno-complex. The chronological age of the specimen is estimated at between 3.5 and 5 years. It is said to display a mosaic of modern and Neandertal features and therefore to demonstrate the occurrence of hybridization between the two groups. Since the first publication, its hybrid nature has been challenged, as have the conclusions drawn from it (Tattersall et al. 1999). According to the description provided by Duarte et al. (1999) and Trinkaus et al. (1999), the observable non-metric morphological features displayed by Lagar Velho 1 are essentially modern. They include a clearly expressed *mentum osseum* with a very prominent *tuber symphyseos*, an exceptionally protruding *tuberculum laterale* on each side, and a deeply excavated *incisura mandibulae anterior*. The mandible also lacks other features most frequently observed in Neandertals, such as a tubercle at the dorsoposterior margin of the medial pterygoid insertion, a mental foramen in posterior position, and an asymmetrical sigmoid notch. The postcranial skeleton shows similar modern conditions with a ventral sulcus on the scapular auxiliary border, an anteriorly rotated radial tuberosity, and little lateral curvature of the radial diaphysis. However, on the preserved temporal bone, the proportions of the mastoid process and juxtamastoid process are said to be "intermediate" between modern and Neandertal conditions. These relative proportions vary, however, with individual development, and both structures are rather variable even in adults. The maxillary incisors display two morphological features reminiscent of the Neandertals. The lingual face displays a basal tubercle and marginal ridges, but these features are not unknown in Aurignacian specimens (Gambier et al 1990). The convexity of the buccal face of the maxillary incisors extending evenly across the labial crown is also considered by the authors as Neandertal. Finally, the cross-section of the upper part of the humeral diaphysis shows an anterolateral to posteromedial elongation in relation to the strong development of the thoracohumeral musculature. According to Trinkaus et al (1999), this pattern seen in Neandertals is usually little developed among early modern humans. It is observed on robust specimens such as Irhoud 4 (Hublin et al. 1987).

The two main arguments for the hybrid status of the specimen arise from the metrical evidence. On the mandible, the proportions of the anterior teeth relatively to the molars (I2 to M1) are modern. But despite its very prominent *mentum osseum*, the mandibular symphysis displays an anterior symphyseal angle (alveolar plane to the infradentale-pogonion line) of 89°. It is close to the mean for early juvenile Neandertals (90.3°±4.4°, N=7) and below that of similarly aged recent humans (101.5°±4.7°, N=15) (Mallegni and Trinkaus 1997). The post-cranial skeleton displays modern proportions of the pollical (thumb) phalanxes and the pubic length is within the recent human distribution. But one feature that aligns Lagar Velho 1 with the Neandertals is its relatively short distal leg segments. The ratio of tibial length to femoral length (in this case, using intermetaphyseal lengths rather than interarticular lengths) places Lagar Velho 1 below a recent human cool temperate sample. The pattern is consistent with the relative robusticity of the tibial and femoral diaphysis. This shortening of the distal leg segments is observed in cold-adapted modern populations and in the Neandertals (adults and juveniles), and contrasts with the tropical proportions found in the early modern humans of the Near East and in the Early Upper Paleolithic modern Europeans, including Gravettian specimens from European middle latitudes, which display longer distal segments (Holliday 1997a; Trinkaus 1981).

Disagreements in assessing the hybrid nature of Lagar Velho 1 are related to its juvenile nature and to the fact that while clearly derived modern conditions are observed on this individual (*mentum osseum* for example), its arguably "Neandertal" features are not represented by autapomorphies of the group but by features occurring in modern humans *sensu lato*. Unfortunately, most of the skull, where the best demonstrated diagnostic features of Neandertals and modern humans concentrate, is poorly preserved on the specimen. It was destroyed during the bulldozing of the site, which resulted in the salvation excavation of

1998. The feature most in contrast to those one would expect on a Gravettian modern specimen is certainly the body proportions reminiscent of arctic adapted populations reconstructed by Duarte et al. (1999). Even if such proportions are known in living modern populations, they are not represented in the Early Upper Paleolithic of Europe, and the published archeological data make the burial unlikely to have been an intrusion from a Solutrean level. However, the juvenile nature of the specimen reduces the possible comparison as little is known about the variability in robusticity and body proportions of Gravettian children of any given age.

For many years, the possibility of a limited gene flow between Neandertals and modern invaders in Western Europe has been contemplated in the perspective of a replacement model for the origin of modern Europeans (see for example Hublin 1990). In this respect, accepting the hybrid nature of the Lagar Velho 1 child does not contradict an "Out-of-Africa 2" model, and in fact, the interpretation of Duarte et al. (1999) is based on the acceptance of an invasion model. Regarding the biological and taxonomic status of the Neandertals, the occurrence of one hybrid (so far the only potential one) does not constitute a definite answer. Nor does it provide evidence for "positive" interactions between the two groups. For most scholars, Neandertals are either a distinct sub-species of *Homo sapiens*, or a very close, sister species. In both cases the occurrence of hybrids is conceivable, however "hostile" or "friendly" the relationships between the two groups. One difficulty with the interpretation of the Lagar Velho 1 child as a hybrid is related to its geochronological position. If some hybridization occurred between Neandertals and modern humans, one would rather expect to see its effects at the time of the Aurignacian spread. From the Lagar Velho evidence, Duarte et al. (1999) conclude the persistence of a morphological mosaic of Neandertal and modern features several millennia after the probable period of transition between the two groups (28–30 ka B.P.) in southern Iberia. In this view, the Lagar Velho child would not be the result of a rare interbreeding but the "descent of extensively admixed populations," and one would expect most of the future Gravettian hominids found in this peculiar area to display the same kind of pattern. Alternatively, one could argue that the real time and process of replacement of one population by another in the Iberian Peninsula is still obscure. As has already been mentioned, the Zafarraya evidence could support the existence of Mousterian toolmakers shortly before the assumed date of Lagar Velho 1. As commented above, archeological evidence from other European areas could also support a late Neandertal survival. Interestingly, while, so far, Aurignacian hominids in Europe do not show any clear evidence for gene flow between Neandertals and modern humans, in two other cases (besides Lagar Velho) Neandertal-derived conditions were arguably recognized in some facial features of Predmosti 3 and Dolni Vestonice 3 (Stringer 1989). The two specimens were in a Pavlovian (Gravettian *sensu lato*) context. Finally, if Neandertals did represent serious and long lasting challenges to the expansion of modern humans, the survival of some pockets of Neandertals after 30 ka B.P., at least in southern Europe is also consistent with the hypothesis that their final extinction mainly resulted from major environmental changes. In this approach, after millennia of relative equilibrium, increased competition with adjacent modern populations developed in relation to the rise of colder conditions at the dawn of OIS 2 and the subsequent reduction of available territories. In this time range, the major deterioration of the climatic conditions in terms of temperature and precipitation in Western Europe developed between 28 and 24 ka (^{14}C), following the Denekamp/Arcy warm event (Guiot et al. 1989).

Discussion and Conclusions

For most of the Late Middle and Upper Pleistocene, the Mediterranean represented a major paleobiogeographic barrier, separating two biogeographic domains. At the western end of Eurasia, hominids evolved in relative geographical and genetic isolation. Located at the limit of the eco-geographical range of the hominids, this area witnessed particular processes that led to the emergence of the Neandertals. Although Neandertals are documented in very different environments, adaptation to the cool/cold conditions of middle latitudes probably played a major role in their evolutionary development. Other features of these populations are related to the fact that they were periodically submitted to climatic crises that dramatically reduced the available territories in the European subcontinent (Hublin 1998a). This situation resulted in two possible phenomena. On one hand, preneandertal populations probably suffered significant demographic fluctuations. The occurrence of several bottlenecks, and subsequent genetic drift may have played a major role in the appearance of some of the Neandertal features which, in this view, would result from random fixation more than from adaptive processes. The evolution of the

Neandertal morphology occurred after at least the middle of the Middle Pleistocene and was the result of accretion and of a shift in the frequency of derived features within the European populations. However, OIS 6 seems to have played a major role in the final emergence of the "classic Neandertals." On the other hand, climatic crises deeply influenced the geographical dispersion of the Neandertals. At the peak of the glacial events, the European population was mainly concentrated in the south of the continent. The eastern and southeastern limits of the Neandertal domain were also modified by these climatic changes. Although preneandertals probably already existed in the northern part of the Middle East by OIS 4, before this stage they are not documented south of the Zagros-Taurus line, or in the south of the Levant, in association with palearctic faunas. However, temperate stages, and particularly OIS 5, may also have played a role in their eastern dispersal through the Ukrainian and Russian plain and eventually toward central Asia.

In North Africa, late middle Pleistocene populations contrast strikingly with their European contemporaries. There are no Neandertal-related hominids in this area. As in other parts of Africa in the same range of time, one finds pre-modern representatives of *Homo sapiens*. Although the exact tempo of their evolution is still unclear, they also seem to display an accretion of derived features over a substantial period of time, eventually leading to the emergence of a virtually modern morphology at the eve of OIS 5. During the Upper Pleistocene, these populations demonstrate a biological and cultural continuity, up to and including the Aterian populations. Although a continuity with later (Ibero-Maurusian) groups has been supported (Ferembach 1985; Debénath et al. 1986), the morphological relations between Mousterian and Aterian hominids are more arguable, and a significant gap may have existed between Aterian and Ibero-Maurusian populations. Although it is difficult to show a direct relation between the northwest African hominids and southwest Asian early modern humans documented in OIS 5, the Moroccan evidence demonstrates that a pre-modern and an early modern morphology was spread throughout Africa from the Cape to Gibraltar, and its emergence cannot be limited to a single geographical area.

Before OIS 3, interactions between Neandertals and early modern humans are hypothesized in the area of the two geographical gates connecting Eurasia to Africa: the Straits of Gibraltar and the southern Levant. Exchanges through the Straits of Gibraltar have mainly been considered on cultural and theoretical grounds. The cultural arguments are mainly related to the spread of the Acheulean in Western Europe, hypothetically from northwest Africa, and to the possible existence of a "Movius line" separating an eastern group of Lower Paleolithic industries without handaxes from a western or southwestern group where handaxes and cleavers are best represented (Alimen 1975; Otte 1996). Similarities between Iberian and Moroccan Mousterian assemblages have been also emphasized (see for example Tixier in Hublin et al. 1987), as have possible Aterian origins for the Solutrean (Debénath et al. 1986; Otte 1996 *contra* Smith 1966). In contrast, as developed above, there is no biological evidence for significant exchanges between southwest Europe and northwest Africa during the second half of the Middle Pleistocene or most of the Upper Pleistocene. Middle Pleistocene specimens clearly representing endemic European preneandertals are indeed associated to Acheulean industries (e.g., Swanscombe). This situation has puzzled many authors who have focussed on the fact that the Straits of Gibraltar is very narrow and "crossed continuously nowadays by windsurfers from Spain and illegal immigrants from Morocco" (Straus 1999). A comparison is also often made with the peopling of Australia 50,000 years ago (or more) by humans crossing some 50 miles of open sea. It is usually answered that the Straits are swept by strong currents, that the crossing is not so easy, and that many "illegal immigrants" are found drowned. Another issue is the difficulty in providing an exact reconstruction of the past configuration of the area. Due to major orogenic movements, this cannot be made from simple sea retreats from the present day coastlines. However, there is ultimately a major difference between the Pleistocene western Mediterranean and Australasian areas. When the first settlements occurred in Australia, even very small groups of humans could successfully colonize the new geographical domain, as their ecological niche was completely empty. Their arrival had a dramatic impact on the local marsupial fauna, isolated not just from humans but from placental mammals for tens of millions of years. Indeed, if human exchanges occurred between northwest Africa and Western Europe during the Late Middle or Early Upper Pleistocene, invaders from both sides discovered well-adapted competitors, established for hundreds of millennia. In this situation, some "contact" is conceivable, resulting in cultural exchanges. However, assuming that biological admixture was possible between Neandertals and their African contemporaries, observable hybridization of the two groups would have needed a massive invasion, which never occurred.

During OIS 5 and 4, early modern humans and Neandertals are both represented in southwest Asia, and it is likely that land borders existed between the two groups. So far, there is no evidence of any local coexistence between the two populations, but rather of successive occupations of the southern Levant. Still, we only have a broad geographical and chronological resolution of this phenomenon, and future discoveries may demonstrate closer contacts at some periods. Modern humans entered this area during OIS 5, in response to the environmental changes driving the northern extension of African faunas, but they are not documented north of the Zagros-Taurus line. Neandertals are well represented in the same area during OIS 4, in reference to this new climatic change, but they were never found in northeast Africa. In the meantime, the fate of early modern humans in southwest Asia remains unknown. Their possible occurrence in South Asia is not demonstrable. Gene flow between the two groups, once supported by some authors (Thoma 1965), is not confirmed by the current fossil record. In addition, common features of the local Neandertals and the early modern humans are interpreted as shared primitive retentions. Although some interaction between the Neandertals and early modern humans in the Middle East is not impossible, there is no clear evidence for it. In terms of culture, both groups occurred in rather similar contexts. It can also be pointed out that no Neandertal burial is known (although cave sites of OIS 5 and 6 are known in Europe) before early modern humans are proved to have developed this practice in the Near East. Cultural similarities between Neandertals and modern humans in the Levant might advocate the long distance diffusion of some innovations in the late Middle Paleolithic, such as the extensive use of pigments in the late Mousterian of Eurasia on the eve of OIS 3 (Hublin 1990; Demars 1992).

The equilibrium existing north and south of the Mediterranean was broken in a more definite way during OIS 3, with the spread of anatomically modern humans throughout western Eurasia corresponding to the development of Aurignacian assemblages. From a biological point of view, more than a century of research has accumulated arguments supporting the model in which modern humans associated with Early Upper Paleolithic industries are invaders with no phylogenetic connection to their Neandertal European predecessors. During the past 20 years, the final argument has been the demonstration of the coexistence of the two groups in Europe for a substantial period of time. From a cultural point of view, despite disagreements on the definition and understanding of the Aurignacian, the assemblages associated to modern humans also appear as intrusive entities in the archeological landscape of the European sub-continent. Although it can always be improved upon, the archeological and paleontological record of Europe remains unrivaled and gives us a detailed picture of this event. So far, it is the best documented example of the replacement of an archaic local population by modern humans of tropical origin, and one must wonder to what extant this example is transposable to other areas of the Old World where the same scenario is assumed. The immediate origin of these modern invaders has not been established. Although genetic and some morphological arguments support an African origin via southwestern and/or western Asia, the exact timing and itinerary of this population prior to its arrival in Eastern Europe is unknown. The resolution of these issues mainly depends on a better knowledge of the archeological and paleontological evolution of Western Asia in the first half of OIS 3. From this perspective, it should be remembered that most of the early upper Paleolithic industries from easternmost Europe and southwestern Siberia are not assigned to the early Aurignacian (Anikovich 1992; Hoffecker 1988; Goebel et al. 1993), but could be of similar age or even predate the spread of the Aurignacian in Europe (Klein 1999). The picture gradually emerging from the European record of the transition is that of a dispersal of Aurignacian groups from east to west in the context of low demographic density and discontinuous settlements (Bocquet and Demars, in press b), followed by a sharing of the European territory. The initial Aurignacian colonization of Mediterranean Europe may have been facilitated by the development of mixed deciduous/coniferous woodland during warm episodes of OIS 3 (Mellars 1998). The pattern of the proceeding sharing may result from the different eco-geographical affinities of the two groups, and/or heterogeneity in the density of settlements of the autochthonous Neandertal populations (Mellars 1999). Due to disagreements on the dating of the earliest Aurignacian sites, the precise time and rate of this colonization is still debated. Confirmed of dates ca. 40 ka B.P. for the first Aurignacian settlements in westernmost Europe would support the model of a rapid dispersal, reminiscent, in some aspects, of that of the Thulean Eskimos over arctic Canada (but see comments by Park 1998). The plain located north of the Alpine arch and Mediterranean coastal areas may represent an early settlement area. In contrast, southwest France, especially in its northern part (Charentes, Vienne . . .), the southeastern Parisian basin, perhaps the Balkans, and more certainly the south of the Iberian Peninsula may have represented areas of the late persistence of the Neandertals. The coexistence of the two groups for several millennia (at least 6,000 years) on the scale of Western Europe does not match the picture of an instant replacement by overwhelmingly superior invaders, but rather a more subtle equilibrium between two groups of hominids probably characterized by different adaptive profiles. Only the environmental crisis related to the development of a new glacial cycle seems to have triggered the final extinction of the autochthonous populations. Even if the late Mousterian assemblages of Europe demonstrate some cultural changes (Demars 1992), it is extremely unlikely that the features demonstrated by "transitional" industries, and especially those of the late Chatelperronian, result from an independent and simultaneous invention of Upper Paleolithic cultural traits by the Neandertals at, or just before, the arrival of allochthonous Aurignacian populations. The acculturation hypothesis remains the most probable. One of the most interesting aspects of this transition is the increasing evidence for a complex process through which different scenarios developed in adjacent, limited geographical areas. In contrast with the evidence for cultural relations, the biological evidence provides little indication of genetic exchange. Neandertal remains from Saint Césaire, Zafarraya and Arcy-sur-Cure post-dating the arrival of modern humans in Western Europe are still identifiable as fully Neandertal. In addition, following the extinction of the last Neandertals, Europe was peopled by robust but fully modern humans. For virtually all of them, the persistence of any Neandertal features is just not demonstrable. If the interpretation of the Lagar Velho 1 child as a modern human displaying some Neandertal retentions is confirmed by further discoveries in the same geographical area, the Iberian Peninsula may, once again, prove an exception. Finally, the European example, with its complex mosaic of local conditions, its coexistence for some millennia of two groups of hominids sharing some behavioral and technical features, and the final extinction of one of these groups, may also provide a model for the replacement process of Neandertals by modern humans (and vice versa) in the southern Levant at earlier stages of the Paleolithic, for which chronological resolution is still rather approximate.

In conclusion, considering the relations of the hominids who lived on both sides of the Mediterranean Sea during the late Middle Pleistocene and most of the Upper Pleistocene, one is struck by the efficiency of this paleogeographic barrier. Geographic and genetic segregation resulted in the emergence of two very distinct biological groups to the north and south. However, at several stages of their evolution they may have been in direct contact: possibly through the Straits of Gibraltar and in the Levant, and certainly eventually in Europe, where they coexisted. However, although in these three cases there are arguments supporting the occurrence of some cultural exchanges between the populations, there is so far no definite evidence for genetic exchange. This statement can probably be viewed as an argument supporting the view that *Homo neanderthalensis* is not only a paleontological species but may have had some biological validity.

Notes

1. In the latter case some contamination of the dated samples may have occurred (see comments by Zilhão and d'Errico 1999b).

2. Vindija 207 displays two features which, *in frequency*, distinguish between Neandertals and modern humans: a horizontal-oval mandibular foramen and an asymmetrical sigmoid notch. According to Stefan and Trinkaus (1998), the retromolar space and the medial positioning of the sigmoid notch crest occur variably in the two groups.

Bibliography

Alimen, H. M.
    1975 "Les "isthmes" hispano-marocain et siculo-tunisien aux temps acheuléens." *L'Anthropologie* 79:399–436.

Allsworth-Jones, P.
    1982 "Comments on F. H. Smith: "Upper Pleistocene Hominid Evolution in South Central Europe: A Review of the Evidence and Analysis of Trends"." *Current Anthropology* 23:607–703.
    1986 *The Szeletian and the Transition from the Middle to Upper Palaeolithic in Central Europe*. Oxford University Press, Oxford.
    1990 "The Szeletian and the Stratigraphic Succession in Central Europe and Adjacent Areas: Main Trends, Recent Results, and Problems for Resolution," in *The Emergence of Modern Humans: An Archaeological Perspective*, P. Mellars, ed., pp. 160–242. Cornell University Press. New York.

Amani, F., and D. Geraads
    1993 "Le gisement moustérien du Djebel Irhoud, Maroc: précisions sur la faune et la biochronologie, et description d'un nouveau reste humain." *Comptes Rendus de l'Académie des Sciences* 316(2):847–852.

Anikovich, M.
1992 "Early Upper Paleolithic Industries of Eastern Europe." *Journal of World Prehistory* 6(2):205–245.

Arambourg, C.
1960 "Au sujet de *Elephas iolensis* Pomel." *Bulletin d'Archéologie Marocaine* 3:93–105.

Arensburg, B., and A. Belfer-Cohen
1998 "Sapiens and Neandertals: Rethinking the Levantine Middle Paleolithic Hominids," in *Neandertals and Modern Humans in Western Asia*, T. Akazawa, K. Aoki, and O. Bar-Yosef, eds., pp. 311–322. Plenum Press, New York.

Ascenzi, A., I. Biddutu, P. F. Cassoli, A. G. Segre, and E. Segre-Naldini
1996 "A Calvarium of Late *Homo erectus* from Ceprano, Italy." *Journal of Human Evolution* 31:409–423.

Auguste, P.
1995 *Cadres biostratigraphiques et paléoécologiques du peuplement humain dans la France septentrionale durant le Pléistocène. Apports de l'étude paléontologique des grands mammifères du gisement de Biache-Saint-Vaast (Pas-de-Calais)*. Vol. 5. Musée de Préhistoire de l'Ile de Franc,. Paris.

Barroso Ruiz, C., and J. J. Hublin
1994 *The Late Neandertal Site of Zafarraya (Andalucia, Spain)*. AEQUA monografias 2 ("Gibraltar during the Quaternary"): 61–70.

Bartolomei, G., A. Broglio, P. F. Cassoli, L. Castelletti, L. Cattani, M. Cremaschi, G. Giacobini, G. Malerba, A. Maspero, M. Peresani, A. Sartorelli, and A. Tagliacozzo
1994 "La Grotte de Fumane: un Site Aurignacien au Pied des Alpes." *Preistoria Alpina* 28:131–179.

Bar-Yosef, O.
1988 "The Date of Southwest Asian Neanderthals," in *L'Homme de Neandertal*, vol 3, E. Trinkaus, ed., pp. 31–38. Etudes et Recherches Archeologiques de l'Université de Liège 30. Service de Préhistoire, Liège.
1995 "The Lower and Middle Paleolithic in the Mediterranean Levant: Chronology, and Cultural Entities," in *Man and Environment in the Palaeolithic*, H. Ullrich, ed., pp. 247–263. Etudes et Recherches Archeologiques de l'Université de Liège 62. Service de Préhistoire, Liège.
1998 "The Chronology of the Middle Paleolithic of the Levant," in *Neandertals and Modern Humans in Western Asia*, T. Akazawa, K. Aoki, and O. Bar-Yosef, eds., pp. 39–56. Plenum Press, New York.

Bar-Yosef, O., and J. Callander
1999 "The Woman from Tabun: Garrod's Doubts in Historical Perspective." *Journal of Human Evolution* 37:879–885.

Bar-Yosef, O., and B. Vandermeersch
1981 "Notes Concerning the Possible Age of the Mousterian Layers in Qafzeh Cave," in *Préhistoire du Levant*, J. Cauvin and P. Sanlaville, eds., pp. 281–285. Centre National de la Recherche Scientifique, Paris.

Belfer-Cohen, A., and O. Bar-Yosef
1981 "The Aurignacian at Hayonim Cave." *Paléorient* 7(2):19–42.

Bergman, C. A. S. C. B.
1989 "Fifty Years After: Egbert, an Early Upper Palaeolithic Juvenile from Ksar 'Akil, Lebanon." *Paléorient* 15(2):99–111.

Biberson, P.
1964 "La place des hommes du Paléolithique marocain dans la chronologie du Pléistocène atlantique." *L'Anthropologie* 68(5–6):475–526.

Bischoff, J. L., K. Ludwig, J. F. Garcia, E. Carbonell, M. Vaquero, T. W. Stafford, and A. J. T. Jull
1994 "Dating of the Basal Aurignacian Sandwich at Abric Romaní (Catalunya, Spain) by Radiocarbon and Uranium-Series." *Journal of Archaeological Science* 21:541–551.

Bischoff, J. L., N. Soler, J. Maroto, and R. Julia
1989 "Abrupt Mousterian/Aurignacian Boundary at c.40 ka B.P.: Accelerator ^{14}C dates from L'Arbreda Cave (Catalunya, Spain)." *Journal of Archaeological Science* 16:563–576.

Bocquet-Appel, J.-P., and P.-Y. Demars
2000 "Population Kinetics in the Upper Palaeolithic in Western Europe." *Journal of Archaeological Science* 27.
in press "Mousterian Contraction and Aurignacian Colonization of Europe: The Pattern Emerging from the ^{14}C Dates." *Antiquity*.

Bon, F., C. Ferrier, D. Gambier, and P. Gardere
1998 "Gisement de Brassempouy (Landes): les recherches de 1995 à 1997, bilan et perspectives." *Bulletin de la Société de Bordeaux* 123(449):203–222.

Bordes, F.
1968 *Le Paléolithique dans le monde*. Coll. l'Univers des connaissances, Hachette, Paris.

Bordes, F., and J. Labrot
  1967 "La stratigraphie du gisement de Roc-de-Combe (Lot) et ses implications." *Bulletin de la Société Préhistorique Française* 64:15–28.

Brauër, G.
  1980 "Die morphologischen Affinitäten des jungpleistozänen Stirnbeines aus dem Elbmündungsgebiet bei HahnöFersand." *Zeitschrift für Morphologie und Anthropologie* 71(1):1–42.
  1984 "The "Afro-European Sapiens Hypothesis," and Hominid Evolution in East Asia During the Middle and Upper Pleistocene." *Courier Forschungsinstitut Senckenberg* 69:145–165.

Brauër, G., and H. Broeg
  1998 "On the Degree of Neandertal-Modern Continuity in the Earliest Upper Paleolithic Crania from the Czech Republic: Evidence from Non-Metrical Features," in *The Origins and Past of Modern Humans—Towards Reconciliation*, K. Omoto and Ph. Tobias, eds., pp. 106–125. Recent Advances in Human Biology, International Institute for Advanced Studies.

Broglio, A., and S. Improta
  1995 "Nuovi dati di cronologia assoluta del Paleolitico superiore e del mesolitico del Veneto, del Trentino e del Friuli." *Atti Istituto Veneto Scienze Lettere Arti* 153:1–45.

Cabrera Valdes, V., and J. L. Bischoff
  1989 "Accelerator ^{14}C Dates for Early Upper Paleolithic (Basal Aurignacian) at El Castillo Cave (Spain)." *Journal of Archaeological Science* 16:577–584.

Cann, R. L., M. Stoneking, and A. C. Wilson
  1987 "Mitochondrial DNA and Human Evolution." *Nature* 329:111–112.

Carbonell, E., J. M. Bermúdez de Castro, J. L. Arsuaga, J. C. Diez, A. Rosas, G. Cuenca-Bescós, R. Salar, M. Mosquera, and X. P. Rodríguez
  1995 "Lower Pleistocene Hominids and Artifacts from Atapuerca-TD6 (Spain)." *Science* 269:826–832.

Cavalli-Sforza, L. L., A. Piazza, P. Menozzi, and J. Mountain
  1988 "Reconstruction of Human Evolution: Bringing Together Genetic, Archaeological, and Linguistic Data." *Proc. Natl. Acad. Sci.* 85:6002–6006.

Champagne, F., and R. Espitalie
  1981 *Le Piagé, site préhistorique du Lot*. Mémoires de la Société Préhistorique Française 15, Paris.

Combier, J.
  1990 "De la fin du Moustérien au Paléolithique supérieur—les données de la région rhodanienne," in *Paléolithique moyen recent et Paléolithique supérieur ancien en Europe. Ruptures et transitions: examen critique des documents archéologiques*, C. Farizy, ed., pp. 267–277. A.P.R.A.I.F. 3. Mémoires du Musée de Préhistoire d'Ile de France, Nemours.

Condemi, S.
  1988 "Caractères plésiomorphes et apomorphes de l'os temporal des neandertaliens européens wurmiens," in *L'homme de Néandertal: vol 3 l'Anatomie*, M. Otte and H. Laville, eds., pp. 49–52. Etudes et Recherches Archeologiques de l'Université de Liège, 30. Service de Préhistoire, Liège.
  1992 *Les Hommes Fossiles de Saccopastore et leurs relations phylogénétiques*. Centre National de la Recherche Scientifique, Paris.

Corruccini, R. S.
  1992 "Metrical Reconsideration of the Skhul IV and IX and Border Cave Crania in the Context of Modern Human Origins." *American Journal of Physical Anthropology* 87:433–445.

Damblon, F., P. Haeserts, and J. van der Plicht
  1996 "New Datings and Considerations on the Chronology of Upper Paleolithic Sites in the Great Eurasiatic Plain." *Préhistoire Européenne* 9:177–231.

Debénath, A.
  1975 "Découverte de restes humains probablement atériens a Dar Es Soltane (Maroc)." *Comptes Rendus de l'Académie des Sciences* 281:875–876.

Debénath, A., J.-P. Raynal, and P. J. Texier
  1982 "Position stratigraphique des restes humains paléolithiques marocains sur la base des travaux récents." *Comptes Rendus de l'Académie des Sciences* 294:1247–1250.

Debénath, A., J.-P. Raynal, J. Roche, J.-P. Texier, and D. Ferembach
  1986 "Stratigraphie, habitat, typologie et devenir de l'Atérien marocain: données récentes." *L'Anthropologie* 90(2):233–246.

Demars, P.-Y.
  1992 "Les colorants dans le Moustérien du Périgord. L'apport des fouilles de F. Bordes." *Bulletin de la Société Préhistorique de l'Ariège* 47:185–194.

Demars, P.-Y., and J. J. Hublin
  1989 "La transition néandertaliens/hommes de type moderne en Europe occidentale: aspects paleontologiques et culturels," in *L'Homme de Neandertal 7: l'extinction*, M. Otte and H. Laville, eds., pp. 29–42. Etudes et Recherches Archeologiques de l'Université de Liège 34. Service de Préhistoire, Liège.

d'Errico, F., J. Zilhão, M. Julien, D. Baffier, and J. Pelegrin
  1998 "Neanderthal Acculturation in Western Europe? A Critical Review of the Evidence and its Interpretation." *Current Anthropology* 39:S1–S44.

Djindjian, F.
  1993 "Les origines du peuplement Aurignacien en Europe," in *Aurignacien en Europe et au Proche Orient*, L. Banesz and J. K. Kozlowski, eds., pp. 136–154. Acts of 12th International Congress of Prehistoric and Protohistoric Sciences, Bratislava.

Duarte C., J. Mauricio, P. B. Pettitt, P. Souto, E. Trinkaus, H. Van der Plicht, and J. Zilhão
  1999 "The Early Upper Paleolithic Human Skeleton from the Abrigo do Lagar Velho (Portugal) and Modern Human Emergence in Iberia." *Proceedings of the National Academy of Sciences USA* 96:7604–7609.

Féblot-Augustins J.
  1993 "Mobility Strategies in the Late Middle Palaeolithic of Central Europe and Western Europe: Elements of Stability and Variability." *Journal of Anthropological Archaeology* 12:211–265.

Ferembach, D.
  1976a "Les restes humains atériens de Témara (1975)." *Bulletins et Mémoires de la Société d'Anthropologie de Paris* 3(2):175–180.
  1976b "Les restes humains de la grotte de Dar-es-Sultan 2 (Maroc), campagne 1975." *Bulletins et Mémoires de la Société d'Anthropologie de Paris* 3:183–193.
  1985 "On the Origin of the Iberomaurusians (Upper Palaeolithic: North Africa). A New Hypothesis." *Journal of Human Evolution* 14:393–397.

Foley R., and M. M. Lahr
  1997 "Mode 3 Technologies and the Evolution of Modern Humans." *Cambridge Archaeological Journal* 7(1):3–36.

Frayer, D. W.
  1986 "Cranial Variation at Mladec and the Relationship between Mousterian and Upper Palaeolithic Hominids." *Anthropos* 23:243–256.

Gambier, D.
  1989 "Fossil Hominids from the Upper Palaeolithic (Aurignacian) of France," in *The Human Revolution: Behavioural and Biological Perspectives in the Origins of Modern Humans*, P. Mellars and C. B. Stringer, eds., pp. 194–211. Edinburgh University Press, Edinburgh.
  1992 "Origine de l'homme moderne en Europe: comparaison des donnes crâniennes en Europe centrale et occidentale," in *Cinq millions d'années, l'aventure humaine*, M. Toussaint, ed., pp. 269–284. Etudes et Recherches Archeologiques de l'Université de Liège 56. Service de Préhistoire, Liège.
  1993 "Les hommes modernes du début du paléolithique supérieur en France: Bilan des données anthropologiques et perspectives," in *El origen del hombre moderno en el Suroeste de Europa*, V. Cabrera-Valdès, ed., pp. 409–430. Universidad Nacional de Educacion a Distancia, Madrid.
  in press "Aurignacian Children and Mortuary Practice in Western Europe." *Anthropologie* 38(1).

Gambier, D., F. Houet, and A.-M. Tillier
  1990 "Dents de Font de Gaume (Châtelperronien et Aurignacien) et de la Ferrassie (Aurignacien ancien) en Dordogne." *Paléo* 2:143–152.

Gambier, D., and D. Sacchi
  1991 "Sur quelques restes humains leptolithiques de la grotte de la Crouzade, Aude." *L'Anthropologie* 95(1):155–180.

Ginter, G., J. K. Kozlowski, H. Laville, N. Siakov, and R. E. M. Hedges
  1996 "Transition in the Balkans: News from the Temnata Cave, Bulgaria," in *The Last Neandertals, the First Anatomically Modern Humans*, E. Carbonell and M. Vaquero, eds., pp. 169–200. Universitat Rovira i Virgili, Tarragona.

Gioia, P.
  1990 "An Aspect of the Transition between Middle and Upper Paleolithic in Italy: the Uluzzian," in *Paléolithique moyen recent et Paléolithique supérieur ancien en Europe. Ruptures et transitions: examen critique des documents archéologiques*, C. Farizy, ed., pp. 241–250. A.P.R.A.I.F. 3. Mémoires du Musée de Préhistoire d'Ile de France, Nemours.

Goebel, T., A. P. Derevianko, and V. T. Petrin
  1993 "Dating the Middle-to-Upper-Paleolithic Transition at Kara-Bom." *Current Anthropology* 34(4):452–458.

González Echegaray, J.
  1980 "El yacimiento de la Cueva de "el Pendo" (Excavaciones 1953–57)." *Bibliotheca Praehistorica Hispana* 17:1–270.

Goring-Morris A. N.
  1987 *At the Edge: Terminal Hunter-Gatherers in the Negev and Sinai*. British Archaeological Reports International Series 361, Oxford.

Grün, R., and C. B. Stringer
  1991 "Electron Spin Resonance Dating and the Evolution of Modern Humans." *Archaeometry* 33:153–199.

Guiot, A., A. Pons, J. L. de Beaulieu, and M. Reille
　1989 "A 140,000-Year Continental Climate Reconstruction from Two European Pollen Records." *Nature* 338:309–313.

Haas, G.
　1972 "The Microfauna of the Djebel Qafzeh Cave." *Paleovertebrata* 5:261–270.

Hahn, J.
　1983 "Eiszeitliche Jager zwischen 35000 und 15000 Jahren vor heute," in *Urgeschichte in Baden-Württemberg*, H. Müller-Beck, ed., pp. 273–330. Konrad Theiss Verlag, Stuttgart.
　1995 "Neue Beschleuniger-C-14-Daten zum Jungpaläolithikum in Südwestdeutschland." *Eiszeitalter und Gegenwart* (45):86–92.
　1996 "Le Paléolithique Supérieur en Allemagne Méridionale (1991–1995)," in *Le Paléolithique supérieur européen. Bilan quinquennal 1991–1996*, M. Otte, ed., pp. Etudes et Recherches Archéologiques de l'Université de Liège 76. Service de Préhistoire, Liège.

Harris, E. E., and J. Hey
　1999 "Human Demography in the Pleistocene: Do Mitochondrial and Nuclear Genes Tell the Same Story." *Evolutionary Anthropology* 8(3):81–86.

Harrold, F. B.
　1989 "Mousterian, Châtelperronian and Early Aurignacian in Western Europe: Continuity or Discontinuity?" in *The Human Revolution: Behavioural and Biological Perspectives on the Origins of Modern Humans*, P. A. Mellars and C. B. Stringer, eds., pp. 677–713. Edinburgh University Press, Edinburgh.

Hedges, R. E. M., R. A. Housley, C. Bronk Ramsey, and G. J. van Klinken
　1994 "Radiocarbon Dates from the Oxford AMS System: Archaeometry Datelist 18." *Archaeometry* 36:337–374.

Hershkovitz, I., M. S. Speirs, D. Frayer, D. Nadel, S. Wish-Baratz, and B. Arensburg
　1995 "Ohalo II H2: a 19,000-year-old Skeleton from a Water-logged Site at the Sea of Galilee, Israel." *American Journal of Physical Anthropology* 96(3):215–234.

Hoffecker, J. F.
　1988 "Early Upper Paleolithic Sites of the European USSR," in *The Early Upper Paleolithic: Evidence from Europe and the Near East*, J. F. Hoffecker and C. A. Wolf, eds., pp. 237–272. British Archaeological Reports International Series 437, Oxford.

Holliday, T. W.
　1995 *Body Size and Proportions in the Late Pleistocene Western Old World and the Origin of the Modern Humans*. The University of New Mexico, Albuquerque.
　1997a "Body Proportions in Late Pleistocene Europe and Modern Human Origins." *Journal of Human Evolution* 32(5):423–447.
　1997b "Postcranial Evidence of Cold Adaptation in European Neandertals." *American Journal of Physical Anthropology* 104:245–258.

Howell, F. C.
　1957 "The Evolutionary Significance of Variation and Varieties of 'Neanderthal' Man." *The Quarterly Review of Biology* 32:330–347.
　1958 "Upper Pleistocene Men of the Southwest Asian Mousterian," in *Neanderthal Centenary 1856–1956*, G. H. R. von Koenigswald, ed., pp. 185–198. Kemink en Zoon, Utrecht, Netherlands.

Howells, W. W.
　1975 "Neanderthal Man: Facts and Figures," in *Paleoanthropology, Morphology and Paleoecology*, R. H. Tuttle, ed., pp. 389–407. Mouton, The Hague.

Hublin, J. J.
　1978a "Le torus occipital transverse et les structures associées: évolution dans le genre *Homo*." Paris VI. Thèse de 3è cycle.
　1978b "Quelques caractères apomorphes du crâne néandertalien et leur interpretation phylogenetique." *Comptes Rendus à l'Académie des Sciences de Paris* 287:923–926.
　1988a "Caractères dérivés de la région occipito-mastoïdienne chez les néandertaliens," in *L'Homme de Néandertal, 3: l'Anatomie*, E. Trinkaus, ed., pp. 67–73. Etudes et Recherches Archeologiques de l'Université de Liège 30. Service de Préhistoire, Liège.
　1988b "Les presapiens européens," in *L'Homme de Néandertal, 3: l'Anatomie*, E. Trinkaus, ed., pp. 75–80. Etudes et Recherches Archeologiques de l'Université de Liège 30. Service de Préhistoire, Liège.
　1990 "Les peuplements paléolithiques de l'Europe: un point de vue paléobiogéographique." *Mémoires du Musée de Préhistoire de l'Ile de France* 3:29–37.
　1993 "Recent Human Evolution in Northwestern Africa," in *The Origins of Modern Humans and the Impact of Chronometric Dating*, M. J. Aitken, C. B. Stringer, and P. A. Mellars, eds., pp. 118–131. Princeton University Press, Princeton.
　1998a "Climatic Changes, Paleogeography, and the Evolution of the Neandertals," in *Neandertals and Modern Humans in Western Asia*, T. Akazawa, K. Aoki, and O. Bar-Yosef, eds., pp. 295–310. Plenum Press, New York.

1998b "Comment on F. d'Errico J. Zilhão, M. Julien, D. Baffier, J. Pellegrin., Neanderthal Acculturation of Western Europe?" *Current Anthropology* Supplement 39:24–25.
1999 "Derniers néandertaliens et premiers européens modernes." *Pour la Science* (h.s.22):110–118.

Hublin, J.-J., C. Barroso Ruiz, P. Medina Lara, M. Fontugne, and J.-L. Reyss
1995 "The Mousterian Site of Zafarraya (Andalucia, Spain): Dating and Implications on the Palaeolithic Peopling Processes of Western Europe." *Comptes Rendus de l'Académie des Sciences* 321:931–937.

Hublin, J.-J., F. Spoor, M. Braun, and F. Zonneveld
1996 "A Late Neanderthal Associated with Upper Paleolithic Artifacts." *Nature* 381:224–226.

Hublin, J. J., and A.-M. Tillier
1988 "Les enfants moustériens de Jebel Irhoud (Maroc). Comparaison avec les néandertaliens juvéniles d'Europe." *Bulletins et Mémoires de la Société d'Anthropologie de Paris* 5(4):237–246.

Hublin, J. J., A.-M. Tillier, and J. Tixier
1987 "L'humerus d'enfant moustérien (Homo 4) du Jebel Irhoud (Maroc) dans son contexte archéologique." *Bulletins et Mémoires de la Société d'Anthropologie de Paris* 4:115–142.

Hublin J.-J, and E. Trinkaus
1998 "The Mousterian Human Remains from Zafarraya (Andalucia, Spain)." *American Journal of Physical Anthropology* Supplement 26:122–123.

Jaeger, J.-J.
1975 "Evolution des Rongeurs du Miocène à l'actuel en Afrique nord-occidentale." Ph.D. Dissertation. Université de Montpellier, France.
1981 "Les hommes fossiles du Pleistocène moyen du Maghreb dans leur cadre géologique, chronologique et paléoécologique," in *Homo erectus. Papers in Honor of Davidson Black*, B. A. Sigmond, and J. S. Cybulski, eds., pp. 159–264. University of Toronto Press, Toronto.

Jelinek, J.
1976 "The *Homo sapiens neanderthalensis* and *Homo sapiens sapiens* Relationship in Central Europe." *Anthropologie* 14(1–2):79–89.

Jouzel, J., N. I. Barkov, J. M. Barnola, M. Bender, J. Chappellaz, C. Genthon, V. M. Kotlyakov, V. Lipenkov, C. Lorius, J. R. Petit, D. Raynaud, G. Raisbeck, C. Ritz, T. Sowers, M. Stievenard, F. Yiou, and P. Yiou
1993 "Extending the Vostok Ice-Core Record of Palaeoclimate to the Penultimate Glacial Period." *Nature* 364:407–412.

Klein R. G.
1998 "Why Anatomically Modern People Did Not Disperse from Africa 100,000 Years Ago," in *Neandertals and Modern Humans in Western Asia*, T. Akazawa, K. Aoki, and O. Bar-Yosef, eds., pp. 509–522. Plenum Press, New York.
1999 *The Human Career: Human Biological and Cultural Origins* (Second Edition). University of Chicago Press, Chicago.

Kozlowski J. K.
1982 *Excavation in the Bacho Kiro Cave (Bulgaria): Final Report*. Panstwowe Wydawnictwo Naukowe, Warsaw.
1990 "A Multiaspectual Approach to the Origins of the Upper Palaeolithic in Europe," in *The Emergence of Modern Humans: An Archaeological Perspective*, P. A. Mellars, ed., pp. 419–437. Cornell University Press, Ithaca.
1992 "The Balkans in the Middle and Upper Palaeolithic: the Gate to Europe or a Cul-de-Sac?" *The Prehistoric Society* 58:1–20.
1996 "Cultural Context of the Last Neanderthals and Early Modern Humans in Central-Eastern Europe," in *The Lower and Middle Palaeolithic: Colloquia 9 and 10*. O. Bar-Yosef, L. Cavalli-Sforza, R. March, and M. Piperno, eds., pp. . 13th International Congress of Prehistoric and Protohistoric Sciences. A.B.A.C.O. Edizioni, Forlí.

Lahr, M. M., and R. A. Foley
1998 "Towards a Theory of Modern Human Origins: Geography, Demography and Diversity in Recent Human Evolution." *Yearbook of Physical Anthropology* 41:137–176.

Laquay, G., and A. Cheddadi
1986 *Nouvelles données sur la faune de vertébrés de la carrière Doukkala II (Rabat-Maroc)*. Société Géologique de France 106. Paris.

Leroi-Gourhan, A.
1959 "Étude des restes humains fossiles provenant des Grottes d'Arcy-sur-Cure." *Annales de Paléontologie* 44:87–148.

Leroyer, C.
1986 "Les gisements castelperroniens de Quinçay et de Saint-Césaire: quelques comparaisons préliminaires des études palynologiques." 125–134.

Lévêque, F., and J.-C. Miskovsky
1983 "Le Castelperronien dans son environnement géologique." *L'Anthropologie* 87(3):369–391.

Lévêque, F., and B. Vandermeersch
1980 "Découverte de restes humains dans un niveau castelperronien à Saint-Césaire (Charente-Mar-

itime)." *Comptes-Rendus de l'Académie des Sciences de Paris* 291:187–189.

Malan, M.
1955 "Zahnkeim aus der zweiten Aurignacien-Schicht der Höhle von Istalloskö." *Acta Archaeologica Academiae Scientiarum Hungaricae* 5:145–148.

Mallegni, F., and E. Trinkaus
1997 "A Reconsideration of the Archi 1 Neandertal Mandible." *Journal of Human Evolution* 33:651–668.

Marks, A. E.
1983 "The Middle to Upper Paleolithic Transition in the Levant," in *Advances in World Archaeology*, F. Wendorf and A. Close, eds., pp. 51–98. Academic Press, New York.

Marks, A. E., Yu. E. Demidenko, K. Monigal, V. I. Usik, C. R. Ferring, A. Burke, J. Rink, and C. McKinney
1997 "Starosele and the Starosele Child: New Excavations, New Results." *Current Anthropology* 38(3):112–123.

Maroto, J.
1994 "El pas del paleolithic mitja al paleolithic superior a Catalunya i la seva interpretacio dins del context geografic franco-ibéric." Ph.D. Dissertation. University of Girona, Girona.

McBurney C. B. M.
1967 *The Haua Fteah (Cyrenaica) and the Stone Age of the South-East Mediterranean*. Cambridge University Press, Cambridge.

Meignen L.
1998 "Hayonim Cave Lithic Assemblages in the Context of the Near Eastern Middle Paleolithic: A Preliminary Report," in *Neandertals and Modern Humans in Western Asia*, T. Akazawa, K. Aoki, and O. Bar-Yosef, eds., pp. 165–180. Plenum Press, New York.

Mellars, P. A.
1973 "The Character of the Middle-Upper Palaeolithic Transition in South-West France," in *The Explanation of Culture Change*, C. Renfrew, ed., pp. 255–276. University of Pittsburgh Press, Pittsburgh.
1986 "A New Chronology for the French Mousterian Period." *Nature* 322:410–411.
1989 "Major Issues in the Emergence of Modern Humans." *Current Anthropology* 30(3):349–385.
1991 "Cognitive Changes and the Emergence of Modern Humans." *Cambridge Archaeological Journal* 1:63–76.
1996 *The Neanderthal Legacy. An Archaeological Perspective from Western Europe*. Princeton University Press, Princeton, New Jersey.
1998 "The Impact of Climatic Changes on the Demography of Late Neandertal and Early Anatomically Modern Populations in Europe," in *Neandertals and Modern Humans in Western Asia*, T. Akazawa, K. Aoki, and O. Bar-Yosef, eds., pp. 493–508. Plenum Press, New York.
1999 "Neanderthal Problem Continued." *Current Anthropology* 40:341–350.

Mellars, P. A., and J. Tixier
1989 "Radiocarbon-Accelerator Dating of Ksar 'Aqil (Lebanon) and the Chronology of the Upper Palaeolithic Sequence in the Middle East." *Antiquity* 63:761–768.

Mercier N., H. Valladas, G. Valladas, and J.-L. Reyss
1995 "TL Dates of Burnt Flints from Jelinek's Excavations at Tabun and their Implications." *Journal of Archaeological Science* 22:495–509.

Movius, H. L., Jr.
1995 "Inventaire analytique des sites aurignaciens et périgordiens de Dordogne," in *Le Paléolithique Supérieur de l'abri Pataud (Dordogne): les fouilles de H. L. Movius Jr.*, H. M. Bricker, ed., pp. 227–313. Maison des Sciences de l'Homme, Paris.

Mussi, M.
1990 "Le peuplement de l'Italie à la fin du paléolithique moyen et au début du paléolithique supérieur," in *Paléolithique moyen recent et Paléolithique supérieur ancien en Europe. Ruptures et transitions: examen critique des documents archéologiques*, C. Farizy, ed., pp. 251–262. A.P.R.A.I.F. 3. Mémoires du Musée de Préhistoire d'Ile de France, Nemours.

Otte M.
1996 *Le Paléolithique inférieur et moyen en Europe*. Armand Colin, Paris.
1999 "The Neanderthal Problem Continued." *Current Anthropology* 40:350–352.

Otte, M., I. Yalçinskaya, J. Kozlowski, O. Bar-Yosef, I. López Bayón, and H. Taskiran
1998 "Long-Term Technical Evolution and Human Remains in the Anatolian Palaeolithic." *Journal of Human Evolution* 34:413–431.

Park, R. W.
1998 "On the Dorset/Thule Analogy for the Middle/Upper Paleolithic Transition." *Current Anthropology* 39:355–356.

Pelegrin, J.
1990 "Observations technologiques sur quelques séries du Châtelperronien et du MTA B du sud-ouest de la France: Une hypothèse d'évolution," in *Paléolithique moyen recent et Paléolithique*

supérieur ancien en Europe. Ruptures et transitions: examen critique des documents archéologiques, C. Farizy, ed., pp. 39–42. A.P.R.A.I.F. 3. Mémoires du Musée de Préhistoire d'Ile de France, Nemours.

Protsch, R., and Semmel, A.
1978 "Zur Chronologie des Kelsterbach-Hominiden." Eiszeitalter und Gegenwart 28:200–210.

Quam, R. M., and F. H. Smith
1998 "A Reassessment of the Tabun C2 Mandible," in Neandertals and Modern Humans in Western Asia, T. Akazawa, K. Aoki, and O. Bar-Yosef, eds., pp. 405–422. Plenum Press, New York.

Rak, Y.
1986 "The Neanderthal: a New Look at an Old Face." Journal of Human Evolution 15(3):151–164.
1990 "On the Differences between Two Pelvises of Mousterian Context from the Qafzeh and Kebara Caves, Israel." American Journal of Physical Anthropology 81:323–332.
1998 "Does any Mousterian Cave Present Evidence of Two Hominid Species?" in Neandertals and Modern Humans in Western Asia, T. Akazawa, K. Aoki, and O. Bar-Yosef, eds., pp. 353–366. Plenum Press, New York.

Raposo L.
1995 "Ambientes, territorios y subsistencia en el paleolitico medio de Portugal." Complutum 6:57–77.

Roberts, R. G., R. Jones, and M. A. Smith
1990 "Thermoluminescence Dating of a 50,000-year-old Human Occupation Site in Northern Australia." Nature 345:153–156.

Roberts, R. G., R. Jones, N. A. Spooner, M. J. Head, A. S. Murray, and M. A. Smith
1994 "The Human Colonisation of Australia: Optimal Dates of 53,000 and 60,000 Years Bracket Human Arrival at Deaf Adder Gorge, Northern Territory." Quaternary Science Reviews 13:575–586.

Roche, J.
1952 "Note préliminaire sur la grotte de Taforalt (Maroc oriental)." Hesperis 40:89–116.
1976 "Cadre chronologique de l'épipaléolithique marocain," in Proceedings of the 9th International Congress of Prehistoric and Protohistoric Sciences, volume 2, V. Giscard d'Estaing, ed., pp. 153–167. Centre National de la Recherche Scientifique, Université de Nice.

Roche, J., and J.-P. Texier
1976 "Découverte des restes humains dans un niveau atérien supérieur de la grotte des Contrebandiers, à Témara (Maroc)." Comptes Rendus des Séances de l'Académie des Science de Paris 282:45–47.

Roebroeks, W., and T. von Kolfschoten
1994 "The Earliest Occupation of Europe: a Short Chronology." Antiquity 68:489–503.

Rognon, P.
1996 "Climatic Change in the African Deserts Between 130,000 and 10,000y bp." Compte Rendus de l'Académie des Sciences de Paris 323:549–561.

Rosas A., and J. M. Bermudez de Castro
1998 "The Mauer Mandible and the Evolutionary Significance of Homo Heidelbergensis." Geobios 31(5):687–697.

Roubet, F.-E.
1969 "Le niveau atérien dans le stratigraphie côtière à l'Ouest d'Alger." Palaeoecology of Africa 4:124–129.

Ruff, C. B., E. Trinkaus, and T. W. Holliday
1997 "Body Mass and Encephalization in Pleistocene Homo." Nature 387:173–176.

Santa Luca, A. P.
1978 "A Re-examination of Presumed Neandertal-like Fossils." Journal of Human Evolution 7(7):619–636.

Schwarcz, H. P., R. Grün, B. Vandermeersch, O. Bar Yosef, H. Valladas, and E. Tchernov
1988 "ESR Dates for the Hominid Burial Site of Qafzeh in Israel." Journal of Human Evolution 17:733–737.

Schwarcz, H. P., J. J. Simpson, and C. B. Stringer
1998 "Neanderthal Skeleton from Tabun: U-Series Data by Gamma-Ray Spectrometry." Journal of Human Evolution 35:635–645.

Schwarcz H. P., and W. J. Rink
1998 "Progress in ESR and U-Series Chronology of the Levantine Paleolithic," in Neandertals and Modern Humans in Western Asia, T. Akazawa, K. Aoki, and O. Bar-Yosef, eds., pp. 57–60. Plenum Press, New York.

Senyurek M. S.
1940 "Fossil Man in Tangier." Papers of the Peabody Museum of American Archeology and Ethnology, Harvard University 16:1–27.

Smith, F. H.
1984 "Fossil Hominids from the Upper Pleistocene of Central Europe and the Origin of Modern Europeans," in The Origins of Modern Humans: a

World Survey of the Fossil Evidence, F. H. Smith, and F. Spencer, eds., pp. 137–209. Alan R. Liss, New York.
1985 "Continuity and Change in the Origin of Modern *Homo sapiens*." *Zeitschrift für Morphologie und Anthropologie, Stuttgart* 75(2):197–222.

Smith, F. H., E. Trinkaus, P. Pettitt, I. Karavanic, and M. Paunovic
1999 "Direct Radiocarbon Dates for Vindija G1 and Velika Pecina Late Pleistocene Hominid Remains." *Proceedings of the National Academy of Sciences* 96(22):12281–12286.

Smith P.
1966 *Le Solutréen en France*. Volume 5. Institut de Préhistoire, Université de Bordeaux.

Sohn, S., and M. H. Wolpoff
1993 "Zuttiyeh Face: A View from the East." *American Journal of Physical Anthropology* 91:325–347.

Stefan, V. H., and E. Trinkaus
1998 "Discrete Trait and Dental Morphometric Affinities of the Tabun 2 Mandible." *Journal of Human Evolution* 34:443–468.

Straus, L. G.
1994 "Upper Paleolithic Origins and Radiocarbon Calibration: More New Evidence from Spain." *Evolutionary Anthropology* 2(6):195–198.
1999 "The Neanderthal Problem Continued." *Current Anthropology* 40(3):352–355.

Straus, L. G., and M. Otte
1996 "The Middle to Upper Paleolithic Transition at the Local Level: The Case of the Trou Magrite (Namur Province, Belgium)," in *The Last Neanderthals, the First Anatomically Modern Humans*, E. Carbonell and M. Vaquero, eds., pp. 157–167. Universitat Rovira i Virgili, Tarragona.

Straus, L. G., J. Bischoff, and E. Carbonell
1993 "A Review of the Middle to Upper Paleolithic Transition in Iberia." *Préhistoire Européenne* 3:11–27.

Stringer, C. B.
1974 "Population Relationships of Later Pleistocene Hominids: A Multivariate Study of Available Crania." *Journal of Archaeological Science* 1(4):317–342.
1989 "The Origin of Early Modern Humans: a Comparison of the European and Non-European Evidence," in *The Human Revolution: Behavioural and Biological Perspectives on the Origins of Modern Humans*, P. Mellars and C. Stringer, eds., pp. 232–244. Edinburgh University Press, Edinburgh.
1990 "British Isles," in *Hominid Remains: An Update*, R. Orban, ed., pp. 1–40. British Isles and Eastern Germany. Université Libre de Bruxelles, Brussels.

Stringer C. and C. Gamble
1993 *In Search of the Neanderthals: Solving the Puzzle of Human Origins*. Thames and Hudson, London.

Stringer, C. B., and E. Trinkaus
1981 "The Shanidar Neanderthal Crania," in *Aspects of Human Evolution*, C. B. Stringer, ed., pp. 129–165. Taylor and Francis, London.

Stringer, C. B., R. Grün, and H. P. Schwarcz
1989 "ESR Dates for the Hominid Burial Site of Es Skhul in Israel." *Nature* 338(6218):756–758.

Suzuki H., and F. Takaï
1970 *Amud Man and his Cave Site*. Academic Press of Japan, University of Tokyo.

Svoboda J., V. Lozek, and E. Vlcek
1996 *Hunters Between East and West: The Paleolithic of Moravia*. Plenum Press, New York.

Tattersall, I., and J. H. Schwartz
1999 "Hominids and Hybrids: The Place of Neanderthals in Human Evolution." *Proceedings of the National Academy of Sciences, USA* 96:7117–7119.

Tchernov, E.
1981 "The Biostratigraphy of the Middle East," in *Préhistoire du Levant*, J. Laville and P. Sanlaville, eds., pp. 67–97. Colloque international du CNRS 598. Centre National de la Recherche Scientifique, Paris.
1992 "Eurasian-African Biotic Exchanges Through the Levantine Corridor During the Neogene and Quaternary." *Courier Forsch. -Inst. Senckenberg, Frankfurt* 153:103–123.
1998 "The Faunal Sequence of the Southwest Asian Middle Paleolithic in Relation to Hominid Dispersal Events," in *Neandertals and Modern Humans in Western Asia*, T. Akazawa, K. Aoki, and O. Bar-Yosef, eds., pp. 77–90. Plenum Press, New York.

Texier, J.-P., J. Huxtable, E. Rhodes, D. Miallier, and M. Ousmoi
1988 "Nouvelles données sur la situation chronologique de l'Atérien du Maroc et leurs implications." *Comptes Rendus à l'Académie des Sciences de Paris* 307:827–832.

Texier J.-P., J. P. Raynal, and D. Lefevre
1985 "Nouvelles propositions pour un cadre chronologique raisonné du Quaternaire marocain." *Comptes Rendus de l'Académie des Sciences Paris* 301(2):183–188.

1986 "Essai de chronologie du Quaternaire marocain." *Bulletin d'archeologie marocaine* 16:11–26.

Thoma, A.
1965 "La definition des néandertaliens et la position des hommes fossiles de Palestine." *L'Anthropologie* 69(5–6):519–534.

Thomas, H.
1981 "La faune de la grotte à néandertaliens du Jebel Irhoud (Maroc)." *Quaternaria* 23:191–217.

Thorne, A., R. Grün, G. Mortimer, N. A. Spooner, J. J. Simpson, M. McCulloch, L. Taylor, and D. Curnoe
1999 "Australia's Oldest Human Remains: Age of the Lake Mungo 3 Skeleton." *Journal of Human Evolution* 36(6):591–612.

Tillet, T.
1984 *Le Paléolithique du bassin tchadien septentrional (Niger, Tchad)*. Centre National de la Recherche Scientifique, Paris.

Tillier, A.-M.
1974 "Contribution à l'étude des hommes fossiles moustériens du Moyen Orient: La pneumatisation de la face." *Paléorient* 2:463–468.
1984 "L'enfant Homo 11 de Qafzeh (Israël) et son apport à la compréhension des modalités de la croissance des squelettes moustériens." *Paléorient* 10(1):7–48.
1991 "La mandibule et les dents," in *Le squelette moustérien de Kébara 2*, O. Bar-Yosef and B. Vandermeersch, eds., pp. 97–111. Centre National de la Recherche Scientifique, Paris.
1999 *Les Enfants Moustériens de Qafzeh. Interprétations phylogénétique et paléoauxologique*. Cahiers de Paleoanthropologie. Centre National de la Recherche Scientifique, Paris.

Tillier, A.-M., and J. Tixier
1991 "Une molaire d'enfant aurignacien à Ksar 'Aqil (Liban)." *Paléorient* 17(1):89–93.

Tobias, P. V.
1967 "The Hominid Skeletal Remains of Haua Fteah," in *The Haua Fteah (Cyrenaica) and the Stone Age of the South-East Mediterranean*, C. B. M. McBurney, ed., pp. 338–352. Cambridge University Press, Cambridge.

Trinkaus, E.
1976 "The Morphology of European and Southwest Asian Neandertal Pubic Bones." *American Journal of Physical Anthropology* 44:95–104.
1981 "Neandertal Limb Proportions and Cold Adaptation," in *Aspects of Human Evolution*, C. B. Stringer, ed., pp. 187–224. Taylor and Francis Ltd., London.
1983 *The Shanidar Neandertals*. Academic Press, New York.
1984 "Western Asia," in *The Origin of Modern Humans: a World Survey of the Fossil Evidence*, F. H. Smith and F. Spencer, eds., pp. 251–293. Alan R. Liss, New York.
1984 "Does KNM-ER 1481 A Establish *Homo erectus* at 2.0 myr B.P.?" *American Journal of Physical Anthropology* 64:137–139.
1987 "The Neandertal Face: Evolutionary and Functional Perspectives on a Recent Hominid Face." *Journal of Human Evolution* 16:429–443.
1992 "Morphological Contrasts Between the Near Eastern Qafzeh-Skhul and Late Archaic Human Samples: Grounds for a Behavioral Difference," in *The Evolution and Dispersal of Nodern Humans in Asia*, T. Akazawa, K. Aoki, and T. Kimura, eds., pp. 278-294. Hokusen-Sha, Tokyo.
1995 "Near Eastern Late Archaic Humans." *Paléorient* 21(2):9–23.

Trinkaus, E., J. Zilhão, and C. Duarte
1999 "The Lapedo Child: Lagar Velho 1 and our Perceptions of the Neandertals." http://www.ommp.abaco-mac.it/stash/stashed/aol.htm. November 17, 1999.

Tuffreau, A.
1984 "Le Paléolithique dans le Nord de la France et la Picardie." *Cahiers de Géographie Physique, Université de Lille* 7:29.

Turner, C. G.
1990 "Paleolithic Siberian Dentition from Denisova and Oklandikov Caves, Altayskiy Kray, U.S.S.R." *Current Research in the Pleistocene* 7:65–66.

Turq, A., B. Martínez-Navarro, P. Palmqvist, A. Arribas, J. Agustí, and J. Rodríguez Vidal
1996 "Le Plio-Pléistocène de la région d'Orce, Province de Grenade, Espagne: bilan et perspectives de recherche." *Paléo* 8:161–204.

Uthmeier, T.
1996 "Ein bemerkenswert frühes Inventar des Aurignacien von der Freilandfundstelle "Keilberg-Kirche" bei Regensburg." *Archäologisches Korrespondenzblatt* 26:233–248.

Valladas, H., J. L. Reyss, J. L. Joron, G. Valladas, O. Bar-Yosef, and B. Vandermeersch
1988 "Thermoluminescence Dating of Mousterian 'Proto-Cro-Magnon' Remains from Israel and the Origin of Modern Man." *Nature* 331:614–616.

Valladas, H., N. Mercier, J.-L. Joron, and J.-L. Reyss
1998 "GIF Laboratory Dates for the Middle Paleolithic Levant," in *Neandertals and Modern Humans in*

Western Asia, T. Akazawa, K. Aoki, and O. Bar-Yosef, eds., pp. 69–76. Plenum Press, New York.

Valoch, K.
1990 "La Moravie il y a 40 000 ans," in *Paléolithique moyen recent et Paléolithique supérieur ancien en Europe. Ruptures et transitions: examen critique des documents archéologiques*, C. Farizy, ed., pp. 115–124. A.P.R.A.I.F. 3. Mémoires du Musée de Préhistoire d'Ile de France, Nemours.

Van Andel T. H., and P. C. Tzedakis
1996 "Palaeolithic Landscapes of Europe and Environs, 150,000–25,000 Years Ago: An Overview." *Quaternary Science Reviews* 15:481–500.

Vandermeersch B.
1981 *Les hommes fossiles de Qafzeh (Israel)*. Centre National de la Recherche Scientifique, Paris.
1995 "Le rôle du Levant dans l'évolution de l'humanité au Pleistocène supérieur." *Paléorient* 21(2):25–34.

Vandermeersch, B., and A. M. Tillier
1977 "Etude préliminaire d'une mandibule d'adolescent provenant des niveaux moustériens de Qafzeh (Israel)." *Eretz Israel, Archaeological, Historical and Geographical Studies* (13):177–183.

Vega Toscano, L. G.
1990 "La fin du Paléolithique moyen au sud de l'Espagne: ses implications dans le contexte de la Péninsule Ibérique," in *Paléolithique moyen recent et Paléolithique supérieur ancien en Europe. Ruptures et transitions: examen critique des documents archéologiques*, C. Farizy, ed., pp. 169–176. A.P.R.A.I.F. 3. Mémoires du Musée de Préhistoire d'Ile de France, Nemours.

Vigilant, L., R. Pennington, H. Harpending, T. D. Kocher, and A. C. Wilson
1989 "Mitochondrial DNA Sequences in Single Hairs from a Southern African Population." *Proceedings of the National Academy of Sciences* 86:9350–9354.

Villaverde, V., and M. P. Fumanal
1990 "Relations entre le paléolithique moyen et le Paléolithique supérieur dans le versant méditerranéen espagnol," in *Paléolithique moyen recent et Paléolithique supérieur ancien en Europe. Ruptures et transitions: examen critique des documents archéologiques*, C. Farizy, ed., pp. 177–183. A.P.R.A.I.F. 3. Mémoires du Musée de Préhistoire d'Ile de France, Nemours.

Vlcek, E.
1995 "Evolution of Human Populations in the European Pleistocene," in *Man and Environment in the Palae-olithic*, H. Ullrich, ed., pp. 167–179. Etudes et Recherches Archeologiques de l'Université de Liège 62. Service de Préhistoire, Liège.

Wendorf, F., A. E. Close, R. Schild, A. Gautier, H. P. Schwarcz, G. Miller, K. Kowalski, H. Królik, A. Bluszcz, D. Robins, and R. Grün
1990 "Le dernier interglaciaire dans le Sahara oriental." *L'Anthropologie* 94:361–391.

Wendorf, F., R. Schild, A. E. Close, H. P. Schwarcz, G. H. Miller, R. Grün, A. Bluszcz, S. Stokes, L. Morowska, J. Huxtable, J. Lundberg, and C. L. Hill
1994 "A Chronology for the Middle and Late Pleistocene Wet Episodes in the Eastern Sahara," in *Late Quaternary Chronology and Paleoclimates of the Eastern Mediterranean*, O. Bar-Yosef and R. S. Kra, eds., pp. 147–168. Radiocarbon and the American School of Prehistoric Research, Tucson and Cambridge.

Wengler, L.
1986 "Position géochronologique et modalités du passage Moustérien-Atérien en Afrique du Nord." *Comptes Rendus à l'Académie des Sciences de Paris* 303(12):1153–1156.
1990 "Economie des matières premières et territoire dans le Moustérien et l'Atérien maghrébins: exemples du Maroc oriental." *L'Anthropologie* 94(2):335–360.

White, R.
1998 "Comment on: 'Neanderthal Acculturation in Western Europe? A Critical Review of the Evidence and its Interpretation,' by F. d'Errico et al." *Current Anthropology* 39:S30–S32.

Zilhão, J.
1993 "Le passage du paléolithique moyen au Paléolithique supérieur dans le Portugal," in *El Origen del Hombre Moderno en el Suroeste de Europa*, V. Cabrera, ed., pp. 127–145. Universidad Nacional de Educacion a Distancia, Madrid.
in press "The Ebro Frontier: A Model for the Late Extinction of Iberian Neandertals," in *Neandertals on the Edge: 150th Anniversary Conference of the Forbes' Quarry Discovery, Gibraltar*, C. Stringer, R. N. E. Barton, and C. Finlayson (eds.) Oxbow Books, Oxford.

Zilhão, J., and d'Errico F.
1999a "The Chronology and Taphonomy of the Earliest Aurignacian and its Implications for the Understanding of Neanderthal Extinction." *Journal of World Prehistory* 13(1):1–68.
1999b "Reply to Straus, Mellars and Otte." *Current Anthropology* 40:355–364.

CHAPTER 8 Afterword

Ofer Bar-Yosef and David Pilbeam
Peabody Museum, Harvard University

"So," said The Master at length, "without laws and without reduction to mathematical formulae, what form should an archaeological explanation take?" (Flannery 1986:314)

Archaeologists and paleoanthropologists, like biogeographers, ask questions about change and interaction within and between populations, taking into account environmental contexts and social patterns. In evolutionary biology, "historical narratives have explanatory value," as cited by The Master from the works of Ernst Mayr (Mayr 1982:72). The papers in this volume were aimed, explicitly or implicitly, at clarifying issues of archaeological sequence (hence helping to build a "narrative") in order, ultimately, to *explain* the sequence of events.

We did not intend in this volume to provide complete coverage for every area in the circum Mediterranean region of the archaeological entities and technologies that potentially bear upon the prehistoric geography of Neandertals and Modern humans. We were primarily interested in producing *archaeological* data sets from selected areas that would form a more balanced geographical basis for addressing questions ultimately related to the nature of the evolving interactions between populations.

Equally, we did not intend to attempt to resolve the issue of whether Neandertals were a separate species or a subspecies of *Homo sapiens*. As the papers clearly express, we need first to map the distribution of human populations as reflected in the archaeological record, and note how it shifts through time, before returning to the very old question of what this means in terms of biological populations. How can we use the archaeological record to address the question of the interactions between Neandertals and early Modern populations? The current, broad dichotomizing of the two populations should in the future be replaced by a more refined identification of several groups within the Neandertals and the Modern humans. Only then would the historical narration of the first part of the Last Glaciation facilitate the explanation of the ensuing millennia. We also feel, as mentioned in the short introduction to this volume, that previously published conferences concentrated mostly on western Europe. (We are, however, fully aware of the limited geographic coverage of this volume, in which large parts of Asia and sub-Saharan Africa receive little attention.)

The two maps (figs. 1 and 2) produced here summarize the TL and ^{14}C dates for the Late Mousterian and the Early Upper Paleolithic manifestations, as recognized through the techno-typological studies. We do not provide a detailed discussion of the dates (as has been done by others, e.g., Mellars et al. 1999, this volume; Zilhão and d'Errico 1999), but have made our own decisions, avoiding as far as possible those we consider dubious dates. We are aware that our conclusions are open to criticism, but we believe that the new dates for the Neandertals of Vindija (Croatia) (Smith et al. 1999), the numerous dates for the late Mousterian in the Iberian peninsula, Crimea, and the Caucasus (Marks and Chabai 1998), and the recently published dates for the Aurignacian in Geißenklösterle (Germany) (Richter et al. 2000), indicate a clear geographic pattern of late-occurring Mousterian entities. This supports the earlier recognized east-west Upper Paleolithic spread.

The change or "transition" from the Middle to the Upper Paleolithic is recorded in many sites in Europe, Western Asia, and North Africa. The shift within the lithic industries, reflected in the most common archaeological finds, was recorded in the various *chaînes opératoires*, as described in the chapters of this book.

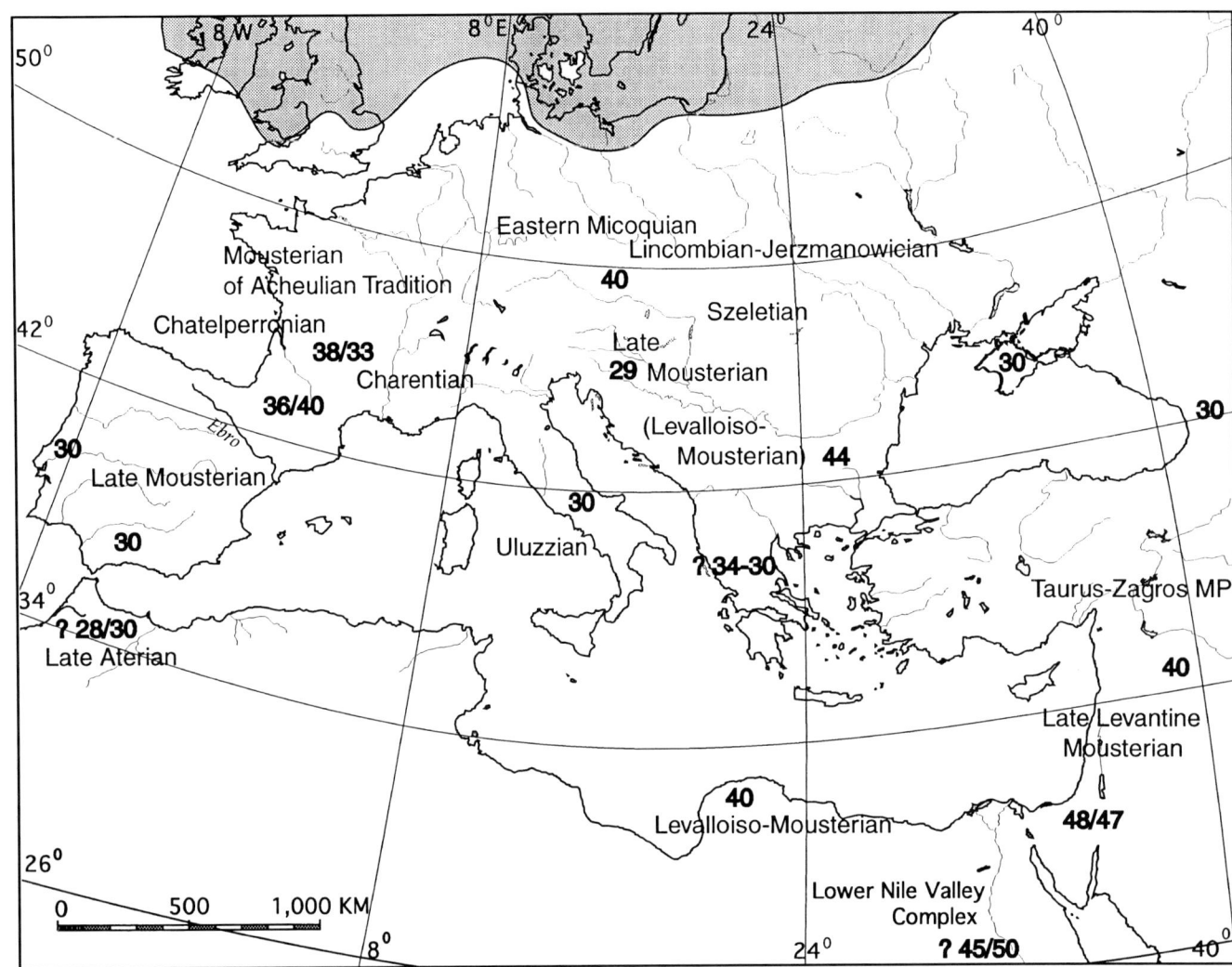

Figure 1. Map showing TL and ^{14}C dates for the Late Mousterian in the Greater Mediterranean region.

This raises an important point. There is no doubt that certain definitions (and here we have in mind "transitional"), whether of "cultural entities" or of "the state of the cultural change," are sometime used loosely. As the history of research in archaeology has demonstrated more than once, paleo-ethnological interpretations will continue to be disputed until we clarify precisely what we mean by a specific term.

A basic term in common usage among archaeologists is the label "Transitional Industries." Unfortunately, "transitional" can be interpreted in several ways. The biological connotation would be that the prehistoric culture, expressed as an archaeological entity, was transformed by a single evolving lineage of related populations into a new culture. Such a view implies biological continuity, difficult if not actually impossible to demonstrate. Alternatively, the lithic characteristics of a "Transitional Industry" are seen by most archaeologists as an intentional admixture—not resulting naturally from post-depositional effects—involving the presence of artifacts bearing the attributes of an older industry, whether as blank production or tool types, together with the newly invented lithic forms.

Archaeologists often do not pay explicit attention to the biological implications when using these terms, but terminology is of fundamental importance, especially when investigating the Middle to Upper Paleolithic transition, or later transitions such as the Neolithic Revolution. In order to make it clear that we are not talking about biological continuity, or the replacement of an older population by a newer, or the

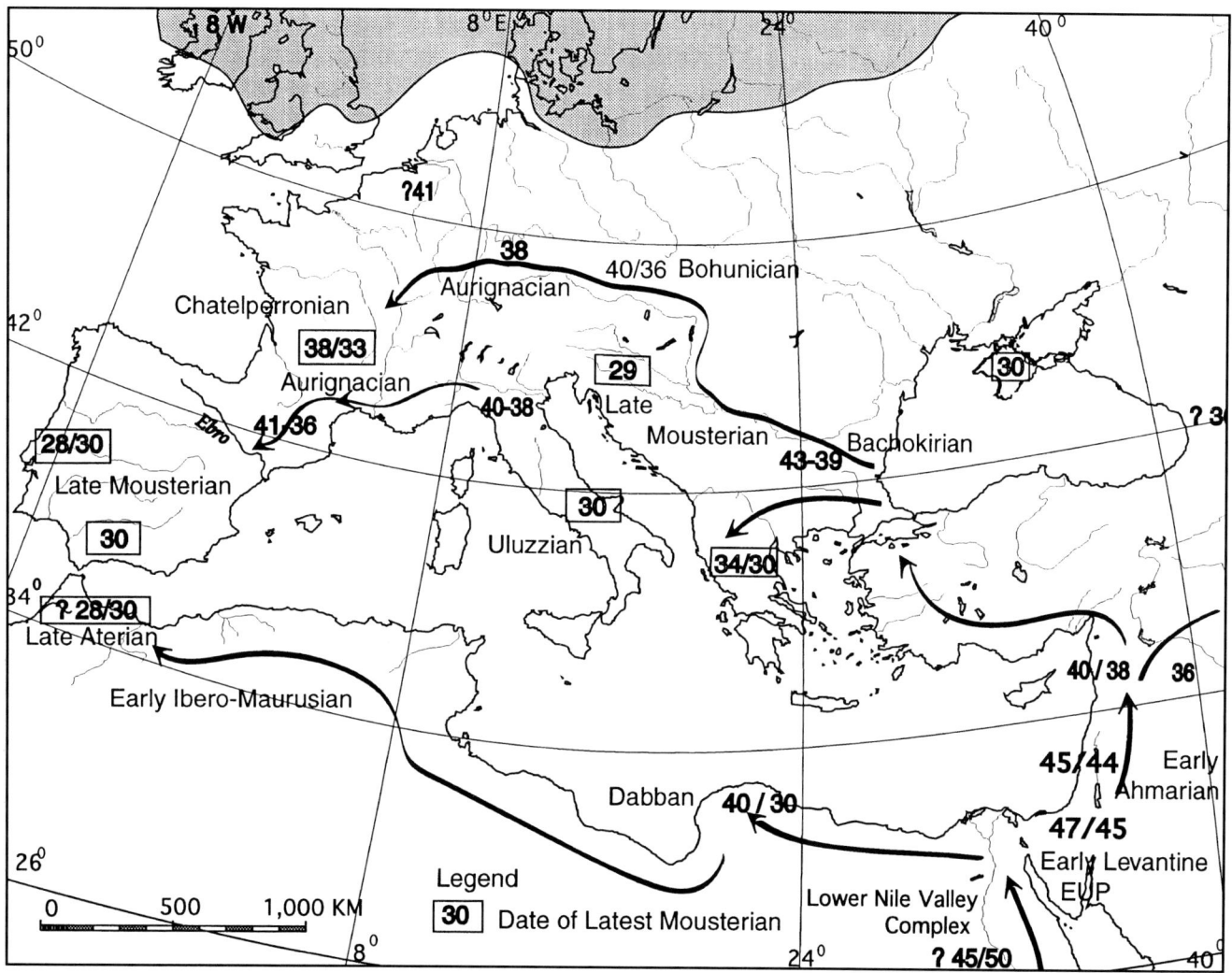

Figure 2. Map showing TL and ^{14}C dates for the Early Upper Paleolithic in the Greater Mediterranean region.

results of interactions between two populations, but simply making descriptive statements, we recommend following the common usage of using names coined from key or type sites. For example, in the Levant, the term "Emiran" would be more suitable than "Transitional Industries." Clustering similar assemblages under a "cultural" label would adequately distance the archaeological entity from unfounded or untested biological interpretations. In cases when the amalgamation of assemblages or sites into a clearly defined entity is simply impractical due to the current paucity of samples, the term Initial Upper Paleolithic (IUP), as suggested by Kuhn et al. (1999), would be preferable.

Describing and discussing the IUP raises the question "do we know who manufactured the lithic industries?" Lithics are always much more abundant than the human fossils. Thus, the rarity or total lack of human fossils in IUP contexts, and especially from the earliest assemblages, does not allow us to test the widely held assumption that these were produced by the Cro-Magnons. Indeed, the association of a Neandertal with the IUP Chatelperronian at St Césaire (Lévêque and Vandermeersch 1980; Lévêque et al. 1993) should urge caution on us all. As regards the latest Mousterian contexts, the most parsimonious assumption is that the bearers of these various industries across Europe and parts of western Asia were Neandertals. We should stress that the only area where the fossils are still the subject of disagreements is the Levant. Opinions differ as to whether one or two populations are being sampled. Perhaps this is due to the fact that this region is located at a boundary of Neandertal distribution. Similar ambiguities are raised concerning the geographic trajectory from Eastern Europe into central Asia, leaving it unclear where the boundaries between Neandertals and Modern Humans lay. Fortunately, no one suggests classifying the humans in North Africa as Neandertals, and this means that the Mousterian and Aterian in this region, and other types of Middle Paleolithic industries in sub-Saharan Africa, were made by non-Neandertal archaic populations (often called archaic *Homo sapiens* although very recently sometimes called *Homo helmei* (Foley and Lahr 1997; Deacon and Deacon 1999)).

The naming of IUP entities demands further attention. Historically, the earliest Upper Paleolithic in Western Europe was named the Aurignacian, and the term thus became a synonym for blade industries, with the implied idea that its bearers were Cro-Magnons. This explains why early blade industries, pre-Mousterian in age, were named "pre-Aurignacian" (e.g., McBurney 1967; Rust 1950). The assumption that these blade industries were the forerunners of true Upper Paleolithic entities, as well as implying relevance for questions of biological evolution, was refuted when the great antiquity of blade and elongated blank production in Eurasia and Africa was recognized (see Bar-Yosef and Kuhn 1999 and references therein).

As figure 2 demonstrates, the emergence of the Aurignacian in western Europe was later than the IUP entities of the Levant. During this period, one notes various industries in the eastern Mediterranean, such as the Emiran and the Early Ahmarian. There is ample evidence to indicate that the manufacturers of the Bohunician in Central Europe employed similar technical solutions to the producers of the Emiran. A similar *chaîne opératoire* possibly relates the Bachokirian, which is not a true Aurignacian industry, to the Early Ahmarian. Only future studies will provide the data to support or refute the proposal that these similarities resulted from human migration from the Levant into southeastern and central Europe.

Chronological precision will be important in showing that the earlier Upper Paleolithic manifestations appear first in the East and arrived later in Europe. What has become obvious is that the Aurignacian evolved in western Europe, and is the earliest definite Upper Paleolithic entity. Its later arrival in the Levant therefore marks the move of a few groups eastward, as proposed by Kozlowski (1992). This would explain why only a few and not the entire array of European Aurignacian cultural traits appear in the Levantine Aurignacian context. The current distribution of other Upper Paleolithic industries in the Levant demonstrates the contemporaneity of the incoming Aurignacian and the local Ahmarian populations.

Population movements and colonizations result in several kinds of interactions: they may be peaceful, which may or may not lead to interbreeding; unresponsive; or violent, resulting in warfare, extermination or enslavement. Interactions can also change over time. It becomes clear from figure 2, that Mousterian-producing populations became isolated from each other. We assume that it was the Neandertal populations across Europe that became disconnected. Isolated populations are more susceptible to extinction than larger, continuous populations; extinction rates in small populations can vary greatly with quite small differences in demographic parameters. Perhaps this explains why the producers of Mousterian industries lasted longer in certain regions, while in other places they quickly disappeared. We reserve our opinion as to whether this disappearance was due to the adoption of the new technologies, to interbreeding, or to replacement, although we favor the last.

BIBLIOGRAPHY

Bar-Yosef, O., and S. Kuhn
　1999 "The Big Deal about Blades: Laminar Technologies and Human Evolution." *American Anthropology* 101(2):1–17.

Deacon, H. J., and J. Deacon
　1999 *Human Beginnings in South Africa: Uncovering the Secrets of the Stone Age.* D. Phillips and Altamira Press, Cape Town, South Africa and Walnut Creek, CA.

Foley, R., and M. M. Lahr
　1997 "Mode 3 Technologies and the Evolution of Modern Humans." *Cambridge Archaeological Journal* 7(1):3–36.

Flannery, K. V.
　1986 "A Visit to the Master," in *Guilá Naquitz: Archaic Foraging and Early Agriculture in Oaxaca, Mexico,* K. V. Flannery, ed., pp. 508–519. Academic Press, New York.

Kozlowski, J. K.
　1992 "The Balkans in the Middle and Upper Palaeolithic: The Gate to Europe or a Cul de Sac?" *Proceedings of the Prehistoric Society* 58:1–20.

Krings, M., A. Stone, R. W. Schmitz, H. Krainitzki, M. Stoneking, and S. Pääbo
    1997 "Neandertal DNA Sequences and the Origins of Modern Humans." *Cell* 90:19–30.

Kuhn, S. L., M. C. Stiner, and E. Güleç
    1999 "Initial Upper Palaeolithic in South-Central Turkey and its Regional Context: A Preliminary Report." *Antiquity* 73(281):505–517.

Lévêque, F., and B. Vandermeersch
    1980 "Découvertes de restes humains dans un niveau Castelperronien à Saint-Césaire (Charente-Maritime)." *Comptes Rendues de l'Academie des Sciences de Paris* (Serie D) 291:187–189.

Lévêque, F., A. M. Backer, and M. Guilbaud
    1993 *Context of a Late Neanderthal.* Monographs in World Archaeology 16. Prehistory Press, Madison.

Marks, A. E., and V. P. Chabai
    1998 *The Middle Paleolithic of Western Crimea*, Vol. 1. Etudes et Recherches Archéologiques de l'Université de Liège 84. Service de Préhistoire, Liège.

Mayr, E.
    1982 *The Growth of Biological Thought: Diversity, Evolution, and Inheritance.* Belknap Press, Cambridge, MA.

McBurney, C. B. M.
    1967 *The Haua Fteah (Cyrenaica) and the Stone Age of the South-East Mediterranean.* Cambridge University Press, Cambridge.

Mellars, P., M. Otte, L. Straus, J. Zilhão, and F. d'Errico
    1999 "The Neanderthal Problem Continued. CA Forum on Theory in Anthropology." *Current Anthropology* 40(3):341–364.

Richter, D., F. Waiblinger, W. J. Rink, and G. A. Wagner
    2000 "Thermoluminescence, Electron Spin Resonance and ^{14}C-Dating of the Late Middle and Early Upper Palaeolithic Site of Geißenklösterle Cave in Southern Germany." *Journal of Archaeological Science* 27(1):71–89.

Rust, A.
    1950 *Die Höhlenfunde von Jabrud (Syrien).* Karl Wacholtz Verlag, Neumünster.

Smith, F. H., E. Trinkaus, P. B. Pettitt, I. Karavanic, and M. Paunovic
    1999 "Direct Radiocarbon Dates for Vindija G1 and Velika Pecina Late Pleistocene Hominid Remains." *Proceedings of the National Academy of Sciences* 96(22):12281–12286.

Zilhão, J., and F. d'Errico
    1999 "The Chronology and Taphonomy of the Earliest Aurignacian and its Implications for the Understanding of Neanderthal Extinction." *Journal of World Prehistory* 13(1):1–68.

Appendix
Radiometric dates available at the time of publication

Nahal Zin, Ein Mor
U-series dates

Layer	Lab number	Date (ka b.p.)	Entity	Ref.
Travertine Blocks:				
Below artifact layer	76NZ3-2	50.7±2.5	Dating the EUP	1 & 2
Below artifact layer	76NZ3-2A	49.0±2.0	MP	"
Above artifact layer:				
upper lamina	76NZ4B-2A	41.8±3.1	MP	"
middle lamina	76NZ4B-3	25.0±1.8	MP	"
lower lamina	76NZ4B-4a	45.2±12.5	MP	"
lower lamina	76NZB-4a	47.3±3.6	MP	"
Above artifact layer	76NZ4A-1	45.2±5.2	MP	"
Travertine block				
0.5m away from 76NZ4	76NZ5-2	46.0±4.2	MP	"
Average (omitting 76NZ4B-3)		46.5±2.9	MP	"

Nahal Aqev
U-series dates

Layer	Lab number	Date (ka b.p.)	Entity	Ref.
fossil spring Layer A	76NZ6e-1	258±86/46	MP	"
fossil spring layer B	76NZ6a-1	228±127/54	MP	"
fossil spring layer B	76NZ6a-2	214±33/25	MP	"
fossil spring layer B	76NZ6a-4	191±5/36	MP	"
fossil spring layer B	Average	211±19	MP	"
fossil spring layer D	76NZ6d-4	85.2±10.0	MP	"
fossil spring layer D	76NZ1	74±5	MP	"

Ein Aqev
U-series dates

Layer	Lab number	Date (ka b.p.)	Entity	Ref.
fossil spring deposit	76NZ8	11.8±0.9	MP	"

Ksar 'Akil
U-series dates

Layer	Lab number	Date (ka b.p.)	Entity	Ref.
XXVI Mousterian level	G-888174S	47±9	MP	3
XXVI Mousterian level	G-888173B	19±5	MP	"
XXXII Mousterian level	G-888177S	51±4	MP	"
XXXII Mousterian level	G-888178B	49±5	MP	"

Radiocarbon dates

Layer	Material	Lab number	Date (ka b.p.)	Entity	Ref.
III	charcoal	OxA-1796	21.1±0.5	Lev. Aurignacian	4
III	charcoal	OxA-1797	26.9±0.6	Lev. Aurignacian	"

Layer	Sample	Lab Number	Date	Entity	Ref.
III	charcoal	OxA-1798	29.3±0.8	Lev. Aurignacian	"
III	charcoal	MC-1191	26.5±0.9	Lev. Aurignacian	"
IV	charcoal	OxA-1803	30.25±0.85	Lev. Aurignacian	"
VI	charcoal	OxA-1804	31.2±1.3	Lev. Aurignacian	"
VI	charcoal	OxA-1805	32.4±1.1	Lev. Aurignacian	"
VI	charcoal	MC-1192	32±1.5	Lev. Aurignacian	"
VIII-VII	shells	GrN-2195	28.84±0.38	Lev. Aurignacian	"
6-7m	shell	GrN-2195	28.84±0.38	Lev. Aurignacian	"
XXVI	dark clay	GrN-2579	43.75±1.5	Mousterian	"

QAFZEH
TL dates

Layer	Sample	Date (ka b.p.)	Entity	Ref.
XVII	13	94.3±8.8	MP	5
XVII	14	106.0±9.6	MP	"
XVII	29	107.2±8.8	MP	"
XVII	33	89.2±8.4	MP	"
XVII	34	87.8±7.2	MP	"
XVII	36	100.7±8.2	MP	"
XVIII	38	87.9±7.2	MP	"
XVIII	40	89.5±7.0	MP	"
XVIII	42	93.4±8.2	MP	"
XIX	45	98.8±8.9	MP	"
XIX	47	82.4±7.7	MP	"
XIX	49	84.9±7.3	MP	"
XIX	77	95.9±8.1	MP	"
XXI	1	109.99.9	MP	"
XXI	2	89.2±8.9	MP	"
XXI	61	90.9±8.7	MP	"
XXII	65	86.6±7.4	MP	"
XXII	66	91.2±8.7	MP	"
XXII	67	85.4±6.9	MP	"
XXIII	76	95.0±7.7	MP	"
Average		92±5	MP	"

ESR dates

Layer	Lab number	EU	LU	Entity	Ref.
XV	370A	92.1	112.0	MP	6
XV	370B	94.2	114.0	MP	"
XV	373	94.7	116.0	MP	"
XVII	372	95.2	103.0	MP	"
XIX	368A	87.7	106.0	MP	"
XIX	368B	99.7	112.0	MP	"
XIX	368C	102.0	117.0	MP	"
XIX	368D	111.0	124.0	MP	"
XIX	371A	107.0	128.0	MP	"
XIX	371B	119.0	145.0	MP	"
XIX	371C	82.0	101.0	MP	"
XXI	369A	95.9	118.0	MP	"
XXI	369B	118.0	143.0	MP	"

Layer	Lab number		Date (ka B.P.)	Entity	Ref.
XXI	369C	73.7	94.0	MP	"
XXI	369D	74.2	89.1	MP	"
XXI	369E	95.3	116.0	MP	"
Average		96±13	115±15	MP	"

KEBARA
TL dates

Layer	Lab number	Date (ka b.p.)	Entity	Ref.
VI	O21,129	45±4.4	MP	7
VI	O21,161	54.5±5.2	MP	"
VI	O21,71	51.3±5.2	MP	"
VI	O21,170	42.9±5.6	MP	"
VI	O21,55	47.1±4.7	MP	"
VI	*Average*	48.3±3.5	MP	"
VII	N21,92b	56.8±5.9	MP	"
VII	N21,92a	53.9±4.6	MP	"
VII	M21,105	52.1±4.0	MP	"
VII	M21,101	45.5±4.3	MP	"
VII	O21,249	53.7±5.0	MP	"
VII	*Average*	51.9±3.5	MP	"
VIII	O21,450	66.7±6.0	MP	"
VIII	N21,109	58.6±4.7	MP	"
VIII	O21,512	58.2±5.4	MP	"
VIII	L21,143	49.3±5.3	MP	"
VIII	L21,12	56.0±6.7	MP	"
VIII	*Average*	57.3±4.0	MP	"
IX	K21,282	59.3±5.8	MP	"
IX	K21,341	59.34.7	MP	"
IX	K21,378	61.6±5.8	MP	"
IX	K21,377	55.2±5.1	MP	"
IX	*Average*	58.4±4.0	MP	"
X	M19,215	58.3±5.2	MP	"
X	M19,117	59.0±4.6	MP	"
X	M19,3	59.8±5.2	MP	"
X	M19,154	67.1±5.6	MP	"
X	N19,342	61.5±5.3	MP	"
X	N19,390	64.9±5.5	MP	"
X	N19,391	62.7±5.3	MP	"
X	*Average*	61.6±3.6	MP	"
XI	L20,222	65.1±5.1	MP	"
XI	L20,803	52.5±3.9	MP	"
XI	L20,225	67.7±6.5	MP	"
XI	L20,580	60±5.0	MP	"
XI	M19,595	63.0±4.6	MP	"
XI	*Average*	60.0±3.5	MP	"
XII	L20,1134	56.0±5.4	MP	"
XII	M20,836	58.9±5.5	MP	"
XII	M20,805	61.9±5.2	MP	"
XII	M20,846	62.5±5.5	MP	"
XII	M20,796	56.1±3.6	MP	"
XII	M20,816	69.2±6.4	MP	"
XII	M20,821	59.2±4.7	MP	"
XII	*Average*	59.9±3.5	MP	"

ESR dates

Layer	Lab number	EU	LU	Entity	Ref.
Units X-XI	H18d(i)	63.3±4.3	66.5±8.3	MP	8
	H18d(ii)	64.9±2.2	69.1±2.3	MP	"
	H17d(i)	60.8±4.3	62.3±4.3	MP	"
	H17d(ii)	65.7±6.0	68.0±6.1	MP	"
	G17c(i)	49.4±5.7	52.9±6.0	MP	"
	G17c(ii)	59.6±7.5	65.0±7.9	MP	"
	H17d:6a	69.0±6.1	71.8±6.3	MP	"
	H17d:6b	61.8±16.3	65.5±16.9	MP	"
	H17d	53.8±13.6	58.3±14.2	MP	"
	H17c	55.8±21.4	63.5±23.7	MP	"
	Average	60.4±5.9	64.3±5.5	MP	"

Radiocarbon dates

Layer	Material	Lab number	Date (ka b.p.)	Entity	Ref.
Limit Unit IV-V, in Q16b/Q15d	charcoal	Pta-5141	43.7±1.8	Early Agmarian	9
IVB	charcoal	Pta-5002	42.5±1.8	Early Ahmarian	"
IVB	charcoal	Pta-4987	42.1±2.1	Early Ahmarian	"
IVB, adjacent to burrow	charcoal	OxA-3978	28.89±0.4	Intrusive	"
IIIB	charcoal	OxA-3976	43.5±2.2	Early Ahmarian	"
IIIBf	charcoal		>43.8	Early Ahmarian	"
IIIBf	charcoal	OxA-3976	>42.5	Early Ahmarian	"
IIIBf	charcoal	OxA-1567	35.6±1.6	Early Ahmarian	"
IIIBf	charcoal	Gif-TAN 90168	>41.7	Early Ahmarian	"
IIIB	charcoal	Gif-TAN- 90028	34.3±1.1	Early Ahmarian	"
IIf hearth	charcoal	Gx-17276	42.8±4.8	Early Ahmarian	"
IIf	charcoal	OxA-1230	36±1.6	Lev Aurignacian	"
IIf above hearth	charcoal	Gif-TAN-90151	32.67±0.8	Lev Aurignacian	"
II, in burrow	charcoal	Pta-4263	31.4±0.48	Lev Aurignacian	"
II, in burrow	charcoal	Pta-4269	28.7±0.45	Lev Aurignacian	"
II top	charcoal	OxA-3975	33.92±0.69	Lev Aurignacian	"
I base	charcoal	OxA-3974	34.51±0.74	Lev Aurignacian	"
I	charcoal	Pta-4268	32.2±0.63	Lev Aurignacian	"
I (contaminated)	charcoal	Pta-4247	22.9±0.25	Lev Aurignacian	"

Skhul
ESR dates

Layer	Sample	EU	LU	Entity	Ref.
	521a	88.1±17.9	102±22.7	MP	10
	521b	86.1±13.1	102±18.1	MP	"
	521c	94.9±15.6	109±20.5	MP	"
	521d	101±19	119±25.1	MP	"
	522a	68±5.4	98.3±10.6	MP	"
	522b	73±7	99.9±12.4	MP	"
	522c	54.6±10.3	77.2±15.7	MP	"

TL dates

Layer	Sample	Date (Ka b.p.)	Entity	Ref.
B	ES1	112.0±16.1	MP	11
B	ES2	133.9±22.3	MP	"
B	ES3	120.2±17.9	MP	"
B	ES4	120.6±19.0	MP	"
B	ES5	166.8±26.8	MP	"
B	ES6	99.4±15.9	MP	"

Amud
TL dates

Layer	Sample	Date (Ka b.p.)	Entity	Ref.
B1	11	49.0±4.6	MP	12
B1	38	59.4±5.1	MP	"
B1	40	51.6±3.7	MP	"
B1	12	70.6±6.9	MP	"
B1	37	61.3±5.2	MP	"
B1	41	58.1±4.1	MP	"
B2	27	59.5±4.5	MP	"
B2	32	52.7±5.5	MP	"
B2	26	55.4±4.0	MP	"
B2	63	45.6±3.9	MP	"
B2	62	52.4±6.8	MP	"
B2	13	44.5±3.9	MP	"
B2	64	44.1±3.1	MP	"
B2	10	53.1±5.5	MP	"
B4	51	75.9±5.3	MP	"
B4	49	70.8±3.8	MP	"
B4	47	55.6±4.4	MP	"
B4	46	64.7±4.0	MP	"
B4	52	66.9±4.9	MP	"

Boker Tachtit
Radiocarbon dates

Layer	Material	Lab number	Date (Ka b.p.)	Entity	Ref.
Boker Tachtit level I		SMU-580	47.28±9.05	Emiran	13
Boker Tachtit level I		SMU-259	46.93±2.4	Emiran	"
Boker Tachtit 4	charcoal	SMU-579	35.055±0.41	Early Ahmarian	"
Boker A	charcoal	SMU-181	>33.6	Early Ahmarian	"
Boker A	charcoal	SMU-260	>33.42	Early Ahmarian	"
Boker A	charcoal	SMU-578	37.92±2.81	Early Ahmarian	"
Boker BE III	charcoal	SMU-188	27.45±1.13	Early Ahmarian	"
Boker BE III	charcoal	SMU-229	26.6±0.5	Early Ahmarian	"
Boker BE III	charcoal	SMU-288	26.03±0.6	Early Ahmarian	"
Boker BE II	charcoal	SMU-227	26.95±0.52	Early Ahmarian	"
Boker BE II	charcoal	SMU-565	24.63±0.39	Early Ahmarian	"
Boker BE I	charcoal	SMU-186	25.61±0.64	Early Ahmarian	"

TOR FARAJ, JORDAN
Amino Acid Racemization

	DATE (KA B.P.)	ENTITY	REF.
	69±6	MP	14

TOR SABIHA, JORDAN
Amino Acid Racemization

	DATE (KA B.P.)	ENTITY	REF.
	69±6	MP	"

SINAI
Radiocarbon dates

LAYER	MATERIAL	LAB NUMBER	DATE (KA B.P.)	ENTITY	REF.
Lagama VII	charcoal	RT-413A	>19	Lagaman	15
Lagama VII	charcoal	SMU-185	31.21±0.278	Lagaman	"
Lagama VII	charcoal	SMU-172	34.17±3.67	Lagaman	"
Lagama VIII	egg shell	SMU-119	32.98±2.14	Lagaman	"
Lagama VIII			30.36/C13/12		"
Lagama IIID	egg shell	SMU-118	30.05±1.24	Lagaman	"
Lagama IIID			30.36/C13/12		"
QB 501	egg shell	Pta-2819	33.8±0.94	Ahmarian	"
QB 601	egg shell	Pta-2964	32.47±0.78	Ahmarian	"
AbuNoshra I	charcoal	B-13198	29.58+1.61-1.34	Ahmarian	"
AbuNoshra I	matrix	B-13897	25.95±0.36	Ahmarian	"
AbuNoshra I	charcoal	B-12125	>30.44	Ahmarian	"
AbuNoshra I	charcoal	SMU-1824	31.33±2.88	Ahmarian	"
AbuNoshra I	charcoal	SMU-2254	35.824±1.09	Ahmarian	"
AbuNoshra I	charcoal	SMU-2007	35.805±1.52	Ahmarian	"
AbuNoshra II	charcoal	SMU-1772	31.023±8.537	Ahmarian	"
AbuNoshra II	charcoal	SMU-1762	31.585±2.275	Ahmarian	"
AbuNoshra II	charcoal	ETH-3075	33.47±0.68	Ahmarian	"

EGYPT, TAHTA AREA
Radiocarbon dates

LAYER	LAB NUMBER	DATE (KA B.P.)	ENTITY	REF.
Shuwikhat I	OxTL-253	24.7±2.5	Shuwikhat	16
Nazlet Khatar 1	GrN-11298	31.65+3.6-2.5	MP	"
Nazlet Khatar 4	GrN-11296	35.1±1.1	MP	"
Nazlet Khatar 4	GrN-11297	32.1±0.7	MP	"
Nazlet Khatar 4	GrN-11299	33.1±0.65	MP	"
Nazlet Khatar 4	GrN-11301	34.95±0.6	MP	"
Nazlet Khatar 4	Lv-1129	30.36±2.31	MP	"
Nazlet Khatar 4	Lv-1140	33.28±1.28	MP	"
Nazlet Khatar 4	Lv-1141D	30.98±2.85	MP	"
Nazlet Khatar 4	Lv-1142	31.32±2.31	MP	"

Umm el Tlel
TL dates

Layer	Lab number	Date (Ka b.p.)	Entity	Ref.
Layer III2a	Gif-A93215	36±2.5	MP	17

Radiocarbon dates

Layer	Lab number	Date (Ka b.p.)	Entity	Ref.
Layer III2a	Gif-A93216	34.53±0.75	MP	"

Üçagizli
Radiocarbon dates

Layer	Material	Lab number	Date (Ka b.p.)	Entity	Ref.
Locus 2, layer H	ch	AA-27994	39.4±1.2	MP	18
Locus 2, layer H	ch	AA-27995	38.9±1.1	MP	"

Mezmaiskaya
Radiocarbon dates

Layer	Material	Lab number	Date (ka b.p.)	Entity	Ref.
2	bone	LE-4735	32.23±0.74	MP	19
2A	burned bone	Beta-53896/ CAMS-2999	35.76±0.4	MP	"
2A	burned bone	Beta-53897/ ETH-9817	36.28±0.54	MP	"
2B	bone	LE-3599	40.66±1.6	MP	"
3	bone	LE-3841	>45	MP	"
1C	wood charcoal	Beta-113536	32.01±0.25	UP	"

Zagros, Shanidar Cave
Radiocarbon dates

Layer	Material	Lab number	Date (ka b.p.)	Entity	Ref.
C-upper	charcoal	L-335H	24.55±1.5	Baradostian	20
C-upper	charcoal	W-654	28.7±0.7		"
C-upper	charcoal	W-178	29.5		"
C-middle	charcoal	GrN-1494	34.01		"
C-middle	bone fraction	GrN-1830	33.9		"
C-lower		W-180	>34.0		"
C-lower		W-650	37.3		"
C-lower	bone fraction	GrN-2016	35.44		"
C-lower	charcoal	GrN-2015	34.54		"
Near base of C	charcoal	L-3351	30.35±3.0		"

Zagros, Yafteh Cave
Radiocarbon dates

Layer	Material	Lab number	Date (Ka b.p.)	Entity	Ref.
200cm	charcoal, ash	GX-711	33.9+2.9-4.5	Upper Paleolithic	
201cm	charcoal, ash	GX-710	32.0+2.4-3.4		"
200-210cm	charcoal	SI-332	29.41±1.15		"

210-220cm	charcoal	SI-333	30.86±3.0	"
250cm	charcoal	SI-336	21.0±0.8	"
250-260cm	ash	GX-709	38.1+3.4-7.5	"
278-280	ash, charcoal	GX-708	>36.0	"
280cm	charcoal	SI-334	29.81±3.0	"
285cm	charcoal	SI-335	>40.0	"
290cm	ash	GX-706	>35.6	"

Sources:

1. Schwarcz, H. P., B. Blackwell, P. Goldberg, and A. E., Marks 1979. "Uranium Series Dating of Travertine from Archaeological Sites, Nahal Zin, Israel." *Nature* 277:558–560.
2. Schwarcz, H. P., P. Goldberg, and B. Blackwell 1980. "Uranium Series Dating of Archaeological Sites in Israel." *Israel Journal of Earth Sciences* 29:157–165.
3. van der Plicht, J., A. van der Wijk, and G. J. Bartstra 1989 "Uranium and Thorium in Fossil Bones: Activity Ratios and Dating." *Applied Geochemistry* 4:339–342.
4. Mellars, P., and J. Tixier 1989. "Radiocarbon Accelerator Dating of Ksar 'Akil (Lebanon) and the Chronology of the Upper Paleolithic Sequence in the Middle East." *Antiquity* 63:761–768.
5. Valladas, H., J. L. Reyss, J. L. Joron, G. Valladas, O. Bar-Yosef, and B. Vandermeersch 1988. "Thermoluminescence Dating of Mousterian 'Proto-Cro-Magnon' Remains from Israel and the Origin of Modern Man." *Nature* 331:614–616.
6. Schwarcz, H. P., R. Grün, B. Vandermeersch, H. Valladas, and E. Tchernov 1988. "ESR Dates for the Hominid Burial Site of Qafzeh in Israel." *Journal of Human Evolution* 17:733–737.
7. Valladas, H., J.-L. Joron, G. Valladas, B. Arensburg, O. Bar-Yosef, A. Belfer-Cohen, P. Goldberg, H. Laville, L. Meignen, Y. Rak, E. Tchernov, A.-M. Tillier, and B. Vandermeersch 1987. "Thermoluminescence Dates for the Neanderthal Burial Site at Kebara (Mount Carmel, Israel)." *Nature* 330:159–160.
8. Schwarcz, H. P., W. M. Buhay, R. Grün, H. Valladas, E. Tchernov, O. Bar-Yosef, and B. Vandermeersch 1989. "ESR Dating of the Neanderthal Site, Kebara Cave, Israel." *Journal of Archaeological Science* 16:653–659.
9. Bar-Yosef, O., M. Arnold, A. Belfer-Cohen, P. Goldberg, R. Housley, H. Laville, L. Meignen, N. Mercier, J. C. Vogel, and B. Vandermeersch 1996. "The Dating of the Upper Paleolithic Layers in Kebara Cave, Mount Carmel. *Journal of Archaeological Science* 23:297–306.
10. Stringer, C., B., R. Grün, H. P. Schwarcz, and P. Goldberg 1989. "ESR Dates for the Hominid Burial Site of es-Skhul in Israel." *Nature* 338:756–758.
11. Mercier, N., H. Valladas, O. Bar-Yosef, B. Vandermeersch, C. Stringer, and J.-L. Joron 1993. "Thermoluminescence Dates for the Mousterian Burial Site of Es-Skhul, Mt. Carmel." *Journal of Archaeological Science* 20:169–174.
12. Mercier, N., H. Valladas, L. Forget, J.-L. Joron, P. Vermeersch, P. Van Peer, and J. Moeyersons 1999. "Thermolescence Dating of a Middle Paleolithic Occupation at Sodmein Cave, Red Sea Mountains (Egypt)." *Journal of Archaeological Science* 26(11):1339–1346.
13. Marks, A. E. 1983. *The Sites of Boker and Boker Tachtit: A Brief Introduction in Prehistory and Paleoenvironments in the Central Negev, Israel. Volume III The Avdat/Aqev Area, Part 3*, A. E. Marks, ed., pp. 15-37. Southern Methodist University, Dallas.
14. Henry, D. O., and G. H. Miller 1992. "The Implications of Amino Acid Racemization Dates on Levantine Mousterian Deposits in Southern Jordan." *Paléorient* 18(2):45–52.
15. Phillips, J. L. 1994. "The Upper Paleolithic Chronology of the Levant and the Nile Valley," in *Late Quaternary Chronology and Paleoclimates of the Eastern Mediterranean*, O. Bar-Yosef and R. Kra, eds., pp. 169–176. Radiocarbon and the ASPR, Tucson and Cambridge.
16. Vermeersch, P., M. Otte, E. Gilot, E. Paulisson, G. Gijselings, and D. Drappier 1982. "Blade Technology in the Egyptian Nile Valley: Some New Evidence." *Science* 216:626–628.
17. Bourguignon, L. 1996. "Un Mousterien tardif sur le site d'Umm el Tlel (Bassin d'El Khowm, Syrie)? Exemples des niveaux IIBase' et III2A'," in *The Last*

Neandertals, the First Anatomically Modern Humans, E. Carbonell and M. Vaquero, eds., pp. 317–336. Universitat Rovira i Virgili, Tarragona.
18. Kuhn, S. L., M. C. Stiner, and E. Güleç 1999. "Initial Upper Paleolithic in South-Central Turkey and its Regional Context: A Preliminary Report." *Antiquity* 73(281):505–517.
19. Golovanova, L., J. F. Hoffecker, V. M. Kharitonov, and G. P. Romanova 1999. "Mezmaiskaya Cave: A Neanderthal Occupation in the Northern Caucasus." *Current Anthropology* 40(1):77–86.
20. Henry, D., and F. Sevello 1974. "Compendium of C-14 Determinations Derived from Near Eastern Prehistoric Sites." *Paléorient* 2(1):19–44.